THE STUDY GROUP READINGS

Edgar Cayce

THE
STUDY GROUP
READINGS

୬ ୧

The Edgar Cayce Readings

VOLUME 7

Compiled by

The Readings Research Department

ASSOCIATION FOR RESEARCH AND ENLIGHTENMENT, INC.

VIRGINIA BEACH, VIRGINIA

Copyright © 1977 by Edgar Cayce Foundation

(ISBN) 87604–094–6

The Edgar Cayce readings are quoted verbatim
from the originals except for minor changes in
spelling and capitalization.

PRINTED IN THE UNITED STATES OF AMERICA

CONTENTS

Foreword vii
The Readings 3

The Study Group readings are in numerical order. The following listing groups the readings according to the chapter in A Search for God *with which they deal.*

Chapter Title	Reading Numbers	Page
Cooperation	262-2—262-5	6–23
Know Thyself	262-5—262-11	20–54
What Is My Ideal?.	262-11—262-16	51–72
Faith.	262-17—262-18	73–80
Virtue and Understanding.	262-18—262-21	77–90
Fellowship.	262-22—262-24	91–101
Patience	262-25—262-27	102–113
The Open Door	262-28—262-31	114–132
In His Presence.	262-32—262-34	133–147
The Cross and the Crown	262-35—262-39	148–165
The Lord Thy God Is One	262-40—262-43	166–177
Love.	262-44—262-49	178–196
Opportunity	262-50—262-54	197–212
Day and Night	262-55—262-57	213–226
God the Father	262-58—262-62	227–252
and His Manifestations		
Desire	262-63—262-73	253–294
Destiny of the Mind	262-74—262-90	295–363
Destiny of the Body		
Destiny of the Soul		
Glory	262-91 —262-95	364–381
Knowledge	262-95 —262-103	379–415
Wisdom.	262-104—262-108	416–432
Happiness.	262-109—262-112	433–450
Spirit	262-113—262-125	451–502
Righteousness Versus Sin	262-126—262-130	503–516
God - Love - Man	262-129—262-130	513–516

Man's Relationship to Man . . . 262-130 . . 515-516
Index 517
Supplementary Index—Affirmations 533
Supplementary Index—Bible References 537

Foreword

Edgar Cayce gave some 14,256 psychic discourses between 1901 and January, 1945. In my opinion, the 130 readings contained in this volume will probably, in time, reach more people and do more good than any other data which he gave.

Twelve to fifteen individuals, making up the first Study Group, sought this information as a group. Each of the readings presented a subject, giving a brief philosophical statement about it. Many of the questions asked by the group are personal and reflect the confusion of average people who became involved in the development of a series of essays on spiritual law. They were charged to submit questions for further clarification of these laws, then instructed to test and work with the laws in their own lives. Each of these readings contains an affirmation which members of the group were directed to meditate on daily before submitting contributions; the latter were eventually compiled into the essays which make up the two slender volumes, *A Search for God,* Books I and II.

The individual members of the group worked for some eleven years, endeavoring to test these concepts in their own lives and compiling the material in essay form. The members of the group prayed and meditated daily. Slowly the individuals comprising the group began to see a little bit more clearly the goals which were suggested in the very first of these readings, and which are summed up in the affirmation, "Let me ever be a channel of blessings, today, now, to those that I contact, in *every* way."

In January of 1976 more than 1,500 small groups, averaging perhaps seven members each, were meeting weekly in various parts of the United States and Canada, discussing essays from the books, *A Search for God,* I and II. Certainly, in the beginning, not one of the original group members imagined the work and the amazing growth of the groups which lay ahead.

Hugh Lynn Cayce
President
Association for Research
and Enlightenment, Inc.

THE STUDY GROUP READINGS

❧ 262-1 ❦

On September 14, 1931, at 8:00 P.M., a meeting was held at the home of Mr. and Mrs. C. A. Barrett, in Washington Manor, Washington Park, Norfolk, Va., for the purpose of forming a group [Study Group #1] to study information received through the psychic forces of Edgar Cayce. Present were: Edgar Cayce; Gertrude Cayce, conductor; Gladys Davis, steno; C. A. Barrett, Minnie Barrett, Mrs. A. F. Black, Hugh Lynn Cayce, Mildred Davis, Edith Edmonds, Florence Edmonds, Mrs. F. M. Freeman, Hannah Miller, Mrs. T. P. W. Morrow, Mr. and Mrs. C. W. Rosborough, Helena Storey, and Esther Wynne.

Mrs. Cayce: You will have before you the group gathered in this room, who desire—as a group—to be guided through these forces as to how they may best be a channel in presenting to the world the truth and light needed. You will answer the questions which this group will ask.

Mr. Cayce: Yes, we have the group—as a group—as gathered here, seeking to be a channel that they, as [a] group, as individuals, may be—and give—the light to the waiting world.

As each have gathered here—as each gathered here has been associated in their various experiences in the earth, as each has prepared themselves for a channel through these experiences —so may they, as a group, combine their efforts in a cooperative manner to give to the individual, the group, the classes, the masses, that as they received, as they have gained in this experience.

To some are given to be teachers, to some are given to be healers, to some are given to be interpreters. Let each, then, do *their* job and their part *well, in* the manner as is given *to* them, knowing—in the forces as manifest through them— they become, then, a light in *their* own respective action and field of endeavor. As the forces manifest in their various ways and manners, to some will be given those of prophecy, to some will be given those of teaching, to some will be given those of ministration, to some as ministers. Then, in the ways as they present themselves; for, as has been given, he that receives shall give, he that cometh together in that name that will give, even as has been promised, "as I have given and am *in* the

Father, so in *me* may *ye* do as *I* have done, and *greater* things than *I* have done shall ye do, for I go *to* the Father, and ye in me, as ye ask in my name, so shall it be *done* unto you!"

Then, as there cometh in the minds, hearts, souls of each, so will there be given—in that selfsame hour—*that* as *ye* shall do!

Ready for questions.

Q-1. Outline for us the steps which we must take that we may become more of one mind, that we may be of the greatest influence for good.

A-1. As should be for each to learn that first *lesson* as should be given unto others: Let all dwell together in mind as of one purpose, one aim; or, *first* learn cooperation! Learn what that means in a *waiting,* in a *watchful,* in a world *seeking to* know, *to* see, a sign. There, as has been given, will only *be* the sign *given to* those that have drunk of the cup that *makes* for cooperation in *every sense* of enlightening a seeking and desiring world. Cast not pearls before swine, neither be thou over-anxious for the moment. *Wait* ye on the Lord; for, as has been promised, he that *seeks* shall find, and ye *will* receive—each of you—powers from on high. *Use* that in a constructive, in a manner as befits that desire of the group, of *each.* Think not of thine *own* desire, but let that mind be in you as was in Him, as may be in all those *seeking* the way.

Q-2. If it be acceptable to the forces, direct us as to how we may best prepare a course of lessons for this and similar groups.

A-2. First let each prepare themselves and receive that as will be given unto each in *their respective* sphere of development, of desire, of ability. The first *lesson*—as has been given—learn what it means to cooperate in *one* mind, in *God's* way; for, as each would prepare themselves, in meditating day and night, in "What wilt thou have *me* do, O Lord?" and the *answer will* be *definite,* clear to each as are gathered here, will they seek in His name; for He is *among* you in this present hour, for all as *seek* are in that attitude of prayer. Pray *ye,* that ye may be *acceptable* to Him in thy going ins and coming outs; for holy is he that seeks to be a light to his brother; and faints not in the trials nor the temptations, for He tempts *none* beyond that they are *able* to bear. Bear ye one another's burdens, in that

each fills his *own* heart—as is *given, answer* when He calls—
"Here am I, send me."

Q-3. What would be the best subject for the first lesson?

A-3. Cooperation. Let each seek for that as will be *their* part
in this lesson, and *it* will be given each as *they* ask for same.

We are through for the present.

This psychic reading was given by Edgar Cayce at his office, 105th Street [now 67th Street] and Ocean, Virginia Beach, Va., on September 20, 1931, at 4:45 P.M., in accordance with a request made by those present: Edgar Cayce; Gertrude Cayce, conductor; Gladys Davis, steno; C. A. Barrett, Minnie Barrett, Mrs. A. F. Black, Hugh Lynn Cayce, Mildred Davis, Florence Edmonds, Edith Edmonds, Mrs. F. M. Freeman, H. H. Jones, Hannah Miller, Mrs. T. P. W. Morrow, Helena Storey, Esther Wynne and others.

≥ 262-2 ≤

Mrs. Cayce: You will have before you the group gathered here, and the subject of Cooperation *as the first lesson for this group. You will answer the questions of each as I ask them.*

Mr. Cayce: We have the group as gathered here. Many of these we have had before, and the desire of the group as [a] group, individuals as individuals *of* the group. As each comes seeking for the understanding of that as may be their part in the lessons as may be given others, in learning cooperation may each—themselves—apply in their own lives, and in the group, *that* they seek.

Ready for questions.

Q-1. [307]: Is not universal love necessary for us in order to have unity of purpose?

A-1. Universal love [is] necessary that there be unity of purpose, or desire, upon the parts of groups *or* individuals in their *presenting* themselves for a oneness of purpose, or to be of aid to others in *finding* themselves; losing self in the love of that as is made the ideal of those seeking.

Q-2. [307]: I offer myself as a teacher of truth. How may I become more spiritual and efficient?

A-2. Practice makes perfect; and as one practices, puts in use, in word, in deed, day by day, so does one grow *in* grace, in knowledge, in understanding; and "He that would be the greatest among you, let him be the servant of all."

Q-3. [307]: Am I led through my dreams?

A-3. Ofttimes.

Q-4. [993]: What is my definite part in the healing group?

A-4. As a leader of prayer in the various supplications that there be accord with those that are aiding in bringing the consciousness of truth, life, light and immortality, *to* those seeking aid through those channels.

Q-5. [*993*]: *Is my method of meditating correct? If not, suggest meditation that would be suitable for my development at this time.*

A-5. This, as we would find, would necessitate first an organization of the purpose of the group. Let these—[the] group—come together, and, as has been given, the needs of an individual—or individuals—will be *outlined* by one of such a group. Then the leader and director would indicate the various *manners* of meditation for that particular character of desire or aid as is to be had *by* the individual seeking same through the group *as* a group. *Group* meditation and individual meditation may be one, or it may be entirely different. That as for self, correct.

Q-6. [*115*]: *How can I best cooperate with this group?*

A-6. Be an emissary of light to those in the group and *out,* bringing those together who may be of aid to, or who may *give* an understanding to the various groups as they go *about* their work. Be a real emissary, as the body *has* been in that called the past—*make* it *now!* For all time is *one* time.

Q-7. [*404*]: *How can I best cooperate?*

A-7. Be, as it were, the secretary, or messenger for the group, aiding each in their respective activities to be of *one* mind.

Q-8. [*404*]: *What is my best time for meditation?*

A-8. At sunrise.

Q-9. [*379*]: *Is there a message for me as to how I can best cooperate with this group?*

A-9. Seek and ye shall find. Do that that is *known* in each meeting, each activity, for it is line upon line, precept *upon* precept, here a little, *there* a little, the leaven that leaveneth the whole lump. In so doing may those blessings that may come to others through thine activities be the *best* service self may give in and with this group.

Q-10. [*341*]: *Please advise us as to how to conduct our meetings.*

A-10. That would depend upon the character *of* the meeting as is to be conducted. In seeking as a group for a lesson as *would* be given for study by the group, and as may be compiled by those of the group for study by other groups—as the various lessons are chosen that are to be presented, let each gain through their *own* concept—of the manner in which they themselves receive—that as may be helpful or directing, and in seeking their answer through these channels this would become a portion of such a lesson. As each should have a part in each lesson, for each *will make* a response to self to another. As *self* receives, so may self give. As may be termed in common parlance, the most interesting thing in life is *self*—yet self must become null and void, as *losing* self *in* love for another, yet self must have a part in the *losing* as in the *giving* of aid to another. In the conducting of meetings where there is to be some special message received, or aid given to an individual in the spiritual healing (to which the body would be a portion of such a group), this has been outlined as to how same should be conducted. Let *everything* be done in decency and in order.

Q-11. [*341*]: *How may I cooperate with this group?*

A-11. In presenting self's associations with the influences as may direct for the good for others in the various exercises or various activities of the group, whether in lesson, in meditation, in healing, or whatnot.

Q-12. [*341*]: *To what advantage may we use the ideas presented in the "Song of Sano Tarot"* [*book by Nancy Fullwood*] *for the benefit of this group?*

A-12. It is to be hoped that the sources would be much higher than these, and that they would seek higher!

Q-13. [*294*]: *Are the seven presented to me* [*in dream—see 294-127, A-3*] *to be the healing group, or was this emblematical?*

A-13. This is both *emblematical* and is, in fact, the portion of the group that should begin their activities in this definite line *and* manner, *aided* by all who may seek or desire to be a portion of same. *These,* as given, leading in their respective places and times, for as each of these gather as a body for aid to another, there will be from time to time a message from one to another. This is not only a promise, it's a threat! Be mindful of it, but be faithful to each as they are received. [See 281-1, 10/5/31, and entire file of prayer group readings as a result. See specifically 281-6, A-11 and 281-8, A-12.]

Q-14. [*69*]: *How may I best prepare myself for the work in hand?*

A-14. In preparing self for that as is to be attempted by a group is a different preparation, as has been indicated by that each should learn the lesson of cooperation, from preparing self for an individual activity. Unless there is the cooperation in intent and purpose in each, as they may be gathered together for some definite action that is to be taken to aid—for remember, as has been said, "Where two or three are gathered together in my name, there am I in the midst of them." Then, in preparing self as a portion of a group, not independent—but not dependent upon any member of the group—be *dependent* upon *God!* In the dependence as is put in individuals, falls short. As may be gained for self through that cooperation that is known as a movement on the part of individuals in a cooperative manner to create by those of the higher forces as may manifest *through* each, so is the power given, the *understanding* given, the *knowledge* given. As was said of old, "In all thine getting, get understanding."

Q-15. [*303*]: *How may I cooperate?*

A-15. In the various manners we find each individual *in* the group has prepared itself through those activities in the material life, in the mental life. They each have passed through their individual trials, that they know better how to present to those seeking for aid and understanding, through a group, a better sympathetic knowledge of the sources of information, whether they be the consciousness that is of that that may be applied through the spiritual realm, or whether through those that are necessary to become more in contact with the spiritualistic influences in an active force. So this body, in its cooperative measures, may meet *many* of those conditions as arise for the group, as an advisory measure; being also the emissary, or one as a *missionary* to many.

Q-16. [*288*]: *Does the dream I had last night, in which I traveled on a ship and arrived at the Statue of Liberty, indicate my part in this lesson?*

A-16. *Emblematically.* That, as the Statue stands for a *spirit* as is supposed to emanate *from* a nation, so do the activities of

the body in recording that as may be received stand as that that
will be the *formulative* spirit in the minds, hearts and souls,
of many—the many thousands that may be reached through
that as may be recorded by the activities of the body itself.

Q-17. [288]: How may I best cooperate?

A-17. Give of thy best to Him. [See 262-12, A-8.]

Q-18. What should be the subject for the next lesson?

A-18. Let's take one at a time! Let's finish this first! Has this
been compiled? Then, in the beginning, *begin* at the beginning!
Do not have so much compiled, or data gathered, that it is
harum-scarum, but—as given—do all things in decency and
order. First make your *first* lesson. Have that complete, by the
completing of that portion each gives—desires to give—would
like to see given—would give themselves with it—to others,
to know what cooperation means. We all in the group have a
smattering as to our part. This has been asked, as *"I* may do
to cooperate"; so, let's put it into practice, and then present
same as a lesson. *Then* we begin with the first lessons in *knowing* self! How may I *know* self?

Q-19. Who should be the leader of the whole group?

A-19. As the spirit moves! As the compiler, Miss Wynne. As
the secretary, Mrs. Miller. As of the groups, as has been given
in their various capacities—as they have asked, they are given.

Q-20. Is there any special message for this group at this time?

A-20. As ye have begun in an active service for self and for
others through a cooperative way and manner, seek ye through
those sources as may give that understanding to each in their
respective knowledge *and* understanding for their part as an
integral unit of a whole to present a light to a waiting world.
As ye seek ye shall find, as ye knock so will it be opened. As
ye practice—not preach! As ye practice, so will thy activities
be. Let thy yeas be yea and thy nays be nay. Be not unstable
in things thou doest, for thou hast asked that thou be guided
by that that may *give* a light to a dying world—not an individual, a world!

We are through.

≫ 262-3 ≪

This psychic reading was given by Edgar Cayce at his office, 105th Street [now 67th Street] and Ocean, Virginia Beach, Va., on October 4, 1931, at 4:15 P.M., in accordance with a request made by those present: Edgar Cayce; Gertrude Cayce, conductor; Gladys Davis, steno; C. A. Barrett, Minnie Barrett, Louise F. Black, Hugh Lynn Cayce, Mildred Davis, Edith Edmonds, Florence Edmonds, Fannie M. Freeman, H. H. Jones, Frances Y. Morrow, Hannah Miller, C. W. Rosborough, M. L. Rosborough, Helena Storey and Esther Wynne.

Mrs. Cayce: You will have before you the group gathered here, and their desire to be guided into the path of greater service through these forces; together with that attempt of each throughout the week to gain through meditation the data for the first lesson on cooperation. Please direct us in the organization of this material, and give to each expansion and interpretation of that received, as presented in questions from each.

Mr. Cayce: Yes, we have the group, as individuals, as a group, as gathered here. As they each seek in *their* way, through their development, to cooperate in being of service to others, so are they lifted up. As the consciousness of the Master is raised in their individual activities, so is the cooperation in a body as was from the beginning, when the cooperation brought into being those forces as manifest themselves in this material world. They each, then, keeping that creative force within themselves in that direction as makes for the continuity of life, hope, peace, understanding, so may it be builded in the lives of themselves first, then in others—as *they*, in *their* way, seek to bring a better understanding in this material world.

Then, as ye are gathered here, let that mind be in you *not* of elementals, but of spiritual forces as may come *through* thine efforts if they are made in accord with His will. Let thy prayer be continually:

NOT MY WILL BUT THINE, O LORD, BE DONE IN AND THROUGH ME. LET ME EVER BE A CHANNEL OF BLESSINGS, TODAY, NOW, TO THOSE THAT I CONTACT, IN EVERY WAY. LET MY GOING IN, MINE COMING OUTS, BE IN ACCORD WITH THAT THOU WOULD HAVE ME DO, AND AS THE CALL COMES, "HERE AM I, SEND ME—USE ME!"

Ready for questions.

Q-1. [*307*]: *How may we have the mind of Christ?*

A-1. As we open our hearts, our minds, our souls, that we may be a channel of blessings to others, so we have the mind of the Christ, who took upon Himself the burden of the world. So may we, in our *own* little sphere, take upon ourselves the burdens of the world. The *joy,* the peace, the happiness, that may be ours is in *doing* for the *other* fellow. For, gaining an understanding of the laws as pertain to right living in all its phases makes the mind in attune with *Creative* Forces, which *are* of *His* consciousness. So we may have *that* consciousness, by putting into action *that* we know.

Q-2. [*560*]: *What is my part in this lesson of* Cooperation?

A-2. That that as is given to those that would seek through these lessons is a *practical* religion in action; for as thine part in the ministry to the Master was as of the practical things of life, so in the lessons these must be *living* words, that they may touch the hearts, the minds, the souls of others. In thine ministry, then, see that each line, each thought, is a *practical* thing, *living,* having its being, in Him.

Q-3. [*560*]: *How may I know self?*

A-3. By the activities of self in the daily walks of life, compared with the thoughts, the activities of Him, will reflect the self—as is *meant* in this query.

Q-4. [*560*]: *A large body of water kept coming into sight* [*during meditation*]. *I could see it plainly.*

A-4. As the activities of self in the relations to others is made active, so will the water of life be made more plain, more active in the experience of self, as was the depth and the activities of that mother of life seen. [See 262-8, A-2.]

Q-5. [*2125*]: *In what way could I best serve this group?*

A-5. In holding one with another, in self's meditation, that of a useful, purposeful, definite aim for those, and for that as is being attempted to be furthered by all active in same, making continually that affirmation, *"His* will—in all things—be done."

Q-6. [*2124*]: *Will my work in the group of healers be made known to me?*

A-6. Be made known, as the activities of the group are centered here or there, or from the directions as come, so will the part of each be made known to them as they seek; for, as is given, "Seek and *ye* shall find," this [is] a promise. Know in self that He is *faithful* to fulfill that as is promised, as *we* are faithful in caring for those to whom, for whom, the promise is made. They that seek *God* may find Him! Would ye have mercy shown, then be merciful *unto* those *ye* contact. Would ye be forgiven, forgive them that know not what they say, what they do; for "As ye lift me *in* thine life, so shall *ye* be lifted *in* the life here, now, and hereafter."

Q-7. [*311*]: *How may I best cooperate with and serve this group?*

A-7. Do with all thy might what thy hand finds to do. Let *this* mind be in you as was in Him, "Not as I will but *Thine* will be done in earth as it is in heaven." Make thine self a channel of blessing to *someone;* so will His blessings come to thee, as an individual, as an integral part of the group. "They that seek my face shall find it."

Q-8. [*2112*]: *Is spiritual healing a gift, or is it a talent we have developed from our past lives?*

A-8. Both. All force, all power, comes from the same source. To some is given the power of healing, to some the speaking of tongues, to some that of ministry, to some that of another — each as they have builded in their experience, and as they seek to be used as a channel of blessing through *that* they have builded for themselves does the blessing come to others. Being free, then let that not become a stumbling block to some. Rather let those efforts of self be in Him, that *all* blessings may come *to* those in their respective ways. He knoweth what we have need of before we have asked. In the asking, in the seeking, as individuals — and intensified in cooperative thought, cooperative intent, cooperative purpose — so do the activities come to each in *their* way.

Q-9. [*993*]: *Before we can have cooperation, do we not have to offer ourselves?*

A-9. In cooperation *is* the offering of self to be a channel of activity, of thought; for as line upon line, precept upon precept, comes, so does it come through the giving of self; for he that would have life must *give* life, they that would have love must show themselves lovely, they that would have friends must be friendly, they that would have cooperation *must* cooperate by the *giving* of self *to* that as is to be accomplished—whether in the bringing of light to others, bringing of strength, health, understanding, these are one *in* Him.

Q-10. [*993*]: *What lack we yet to cooperate as a group?*

A-10. *Beautiful* is the cooperation of the group in purpose; needs be put in action!

Q-11. [*993*]: *How can we as a group get in accord with those that are aiding us?*

A-11. Open thine hearts to those of the unseen forces that surround the throne of grace, and beauty, and might, and throwing about self that protection that is found in the thoughts of Him—so may the activities be that bring about the work that may be accomplished, the thought as may be made active in the lives of others, the health, the prosperity even that may be brought to those through those efforts of individuals, group, as an active force *with* Him *in* this material plane. [See 262-19, A-7.]

Q-12. [*288*]: *Is not cooperation a natural result when self is lost in the ideal?*

A-12. This is a natural consequence of self-service, self-sacrifice, self-*bewilderment,* in Him. Being the channel is cooperation. Being a blessing is it in action. In whatever *state* of being, meet that upon the basis of *their* position—and *lift* up, look up —and *this* is cooperation.

Q-13. [*288*]: *What does my dream of the group on desert sands signify?*

A-13. A harking back to periods when many gathered here aided *upon* the sands, *through* the activities of many a one— and easy will be the gathering of others as the active forces are put *into* operation, for *like* begets like. Let the seeds sown be cooperation with Him, that the harvest may be a looking up to the leader—the *Giver* of light.

Q-14. [*341*]: *Please interpret and expand upon, "Cooperation is the soul of any organized group of individuals."*

A-14. This is a philosophical truth; and in activity must be that the *spirit* be that that *gives* life. As the soul is made one in purpose, let the spirit that motivates that purpose be in that channel, that position, that is sure that the harvest is in Him; for *man* labors—but *God* giveth the increase. Is the spirit that

that has come from Him? Then the increase must be in Him. As a group gathers to make for cooperative measures in a material plane, so may the soul of that be divided or united in Him, dependent upon the spirit that gives the motivative force *to* the activities of *such* a group; for that as may be sounded here, through the activities of these gathered here—as of old, were heard around the world—so may the activities of *this* group again go through the ages yet unborn, *regenerating* them to that awakening that makes for the *souls* of men safe in the knowledge of Him.

Q-15. [404]: *Are my ideas of taking the right attitude of mind correct for this first lesson?*

A-15. The attitude of mind makes for that which gives the birth, or the rising up of peace, harmony, understanding, or it is as the children *of* the mind—that which brings contending forces that may be warred against; for as *all must* find, "When I would do right the spirit of unrest is ever present." As day by day this is put out of the mind, and more and more the mind of harmony, peace, understanding—not a latent kind, but an *active* force—so does this become the manner in which self is giving expression of that being sought.

Q-16. [404]: *Where must I begin in order to have full coordination in my own body, soul and spirit?*

A-16. Begin with making of self—and self's *own* efforts—as naught but a channel of blessings from the *source* of good to others.

Q-17. [538]: *I seemed to see the following words: Cooperation foundation on which all should be built. In unity is strength.*

A-17. This is as an axiom for all to find in their various expressions the *unity* of purpose, the *oneness* of heart, the *oneness* of mind, in that *"His* will, not my will"—nor my personality—but *losing* self in *His* will. When ye meditate, when ye pray—*not* for self, but that self may be a blessing for others, through this given group—not as personality of same, but as a oneness of purpose in Him, the Giver of all good and perfect gifts.

Q-18. *Is there a message for us now that we may use as the center about which to build the first lesson on* Cooperation?

A-18. As ye have gathered through that meditating of mind,

or in putting self first in the channel of being a blessing, give active *words* for that that thou hast received. This becomes a blessing to self *through* becoming a blessing to others. Seek to know *His* way, and "As I am lifted up in thine consciousness, so will I be lifted in the consciousness of others."

We are through.

ᘒ 262-4 ᘒ

This psychic reading was given by Edgar Cayce at his office, 105th Street [now 67th Street] and Ocean, Virginia Beach, Va., on October 18, 1931, at 4:50 P.M., in accordance with a request made by those present: Edgar Cayce; Gertrude Cayce, conductor; Gladys Davis, steno; C. A. Barrett, Minnie Barrett, Mary Louise Black, Annie Cayce, Hugh Lynn Cayce, L. B. Cayce, Mildred Davis, Edith Edmonds, Florence Edmonds, Fannie M. Freeman, Sarah Hesson, Hannah Miller, Frances Y. Morrow, C. W. Rosborough, M. L. Rosborough, Helena Storey, Esther Wynne, and Marie D. Zentgraf.

Mrs. Cayce: You will have before you the group gathered here who seek guidance and direction in carrying forward the work which we have undertaken. Consider the activity and the progress this group has made and please give us any individual or general suggestions that will aid us in understanding the way Thou would have us carry on. We present at this time three specific conditions for consideration: First, the work and progress on the lesson of Cooperation; second, the time and type of a meditation for the group; third, the presentation of a series of lectures by Edgar Cayce to be given in Norfolk and sponsored by this group. Please answer the questions asked on these.

Mr. Cayce: Yes, we have the group, the individuals, as gathered here; the work as is to be done, that as has been accomplished thus far.

In the considerations of individuals, or of the work to be accomplished by the group, as has been given, there are individuals chosen for—and to be—specific channels through which various phases of that attempted *would* operate or be done.

In the manner as has been begun is well, if all will be of one mind, one purpose, as they gather to consider the various aspects of the work, the lessons to be given.

As is indicated in the first of those lessons, in making preparation for a study group, or a group to perform any given work, there *must* be the wholehearted cooperation, whether in meditation, in thought, in act, or what; for, as is given, the *union* of strength may accomplish much, even as in the activities that may be accomplished in *any* phase of life, whether the spiritual

-17-

life, the material life, the imaginative life or the spiritual; for, as the forces run, in the active principles they must be that as is motivative, that as is the carrier, that as is accomplished.

So, keep *in* the way and manner as has been *outlined,* and be faithful—*each*—*to* that portion. Think none that their dependence must be upon another. Put rather the dependence in the *Father,* and as the spirit moves thee to speak *express* thine self! for *thou* art a child *of* the Creator! and each *has* its portion in that that may be accomplished.

In the meditations—we would set as a specific time for all to meditate; for he that may not cooperate one with another has little part in that that may be accomplished; for whether these be much or little, *their* activity—in *accord*—keeps harmony; harmony makes for peace; peace for understanding; understanding for enlightenment. In *this,* then, let *all* be active.

As to sponsoring those of discourses, that should be activated as the portion of a definite portion of group's *work,* and *these should* study the situations, the individuals—as is seen, as is felt by *them*—and so act that their part may be as the emissary or missionary in the active forces of that being gained by the group, by the group activity; for *all* have their part, and God is no respecter of persons. "As to whether ye shall sit on the right hand or the left is *not mine* to give," said He who would *guide* thee, wilt *thou* be led by the Lamb of life.

Ready for questions.

Q-1. We present the following outline of the first lesson and ask for corrections and suggestions on the fuller preparation of this:

    1. Definition of cooperation
      (a) Physical
      (b) Spiritual
    2. Needs of cooperation
    3. Methods of obtaining cooperation
      (a) Recognition of essential factors
         (1) Seeking physically to be of one mind and purpose
         (2) Losing self in Him and seeking His way

A-1. Change those to A—B, you see.

Q-1. [Continued]

(b) (1) *Physical methods*
    (a) *Daily acts and thoughts towards others*
(2) *Spiritual*
    (a) *Meditation—prayer*
    (b) *Seeking to have the mind of Christ*
(3) *Illustration of the relation of these two methods*
4. *Realization of cooperation; self-elimination, spiritual ecstasy, joy, peace*
5. *Able to give this to the world by becoming channels for His forces to work through*
Any other corrections?

A-1. [Continued] This as outlined, *as* given, is the manner in which this *should,* or would, be presented, they each having *their* part *in* the presenting of same. Hence it becomes not *only* a *living* lesson in each of this *individual* group (if they'll let it grow), but will *be* a living truth in the minds and hearts of those who may seek *through such* an outlined lesson for truth and understanding. Well begun!

Q-2. What points should we emphasize in this lesson?

A-2. As each heading is set, the *emphasis* will be made *by* the *individuals* to whom it is sent. Let this be rather a well-rounded, well-*balanced,* outline—and that of the truth *answering* each as they are set forth here.

Come, ye that are here; for the way is being opened *for all to have a part in the* redemption *of* many *an* individual *in this work. Keep the heart* singing; *not as of sorrow but gladness, in purpose, in deed; for—of* all— *those chosen of Him should be the* gladdest *group of all!*

Q-3. Please suggest a group meditation for this group.

A-3. As the group *gathers* in the various lessons as are *to* be given out, we would *find* that these *should*—and *would* of themselves— *vary* as to that phase of experience that each would seek enlightenment upon. Hence, as has been given in this, this is *well* to be kept until the *lesson* is complete, that ye may *be* of one mind, ye all may *be* a channel, ye all may *have* one purpose.

Do that.

We are through for the present.

⋊ 262-5 ⋉ *This psychic reading was given by Edgar Cayce at his office, 105th Street [now 67th Street] and Ocean, Virginia Beach, Va., on November 29, 1931, at 4:00 P.M., in accordance with a request made by those present: Edgar Cayce; Gertrude Cayce, conductor; Gladys Davis, steno; C. A. Barrett, Minnie Barrett, M. L. Black, Annie Cayce, L. B. Cayce, Mildred Davis, Edith Edmonds, Florence Edmonds, F. M. Freeman, Sarah Hesson, Hannah Miller, F. Y. Morrow, C. W. Rosborough, M. L. Rosborough, and Helena Storey.*

Mrs. Cayce: You will have before you the group gathered here, who seek guidance in carrying on Thy work. We pray that each may be directed that they may contribute of their best to the whole, and that the cooperative work of the group may be kept close in the path of Thy will. You will please answer the questions of the group as a unit and as individuals.

Mr. Cayce: Yes, we have the individuals—and as a group—as gathered here for a purpose. In the way and manner as they each contribute of themselves in a cooperative manner towards being, themselves, a light to others, in magnifying His name in their lives to others, may the work as contemplated, as desired, as sought for, be carried on.

In the lessons as they each have gained through their attempt to cooperate one with another, they each have gained something for themselves, that—if same will be put in a practical, applicable manner in their lives—it will bring to each that as will make life in this experience more worthwhile to each.

Ready for questions.

Q-1. We present the lesson Cooperation compiled by the group, which I shall read. Please make such corrections and suggestions that will clarify, complete or strengthen this lesson. [The lesson is read.]

A-1. The lesson is well.

Q-2. Is this lesson acceptable to the forces, without any correction, just as it is?

A-2. The lesson is well.

Q-3. Are we now ready to begin work upon the second lesson, How to Know Thyself?

A-3. Ready, as each puts into effect that as has been—and

may be—gained through the application of the lesson prepared, to begin to *know* self.

Q-4. What special meditation should we hold in preparing ourselves for work on this lesson? Please suggest the thought we should hold.

A-4. FATHER, AS WE SEEK TO SEE AND KNOW THY FACE, MAY WE EACH—AS INDIVIDUALS, AND AS A GROUP—COME TO KNOW OURSELVES, EVEN AS WE ARE KNOWN, THAT WE—AS LIGHTS IN THEE—MAY GIVE THE BETTER CONCEPT OF THY SPIRIT IN THIS WORLD.

Q-5. Are we handling our work in the correct manner? Please give any specific suggestions that would clarify our understanding and help us at this time.

A-5. Wait ye upon one another. Work ye as a unit. Let *all* be done in order. Wait ye oft on the Lord before speaking the word that would give an improper relationship of that *thou* would present. In this manner may the work be expedited, may it be in unison. Depend not *one* upon another; rather depend upon Him, working together each in their respective sphere. To all are given a portion, a part, in this work. Let each look not upon that that would exalt themselves in any manner; rather that the feeling, the thought, may be the better expressed, that those who seek may gain the closer vision of the Master's face, may have in their hearts, their souls, that peace that comes only from being close to Him; for when He speaks, only peace may abound. Others may make afraid. Others may bring that force that would sound far, yet *He*—the *Prince* of Peace—brings cheer, gladness, to the hearts and souls of those who seek to be a channel of blessing *through Him!*

Q-6. Is there any special message for the group at this time?

A-6. Children, as ye seek in His name to know the *Father's* way, come ever then in singleness of purpose. Think not of the hindrances that are of the man-made nature; rather know in whom thou hast believed, knowing He has brought all things into being, and as ye seek—*and* use—*His* strength, in *His* name, ye *are* His, and will become—and be—the lights that will bring that light into the shadowy places, and—though turmoils and strifes, and contentions, are about you—that peace, *His* peace, will keep thee *safe* in Him.

Q-7. [2124]: Are the readings as have been given sufficiently understood by the group?

A-7. As they each seek in their own hearts and minds, as will be seen in that as will be given in each knowing themselves, each will gain the better understanding, the better insight into that as *is* given from day to day; for as He gave, "Sufficient unto the day is the good—or the evil—thereof." As ye apply His love, His light, in thine *own* life, so does the understanding come of that He would have *each* of *you* do day by day. Tell not thine neighbor how he, or she, should act. Hast thou been put under the same circumstance? Rather give each that standard they may measure themselves by, and be equal— *through such measurements* to the needs of each hour, each circumstance. Walk thine self circumspect in the knowledge thou hast of thine *own* God. Seek as children to know *His* love, His law, His biddings, and as ye seek so shall ye find; for He is in His *holy* temples. Art thou holy? Art thou *desirous* of being holy? Art thou seeking rather the good of thy brother than thine self? Then, as ye know Him, His way ye know— *be* on speaking terms with thy brother.

Q-8. [288]: Tuesday morning, November 24th, I dreamed there was war. We were all on the roof of a building shooting from cubbyholes. Each of us had a post. I noticed a strip, or band, up in the air, about to break, and recognized it was holding up the building, that if it did break the whole structure would crumble and thousands underneath would be destroyed, besides ourselves. I got permission to leave my post and went down and out of the building. I influenced people of higher authority to come and fix the strip so that the building would still stand. What is the significance of this dream?

A-8. That within self there are those needed corrections that can only come from the source of all love, force, power, that the structure that is builded for others may be a unit, a whole. Look to thine own conscience within.

Q-9. [288]: Will I be able to prophesy through dreams?

A-9. Rather interpret.

Q-10. [288]: Will I be able to interpret those that come through me?

A-10. If thou will only open self to be a channel.

Q-11. [*69's husband*]: *What is my duty as a member of this group, and how can I best cooperate?*

A-11. As the light comes in thing own life as respecting the various duties in a secular and spiritual life, so will the body-consciousness be able to be the *balance* as would keep a union of purpose, keeping all in order. As thou wast in the days of old, when in the temple thou ministered to the needs of those—and *prophesied* under the spirit of the office held—so wilt thou be able to minister in this direction, as the light opens through the associations of the cooperation of self with others, in studying to *know* His way.

We are through for the present.

≽ 262-6 ≼

This psychic reading was given by Edgar Cayce at his office, 105th Street [now 67th Street] and Ocean, Virginia Beach, Va., on December 13, 1931, at 4:20 P.M., in accordance with a request made by those present: Edgar Cayce; Gertrude Cayce, conductor; Gladys Davis, steno; C. A. Barrett, Minnie Barrett, M. L. Black, Hugh Lynn Cayce, Mildred Davis, Edith Edmonds, Florence Edmonds, F. M. Freeman, H. H. Jones, Hannah Miller, F. Y. Morrow, C. W. Rosborough, M. L. Rosborough, and Helena Storey.

Mrs. Cayce: You will have before you the group present in this room. We seek prayerfully as individuals, and as a group, to come to a better understanding of ourselves and be able to present this to others through the lessons we are preparing. You will please answer the questions we ask.

Mr. Cayce: Yes, we have the group, as a group, as individuals, and the manner in which each comes seeking that they may know His face, that as individuals, as a group, they may be the more perfect lights in His name.

In coming, each should first know these as the marks of judgment; that there must by each individual be set that as is to be a standard of measurements, of valuations, of percepts, precepts and concepts. Knowing first, then, that self is not other than that it, as an individual, may receive from without or from within. As the conditions then arise, each is dependent one upon another in the *material* phases of life, and as such each must be their concept of that they have accepted as being a standard, a measurement, an active force within their own experience. *Measure* then not *by* self, for he that doeth such is not wise. Measure not by earthly standards, would ye know self; rather by that as has proven within self as a criterion, as an ensample, as a guide. *Know* in what ye *have* believed, and *act* that way.

Ready for questions.

Q-1. Please interpret the following dream had by Edgar Cayce, Saturday morning, December 12th, in which he was in meditation with this group. He heard a voice calling but was prevented from answering by the group.

A-1. As has been indicated, that there are needs in the

spiritual and the material world for the *efforts* of this entity, and that there must needs be those activities in the one or the other for the concentration of the *actions* of the entity. Where the need is most, there the body, there the activities of the entity, will be. There is the stage of transformation coming, then, to the entity, will this be held in the material plane or in spirit—and the actions depend upon the group, as was seen.

Q-2. What can we as individuals, and as a group, do to aid in expressing that which will create the force necessary to counterbalance the call from the other side?

A-2. Work!

Q-3. [993]: Dream, Saturday night, December 12th, in which Mr. Cayce was testing or raising vibrations of individuals in the group. Interpret.

A-3. This another expression of the same experience, that the activities of the group in their *individual* lives, as *well* as group, may be measured by those vibrations or activities of the body, or *entity,* so testing same. As seen, that each in their *respective* way *responded* to the test made. So each, in that that is given by those sources from whom, or the measure by which each measure themselves, are they able to give that strength, or that aid, in that being attempted—in the awakening of selves, as *well* as others!

Well were it that *all* not only *know* but understand, what it means to be measured by not that which one *has,* but that each is able to give out; or, to be better put, know what it *means* to *be* a *channel* of blessing to someone! As ye have received, give; for Lo, I stand and knock! Who will open and let that peace, that joy, enter, that there *may* be more light in thine own soul? Think not on the cares of the day nor the hour. Be not blinded by those things that make the physical body afraid; for He that will come will *not* be denied. "Not everyone that saith Lord, Lord—but he that doeth the *will* of the Father." As I *in* Him, and ye *in* me, so shall *His* will be done *in* earth as it is in heaven.

Q-4. [993]: Through which one of its members can the group best aid Edgar Cayce in the present situation?

A-4. Each in their own *respective* way and manner, and let not *one* depend upon the other! Good way to know yourself also!

Q-5. How may I, [538], best aid?

A-5. In awakening that that brings, as has been seen, the desires to do that the love, physically, spiritually shown, may find as a renewing strength. Does love wane through over-activity, or grow by use? Does love fail or wear away, or is it not that, that in *blossoming,* in growth, in use, *magnifies* and so brings into being those forces as overcometh all things? Do as thine *heart,* thine inner self, as thine *soul,* dictateth. Be not *ashamed* to be what you are! If you *are,* there is something amiss! The standard is shortened or lengthened, and does not fit the pattern!

Q-6. How can [341] best aid?

A-6. Even as has been seen, that here a little, there a little, is added in the material activities of individuals that, that shows a growth. Has self grown by association? Has self been neglected by the association? Then demand, or give, as self is found to be.

Q-7. How may [288] best aid?

A-7. Keeping in accord those things known to be the *uplifting,* the *opening,* to those of *many* conditions that makes for *creative energies,* even as *has* been oft in associations. Not in *any* selfish or unseeming manner; but keep thine heart pure, thine actions unquestioned, thine self free from condemnation!

Q-8. How may [295] best aid?

A-8. In keeping those of the precepts in activity *known* as from *His* own self, that he that would aid must show forth the desire in self, as well as in others. Keep thine heart *singing!* Make for the needs *of* the abilities of each to be able to *accomplish something* in the now! Making, then, demands for that as may be of help to others.

Q-9. [462]: Have I any part in the work with this group; if so, please give it.

A-9. Whosoever *will* has a part, or parcel, in *His* work. This is *His* work! He that has *called to* thee! If one heeds not, or hears not the invitation, then one has only missed an opportunity and it must all be done over again. As self finds in contemplation of that brought in the lives, the activities, of those contacting those experiences in the group, this *must* of itself (if it be alive) *awaken* a desire, that—measured or acted upon by that arising within self through its *own* meditation—will find what willing

hands are *willing* to do. Each are called in *their* respective
sphere. Each must find the *answer* in their own selves. Remember thou not, "Come ye with *me,* and I will make you fishers
of men"? Again, "Lord, wilt thou grant my request when thou
comest in thy kingdom, that I and my brother may sit the one
on the right hand, the other on the left?" "Art thou able to
drink of the cup?" "We are able." "Indeed ye *shall* drink, *but*
to sit on my right or my left is not mine to give." "He that *doeth*
the will of the Father, the same is my mother, my brother, my
sister."

We are through.

≈ 262-7 ≼

This psychic reading was given by Edgar Cayce at his office, 105th Street [now 67th Street] and Ocean, Virginia Beach, Va., on December 15, 1931, at 8:30 P.M., in accordance with a request made by those present: Edgar Cayce; Gertrude Cayce, conductor; Gladys Davis, steno; C. A. Barrett, Minnie Barrett, M. L. Black, Hugh Lynn Cayce, Mildred Davis, Edith Edmonds, Florence Edmonds, F. M. Freeman, Hannah Miller, F. Y. Morrow, C. W. Rosborough, M. L. Rosborough, Helena Storey, and Esther Wynne.

Mrs. Cayce: You will have before you the group gathered here, who seek a clearer understanding of the directions given all, in the reading of Sunday, December 13th, to work in order to meet the conditions which have arisen in connection with this channel of the forces, Edgar Cayce. As I name each individual, please give them explicit directions and work which will relieve this present situation.

Mr. Cayce: Yes, we have the group as gathered here, as individuals, as a group. In seeking understanding is well; in application of that *already understood* is better. As given, each in their own way and manner may aid, or hinder, according to the application of their own abilities, own talent, own understanding. Each have indicated their desire to know the manner and way of a clearer approach to the continuity of *life,* or the origin of life, light, that they might be a better channel of manifesting same as individuals, as a group. In this individual situation, many in their own way and manner have sought to apply that known or felt in self to be the manner or way to aid in the existent situation or condition. Then, as they seek for an individual interpretation of *their* work, *their* portion in same, each *should* apply that known, and in the application gain a clearer, a better understanding, in experience.

Q-1. [2124]: When will I be ready to begin my spiritual work under your instruction?

A-1. When the light has come sufficient in self to know the awakening that gives strength, power, understanding. As that known is used, the light cometh. When will that be put in more perfect activity? Do not become confused in waiting. Be not overanxious, that *any* source, any channel, would do. Know

-28-

that He whom *thou* hast *named* has directed, for "My sheep will hear my voice, and not heed *any* other."

Q-2. [307]: *What more specific work can I do?*

A-2. This may be as in a specific condition or as a general condition as for all. In the specific manner much has been accomplished in the activities of the mental *and* spiritual self. In the general, continue to be a light-bearer to others, as *has* been *indicated* in thine work.

Q-3. [2125]: *What is my definite work?*

A-3. Keep in the way and manner as has been indicated as the manner in which self may be awakened to the possibilities in self. In general, keep that known in *applying* self *to* that as is known, being more gentle, more loving, more in kindness to all; for little by little we gain that understanding that comes from keeping a heart, a mind, a life in the light.

Q-4. [379]: *What can I do at this time?*

A-4. Think not that the abilities of self are lacking in such conditions. Doubt not that thine own supplications reach the throne of grace or mercy. *Show forth,* then, that in thine activities day by day, that in the union of strength *comes* a greater understanding in all.

Q-5. [404]: *Is there more that I can do at this time?*

A-5. Keep on *keeping* on, and—as this, that or the other experience opens the understanding of that necessary for spiritual or physical activity—be *willing* and *ready* to answer.

Q-6. [69]: *What more specific work can I do at this time?*

A-6. Doubt not self nor self's abilities, for in *doing* does strength come. Keep that consciousness that answers to self, as face answers to face in the water, and this will bring the answer in self as to whether the Spirit of the Creative Forces bears witness with thine *own* spirit. Not that any should chide another, unless self's own self answers for that as *is* felt or acclaimed in self.

Q-7. [69's husband]:

A-7. As has been given in that the entity, the *inner* self, seeks, knows intuitive forces much more than is *often* expressed in action, or that the word of the moment covers much that is felt *to* be true in the inner self. *Cultivate* rather that spiritual insight ability in self, that the analysis of disorder, disruption, distress, may be thine to correct at a *moment's* thought or activity; for he that has *been* anointed to the priesthood in the *living* God's activities, *loses* little of abilities in *many* of the appearances. Then, *save* thine activities in that that may *be* accomplished in self. How? Open thine understanding, that those forces as may manifest, even through that anointing, may bring that of an *understanding* heart, mind, soul, and *much* may be accomplished by the activities of the entity.

Q-8. Interpret the word "work" for me in this connection.

A-8. As ye have chosen, as ye have *been* chosen, know ye not that ye should be about the *Father's* business? *Work!* As each *are* given, and each interpret their own activities, so apply self in *that* direction as to answer that consciousness, or the mind of the soul, as to know *all* is well, and as the answer comes— know *work* has been accomplished.

Q-9. [560]: What more specific work can I do at this time?

A-9. Keep on in the manner as thou hast set before thyself, for the way is opening, the light *is* dawning, for thee.

Q-10. [303]: What can I do at this time?

A-10. Doubt not in self that the seeking, as self would apply self, has its own reward in that as *is* being, as *may* be, accomplished in the whole. Each should learn, in the attempts as is being made by each, the *lesson* as *has* been set by the *group* as the *lesson* of cooperation toward one thing to be accomplished; remembering, there has been given, "Who can, by taking thought, add one whit or one cubit to his stature?" but "When thou prayest enter into thine closet and *pray,* and He that heareth in secret will reward thee openly." Then remembering, the giving, the understanding, *comes* from Him.

Q-11. [993]: Is there any more definite work for me at this time?

A-11. As was seen in the testing of those that had raised their vibrations for an understanding, then pray *ye* that *all* may *hold* as one. A group, a chain, a band, is as strong as its weakest member.

Q-12. What should I do in connection with aiding the organization?

A-12. Speak, act, when the *spirit* gives utterance, where the way is opened; then fill that necessary for a spreading an understanding of that as has been tested and tried by self.

Q-13. Explain what is meant by the transformation taking place or to take place in connection with the work of Edgar Cayce.

A-13. In an explanation, let's all understand in their own speech. To some, an awakening to the greater channels of power; to others, more spirituality *than* materiality. To others, the karmic influences have reached *their* changing point, that the vibrations may be brought one to another. In transformation comes a light for those that *look* for same.

Q-14. Any special message for us as a group at this time?

A-14. Hold fast to *that* thou hast, pressing on to the mark of the higher calling as is set in Him; keeping thine own garments white, and *seeing* less and less fault in the other fellow.

We are through.

≽ 262-8 ≼

This psychic reading was given by Edgar Cayce at his office, 105th Street [now 67th Street] and Ocean, Virginia Beach, Va., on December 27, 1931, at 4:00 P.M., in accordance with a request made by those present: Edgar Cayce; Gertrude Cayce, conductor; Gladys Davis, steno; M. L. Black, Annie Cayce, Hugh Lynn Cayce, L. B. Cayce, Mildred Davis, Edith Edmonds, Florence Edmonds, F. M. Freeman, L. J. Hesson, Sarah Hesson, Sarah E. McPherson, Hannah Miller, F. Y. Morrow, C. W. Rosborough, M. L. Rosborough, and Esther Wynne.

Mrs. Cayce: You will have before you the group gathered here who seek further guidance in working upon the lesson of Knowing Self. *Please give us that which we need at this time in carrying on Thy work. Please answer the questions asked by each at this time.*

Mr. Cayce: We have the group, as a group and as individuals, as gathered here. In the preparation of lessons, as has been outlined, well that they each prepare themselves to be a channel that they may be the better able to minister through their selves to others in the studies or lessons as being prepared.

As has been given, there must be considered the self as an entity, an integral factor in the seeking to know that as goes on from within and from without.

As this should be a practical lesson in the study of self first, then let each consider the factors within self that must reason with, or reason from, those factors from without. There is, then, the physical body with its physical attributes. The various members must function one with another in the lesson of cooperation, and would one member war against another then disorder must naturally ensue.

There are, then, the organs and their functionings of the physical or natural body, that have their individual desires that are taken into consideration when the body functions in its physical sense as a unit of creative forces that are manifesting in a material world, in the body with its senses, that make known to the physical body those magnified desires or natures of that physical body. These are registered in the activities of the physical body in such a way and manner as to stamp upon the very face of the body that which has been magnified through its own physical senses. These senses are but attunements within a physical body, each vibrating according to the training of, or elements of concentration by the physical forces of the body as pertaining to attunements of the development of that, of which the physical body is a *material* representation; for not only do these show forth that which *is* magnified in a single appearance or experience, but of the whole impressions as have been received through those varied experiences of that entity; the registering being in the soul of the entity, the same as in the material sense it is in the physiognomy of the individual upon which the activities of that environ in which the entity has placed itself, by its attunement to the various elements about that entity. In the same sense these elements, then, are made up of the *physical* body, the *mental* body, the *spiritual* body, each with their attributes and associations and connections that must all work in unison in much the same manner as the organs of the physical body must *attune* themselves in their ratio or relative active forces with a normal physical functioning body. This lesson! [See 262-10, A-15, A-16.]

Ready for questions.

Q-1. [115]: *After group meditation for the folks in New York, I dreamed I was talking to and walking with Gladys. She said, "They do not pay their rent." I asked who owned the place (we seemed near a house). Gladys said, "Mr. Cayce." The building seemed quite large and rambling and was at the Beach. We wandered around the place, and I noticed much iron rubbish, both old and new. Gladys seemed to fade out of the picture. I still wandered around the place, discovered a lovely lake, clear as crystal, beautiful white swans swimming around and being fed by loving happy children. Looking over the lake I saw there beautiful houses like a new settlement of beautiful happy homes, a white village, flowers, etc. Then I was so happy, felt uplifted, etc. What is the significance of this dream? [Gladys Davis felt that this dream may have also been prophetic. She related that in the Spring, 1932, Mr. Cayce moved into a house on Arctic Crescent: "big, rambling old house, very dirty and mis-used . . . Beautiful Holly Lake was in the back; often swans could be seen. Years later little white cottages appeared across the lake."]*

A-1. This, as is indicated, is emblematical of conditions within the development of the individual, or *entity*-individual itself, as to the individual ideal in that as is held in its consciousness. Now apply that as has been given, as to how the activities of a body-consciousness or mental body acts upon incidents or happenings in a material plane, and we will find the answers in the material sense; that is, *sense* conditions of material nature represent the spiritual, or mental and spiritual aspects, and as the body viewed those of disorders, representing in the body-consciousness that of laxness, or inability in directions that made for disorders; yet as these are turned into directions that become of more the mental and spiritual aspect, the visions of that as would *again* be held by the *entity,* or *individual,* as ideal, or idealistic, arise from the rubbish of those things material. *Dreams* are such of which buildings come into the material aspects of life. First as visions that are as to some visionary, unreal. They are crystallized in the lives and activities of others through those constant actions upon the various elements in the body of an individual entity, which is as being studied. Then they act upon those in such a manner as to bring into being realities, that in a material plane represent those; as the peace and tranquility of the lake with its crystal fountains, and the swans as representing peace and serenity as come with such surroundings, and with the *hope* as in flowers and blossoms and children. Then the whole as *emblems* in the body-consciousness, seeing, visioning, that to which its own self *is* raising, *may* raise, those *around* self. Hence the entity, the body, *truly* the missionary, the emissary.

Q-2. [560]: *Please interpret, "As the activities of self in the relations to others is made active, so will the water of life be made more plain, more active in the experience of self, as was the depth and the activities of that mother of life seen."* [*See 262-3, A-4.*]

A-2. Again an emblematical opening of the entity's consciousness as to that practical applicability of things unseen upon the relative forces, of force within individuals being raised in their consciousness to the awakening of the universality of the continuity of life, God, *in* human experience; and as the lesson — as is and will be awakened in the consciousness of each entity — is aroused in the study of self, these awarenesses *of* the activities become more and more real. As is conceded, even by the most pessimistic, that *unseen* forces are the more powerful than those seen—or realities, as to some. The dreamer, the visionary, those who attune themselves to the infinite, the more often receive the more infinite power, for those attunements that will bring into being those as of the realities of the *unseen* forces being as *coordinant* in their activity, as the night follows the day, the moon sheds its light from the activity of the giver of light, the sun.

Q-3. What service did Isusi [560] render in the temple in the Egyptian period?

A-3. As those in the temple were raised in their understandings, through the applications of the laws (of love) as meted or measured, the entity was in the capacity of making *practical, personal* application of such in the lives of those who sought to be channels for such laws, such loves, such manifestations as raised the attunements of those seeking to be channels in the *spiritual* sense.

Q-4. [993]: Am I drawing near to the time when through knowing self I can know the voice of the teacher within?

A-4. As self keeps self nearer in attune, in accord, in vibration, in *coordinating* of vibration, nearer the awakening, nearer the ability to heal self and give life, light, understanding, to another. Each individual (as this entity) should know, first is the application, then the *understanding* and the *knowledge* of *that* applied. As in the life, so in the actions, in thought and body of an entity, that this *is!* Then how is *its* manner of executing that function it performs? As these are in action, the awakening is soon to come to the entity of the *life* within. [See 262-10, A-15.]

Q-5. [993]: Were my two dreams on Sunday, December 7, 1931, one at morning, the other at night, a glimpse of self-awakening?

([993's] dreams, not read in the above: "The first dream was a miniature statue of an adult. It seemed to have its place near me. I had a desire to take it in my aura, as I did. It seemed to have life. I called [560] to take it in her aura. She came but did not take it. She seemed afraid. I received joy by holding it in my arms and wanted her to have the same experience.

"The second dream, I felt something being driven through the

center of my left hand and on awakening there came the Master's hand before me. ")

A-5. A glimpse of self-awakening. As in the visions as seen, as to how the light, or lights in their variation, brought those various effects upon not only the surroundings but upon the individuals upon whom they shone, so does the awakening in self act not *only* upon self but upon the *activities* of self and those to whom, *with* whom, *through* whom, self ministers.

Q-6. Please explain the second dream.

A-6. This as a continuation in its *varied* activity upon those who, not seeking—yet become *aware* of that awakening. To turn back for a moment, may all understand the explanation of an awakening from within: In self, as has been given, is those of the material natures in an entity without as yet considering that that *awakens* a desire to know, not only that of the without but that that *awakens* a desire for a *continuity of* self other than from a selfish viewpoint. Get the variation and difference now! As seen in the second vision, those from without are being acted upon in much the same manner as an individual that is not aware of the holiness of a brother, yet in contact *with* such an one feels or experiences, through not a feeling, not a hearing, not a tasting, not a vision of, an aweness of a presence! So, as in the vision as seen, those without *will, are, must* become awed by the activities of self, of the group—of *what* it stands for!

Q-7. [379]: What do I need most to further my development, also to know self better?

A-7. As self will meditate upon that as has been given, then in seeking those answers to that as *comes* to self, in the awareness of the various conditions physical, mental, spiritual, that are awakened through the study of that given, will there be seen, felt, known, understood, that that will *awaken* self to a more close *unison* of purpose; for indecisions have often racked the *mental* body of this entity, but with *unison* of the mental visions will there come more peace, more harmony, more unison of purpose.

We are through for the present.

≈ 262-9 ⧏

This psychic reading was given by Edgar Cayce at his office, 105th Street [now 67th Street] and Ocean, Virginia Beach, Va., on January 10, 1932, at 4:10 P.M., in accordance with a request made by those present: Edgar Cayce; Gertrude Cayce, conductor; Gladys Davis, steno; Hugh Lynn Cayce, L. B. Cayce, Mildred Davis, Edith Edmonds, Florence Edmonds, F. M. Freeman, Hannah Miller, F. Y. Morrow, Eloise Potter, C. W. Rosborough, M. L. Rosborough, Helena Storey, and Esther Wynne.

Mrs. Cayce: You will have before you the group gathered here who seek guidance in preparing the lesson on Know Thyself. *We pray that we may receive·that which we need to guide us in our work at this time. Please answer the questions each will ask.*

Mr. Cayce: Yes, we have the group—as a group, as individuals—gathered here. As the group comes as a unit, so may each receive—through their desire to give out—that that is necessary for the lessons that may awaken in others seeking the light. Each should know this: That as is self's own ideal is the standard by which the will is controlled or measured. *WHAT Is Thy Ideal?* then, would be the next lesson.

Ready for questions.

Q-1. [2112]: Where can I find a record of my work in spreading the glad tidings to those in Mt. Seir during my appearance at the time of the Christ?

A-1. There is in the common version of the incident of the woman at the well, the sister of the entity, which gives, "Ye say in Jerusalem [is] the place of worship, *our* fathers [say] Mt. Seir." The answer was, "The day will come when neither in Jerusalem nor in the mount, but in each individual's heart." As for the tidings as given by the entity in that period, there may be found a record in that of Josephus, as well as in the stories that are among the writings of one Bartimaeus in the Jewish history, page forty-five. In this there is given as the variation of how, or what effect is had upon those of that particular peoples, that is the mixture of the Edomites and the Jewish peoples left when the first of these were carried into captivity. With the return of those first under Zerubbabel, and the dispersing as happened by Sanballat and Loti [?], as teachers in Seir, these were then called the Samaritans, and *Seir—*

where Jeroboam had builded an altar—was chosen as the place for these peoples to worship. With the teachings, now, of the Man of Nazareth to these peoples, began with this household —Selmaa and Nina[?], and Nola[?], with the changes in the peoples of the establishing of groups nearer akin to those of the synagogue, or that of what would be termed the daily or cottage prayer meetings—see? These will be found, or as reference to these, in that given. Josephus makes one reference. Those in the others are among the stories in Jewish literature. The intent, as is seen, is to influence the different effects had upon individual minds by the teachings of this man, teacher, leader. [See 2112-1.]

Q-2. [288]: *Is the interpretation and lesson correct, which I have written on the vision presented through me on the morning of January 9, 1932?*

A-2. In part, correct. Better, in the interpreting of vision, that is evident in itself of being emblematical, that there be sufficient of collaborations of events as *is* affecting individuals seen. Then a more nearer the interpretation may be had.

Q-3. *What is the deeper significance of this dream?*

A-3. Better wait and see! [See detail of dream published in Volume IV of this publication series.]

Q-4. [2673]: *Is this an open group, and may I become one of the group at this time?*

A-4. The open group had best be sought as from the individuals. To make one with that the group seeks is different. In seeking, ye shall find. Know that there are the openings ever for those that seek to know His face, for those who will wait upon the Lord. Be not overanxious. *Wait* ye on the Lord. In seeking, do not seek something afar, nor yet something new; rather that there are the proper ideals, the proper valuations of that *already* in hand. In using the opportunities in hand comes the understanding of larger, better, greater things; for whom the Lord loveth, to him is given *in hand* that which, if used, brings understanding and peace.

Q-5. [379]: *Are my dreams ever significant of spiritual awakening?*

A-5. As is experienced by the entity, there are dreams and visions and experiences. When only dreams, these *too* are significant—but rather of that of the physical health, or physical conditions. In visions there is oft the *inter-between* giving expressions that make for an awakening between the mental consciousness, or that that has been turned over and over in the physical consciousness and mind being weighed with that the self holds as its ideal. In visions where spiritual awakenings, these most often are seen in symbols or signs, to the entity; for, as the training of self's consciousness in a manner of interpreting the visions would be in expressions of eye, hand, mouth, posture or the like, these are *interpreted* in thine own language. When these are, then, in symbols of such, know the awakening is at hand.

Q-6. [*2673*]: *In what way can I best serve?*

A-6. Much might be said to the body as to manners or ways. Much may be gained by the body, by the entity, in considering that as was said to the young ruler; not gifts but *self* is that necessary to be used in aid to others; not my will but Thine be done in me! Use me! as Thou seest fit; not as I *would* be used, but as Thou seest fit! As the body-consciousness and mind lends a stability to others, then doubt not self; for to doubt self is to create that of a negative force that brings upon its *return* to self discontent—see? For, as ye seek, ye *shall* find! Faint not at the long tarrying, nor be not unmindful that he that is faithful unto the end shall wear the *crown* of life.

Q-7. [*303*]: *How may I learn to know self as I am known?*

A-7. Being able to, as it were, *literally,* stand aside and watch self pass by! Take the time to occasionally be sufficiently introspective of that, that may happen in self's relation to others, to *see* the reactions of others as to that as was done by self; for true—as it has been said—no man lives to himself, no man dies to himself; for as the currents run to bring about the forces that are so necessary to man's own in these material things, so are those forces in self active upon those whom we act upon. Being able, then, to see self as others see you; for, as has been given, "*Now* we know in part, then shall we know even as we are known." Then, in Him so let thy life be in Him, in thought, in deed, that, "Ye that have known me have known the Father also" may be truly said of self. Stand aside and watch self pass by!

*Q-8. What definite work may I do as an emissary or mission-
ary?*

A-8. As the opportunity, day by day, is given, be not unmindful of speaking when there is the opportunity; not that self
becomes offensive, no! Kindness has *never* been offensive, will
never be offensive to anyone! The kindly thought, the kindly act
—for "He that gives the cup of cold water in my name shall
not lose his reward." This is oft interpreted as reward for self.
Rather is it the knowledge that comes from a true within, that
"His Spirit beareth witness with thy spirit" that ye are *known*
of Him *among* men. In this manner may the body act as the
missionary, as the emissary. That there may be harsh words,
there may be slight remarks oft, is apparent—but be so *close,*
that you can smile with those that would make of thy acts puns,
even. Be able to make them with them, yet so kindly that they
heap coals of fire upon the heads of those that laugh.

*Q-9. [307]: Explain the subject of the second lesson, "Know
self as I am known."*

A-9. As each gains, through their own meditation or prayer,
that they may be known among men even as they are known
with Him, this *takes* on an import. Would ye act before thy God
in the manner ye act before thine brother? Love one another.
"A new commandment I give, that ye *love* one another." In *this*
manner may each see themselves as others see them. Let not
thy words and thy actions be so different that they are not
children of the same family. Let thy deeds, let thy words, be
in keeping with that others see in thee.

*Q-10. Give the best means by which I may know myself as I
am known.*

A-10. By measuring self by that standard that is thine own
ideal.

Q-11. Explain more fully my work as a light-bearer to others.

A-11. As the body-consciousness goes about giving that as
received day by day, so does the body become a bearer of tidings
to others, so that, as the body is seen and known among others
as one that bears tidings of that as *has* come, is passing, will
come to pass among men. In the thoughts, in the acts, keep self
in attunement with the ideal, and you'll always know what's
passing on in your own self!

Q-12. Is there any message to the compilers?

A-12. Be patient with those that are lax, but be positive *ever*. Keep thine own counsel oft, and counsel oft with others. Be sure each gives of themselves in the lessons from week to week, for in this is the *hope* of the lessons becoming the light to many in many a place, many a land; for there is being made such as has not yet *been* made in the whole of meditating in group or cooperation of a body.

Q-13. [404]: What must I do in order to know self better?

A-13. As self meditates upon the various activities of self, as to how oft self becomes the impetus of another's activity, then there may be seen that self is understood, or *not* understood, as the *activities* of self have been. How oft in thine own self has *thou* been that, that *impelled* another to look within themselves as to whether they were in accord with that *He* would have them do? How *oft* hast thou made another think better of themselves? Not *laud* themselves, but think *better* of themselves? In this may one see self; for in magnifying Him self sees self as *others* may see self in self's activities.

Q-14. [560]: Upon awakening I remembered the following. Was it imagined or a dream or a realization? I seemed to realize that I was in a boat, suspended quite high from the deck, seemingly in a hammock which rocked to and fro over the side of the deck. I realized there was an ocean beneath and if I was thrown out what the result would be. Then the words came, "Not my will but Thine, O Lord, be done." I then saw, as it appeared to me, in the heavens a beautiful white-robed angel. Please interpret.

A-14. As seen, an emblematical vision of self's own awakening to the conditions about self, those associated with self, and the source of help and aid as may come through the combined efforts of those as indicated by the character of the group, and by the character of the hammock or boat as seen. In a sea, or maze, are many. As the white light of truth is made manifest in the hearts and souls of many, will peace, harmony, contentment, joy of service come to all.

Q-15. [993]: Please explain the message of the dream I had the last part of December, in which there was a beautiful white horse climbing up the side of a high wall. I seemed to be looking down upon him, and as he came nearer I became afraid and put

*my hand upon his head, and as I did his head became that of
a man.*

A-15. As indicated, there is, has, will come to the consciousness of the entity, in the service being given upon the wall of
faith, those messages time and again of the various effects had
upon the minds, the bodies of individuals in their various stages
of attunement or development, and oft these may become confusing; yet—as seen—with the touch that comes from the
closer associations of self and those that aid, or would aid in
these closer communions for those that are suffering in body
or mind, or in the various vicissitudes of their experience, these
become more gentle—as their awakening that they, *too,* may
be the *Sons* of God!

We are through.

This psychic reading was given by Edgar Cayce at his office, 105th Street [now 67th Street] and Ocean, Virginia Beach, Va., on January 24, 1932, at 3:50 P.M., in accordance with a request made by those present: Edgar Cayce; Gertrude Cayce, conductor; Gladys Davis, steno; C. A. Barrett, Minnie Barrett, M. L. Black, Annie Cayce, Hugh Lynn Cayce, L. B. Cayce, Mildred Davis, Edith Edmonds, Florence Edmonds, F. M. Freeman, Lu Hesson, Sarah Hesson, S. E. McPherson, Hannah Miller, F. Y. Morrow, Anne Penn, C. W. Rosborough, M. L. Rosborough, Helen Storey, and Esther Wynne.

⩗ 262-10 ⩘

Mrs. Cayce: You will have before you the group gathered here and the work which they have done on the lesson of Know Thyself, *the first draft of which I hold in my hand. You will give such counsel as will be helpful to the group at this time, and will answer the questions which will be asked concerning this lesson or other phases of the work of the group or their experiences.*

Mr. Cayce: We have the group as gathered here, as a group, as individuals; also those conditions as surround the group in the activities respecting the preparation of lessons that have been contemplated. There is not as wholehearted cooperation on the preparation of lessons as there should be! Each should contribute their portion to such lessons, that it (the lessons) may be complete as a whole. Do not start and then turn back. Remember, as has been given, he that putteth his hand to the plow and looketh back, better that he had never begun! In the preparations, these have been given for the use of each individual's application, and—as each will apply that given— there will come that which will be helpful to another. As ye have received, so give!

Ready for questions.

Q-1. As I read the first draft of the lesson as prepared, please make such corrections, expansions or suggestions, that may be helpful in clarifying this subject. [Mrs. Cayce reads the first paragraph:]

*Man is endowed with no greater ability than of being able to step aside and study self. Down through the ages there has come the command from the great teachers—*know self. *It is the key*

-43-

*to the door which bars the way to the path of light and under-
standing of universal law and its creator.*

A-1. This correct, yet may be altered in the first lines to
clarify those functionings of the spiritual and mental mind; as,
the ability being a functioning of that which enables entity to
know himself, herself, to be a part of the whole, yet not the
whole—which gives the ability of an individual to see self as
self is! Few there are, to be sure, that often desire to see themselves as others see them! But he, or she, that would be a
channel of blessing, an avenue of expression of the Son, of the
Teacher, of the Father, will keep *that* temple, that self, clean!

*Q-2. [Mrs. Cayce reads the second paragraph:] To know self
is not only to be cognizant of the acts of the physical body, but
to know self as an entity, a complete factor capable of knowing
all that goes on within and without of self. This spring of knowledge is tapped only by those who are willing to pay the price.
The price is a complete surrender of self with a purification and
dedication that comes only through prayer, service and meditation. While it is along the straight and narrow way, it is open
to all and freely is the water of life offered to all.*

A-2. Well given.

*Q-3. [Mrs. Cayce reads the third paragraph:] Each as an entity
is a miniature copy of the universe, possessing a physical body,
a mental body and a spiritual body. These bodies are so closely
associated and related that the vibrations of one affect the other
two. The mental especially partakes of the other two; in the
physical as the conscious mind and in the spiritual as the super-
conscious mind.*

A-3. Well.

*Q-4. [Mrs. Cayce reads the fourth paragraph:] In the study of
self, beginning with the physical body we should recognize that
it is the temple of the living God, that it has pleased God to
manifest Himself through this medium to the world. This physical body is a composite unit of creative force manifesting in the
material world.*

A-4. Good.

*Q-5. [Mrs. Cayce reads the fifth paragraph:] The members of
the body must all work in unison, for should one war against
another, discord naturally follows. Each member has its office*

and so important is its office that no other member can be it, neither can it be counted useless and insignificant and as we know ourselves each member is cherished and blessed.

A-5. Good.

Q-6. [Mrs. Cayce reads the sixth paragraph:] Each organ has its individual office and desires which are in themselves holy. Keep them so. The senses make known to the physical body those magnified desires or natures of the physical body. These are registered in the activities of the physical body in such a way and manner as to stamp upon the very face of the body that which has been magnified through its physical senses. These senses are but attunements with the physical body, each vibrating according to the training of, or elements of concentration by the physical forces of the body, as pertaining to attunements of development of that of which the physical body is a material representation; for not only do these show forth that which is magnified in a single appearance or experience of the entity, but the whole impressions that have been received through the varied experiences of the entity; the registering being in the soul of the entity, the same as in the material sense it is in the physiognomy of the individual.

A-6. Very good.

Q-7. [Mrs. Cayce reads the seventh paragraph:] In the same manner the desires of the mental and spiritual bodies build that which becomes apparent to others and to yourself as you. This process of building up the entity has been going on for ages. The great factors of heredity, environment, karma, thought vibration and the actions of universal law and in the planes beyond the physical, all have their influence upon the entity just as the desires and vibrations of the physical organs attract and build the composition of the physical body. You are a result of not only the development of the race before you, but also the individual development which has been going on since your creation as an individual soul.

A-7. Well said.

Q-8. Please outline the paragraph for the material on the mental body.

A-8. This may be builded upon that as may be received by each individual, upon their reactions to the effect that cooperation and knowing self gives to their mental beings in preparation. The *lessons* are to be prepared by those that *magnify* that they receive, that it may respond or find response *in* the mental, and the material, and the spiritual minds of those who seek. Do some work!

Q-9. The spiritual body.

A-9. The same.

Q-10. [Mrs. Cayce reads the eighth paragraph.] Study self in its relation to others. Literally stand aside and see self pass. Take the time to be occasionally introspective of that, that may happen in self's relation to others, to see the reaction of others to that as was done by self; "For no man liveth to himself and no man dieth to himself." Take into account the acts, thoughts and words for the day, for these reflect your concept of God. Would you act before God as you do your brother? "A new commandment I give unto you, that you love one another." Dare to realize that you now, today, begin to reflect a full development of your soul, that you now manifest God's love and are known before man as you are known of God. Self only stands in the way. Then begin to study and discipline self, that your words and actions may not be so different that they are not children of the same family.

A-10. Good.

Q-11. [Mrs. Cayce reads the ninth paragraph.] In seeking to know self through meditation, or by taking inventory of self, one is passing, as it were, a "signpost," seeing a little, catching a word here, an idea there, from those we contact day by day, which shows we are all closely related and are traveling somewhere along the same road. Truly, therefore, in knowing self is knowing the other fellow also, for all are parts of one mind. Should it not make us more tolerant of the weakness of our brother as we view him as we are, or as we have been? Service being the means of fulfilling our mission here, the question will naturally arise, "Am I doing all that I can for my brother? Am I giving freely of self to help others? Is every moment of my life lived as He would have me live? In other words, am I a channel of blessing to others?"

A-11. Also use the illustration here of, "Who is my mother, my brother?"

Q-12. [*Mrs. Cayce reads the tenth paragraph:*] *Know self by activities of self in the daily walks of life, by comparing each thought and activity by your standard* The Christ. *"Be what thou seemeth, live thy creed. Hold up to the earth the torch divine. Be what thou prayest to be made. Let the* Great Master's *step be thine."*

A-12. Well.

Q-13. [*Mrs. Cayce reads the eleventh paragraph:*] *Keep in tune with the creative forces, getting beyond the state of consciousness where the blind lead the blind. "Stand still and know that I am God, and that I dwell within you." Find that place. It is there that self is known. It is there His spirit bears witness with your spirit that ye are sons of God.*

A-13. Well.

Q-14. [*Mrs. Cayce reads the twelfth paragraph:*] *In your daily periods of meditation hold this prayer: "Father, as we seek to see and know Thy face, may we as a group and as individuals come to know ourselves, even as we are known, that we—as lights in Thee—may give the better concept of Thy spirit in this world."*

If your actions and thoughts are of God, hold them fast. If they are not, drive them from you. Let not will drive you from the path of understanding. The voice of the soul is seeking its creator. "Behold I stand at the door and knock. He that will hear my voice, I will come in and dwell with him and he with me." There is no way to be pointed out save the "I AM." It is a birth of the spirit. The wind bloweth where it listeth, and thou heareth the sound thereof. Thou canst not tell whence it cometh or whither it goeth. So it is with everyone born of the spirit. That soul lost in spirit, universal love, will know self even as it is known.

A-14. Well.

Q-15. [*993*]: *Please expand on what the readings mean by "entity," and tell us how to explain to another seeking what it means to consider themselves as an entity, and interpret Q-4 in reading of December 27, 1931* [262-8], *where it said, "and give life."*

A-15. As given in the information, the entity is that combination of the physical body throughout all its experiences in or through the earth, in or through the universe, and the reactions that have been builded by those various or varied experiences, or the spiritual body of an individual. That that *is* individual; that that is the sum total of all experience. Then for the *entity* to create, or give, or be life, it must be a living, acting example of that it is, and not as something separated, inactive, inanimate, not giving but gradually deteriorating. There is the variation that may be seen in the material world as an example: As long as life is in whatever may be a manifestation in the material plane, it *is* a *growth*. As soon as it becomes an inanimate object (though it may be serving a purpose), it *immediately begins* to deteriorate, disintegrate. *Be* an entity! *Be* a *living* entity! See?

Q-16. Please explain more fully the following: [*Mrs. Cayce reads the last half of first page in lesson of December 27, 1931, 262-8.*]

A-16. That is as itself. The confusion that comes to those seeking the expansion of it is the relative relation of the physical body as a unit, yet a portion of the whole. The entity or soul body and its experiences that it may receive, in the clarifying of that which is builded by an entity as it passes from plane to plane. Let's begin with that which was given by Him, "Not that which entereth into a man defileth him, but that which cometh forth. Many are as whitened sepulchres, beautiful without but within full of dead men's bones!" This is referring to the activities of a physical being, but taking into consideration the activities of a physical body, a mental body, *and* spiritual body. One that lives to gratify the desires of the fleshly body *alone* may be beautiful without (and often is!), but within is as of those foul, that make for the belittling of the soul—for it must become corruption, and that able to be given out by such an one then is that which brings for that, in its seed, that makes for discord, corruption, disorder. Such an entity, such a soul, passing in—as the tree falls, so must it lie, and the whole shall be paid *every whit!* "My word shall *not* pass away." The soul, the entity, goes to meet that it has builded in that atmosphere, that surrounding, that environ, that vibration it has created or builded for itself; not in the material, but in the spiritual, in the universal plane. Then again it enters in the physical plane

for the experimenting, or developing, or magnifying, or showing forth that it may build. Just as given in the illustration, that
each functioning of the organs of the physical body is dependent
one upon another, and — as was given — who finds fault that the
hand is not the eye, or the head that it is not the foot, or the
comely part that it is [not] the uncomely, and the like? All must
be made in attune, in accord, that the *whole* may be saved,
rather than that a portion should suffer through that it may
build in this activity through the world. See? This may be clarified most with individuals taking their own *experiences* in the
various spheres that brought from one to another position, element, understanding, and meet each as they find in that environ, that surrounding, that which must bring that knowledge
of the whole, that "the Father and I *are* one." For the physical
body, the mental body, the spiritual body, to rebel, is as for the
foot to *rebel* that it is not the head, or the hand; or as for the
organs to rebel because they have become *poisoned* by that
which *unseemingly* has been fed the body for its sustenance.
See? To some the explanation is worse than that first given! But
study self in the light of that which is given in knowing self.

Q-17. [404]: *In the training of the subconscious mind, which
is more effective, thought or the spoken word, and why?*

A-17. In the training of the subconscious mind, first let it be
considered as to *what* is being acted upon. Then the question
will answer itself. The subconscious mind is both consciousness
and thought or spirit consciousness. Hence may be best classified, in the physical sense, as a habit. Should such an one being
acted upon be one that thinks thought would act quicker than
the spoken word, then to such an one it would! When it is
necessary to reach the subconscious of an individual through
the senses of the physical *body,* before it may be visualized by
such an one, then the spoken word would be more effective —
and you may see why. Hence, that which is spoken (for why
the question is asked) to a growing, developing body in oral
manner to the sleeping or semi-conscious mind will act the
better still! That answers the question for *this* body!

Q-18. *Please explain, as to a little child, the method of introspection.*

A-18. As the body-consciousness may view how that one word

of a conversation led to another in an evening, so may the body-consciousness see from introspection, "What caused me to think or act in such a manner under such and such a circumstance? Why answered I sharply under *this* particular experience and gentle in another?" The introspection gives the body that insight into the mental forces of the physical and soul-consciousness of a body, *by* such introspection.

Q-19. Is there any message to me as secretary?

A-19. There has been a *wonderful* awakening to the body in the activities in which the body has been active, since the last question was asked, and—as that joy comes *with* such—then use the *abilities* to expand in *every* way and manner. It is well!

Q-20. Please give a prayer which may be sent to individuals seeking aid through the healing group [281] for them to hold in the daily meditations.

A-20. MAY THERE BE MAGNIFIED IN ME THAT AS THE FATHER SEES I HAVE NEED OF. THY WILL, O FATHER, BE DONE IN ME, AS THOU SEEST I HAVE NEED OF!

Q-21. Any other special messages for the group, or any individual?

A-21. As ye seek, my children, to give life, light, understanding to others, faint not. Be not double-minded, but keep ever that which has been committed unto thee as thou *would* present it before the throne of grace, of mercy. And His peace abide *with* you always!

We are through.

This psychic reading was given by Edgar Cayce at his office, 105th Street [now 67th Street] and Ocean, Virginia Beach, Va., on February 7, 1932, at 4:00 P.M., in accordance with a request made by those present: Edgar Cayce; Gertrude Cayce, conductor; Gladys Davis, steno; C. A. Barrett, Minnie Barrett, M. L. Black, Annie Cayce, Hugh Lynn Cayce, L. B. Cayce, Mildred Davis, Edith Edmonds, Florence Edmonds, F. M. Freeman, Mrs. and Miss Gresham, Lu Hesson, Sarah Hesson, Anne Penn, Eloise T. Potter, C. W. Rosborough, M. L. Rosborough, and Esther Wynne.

≫ 262-11 ≪

Mrs. Cayce: You will have before you the group gathered here and their work upon the lessons they are preparing, both that as presented in Know Thyself, *a copy of which I hold in my hand, and the subject* What Is Your Ideal?, *on which they will now seek to form the next lesson. Please advise them and give that counsel which they need at this time in carrying forward the work. Answer the questions they will ask.*

Mr. Cayce: Yes, we have the group as gathered here, as a group, as individuals. The lesson that is prepared on *Know Thyself,* as we find, with the minor changes that will come in the preparation, is very good. The presentation of the spiritual body presents to many a variation in those things as make for the spiritual life. Were there added somewhat in this connection, that as relates the mental *and* spiritual life to that of the Christ Consciousness, as may be had in Him through that *applying* of self in act, in thought, to those lessons as bring to individuals that consciousness, then the greater effect may be in this connection.

In preparing a lesson upon that of having an ideal, as may be seen from the proper consideration of the lessons that have gone before, there must of necessity be *oneness* of purpose in a cooperative manner, which *gives* then a group a one ideal. Though there may be many ideas in the approach to the one, the differentiations are lost in the purpose of the ideal. An ideal, then, *cannot, should* not, *will* not, be that that is man-made, but must be of the spiritual nature—that has its foundation in truth, in God, in the Godhead, that there may be the continual reaching out of an individual, whether applied to the

-51-

physical life, the mental life, or the spiritual life; knowing that *first* principle, that the gift of God to man is an *individual* soul that may be one *with* Him, and that may know itself to be one with Him and yet individual in itself, with the attributes *of* the whole, yet *not* the whole. Such must be the concept, must be the ideal, whether of the imaginative, the mental, the physical, or the spiritual body of man. All may *attain* to such an ideal, yet never become the ideal — but *one with* the ideal, and such an one is set in Him.

Ready for questions.

Q-1. Please give a prayer or meditation which the group may hold in seeking the preparation of this coming lesson on What Is Your Ideal?

A-1. GOD BE MERCIFUL TO ME! HELP THOU MY UNBELIEF! LET ME SEE IN HIM THAT THOU WOULD HAVE ME SEE IN MY FELLOW MAN! LET ME SEE IN MY BROTHER THAT I SEE IN HIM WHOM I WORSHIP!

Q-2. As a group are we doing anything that we should not do, or leaving undone anything that we should be doing in seeking understanding that we may be used in Thy service?

A-2. This is a question that each shall answer within their individual lives. Who has been made a judge? Who showeth mercy, patience and understanding? Pray that each may have that light as is necessary for them, as an individual, as an integral part of the whole group, that would give life, light and understanding to others; for he that would be patient must show patience with those even that have a *different* understanding or concept of life. He that would teach, he that would minister, he that would heal — all likewise must be able to demonstrate in themselves that they would *give* another; for, as was given, "As I am in the Father and ye in me, so shall ye know the way, for so *is* my Father magnified in the world." Art thou a channel of blessing to *someone* today? Then that will answer in thine own behalf, that as will give that understanding that enables individuals, the group, to give to others that light, that awakening, that must be *found* in Him. As was given of Him, that the *awakening* may be done by the words and the acts of individuals; the increase, the *understanding,* is God's work! Expect *not* that to be *thine* work, but bringing the *oppor-tunities,* the awakening, the light, the knowledge—and *God* gives the increase; for those that are called, those did He predes-tine.

Q-3. *[307]*: *How may I attain to and realize my true ideal?*

A-3. Study to show thyself approved unto God, rightly divid-ing the words of truth, avoiding the appearance of evil.

Q-4. *In what person, first, second or third, should the lessons be written, in order that they may best express the truth and help the greater number of people?*

A-4. First person, I AM! "I *am* the way, I *am* the truth, I *am* the light." That as is manifested, that as is experienced in the life of each individual, is a personal application of that truth as would be imparted unto another. Hence should be in the first person.

Q-5. *[2112]*: *What was meant in my reading when it said I might heal by the "pouring in of the oil"?*

A-5. That as applied in many instances where the individual understands that individual to be healed needs something con-crete, physical, that *represents*—as the oil of truth, the oil on troubled waters, the oil of understanding, the oil of awakening. To some prayer means much. To others an awakening must be through their five senses. *All* are equally dear in the eyes of the Maker. Be patient. Endure all things. "I will be all things unto all men that I may thereby save the more," is applicable in this light also.

Q-6. *[115]*: *Was there any special word of power given me in my Egyptian period that would be of help to the class at this time?*

A-6. As an emissary in this particular experience, the power of *persistence* is *magnified* in the present. Patience and endur-ance is a good lesson to teach in the present.

Q-7. *[379]*: *How may I attain my ideal?*

A-7. In each there is, as was given, ever has there been, prepared a way of escape for each and every soul. To this entity, that of an ideal must be attainable in a concrete manner. Then little by little, line by line, may the body-consciousness become conscious of the Spirit of the Master working in and through the acts, the thoughts, the *life* of the body. *See* in each individual that they represent of the ideal set by self, and live the life, the whole concept, of thine own ideal.

Q-8. [993]: *What should be our true ideal, and how may I reach it?*

A-8. Ideal should be as given, as is set in Him. See that *coming* to pass in the lives, the hearts, the minds, the souls, of those the body works with, the body labors with, and work—work! For the night cometh, and in *Him* will be that light that gives rest unto the soul. [See 262-12, A-4.]

Q-9. [69]: *How may I reach my ideal?*

A-9. As each lifts in themselves that as is their ideal, as each measures another—whether a physical, a moral or a spiritual act—so may self measure self by that as is set as the ideal *in* self *for* self, and see the Christ Consciousness raised in the heart, the mind, the soul of others. Keep before self, "Judge not that ye be not judged, for as ye measure so is it measured again." That signifies that with the *measure* ye mete is thy ideal. Let that, then, be in Him.

Q-10. [560]: *How may I come to the realization of my true ideal?*

A-10. As there is raised in self more and more the [Christ] Consciousness does one become free indeed, and *free* gives that awakening that comes with the realization of the ideal as set awakening more and more in the hearts, the minds, the souls of others. Not in long-facedness, not in moral aptitudes that make for shadows—but free in the love that makes not afraid, that makes for that that would make self dare to do for Him.

Q-11. [2125]: *How may I come to the realization of my true ideal?*

A-11. As there is applied in the conversation, in the acts, in the thoughts of self as respecting others, and measure then by that ideal that is set in self, be as patient and as forgiving, and as long-suffering as He was. Then there comes that peace that gives understanding.

Q-12. *Is there any message for the group at this time?*

A-12. Is there set in this group that one ideal that has been set, before the lesson is finished, a sign will be given thee.

We are through.

This psychic reading was given by Edgar Cayce at his office, 105th Street [now 67th Street] and Ocean, Virginia Beach, Va., on February 21, 1932, at 4:00 P.M., in accordance with a request made by those present: Edgar Cayce; Gertrude Cayce, conductor; Gladys Davis, steno; C. A. Barrett, Minnie Barrett, M. L. Black, Annie Cayce, Hugh Lynn Cayce, L. B. Cayce, Mildred Davis, Edith Edmonds, Florence Edmonds, A. T. Ellington, Helen Ellington, Lu Hesson, Sarah Hesson, S. E. McPherson, F. Y. Morrow, Anne Penn, Eloise Potter, C. W. Rosborough, M. L. Rosborough, Helen Storey, and Esther Wynne.

⊰ 262-12 ⊱

Mrs. Cayce: You will have before you the group gathered here. Please give them at this time that which they need in continuing their work on the lesson which they are preparing on What Is Your Ideal? *You will answer the questions which will be asked in regard to this by some of those present.*

Mr. Cayce: We have the group as gathered here. Also that as has been given in *What Is Thy Ideal?* Each, as given, should apply that in their daily experience as has been given in *Cooperation* and *Know Thyself,* for there comes then to each that as has been set as their ideal. Many an individual is able, or do express themselves as to the secular things in life as their ideal —or idea of a standard. Have *ye* chosen that *spiritual* ideal? Are the things in thine own life measured by that ideal? Are there the continued efforts on thy part to put into practice, or to count as worthy of self *being* the channel that may bring a blessing to another? As has been given, there will come a sign to the group, or to members of same—will they make the ideal that as is one with Him. The promise is, as was given of Him, "for I will bring to remembrance all things whatsoever has been my part with you, for in such manifestations is my Father glorified in you."

Ready for questions.

Q-1. [303]: Please explain to me how I should proceed in order to attain my true ideal.

A-1. As is given, in seeking the Father's face, grace, mercy and peace is added in the seeking. Know that thou would worship, and self a part of same, seeing in others then that thou

-55-

would worship in the Father; for the prayer was, "May they be one, even as Thou and I are one," for, as given, a *spiritual insight* brings the *seeing* of the best in each life. There is good in all, for they *are* of the Father, and have been bought with the price, even of the Son, in that flesh may know the *glory* of the Father that may be manifested even in thee!

Q-2. What can we do as individuals and as a group that we may come to a oneness of purpose, in a cooperative manner, which will then give the group a one ideal?

A-2. This must be found in the Father, for "Ye I have chosen, as ye have chosen me. He I have called, him did I also predestine—and they hear my voice, and *answer* by *my* name." In that name alone may the *calling* and *election* be sure; presenting selves, each, in a way and manner that is holy and acceptable unto *thee,* according to thine *own* understanding, doing each day that as thou knowest is in accord with that ideal, and the *way* is shown thee! Be not overhasty in word or deed, for it *is* line upon line, here a little, there a little; for it is the *little* leaven that leaveneth the whole lump, and such compared He to the *kingdom* of God. The kingdom, then is within. Go. Do. That as I have shown thee, so do ye, and there will be peace, harmony, understanding, light, that saves—even unto the end.

Q-3. [993]: What would be the most important work for the group or individual to do at this time, that would help us to attain the ideal as is set in Him?

A-3. Each show forth in their own way of manifesting His love day by day. "A new commandment (said He) give I unto you: Love one another." Even as ye would have spoken of you, so speak of one another. In this manner may the greater work, may the greater blessing, *come* to one and all. *Be patient,* and *see* the glory of God!

Q-4. In the reading of February 7th in Knowing Self, *please explain what was meant by "work, work! for the night is coming, and in Him will be that light that gives rest unto the soul."[See 262-11, A-8.]*

A-4. In this is seen that as was expressed by Him, "Behold the fields are white unto the harvest, but the laborers are few." Ye have signified the willingness to be a laborer with Him. Then work, work! for the night, for the shades of those things that bring doubt, darkness, dissimilitude, will come—unless one is busy with that they *know* to do; but with the labor comes that rest as promised in Him.

Q-5. [404]: How may I best attain to that ideal as is set in Him?

A-5. Put into active, prayerful, working service, that thou knowest to do day by day. See in others something that may be glorified by Him, and see in self that thou would consecrate to Him. Thine daily acts, thine words, thine speech—these will bring that understanding, and the realization of the ideal *being* manifest in thee, as *well* as in others. Look for the *good* in *everyone*. Speak neither evil, harsh, nor unkind, to any.

Q-6. Please explain what is meant by the Godhead.

A-6. That as from which the impulse flows, or returns to. The beginning—the end—of all.

Q-7. How may I increase my faith?

A-7. Use that thou hast in hand, has been the command from the beginning, will be unto the end, as to how to increase faith. Faith, the substance of things hoped for, evidences of things unseen. Using that known brings those attunements, those emoluments in every form, that makes for *Creative* FORCES in themselves—which is, must be, the basis of faith.

Q-8. [288]: Just how is it meant that I should give of my best to Him? In what manner may I do that? [See 262-2, A-17.]

A-8. Study that thou sayest, that thou doest, and reserve *nothing*—in strength of body *or* mind—in service to others, *that is* a reflection of that He would have thee do, as thou knowest how. As was given by Him, let thine works, thine efforts, be even as was said by Him—"If ye will not believe me, ye *will* believe for the very works' sake—for the things I do bespeak *that* I believe I AM!"

We are through.

[See Volume IV of this publication series for an account of the dream Mr. Cayce had during this reading.]

≫ 262-13 ≪ *This psychic reading was given by Edgar Cayce at his office in Pinewood on Lake Drive, Virginia Beach, Va., on March 6, 1932, at 4:00 P.M., in accordance with a request by those present: Edgar Cayce; Gertrude Cayce, conductor; Gladys Davis, steno; C. A. Barrett, Minnie Barrett, M. L. Black, Hugh Lynn Cayce, Mildred Davis, Edith Edmonds, Florence Edmonds, Hannah Miller, F. Y. Morrow, Helen Storey, and Esther Wynne.*

Mrs. Cayce: You will have before you the group gathered here and their work on the lesson of What Is Your Ideal? *Please guide and direct this group in their work on this lesson. You will answer the questions which will be asked.*

Mr. Cayce: We have the group as gathered here, as a group, as individuals, contributing to the lessons in the varied ways and manners in keeping with that which has been given in that pointing to the beginning of the work in the building of the lessons. As in the cooperation, as in the developments that do necessarily come to each in applying those things (for they become things, ideas in the application), as they—the ideas—work upon the activities of each individual, then as in this the ideal or the standard that each not only measure themselves by—but see in others *through* that standard that they worship, that they may honor, in *their* ideal. Knowing first all is one. Then should come the lesson of faith, that is as one of the stepping-stones in balancing self to the labors, as each applies self in that as they, as individuals and as a group, set before themselves to work toward; that that may bring the understanding, that understanding of the source of the good, or brighten the lives of others through those things that have been builded, are builded, may be builded, through the application of those things as make up the lessons that are studied; for in the *beauty* of service comes the knowledge and understanding that *makes* the living worthwhile. Setting aside those things that so easily beset, looking forward to that mark of the higher calling as is set in Him, knowing that the greatest service that may be done is the little word here and there, the kindly thought, the little deeds that make the heart glad, and the brightness of the Son come in the lives of all.

Ready for questions.

-58-

Q-1. I hold in my hand an outline of the lesson on What Is Your Ideal? *Advise us as to the expansion of this.*

A-1. Insofar as each has contributed their portion, then, in the joining of each link let these be in the same manner or temperament of thought, that there are no stumbling stones between the truths as are presented by each individual, that there may be unison, that there may be oneness of purpose, that there may be wholehearted cooperation by all to whom same may be presented. Let each individual, themselves, apply in their own daily life that they have contributed toward the awakening of someone through *their* thought. So does the lesson become a *living* example known and read of men. So will the lessons, the studies, be given a soul, with life, that may live in the hearts and minds of others. Beautiful truths without personal application by the one presenting them is indeed casting pearls to swine, and will turn again to its own wallow.

In the outline, well has been much of that prepared. Let each know and feel, understand, that same is a part of them. Unless same *is* a part of them, they have little or no part in same; for, as has been given, many are called but few have answered. The harvest indeed is ripe, the laborers are few! The lords have called, do call, for laborers in His vineyard. *Who* will work today? He that has seen a vision of the love of Him that has been set as thine example, as thine ideal. These founded in those that are of man's making *must* come to naught! With the cooperation of the spirit of truth it is *made* alive in Him, even as the overcoming of death itself through the applying of self to *His* will. Not *my* will but Thine, O Lord, be done in me! As the meditations should be, in the preparation of faith in self, in God, in thy ideal: CREATE IN ME A PURE HEART, O GOD! OPEN THOU MINE HEART TO THE FAITH THOU HAST IMPLANTED IN ALL THAT SEEK THY FACE! HELP THOU MINE UNBELIEF IN MY GOD, IN MY NEIGHBOR, IN MYSELF!

Q-2. May this group obtain through this channel at this or some other time in the near future information which will be of help in locating Charles Augustus Lindbergh, Jr., who has been kidnapped?

A-2. This has already been approached in *many* ways and manners. Already is there set in motion that that will give the understanding to those so deeply concerned, as to what has come about.

Q-3. Is it meant that we should not seek this information through these channels?

A-3. Information has *already* been sought, *oft,* through these channels—and that that has come about has been set in motion, and will be known to those so deeply interested.

Q-4. Please explain just what is meant, as we do not understand.

A-4. The conditions as surrounding same are such that already there has been set in motion, through these channels, that which will bring to the attention of those so deeply interested as to *what* has come to pass. [See 4191 series.]

Q-5. [2124]: In what way may I best attain my ideal?

A-5. Well that an individual know that in the *attaining* of an ideal of an earthly making is satisfaction, and if of spiritual making is obtained only in *spiritual* understanding—which gives contentment. Then be content with that thou hast, and use with honor, praise, glory *to* thine ideal that thou hast, and more and more is given as there is proper use made of that in hand; for, as was given by the Master of masters, "The kingdom is likened unto a man that making a journey called his servants. To one gave five talents, to another two talents, to another one talent." As they applied themselves, so did they obtain that *not* as favor, but as understanding—and so rewarded, as called to *account* for that held in hand. So, obtaining the ideal is making use—spiritual use, first—for, "Seek first the kingdom and all these things are added unto you." [See 262-17, A-12.]

Q-6. [69's husband]: In what way may I best attain my ideal?

A-6. In the applying of self day by day in every way, that thou *knowest,* that makes a personal application of that thou knowest to do, without questioning of the morrow; for the *morrow* has *its* evils and its goods, sufficient unto self. Today is! Use that thou hast in hand. So does the awakening come. Even as called by God to lead a peoples, as was Moses, a shepherd and the flocks in Moab. Use that thou hast in hand, for the *ground* whereon thou standest is holy! Do *thou* likewise! Even as Ram, even as Phares [?] or Tama[?], each under their *own* vine and fig tree, learned first that opening self to be a channel of the *living* forces, not the dead past—nor that that makes afraid, but *Thy* will, O God, be done *in me*—*Use me* as *Thou* seest fit! *Fit* me for *Thine* own! [See 262-15, A-3.]

Q-7. Are we submitting the paper, "Present World Conditions," for publication in the manner we should? If not, please offer suggestions. [See readings numbers 3976-8 through -11.]

A-7. Do with might what thine hands find to do, through the channels that have been set before thee; knowing that many minds have many ideas—and *all* are not of thine own channel, yet give each the opportunity in *their respective* place. "Woe unto thee, Chorazin! Woe unto thee, Bethsaida! for if the mighty works that have been in *thee* had been done in Sodom and Gomorrah, they would have repented in sackcloth and ashes." How *many* of the group have repented, or been in sackcloth and ashes? [See 281-5, A-9.] How are such cast out? Why could not we, who have been endued with *Thine* own power? *Fear* has crept in! Ye have neglected to pray. Ye have neglected to fast. Keep that as is given, and parade nor flaunt not that as given, but know that there is need for an awakening and it comes.

We are through.

This psychic reading given by Edgar Cayce at his office in Pinewood on Lake Drive, Virginia Beach, Va., on March 20, 1932, at 4:30 P.M., in accordance with a request made by those present: Edgar Cayce; Gertrude Cayce, conductor; Gladys Davis, steno; C. A. Barrett, Minnie Barrett, M. L. Black, Hugh Lynn Cayce, L. B. Cayce, Mildred Davis, Edith Edmonds, Florence Edmonds, Helen Ellington, F. M. Freeman, Sarah Hesson, Mrs. LeNoir, S. E. McPherson, F. Y. Morrow, C. W. Rosborough, M. L. Rosborough, Helen Storey, and Esther Wynne.

⤳ 262-14 ⤶

Mrs. Cayce: You will have before you the group gathered here, and their work on the lessons which they are preparing. You will please answer the questions regarding this work that they will ask.

Mr. Cayce: Yes, we have the group as gathered here, as a group, as individuals, and the work as is being done in the preparation of the lessons.

Ready for questions.

Q-1. We present at this time the lesson on What Is Thy Ideal?, *a copy of which I hold in my hand. Please make suggestions, any corrections or expansions that should be made, as I call each paragraph under the various headings. First, paragraph one, under Meaning of an Ideal.*

A-1. Correct.

[Questions 2 through 15 are a continuation of checking various paragraphs from the lesson *What Is Thy Ideal?*, to each of which Mr. Cayce gave an affirmative answer.]

Q-16. Any other suggestions regarding this lesson?

A-16. Well that the ideal in the suggestions as given be that rather of the personal nature, as *individual*, than personality presented in same. In the lesson as has been outlined, as given there would come the sign for each as they applied themselves in knowing their *own* ideal and how same is applicable in their own experience: To some has come in the form of tests, that that as is proclaimed, or claimed by them, must be acted in their own experience, as to relationships to others. In some in the form of greater opportunities, in the manner in which there may be given more and more of that which will arouse in the inner beings of others a closer concept of an ideal. In others a vision of those forces as may manifest in the activities of their *own* selves towards others, as well as to those who have experienced the presence of that consciousness that His abiding promise is true in this period of their experience.

Q-17. Please give us at this time that which will aid us in beginning our next lesson.

A-17. Faith. As each have their own concept of faith, as to whether this is grounded in experience in relationship to life's activities in the material, or to the activities in the mental, depends much upon what has been held as the ideal of that individual. In the beginning, then, as we would find, the analysis of self as to whether this that is held is confidence or faith is the first question as would naturally arise in the minds of each individual. Faith, as has been defined by Barnabas, is the substance of things hoped for. Then there is illustrated the activities of individuals as to how, through the exercising of that prerogative, that through which is brought into being the worlds as is manifest before each individual that looks about them with the view to ascertaining that they are a portion *of* the whole, yet with the abilities to discern all, and able to use that that will bring the same exercising of that prerogative as the spirit of the Father brings through faith into that *being* where this may be of this or that sphere of man's own perception. Brought into material aspects, we find the greater portion as partakes of that as has been termed the sensing, or that of the whole of the nervous system in a physical, living organism, that makes such an individual aware *of* that concept. This is rather confidence. That that has been brought into the consciousness through the activity *of* the spiritual forces manifesting in and through that of the spiritual force of the individual. Then becomes the essence of faith itself. Hence, as has been termed by many, that *faith*—*pure* faith—accepting or rejecting without basis of reason, or *beyond* the ken or scope of that as is perceived through that that man brings to his own activity through that of his five senses; yet to most individuals there is seen that *little* becomes in the scope of acceptance except they *live* by faith that they become aware of; for, as has been said, ye with faith as much as a mustard seed may say unto the mountain be thou removed and cast into the sea. *Most* say they believe, and yet begin at once to explain as to how this means in the mental rather than in the material source. Hence we find faith not of the senses, else it becomes confidence in personalities of the experiences of the senses within themselves or others. Then, when troubles and doubts arise, they immediately begin to sink, even as Peter in the presence of Life itself. [See 262-15, A-7.]

In the concepts then, as individuals in the group, in the first portion of this lesson let each so examine themselves in the light of that they have attained with the concept of their individual ideal, and we will find upon what faith is founded in *their* experience.

Ready for questions.

Q-18. Is there anything more this group may do in aiding in finding the Lindbergh child?

A-18. Those have been set in motion, as has been given. Be thou *not* of little faith.

Q-19. Should we begin to distribute the lessons as already prepared?

A-19. *Well* that first there be found those in the various outlined principals that are to be teachers, ministers, or one *forming* such groups, and prepare *them for* that they *are to* do in their respective spheres; else it will turn again with that as is poorly prepared.

Q-20. [333] and [602]: How may we as members of the group through cooperation grow stronger in faith, and through a knowledge of self attain to those ideals as are set in self for the part in this great work that each would accomplish with the help of all?

A-20. Studying to show thyself approved unto God day by day, rightly dividing the words of truth, and keeping self unspotted from the world. There is builded in the meditations, and in the gathering of others here, there, to gain the understanding necessary to bring about a revolution, a revelation, an awakening in *this* place as *has* not been seen in many a day! Making those truths as are known in self *living* truths, through the active force of the *spirit* of *truth* itself. Do that.

Q-21. [*255*]: *Is the faith of man in Buddha or Mohammed equal in the effect on his soul to the faith in Jesus Christ?*

A-21. As He gave, he that receiveth a prophet in the *name* of a prophet *receives* the prophet's reward, or that *ability* that that individual spiritual force *may* manifest in the life of that individual. Hence, as each teacher, minister or seer, or prophet, receives that obeisance as is giving the life from that faith and hope as held by that as an individual, in the Christ is found that as the advocate *with* the Father and the spirit of the Father glorified in him that approaches through that manner, without that as is approached in the spiritual activity of any individual; for individuality is last lost, even as man in spirit overcomes death in the material; even as He overcame death in the material, and able to put on immortality in a material world, bringing to man not only of flesh that endowed *with* the ability to be one *with* the Father but magnifying the Father *in* the individual yet in the material plane. Hence, as we find, each in their respective spheres are but stepping-stones to that that may awaken in the individual the knowledge of the Son in their lives.

Q-22. How can I so strengthen my faith so as to become a fitting channel of help in God's healing of my daughter, [*275*]?

A-22. Magnify in the words of mouth, the acts of the body and hand, that as is *given* day by day. As the ideal is a growth, as the activities of the physical and mental consciousness through confidence brings that seeking of the mental and material body to awaken to the spiritual activities, so may the *growth* in faith *bring* the activating forces of the spirit that makes alive in the flesh.

We are through for the present.

This psychic reading was given by Edgar Cayce at his office in Pinewood on Lake Drive, Virginia Beach, Va., on April 3, 1932, at 4:35 P.M., in accordance with a request made by those present: Edgar Cayce; Gertrude Cayce, conductor; Gladys Davis, steno; C. A. Barrett, Minnie Barrett, M. L. Black, Annie Cayce, Hugh Lynn Cayce, L. B. Cayce, Mildred Davis, Edith Edmonds, Florence Edmonds, Lu Hesson, Sarah Hesson, S. E. McPherson, Hannah Miller, F. Y. Morrow, Anne Penn, C. W. Rosborough, M. L. Rosborough, Helen Storey, and Esther Wynne.

⩘ 262-15 ⩗

Mrs. Cayce: You will have before you the group gathered here, and their work on the lessons which they are preparing. Please give us at this time that we need in continuing work on the lesson on Faith *and answer the questions which will be asked.*

Mr. Cayce: Yes, we have the group as gathered here, as a group, as individuals, and the work and preparation as the group, and as each have contributed, do contribute, to the lesson.

As has been given, in the exercising of the faith does there come to each that as may be given another for their enlightenment.

In the preparations of self, as individuals, as [a] group, these are of the exercising of that talent or ability as is the heritage of each, plus that as may be gained by the cooperation of one with another in the light of that as is seen in self through that as chosen as the ideal of [the] individual, of the group.

In the manner of presenting same, that as has been chosen that comes through the concerted action of self in response to those surrounding environs, and the seeking of self for that knowledge as will enable self to give expression to that as is experienced within the individual in responding to those opportunities as are presented from day to day to put that as is the experience into active thought, active being; activating, then, one with another, toward that as may be given out to others to enlighten them as respecting their relationships with the creative forces, with their fellow man.

As is seen by those of the first of the lessons, these are builded step by step, that there may be seen that which may become

-66-

a living truth in the lives of individuals, known and seen of those who may come in contact either with the life of the individuals so applying same, or that as may be given by the group as a whole.

Ready for questions.

Q-1. [993]: *In passing through the test that has come with the sign that was promised, has my faith been sufficient? Would appreciate more light regarding same, and how I should act.*

A-1. As has been promised, "My grace is sufficient," and, "Take no thought of what ye shall say in the hour of trial or test, for it will be given thee that as is necessary for the renewing of that spirit that makes for the understanding of 'His Spirit beareth witness with thy spirit.' " Then, meet each step as is shown thee, remembering that He has promised, "I am with thee always, even unto the end of the world. I will not leave thee comfortless, but will come to thee, and he that takes my cross shall not bear it alone."

Q-2. [560]: *Could the entity receive a message at this time that her faith may be strengthened?*

A-2. Add unto thy faith works, that showeth forth those attributes that are expressions of His Spirit in the world. So shall it, the faith, become the evidence of things not seen, and His grace, His mercies, will abide with you whithersoever thou goest. Peace be with thee! Not as the world gives peace; rather as that that has lost self, self's personality, in Him.

Q-3. [69's husband]: *Please explain what was meant in reading of March 6th* [262-13, A-6], *by "Use that thou hast in hand, for the ground whereon thou standest is holy!"*

A-3. As each individual uses that knowledge and understanding as pertains to the attributes of the spirit of truth, life, light and understanding, so does there come that growth, even as brought the worlds into being; and being, places, things, spots, that are brought into being through such activity of an entity, self, is indeed holy. There is that, then, in the self, in the entity, seeking that may find, and may come to know the closer relationships with the holy activating forces in a material world.

Q-4. *We present the outline on* Faith, *which I hold in my hand. Please suggest any further headings which should be added.*

A-4. Rather would we fill those that have been outlined with that as may be furnished as experiences of individuals, as to the tests whether of faith or confidence, according to that held as the ideal; and, as given, whether it partakes of the physical conscious sense or that of the spiritual intuitive forces as comes from close communion with the Holy Spirit, the promised Comforter, the consciousness of the Christ.

Q-5. When in the meditation of Faith, *we are told to pray, "Create in me a pure heart, O God," does the word "heart" refer to the subconscious mind? Please give some light on the word "heart."*

A-5. As in the physical body the heart considered the seat, or the source of that which impels life to all portions of the body. In that sense, then, in creating in me a pure heart, a pure soul, a pure purpose, that in all forces, all circumstance, all conditions, in all the active forces of the body, in mind or in physical contact, may bring as life, light, understanding, to those contacted—as does the heart to the body. This as an attribute, or a representation then, as is used to signify that purpose, that intent, that life, that characterization, of the active forces of an entity, a body, a mind, the imaginative forces, the conscious forces, the subconscious or soul forces. Not as of the subconscious alone; rather that that illustrates, as of the seat, the source, the activating forces that *impel* those as would do His biddings. As: "Create within me a pure heart, O God, and *renew* a right, righteous, holy spirit within me."

Q-6. Please give some information as to how we come to have faith; is it a gift of God and developed through the use of it?

A-6. As there is brought into creation, as in the beginning, there are the attributes of every force, power, as it may be magnified in whatever source of creation as is exemplified in the act. In man given that as of will, and the soul, with that as is the attribute to keep those forces in a line with that that takes of the source of its emanation, and in faith—then—grows (the will) to be one with; or going away from, by the exercising of same in another direction. So does the soul, or that as separates an entity from the whole, grow in whatever direction the exercising of the attribute, as gift, as a force, as power, magnified in the creation of forces in the beginnings. So does it show forth in individuals according to that as the manner or way in which it, the faith, is used as respecting those attributes of individuals as related to the Creative Force, or God Himself.

Q-7. *Please explain by illustration, "Most say they believe, and yet begin at once to explain as to how this means in the mental rather in the material source."* [*See 262-14, A-17.*]

A-7. As has just been outlined as to how faith, as an attribute that came into being as the Son—in which the faith is magnified as to make those active forces in will, and the growth of the soul. So, as is seen in individuals as would say, "Yes, I believe—but"—"but" meaning there is that doubt, that by the comparison of some individual, individuals or circumstances in their experience, when, where, or how, that individuals spoke yet acted in a manner as if that did not exist! Then, creating that doubt for self, applying to self, brings about that as is the opposite of faith, or else partakes of that within the conscious mind that begins with the lessons that must be answered by the attributes of the physical consciousness, that seek for a demonstration through those senses of the body that makes for an awareness to the physical being; yet, as is seen, these are the manners in which the variations to individuals reach those various conditions or circumstances in their experience.

We are through for the present.

This psychic reading was given by Edgar Cayce at the home of Misses Florence and Edith Edmonds, 611 Pennsylvania Avenue, Norfolk, Va., on April 4, 1932, at 9:40 P.M., in accordance with a request made by those present: Edgar Cayce; Gertrude Cayce, conductor; Gladys Davis, steno; C. A. Barrett, Minnie Barrett, M. L. Black, Hugh Lynn Cayce, Mildred Davis, Edith Edmonds, Florence Edmonds, Helen Ellington, Ruth LeNoir, Hannah Miller, F. Y. Morrow, Helen Storey, and Esther Wynne.

⋊ 262-16 ⋉

Mrs. Cayce: (Dream Suggestion)[You will have before you the body and enquiring mind of Edgar Cayce, present in this room, and the dream this body had on Sunday, February 21, 1932, in which he went everywhere, in every imaginable vehicle, and presented a box to a member of the group at each place.]

Mr. Cayce: Yes, we have the body, the enquiring mind, Edgar Cayce, present in this room, the dream, or vision and experience of the entity, as in the visit and travel to various portions of the country, and the meeting and presenting to the various members of the group the message.

In this there is seen not only the individuality of each person or member of the group, but also the one message as is being builded in the experience of all. Also there is seen the various portions of the country to which, in which, the appeal of the individual contribution to those of the lessons will receive their import.

As these, then, are gathered, there will be seen that the day will come when each as seen may in that particular region seen present that message as is being builded in each in the present.

As to the individuality as manifested by the manner in which each are approached, this rather the lesson that as in the form of bringing the message to those of the groups seen in the various modes or manners of traveling to each, see?

Ready for questions.

Q-1. What is the one message developed and given?

A-1. That of the compilations of the studies, as indicated by the asking of each, "Have you the little box or package?", showing the compilation of those truths as will be presented in the various portions of country as seen.

Q-2. *In what particular portion of the country was* [69], *and what is the message?*

A-2. In the Middle West, or in Denver, as was seen. There the aid may be the greater as presented by the body. The message, that as compiled by all seen.

Q-3. [307]:

A-3. Was in that of Cleveland, or that portion of the country, and in the presentation as of studying, or as presenting in the logic of same.

Q-4. [993]:

A-4. In the Southland, or New Orleans, as seen, and among such groups may the body present the greater message.

Q-5. [560]:

A-5. In Kentucky and Tennessee, that portion where the studies of same have been for many the day as those of the *orthodox* forces, or church ritualistic forces. These will be hard; but truth prevails!

Q-6. [404]:

A-6. These presented in the eastern portion and northern portion of the country, as of southern New England, among those especially of the spiritual faith.

Q-7. [413]:

A-7. These were in the eastern portion of the South, and in that of southern Georgia and Flordia, but as in the peach orchard section.

Q-8. [341]:

A-8. These presented more in the Far West.

Q-9. [295]:

A-9. In the Southwest, or San Antonio and that portion of the country, and among those of the particular sect or sets of people.

Q-10. [303]:

A-10. These were in the Carolinas, and especially that portion about those of the student body, or peoples.

Q-11. [585]:

A-11. This was seen in those of the valley country of West Virginia, or the northwestern portion of that part of the country, and as the travel indicated there, in that that pertained most to the waterways.

Q-12. [379]:

A-12. These were in Oklahoma, and those portions of southern part of Missouri, or—as what would be called—in the Ozark portion of the country.

Q-13. [115]:

A-13. Among those of the southwestern portion, and especially of that as pertained to those of the cult natures.

Q-14. [69's husband]:

A-14. Those of the harder-headed portions, in the north and northwestern portions of Texas.

Q-15. [288]:

A-15. In that portion of the northeastern portion of the country, as in the vinelands of New York.

Q-16. [2112]:

A-16. In Indiana and Illinois, or as to that portion in which there is seen those of a peculiar peoples, as termed by many. Most of them holding to that of folklore, or of the Zionists.

Q-17. [2125]:

A-17. Among the peoples at home!

Q-18. [2124]:

A-18. In that portion of the Southwest, as in Arizona and New Mexico, especially in that portion among the miner and the rodeo peoples.

Q-19. [2673]:

A-19. She in that portion now called the far Northwest, as in Oregon, Washington, and that portion of the land.

Well that these be understood, that that portion of the lessons as are compiled in the whole will be most *appealing* to that section from these of the group seen.

We are through.

≫ 262-17 ≪

This psychic reading was given by Edgar Cayce at his home in Pinewood on Lake Drive, Virginia Beach, Va., on April 17, 1932, at 4:40 P.M., in accordance with a request made by those present: Edgar Cayce; Gertrude Cayce, conductor; Gladys Davis, steno; C. A. Barrett, Minnie Barrett, M. L. Black, Hugh Lynn Cayce, L. B. Cayce, Mildred Davis, Edith Edmonds, Florence Edmonds, Helen Ellington, F. M. Freeman, Sarah Hesson, Mrs. LeNoir, S. E. McPherson, Hannah Miller, F. Y. Morrow, Eloise Potter, C. W. Rosborough, M. L. Rosborough, Helen Storey, and Esther Wynne.

Mrs. Cayce: You will have before you the group gathered here, and their work on the lesson of Faith. May we receive at this time guidance in understanding faith, that we may make this lesson a living lesson? You will answer the questions as we ask them.

Mr. Cayce: Yes, we have the group as gathered here, as a group, as individuals. In the study of lesson on *Faith,* this becomes a living truth as each applies in their experience that gained in meditation and prayer upon that attribute of creative forces, for it in essence *is* creative in its active principle in experiences of individuals in their lives. Then, as one applies that as known, is there given the understanding as to that that may increase or enlarge, or make same become living in their experience.

Ready for questions.

Q-1. [413]: What is the comparative extent of my faith, and how may I extend and use it to achieve the most benefit?

A-1. Just as given, faith is the essence of creative forces within the active force of that of an individual to which they apply themselves in the spiritual activity of their experience. So, in the application of that known to self as an expression of that faith as is manifest in every child of God — that in its active force puts that known into operation — does this grow, expand, or *become* the basis *of* the activities of self in those directions as necessary. As the ensample, or examples, as were given by those patriarchs of old, or as has been experienced in self's own experience, that once awakened to the abilities within self *dare* to do for Him that as has been done even for self!

Q-2. [*255*]: . . . . *Should faith healing be included in the teachings of theology? If so, who is best qualified to teach it?*

A-2. There has been given by those in the orthodox manner those who *should, through* faith, laying on of hands, anointing with oil, praying over same. There is, in the broader sense, that innate in each individual that may be awakened to those abilities in their activity, are they willing to attune themselves to the laws as pertain to the active forces in self's *own* experience, keeping self unspotted and clean from the world, and *keeping* that that brings according in the body that necessary for its awakening to its own spiritual activity. Who shall do such? Such as are called in their own experience. Knowing that as has been given, to some is given teaching, to others healing, to others ministry, to others on the various forces as are attributes of His love, His force, in a material world. One that is so given, then, let them *sanctify their* selves, *their* bodies, *their* minds, to his *fellow man's* service; for he that lendeth to the Lord covers a multitude of sins.

Q-3. [*115*]: *Is my faith manifested in my East Indian incarnation sufficient for today?*

A-3. Sufficient to the day is the evil or the good thereof. Putting rather in practice that as is known in the present is sufficient to make the growth attain that as *may* be even *greater manifested* in the present; for that as experienced in the various spheres of activity is as the background and the *staying* forces, that through faith, through the promise, all things are brought to remembrance in thy spiritual activity.

Q-4. [*288*]: *Are my attempts at meditation accomplishing anything outside myself?*

A-4. These are but questionings of self, and questionings of the promises as are given! Might be termed lack of faith in self or the promise! For each thought, each atom, has its own weight as is expended in whatever direction it *may* be guided by the thought of self! To be sure, it *accomplishes,* then, that in self and that outside of self. He that doubteth, then — doubteth self, doubteth Him!

Q-5. In what position may I best meditate?

A-5. As has been given, there are given to each their own respective manners, from their varied experiences, as to *how,* as to form. If *form* becomes that that is the guiding element, then the hope or the faith is lost in form! He that made long prayer, or he that not even raised his eyes but smote his breast and said, "God be merciful to me, a sinner!" *Who* was justified? He that in humbleness of self, humbleness of mind, humbleness of the whole *individuality* (*losing* personality in Him) comes; and in *whatsoever* manner that—whether prone, whether standing, whether walking, or whether sleeping—we live, we die, in the Lord.

Q-6. How can I make my faith more active and worthwhile in the lives of others?

A-6. By exemplifying it in self; for we individuals are as reflections to others of that we worship in *our* own selves. Let your light so shine that others, seeing their light, may *glorify* God.

Q-7. [303]: How can I increase my faith?

A-7. Continuing to lose self in the thought of Him who is able to make the tiny seed bring forth the great tree. As self is lost in doing *His* biddings does the *faith* grow; for growth is made through the exercising of, the *losing* of, self in Him. In Him, then, as we see the *attributes of* the Father in the daily walks of life. By *faith* a cup of water given brings its reward to self, and quenches the thirst of the thirsty. By *faith* a kind word brings that joy to the one spoken to, and to self that knowledge of—in *His* name. Not that it *brings* to self as a reward, but the *reward* is as of that *brought* to self by the act. Great difference!

Q-8. [404]: In praying, should a prayer be kept up persistently until a definite answer is given, or should one only ask and leave the rest with God?

A-8. Seek and ye shall find. Know in whom thou hast believed, and believe—in faith—He is able to commit that *thou* hast committed unto Him against *any* condition in thine experience. *Thy* will, O Lord, be done—not mine! *Ask*—leave the result with Him. His promises are sure. "Heaven and earth may pass away, but my promise shall *not* pass away."

Q-9. [2125]: What is the meaning of the name "Abercrombie" that so often comes to me?

A-9. An associate of the entity in its activity through its spiritual forces, or those that come *with* its activity in itself.

Q-10. Please explain further regarding the name "Abercrombie."

A-10. Just as given.

Q-11. [379]: How can I strengthen my faith?

A-11. Put that thou hast to the test in thine self. Know that, as it is used, it grows.

Q-12. [2124]: Please explain more explicitly the following answer to my question. [See 262-13, A-5.]

A-12. As the ideal of an entity is set, and the entity knows or gives that activity, or the abilities of its ideal in a given direction, then the use of that as *is* in hand as respecting such an ideal strengthens *all* attributes as *respecting* the *activities* of same in self. So, as is given, use that thou hast in hand, for the more *perfect* understanding comes with the more knowledge of that as is known that may be used in the daily experiences of self.

Q-13. Can this group aid further in the Lindbergh case?

A-13. Leave it as it is.

Q-14. Is there any message for this group at this time?

A-14. Prepare ye the way for the next lesson, that should come with this— *Virtue and Understanding;* and as ye meditate, as this:

LET VIRTUE AND UNDERSTANDING BE IN ME, FOR MY DEFENSE IS IN THEE, O LORD, MY REDEEMER; FOR THOU HEAREST THE PRAYER OF THE UPRIGHT IN HEART.

We are through.

This psychic reading was given by Edgar Cayce at his home in Pinewood on Lake Drive, Virginia Beach, Va., on May 1, 1932, at 4:30 P.M., in accordance with a request made by those present: Edgar Cayce; Gertrude Cayce, conductor; Gladys Davis, steno; C. A. Barrett, Minnie Barrett, M. L. Black, Hugh Lynn Cayce, L. B. Cayce, Mildred Davis, Edith Edmonds, Florence Edmonds, Helen Ellington, Lu Hesson, Sarah Hesson, Ruth LeNoir, Hannah Miller, F. Y. Morrow, C. W. Rosborough, M. L. Rosborough, Helen Storey, and Esther Wynne.

≈ 262-18 ≈

Mrs. Cayce: You will have before you the group gathered here and their work on the lessons which they are preparing. You will first tell us if any changes or additions should be made in the lesson on Faith, *a copy of which I hold in my hand. You will then answer the questions on the continuance of our work.*

Mr. Cayce: Yes, we have the group as gathered here, as a group, as individuals; also that as prepared on *Faith,* and the work.

Ready for questions.

Q-1. Regarding lesson on Faith, *paragraph one.*

A-1. This is very good, and the proper presentation of the subject.

[Questions 2 through 23 are a continuation of checking various paragraphs from the lesson on *Faith,* to each of which Mr. Cayce gave a simple affirmative answer. Regarding paragraph eleven (Q-11), he added: "There will be necessary for some little changes in the punctuations, rather than the matter itself, as is written here. Very good."]

Q-24. Any advice regarding this lesson?

A-24. This is very good, with the minor changes. No transpositions, nor would we add any, save that as may be the questions that may arise in the study of same.

Q-25. Are the divisions correct which Florence Edmonds has made of those seeking aid from our healing group [281],[1] *a copy of which I hold in my hand? [See 281-5, A-17.]*

A-25. These are very good. Only will there be necessary for

[1] This is the identification number assigned to the series of readings given for the Healing Group. These readings are published as Volume II (*Meditation,* Part I) in this publication series.

changes as conditions develop with individuals and circumstances necessary for the carrying out of the variations as will
appear from time to time. The commencing is the best thing.

Q-26. *Will you give us the position of the hands for* [146]?

A-26. In the right hand, on the third and fourth cervical. The
left on the auditory plexus, or that as about the lower portion
of the ear—thumb and finger on either side, see?

Q-27. *Please give us that which we need in understanding and
beginning work on our next lesson, on* Virtue and Understanding.

A-27. In the beginning of the study of this lesson, would be
well that each individual of the group, or students of same,
review that as has been the preparation for the study of the
attributes that are now to be set before such students. In the
beginning was that as would apply to the individual's cooperation with a group, or concerted effort on the part of individuals
with one mind, or aim, or purpose. The understanding, or looking into self, and the preparation of self in the light of that of
the cooperation. Then as to become active with that as had been
gained. Then the basis with which an entity approaches the
forces within each individual, that there may come forth those
works, that are through the activity *of* that force of faith in the
material activities of an individual. Then there begins as in
this: Adding to thy faith virtue and understanding. Virtue, in
this study, then, is to be as the criterion with which thine faith
is to be put into active service; for without that pureness of the
virtue of self's own mental, material and spiritual self, there
can come little understanding. Know, then, these are to be that
as is the beginning of the opening of self to the activity of those
forces as emanate from that which has been applicable from
the studies that have gone before; for with faith comes then the
working forces that make for an activity upon the part of each
towards that being manifested in the lives of each who have set
their face towards an activity. So these, then, are the *beginnings*. Study to show that within self which is an exemplification of that which has been gained by each, and as a group, and
then comes understanding. With that same pureness in self
that is demanded by self of thy brother.

Q-28. [307]: I greatly desire to be filled with virtue and understanding. Is there any message for me?

A-28. Keep in line with that as has been set before self, and *sure* is the way—for this is as *His* way.

Q-29. [303]: Please lead me more into the way by which I may get true virtue and understanding.

A-29. In the application of that as has been gained comes the understanding. Be true to that that is pure in thy purpose, for *this* IS virtue. In virtue comes understanding; for they are as the tenon and the mortise, they fit one with, one to, another.

Q-30. [404]: Does understanding come only with experience?

A-30. Understanding comes with application. Application may be experience mental or physical, or spiritual. With the ideal that is set before self there comes the awakening. As to whether this is shaken by doubts or fears, or there is the inroads of a doubt that makes for muddying of thine experience, this then makes for a less understanding.

Q-31. Please define spiritual faith.

A-31. The application of that that is awakened by the spirit within self.

Q-32. [341]: Please tell us how we should define virtue.

A-32. As that is applied in the daily life of individuals as respecting the cooperation, self, the ideal, and the faith, to each it is given; for each individual is an entity in itself, and all work together for the proper understanding and definition—but to *each* is their *own* approach. Not that God is many, but the attributes *of* the Creative Forces *respond* according to the development *of* that entity.

Q-33. [585]: Would the interpretation of my dream of several weeks ago, in which I was permitted to see the world from a distance as being lifted in space, be helpful in any way to this group? If so, please give it.

A-33. Each individual experience is helpful to another, provided the experience is of such a nature that it gives an impetus for activity upon the part of another. In this experience to the entity, as a real experience—and may be set as for others in *their* seeking. Some seek an experience of like nature, some seek an experience that is within line with their individual

thought. Then *all,* when they have put themselves in that position, attitude, or attunement, to *receive* the lesson through an
experience, receive same in their *own* language or tongue; for
so is the activity of the spirit in the material world, that each
hear, or feel, or know, or understand, in their *own* language,
their *own* experience, their *own* interpretation, of the One; yet
all are one, as was learned from the beginning, as the ideal
must be one in Him, as the relationships of self must be as of
one purpose and one aim, as in faith there comes the awakening
to the virtue in that thou hast believed and hast set before self,
so does each experience find in the life or activity of individuals
that which enables them to come to a greater understanding
[of] "What is it all about?" [* Gladys Davis's note: Mrs. 585 told
me, 2/23/66, that she and Mrs. 413 came late into the group.
Mrs. 2125 said to them, "Why don't you start your own group?"
Mrs. 585 said to Mrs. 413, "I don't think I'll go any more—they
don't seem to want us." At another meeting she told Mrs. 413
afterwards, "I don't think I'll go any more—I don't know what
it's all about!" She then submitted Q-33 at the next rdg. for the
group and was convinced beyond question of the divine source.]

Q-34. [*288*]: *Just what should I understand and gain from my
experience Wednesday afternoon, April 20, 1932, [during reading 1800-18] of seeing a prophet, Christ on the cross, and the
all-seeing eye?*

A-34. This as the vision to self, as was given to the prophets
of old, that thy prayer and supplication have been heard [see
288-30, A-3], and that there is the way as of the cross being
opened for the greater activity through the all-seeing eye; for,
as each figure seen represents a portion in the experience of
self, so make thine self more and more the channel for blessings
to others.

Q-35. Any message at this time for the group?

A-35. Keep the way open. Do not become a stumbling block
to any. *Know* in what thou hast believed, and *where* thy faith
has been placed. By the works ye shall know them, as by their
fruits; for as virtue is a fruit of faith, so does the *understanding*
come—as the full-grown seed ready for planting.

This psychic reading was given by Edgar Cayce at his home in Pinewood on Lake Drive, Virginia Beach, Va., on May 15, 1932, at 4:00 P.M., in accordance with a request made by those present: Edgar Cayce; Gertrude Cayce, conductor; Gladys Davis, steno; C. A. Barrett, Minnie Barrett, M. L. Black, Hugh Lynn Cayce, L. B. Cayce, Mildred Davis, Helen Ellington, Edith Edmonds, Florence Edmonds, F. M. Freeman, Ruth LeNoir, Hannah Miller, F. Y. Morrow, C. W. Rosborough, M. L. Rosborough, and Helen Storey.

༔ 262-19 ༂

Mrs. Cayce: You will have before you the group gathered here and their work on the lesson of Virtue and Understanding. *You will continue the information on this subject which will aid us in continuing our work, and will answer the questions which various individuals will ask.*

Mr. Cayce: Yes, we have the group as gathered here, as a group, as individuals. In the study of this particular phase of that necessary preparation within individuals that they may know and understand themselves, their relationships to the Creative Forces, these as lessons are then the preparations for the relationships that are to be studied as respecting their fellow man. Hence the next lesson must be *Fellowship.* In the preparations of self virtue and understanding are necessary requisites for the relationships that are to be further studied.

Ready for questions.

Q-1. Is the following outline of Virtue and Understanding *complete and inclusive enough to cover the lesson which we should present on this subject? Please suggest any advisable additions or changes, as I read this to you:*

VIRTUE AND UNDERSTANDING

1. Introduction

2. Both Virtue and Understanding Essential to Right Living

3. Virtue and Understanding Are Spiritual and Can Be Found Only in the Spiritual Way

4. The Way to Virtue and Understanding Open to All Who Will:

a. Become a channel of blessings to others

b. Thoroughly acquaint self with self

c. Have their ideal set in Him: The One Way — the Straight and Narrow Way

5. *Faith, the Chief Cornerstone in Acquiring Virtue and Understanding*
6. *Virtue, a Defense; Understanding, a Weapon*
7. *The Effect of Virtue and Understanding upon Self and Others*

A-1. This is well. Well that this be understood, that virtue and understanding deals primarily with self and self's relationship to the Creative Forces, or God, and that virtue and understanding in self is *reflected* in self, rather than a *judgment* upon another. Judge self by thine understanding and thine own virtue, *not* another—for these are of the spirit and must be judged by the spirit. "Judge not that ye be not judged."

Q-2. [*993*]: *Would appreciate a message from the Master that may guide me now in virtue and understanding.*

A-2. As there is set before thee that thou hast builded and chosen in thine service, thine work, so *will* the harvest be, if there will be kept that faith in Him who gives that necessary understanding for the comprehension of the varied conditions as present themselves as problems in thine daily experience. There will not be those things that are not understood, if there will be the opening of the heart to that consciousness that comes from the closer walk with Him. Keep the way thou knowest; keep the path thou hast trod in, for He is able to *deliver* thee in every trial, in every way, for unto him that is faithful comes the crown of life.

Q-3. [*69*]: *Through what source may I gain a greater understanding?*

A-3. Through prayer and meditation in Him, for He *is* the way, He *is* the understanding, and the approach to all understanding must come from the proper concept of the relationships of conditions in the physical, the mental and the spiritual phases of an individual's existence. In *Him*, then, is understanding. The approach to the Father through Him.

Q-4. *What is the meaning of the words I got in meditation, "eighteen-karat gold," that was repeated over and over?*

A-4. That as had been that criterion with which the judgment had been passed on those concepts that were in the mental being of self, *rated* as such from material standards.

Q-5. [379]: Is there a message for me regarding virtue and understanding?

A-5. In making those parallels, or those analyses of what are the requisites for the closer relationships to faith, to knowledge, to self, to cooperation, to the knowing of self, to that of thine ideal, *measure* these by the spiritual aspects; *not* as man-made, or man's concept from the material viewpoint, and there will come the more perfect understanding. *Knowledge* is not *always* understanding; for these are as knowledge in the daily experiences that are as miracles, yet they become so often as everyday facts that there is no understanding in the mercies or the glories that are showered upon the sons of men from an All-Wise Creator. Few get understanding that have mere knowledge. Then the fault lying in that which is as the standard of measurements, in judgments; but get the understanding through the closer approach to the throne, for he that has understanding may move mountains.

Q-6. [404]: Please expand on the statement, "Truth is not learned, it is earned."

A-6. *Truth* is as experience. Hence *is* an earning, through the manners in which a finite mind becomes conscious of what truth is. Hence truth is a growth, and hence an *earning*, a yearning, a growing, and is *earned* by he or she that applies that known in the manner that *is* in keeping with His will, rather than that there may be the satisfying of self's own desires. Not that man should deny that this or that force exists, to make self believe, but rather that the truth is as that which may be earned through the *experiencing* of the knowledge and understanding concerning the laws of truth; for HE is *truth!*

Q-7. Please expand on the statement: "Open our hearts to those unseen forces that surround the throne of grace, and beauty and might, throwing about us the protection found in the thought of the Christ." [See 262-3, A-11.]

A-7. These expand by doing it! That's the best expansion!

Q-8. [2125]: Am I pursuing the right course for my development?

A-8. As ye sow, so *shall* ye reap. As ye remain in that attitude of seeking, so will there be opened unto thee *that* as is sought.

In Him is the light, and no darkness at all. Seek the way, and it will be opened unto thee.

Q-9. [*2124*]: *Am I still on the straight and narrow path?*

A-9. That must be answered from within, to Him in whom thou hast put thy faith, thy trust, thy hope, thy hereafter. *Who am I* to judge thee? " *Who* is good?", as He gave, "*None* save the Father," not even the Son of man. Rather in *Him* is the way, and "My Spirit," saith He, "beareth witness with thy spirit whether ye be the sons of God or not."

Q-10. Compilers: We have sent the paper on "Present World Conditions" to The Westerner, *The Westerner Limited, Calgary, Alberta, Canada, some weeks ago for publication. We have received no reply from our letter in regard to the paper. Should we write to publishers again?*

A-10. It has gone abroad. Wait at least a week.

Q-11. Any message for the group at this time?

A-11. Keep in the way as is set before thee, for much may be accomplished in that *thou* hast undertaken.

We are through.

≫ 262-20 ≪

This psychic reading was given by Edgar Cayce at his home in Arctic Crescent, Virginia Beach, Va., on June 5, 1932, at 4:00 P.M., in accordance with a request made by those present: Edgar Cayce; Gertrude Cayce, conductor; Gladys Davis, steno; C. A. Barrett, Minnie Barrett, M. L. Black, Annie Cayce, Hugh Lynn Cayce, L. B. Cayce, Mildred Davis, Edith Edmonds, Florence Edmonds, Helen Ellington, F. M. Freeman, Lu Hesson, Sarah Hesson, Ruth LeNoir, Hannah Miller, F. Y. Morrow, Eloise Potter, and Helen Storey.

Mrs. Cayce: You will have before you the group gathered here and their work on the lessons which they are preparing with the aid of the forces through this channel. You will give us at this time any further counsel which we need in completing the lesson on Virtue and Understanding, *a copy of our work so far [which] I hold in my hand.*

Mr. Cayce: Yes, we have the group, as a group and as individuals, as gathered here. Also the work in preparing lessons.

In the preparation of the lesson *Virtue and Understanding,* well has it been thus far. In the preparations, as has been given, the group as a group, in the preparation, depends one upon another, as does the lesson depend upon the activity of each individual contributing to same. As has been given, each should feel, should know, they—as individuals—are a portion of the whole, and must contribute their part that the whole may be the more applicable in the lives of individuals who will be interested in that lesson from such preparation; for, as given, no one finite mind may contribute that even of interest to the many who may be reached through such lessons, yet individual contribution makes for the whole that which will find a responsive chord in the lives and hearts of those who contact same; for these are as experiences, *living* truths, known and read of many, and will thus make for that which will become the more worthwhile in the lives of others. Then let each give that which will aid in making the whole complete, for each should recognize their individual responsibility to themselves, to the group, to their Maker whom they reflect their conception of in the minds of those who would apply the lesson in *their* daily experience.

-85-

As given, virtue and understanding are the attributes that make for the relationships with the Creative Forces, as making for preparation of contacts with the fellow man as individuals, personalities that must be dealt with, that the relationships may become such as to make the understandings of individuals compatible with daily life, daily experience, that the lesson may be the more worthwhile.

Ready for questions.

Q-1. [2112]: *What is the difference between psychic forces and occult forces?*

A-1. These have oft been explained. Well that these be studied in the light of that which has been given. One is the study of the other. One is the essence of the sources, and the other the channels through which, of which, the study.

Q-2. [69]: *Please explain what was meant by the spiritual eye, or third eye, in relation to psychic development. Should we today seek to develop this particular facility? If so, how?*

A-2. As has been given, there is ever a channel or manner in which the expressions of a force may manifest in a material world. Hence the term, "Angels took form," that there might be the expression of, or vehicle for, the activity of an individual force manifestation in the *material* plane. In the psychic forces, or spiritual forces (which are psychic forces), there has ever then been a vehicle, or portion of the anatomical forces of the body, through which the expressions come to individual activity, and these may find various forms of manifestations, or *movements* of—as has been given, that finds its seat in the creative energies and forces of the body. In the eye, "Let thine eye be *single*" may be the interpretation of same, or vehicles, or channels, or glands through which man has lost his vision, or the ability of seeing the self-expression in same in the pituitary forces, as in the lyden and the others—we find expressions in various forms of the body. These become, as has been seen or given, in the feminine body more manifested than ordinarily in the male, in man forces, in that called intuition, or that which is active in that portion of the system. These are but one expression of that portion of the body, for these may be added to by the feeding of same, that partake of other forces of the body in such quantities, or such character of development, as to produce other conditions in the body, as the growing of portions of the body that have become lax, or lacking in their activity in the system, but development in the spiritual sense —by meditation, prayer—dependent upon the external forces, or the Creative Energies, for its food, rather than upon that which is wholly of the material, develops that as may be termed the psychic development of individuals. Well that psychic forces and occult influences be developed in the individuals that so find within their individual selves that which makes for a closer relationship with that they individually worship as their ideal! That does not indicate that every individual should make of themselves a psychic channel that may be used to their own destruction; for, as has been given, there be many things hard to be understood that many wrest with to their own destruction, but that which gives more understanding of the relationships of self with the Creative Forces of a universal experience, rather than individual, makes for a closer walk with God, that from which the essence of Life itself has its emanation. In the body we find that which connects the pineal, the pituitary, the lyden, may be truly called the silver cord, or the golden cup that may be filled with a closer walk with that which is the Creative Essence in physical, mental and spiritual life; for the destruction wholly of either will make for the disintegration of the soul from its house of clay. To be purely material-minded, were an anatomical or pathological study made for a period of seven years (which is a cycle of change in all the body-elements) of one that is acted upon through the third eye alone, we will find one fed upon spiritual things becomes a light that may shine from and in the darkest corner. One fed upon the purely material will become a Frankenstein that is without a concept of any influence other than material or mental.

Q-3. Regarding the lessons, at this time, we seek individual guidance and advice in enabling us to better cooperate in carrying forward this work of our group.

A-3. Study, then, that which has been given on cooperation! For that applied in the individual life will make for that necessary for carrying on. Do not become weary in well-doing, for soon we must come to that lesson of *Patience* as following *Fellowship.*

Q-4. Any special message for the group at this time?

A-4. As has been given, let each—each—know themselves a link in the chain, a spoke in the wheel. Do not be the whole, but fulfill that *thou* may do, that there may be the perfect accord; for he that giveth a cup of water in His name is greater than he that conquereth a city for his own aggrandizement.

We are through.

This psychic reading was given by Edgar Cayce at his home in Arctic Crescent, Virginia Beach, Va., on June 12, 1932, at 4:00 P.M., in accordance with a request made by those present: Edgar Cayce; Gertrude Cayce, conductor; Gladys Davis, steno; C. A. Barrett, Minnie Barrett, Annie Cayce, Hugh Lynn Cayce, L. B. Cayce, Mildred Davis, Edith Edmonds, Florence Edmonds, Helen Ellington, Ruth LeNoir, Hannah Miller, F. Y. Morrow, and Esther Wynne.

➢ 262-21 ⬧

Mrs. Cayce: You will have before you the members of the Norfolk Study Group #1, present in this room, and their work on the lessons which they are preparing. We present the lesson on Virtue and Understanding, *a copy of which I hold in my hand. As I call the number of each paragraph you will suggest any changes or additions that would be advisable. You will please answer the questions which will be asked.*

Mr. Cayce: Yes, we have the group as gathered here, the work, the lesson as prepared. In this we find there has been work that is well, acceptable, and will give much understanding to many of that which has heretofore not been considered in the light as presented here. Very good.

["Very good" was the answer given to each paragraph named.]

Q-1. Please give us the meditation for our daily prayer on Fellowship.

A-1. HOW EXCELLENT IS THY NAME IN THE EARTH, O LORD! WOULD I HAVE FELLOWSHIP WITH THEE, I MUST SHOW BROTHERLY LOVE TO MY FELLOW MAN. THOUGH I COME IN HUMBLENESS AND HAVE AUGHT AGAINST MY BROTHER, MY PRAYER, MY MEDITATION, DOES NOT RISE TO THEE. HELP THOU MY EFFORTS IN MY APPROACH TO THEE.

Q-2. Please outline the central thoughts and basis upon which we should begin our meditations and questions on Fellowship.

A-2. As each will find in their own searching of their hearts, fellowship with the Creative Forces is making ever a balance in the activities of self towards thy fellow man; for would we seek grace, mercy, understanding, would we have faith, knowledge, there must be the exercising of same in our fellow man. As we have dealt with those attributes necessary in the preparing of self to deal with, or know the heart of self, so must the acts, the judgments as would be builded in ourselves, be found in our fellow man, would we seek to be in the position of communion with the spirit within; and the fellowship is the promise of the Father through the Son, that—would ye seek to know His face, be kind and gentle, compassionate and loving, to thy fellow man. In this manner, then, let each purge their own minds and hearts, and he that has aught against any, present it to the throne of grace, and His mercy is sufficient unto all. "As ye would that men should do to you, do ye even so to them." "Forgive me, Father, even as I forgive my brother" should be that lesson, that exercising of the position each would take, would they know the face of Him who seeks fellowship with His creatures; for as the Father pitieth His children, so in that manner may the Father gather those close that would seek fellowship with Him. *Know* that as ye forgive will ye be forgiven; for "Inasmuch as ye have done it unto the least of these my little ones, ye have done it unto me."

As we deal, then, with our fellow man, may there be expected —and may we expect—those blessings to come to us. In the way and manner as we deal, so must it come again to all.

In the preparations, then, let each set their minds, their hearts, their souls, at peace with Him; and there will come that light that will shine in the darkest hour, in those periods when needed most. Approach the throne of mercy with mercy to all.

Q-3. Please give each member of the group, as I call their names, an individual message on true fellowship.

A-3. Let each examine themselves first, that they may know that within their own hearts and minds that must be purged, that there may be true fellowship with Him.

We are through for the present.

This psychic reading was given by Edgar Cayce at his home on Arctic Crescent, Virginia Beach, Va., on June 26, 1932, at 4:15 P.M., in accordance with a request made by those present: Edgar Cayce; Gertrude Cayce, conductor; Gladys Davis, steno; C. A. Barrett, Minnie Barrett, M. L. Black, Annie Cayce, Hugh Lynn Cayce, Mildred Davis, Edith Edmonds, Florence Edmonds, F. M. Freeman, Lu Hesson, Sarah Hesson, Ruth LeNoir, Hannah Miller, F. Y. Morrow, C. W. Rosborough, M. L. Rosborough, and Esther Wynne.

≈ 262-22 ≪

Mrs. Cayce: You will have before you members of the study group present in this room, and their work on the lesson of Fellowship, *an outline of which I hold in my hand. You will please give us that information which we will need in expanding this outline, and suggest any changes or additions that would be advisable in the approach to this subject. You will answer questions which various members will ask.*

Mr. Cayce: Yes, we have the group as a group, as individuals, as gathered here; also those preparations regarding preparation of lesson.

In carrying on, it would be well that the spirit of fellowship among the members of the group be in accord with that which has been and may be given. Well that this be in unison of purpose, as well as said outwardly. In all things *Fellowship* as the lesson that begins, as has been given, that each must clarify themselves that their relationships between their fellow man and the Creative Forces be such as to make a cementing of the purposes for which the lessons are given to others. Then, let their meditation be as this:

IN PREPARATION FOR THE TASK BEFORE US, LET EACH BECOME MORE CONSCIOUS OF THE DIVINE SPIRIT IN EACH, THAT WE MAY GO ON. MAY WE FACE THE ISSUES AS ONE CALLED FOR A PURPOSE. MAY WE RELY ON HIS PROMISES, FOR WHILE WE ARE OFTEN WEAK AND SELFISH—AND THE WORK IS GREAT—MAY HE ENCOURAGE OUR SPIRITS, OUR HEARTS, WITH THE PRESENCE OF HIS HOLY SPIRIT, THAT THERE MAY BE NO IDLENESS OR DELAY IN US.

In this manner may these truly become the living lessons. Not one dependent upon another, but all conscious that they have been called, and unless they answer in person they may *not* have that whole fellowship with Him that is promised to those who have vowed and bowed unto Him.

The outline as set is well, and with this in the minds, the hearts, the understandings of all, there must come an awakening that has not yet come to all.

Ready for questions.

Q-1. [993]: In what way am I best adapted to express fellowship?

A-1. As has been given, the talents are in the expressions of bringing to others that consciousness which leaves in the spiritual and mental body those things that bring for the reliefs in that reflected in the physical being. Then, through these channels may there be the greater fellowship with Him, brotherhood with thy fellow creatures. [See 262-23, A-4.]

Q-2. [115]: Please describe the difference in fellowship and brotherhood.

A-2. One to God, the other to man.

Q-3. [404]: Ofttimes when one gives of his service, either materially, morally or spiritually, unselfishly to others, those served seem to use it for purely selfish purposes. Please advise.

A-3. Who has judged? Judge ye not that ye be not judged! For with what judgment ye judge it shall be meted to you again! The *abilities* oft of individuals to express or manifest appreciation, and their trust, is not capable of being manifested in such a manner as to be interpreted in the material sense by those in a different vibration or environ from those ministering or ministered to. Hence understandings often produce those conditions in the hearts, the minds of individuals, and thus warped conditions arise. Rather let that mind be in you as was in Him. "Were there not ten healed? Where are the other nine?", but the healing was just as true for the nine as the one. They that are whole need not the physician, but who having a herd of sheep and loses one does not leave the ninety and nine and seek for that one lost? So, in thy ministering be rather in that of *daring* to do even for those that would not understand, but doing rather for Him, in that "As ye have done it unto the least of these my little ones, ye have done it unto me." *Reserve*, then, that the thanks will come from Him who knows!

Q-4. Is there any message to me [404] as secretary?

A-4. Be thou faithful unto those that thou ministereth to in every manner, for he that serveth with the might receives the reward from and through the Giver of all good and perfect gifts.

Q-5. [69]: What is the extreme test of fellowship?

A-5. Doing unto others as ye would have them do unto you is the extreme test of fellowship. Without same ye may not wholly please God.

Q-6. Compilers: Is there any message to the compilers in regard to the lesson on Fellowship?

A-6. Let there be unison of purpose from those ministered unto and those ministering, to those that the group as a group and as individuals minister to the needs of, those who are and who will be seeking through these channels. That the way is being opened is evidenced by all of the group. Be not afraid, for He will guide, direct. Trust in His graciousness, in His support, in His understanding.

Q-7. What should be our next step in regard to our paper on "Present World Conditions" that was sent to Alberta, Canada?

A-7. This, as we find, should keep on its round until there is given the opportunity for all to have accepted or rejected.

Q-8. Shall we write to them again about it?

A-8. Write again. It hasn't been received back as yet.

Q-9. Please explain to the group what made possible the attunement when the information was given on the Lord's Supper, June 14, 1932, and why was this given at that time? [See reading 5749-1.]

A-9. The attunement of those present, and the conditions that surrounded same as respecting the test through which many were passing at the period, as compared to those in the room at that supper.

We are through.

This psychic reading was given by Edgar Cayce at his home on Arctic Crescent, Virginia Beach, Va., on July 10, 1932, at 4:00 P.M., in accordance with a request made by those present: Edgar Cayce; Gertrude Cayce, conductor; Gladys Davis, steno; C. A. Barrett, Minnie Barrett, M. L. Black, Hugh Lynn Cayce, Mildred Davis, Edith Edmonds, Florence Edmonds, Helen Ellington, F. M. Freeman, Lu Hesson, Sarah Hesson, Ruth LeNoir, F. Y. Morrow, C. W. Rosborough, M. L. Rosborough, and Esther Wynne.

≫ 262-23 ≪

Mrs. Cayce: You will have before you the group gathered here and the work which they are doing. You will please give us further data and information on Fellowship *upon which we are preparing our present lesson. You will answer the questions which various individuals present will ask.*

Mr. Cayce: Yes, we have the group as gathered here, as a group, as individuals. These, as we find, in their preparation for the study necessary in preparing such lessons, are well. These show some improvement in their activity. Some are still rather backward—yea, indolent—in the accepting of that as is necessary for their part in the undertaking; for as these are to give a definite outline for individuals, there must be the concerted effort on the part of each to act in the manner toward the preparations as they would desire were the conditions reversed.

In consideration of fellowship, this should mean a great deal to each and every member of this or such a group; for with the application in their own experience there may be expected, and there may be received, that true fellowship in the experience of the individual; and when such is *not* one's experience, then such ones may know they are lacking in *their* efforts in being what they should in their relationships to themselves, their Maker, the group.

Then, make for that which is sincere in purpose, pure in mind, reasonable even to self, walking in the way that brings a more close union with Him, that "Will ye be my people, I will be your God." He seeks to find that expression even in all who are called in the I AM THAT I AM, and is an ever active force that through all ages, all peoples, may be a memorial that one has fellowship with Him, that brought the Pleiades into being, that set the bands of Orion, or the waters in the deep that are cast upon the land, or brings breath into the life of all creatures, and supplies the union with those Creative Forces that makes for the *songs* of the spheres—the Lord is His name!

Ready for questions.

Q-1. [307]: Can brotherhood exist among men without true fellowship?

A-1. Fellowship is first brotherhood, a pattern of—or a shadow of—what fellowship is; for, as has been given, all one sees manifest in a material world is but a reflection or a shadow of the real or the spiritual life. Brotherhood, then, is an expression of the fellowship that exists in the *spiritual* life.

Q-2. [585]: Please explain to me what is meant by the awakening. Have I fully realized it?

A-2. The awakening is the consciousness of a relationship that exists in animate or inanimate, finite or infinite. Becoming conscious of, aware of, the existence of conditions, relations, and such, is an awakening. As to self's being awakened, or aware of, that depends upon what is referred to. As to the *abilities* of self to become conscious of, or aware of, all are endowed with that, will they but be awakened or aroused to the necessity of becoming aware of.

Q-3. Interpret the meaning of the drops of blood which I saw in meditation last week.

A-3. As there has been builded in self that consciousness that *without* the shedding of blood there is no remission, or without the shedding of blood there is no purification, then this is rather the using of symbols within self's own consciousness to bring about that awareness of self's position. This rather confuses the body!

In making self aware of that that is a portion of self's own development, as in the drops of blood brought with same the idea of the purifying of the mental and spiritual self that there might be the more awareness of, in the conscious or material self, of that awareness received in the mental and spiritual self; so, as we would speak of omens, know that self is aroused! Then don't let yourself go back to sleep!

Q-4. [993]: Please interpret the meaning of the lights which

I saw about Mr. Cayce's head during the last reading on Fellowship [*262-22*].

A-4. This, too, may be as a symbol of the awareness of, the closeness of, relationships of the entity and the subject through which these were being brought to the consciousness of individuals during such a period; for, as there has oft been seen by the entity, those manifestations in the material plane of the spiritual essences as manifested through the activities of the entity seen, then those expressions as seen at the period are a reflection of the spiritual. Remember those laws as just given! That made manifest in a third-dimensional plane, or materialization, is a shadow or reflection of that from which it has its emanation! Then, there is seen in this that it is a harkening to those experiences of the entity in the various periods of its existence in association with those conditions being considered in that particular moment or period as is called time. An attunement of self to the presence of that being manifest. All are wading in rather deep water! But learn what you are doing! [See 281-8, A-19.]

Q-5. [2124]: Is the present method of healing I am using the best for the fullest development of my abilities in this field of work?

A-5. Provided they are kept wholly upon the spiritual plane, and because they *can* become mechanical are not allowed to partake of the carnal influences that oft are aroused at the same time or periods. This is a development. This is an ability of self, that is harkened from the experiences of self through the sojourn in the earth's experience, and may be made to become a manner and way of manifesting that love that is and was shed upon self. Be true to that as is given thee!

Q-6. [560]: Please interpet the following which I received during meditation: "That I may touch the hearts, the souls, the minds of others."

A-6. A message of the Infinite to the infinite of self, seeking to use self as a channel of expression to others. A call. Then, be true *to* that, even as the opportunity and the abilities are increased by the power of the might that would touch the hearts, the souls, the minds of those that self may contact in the various experiences in the preparation of truths, that may go in lessons or in thought that may be carried in unison for the awakening of the Christ Consciousness in the lives and hearts of others.

Q-7. [341]: How should we explain to others how to interpret their experiences as signs of development towards a true realization of fellowship?

A-7. This has been given in how ones may answer their experiences, have an answer to their experiences, in the way of *training* the child (for we all are children) in its development. Or, as this: When an experience of self is in question, then ask self in the mental being so that the answer may be yes or no, and with sincerity. Then, whether the answer is yes or no, as to any question with spiritual forces, then *accept* that. Then in meditation and prayer *ask* the spirit whether *that* answer *received* in the mental is yes or no, and *know* the spirit answers! Doubt not! For he that looks back, or doubts, is worse than the infidel. Remember Lot's wife!

Q-8. [2112]: Is the handwork referred to in the Egyptian period of my life reading located in the same tomb as the records of the Christ?

A-8. They are!

Q-9. Was I associated with Mr. Edgar Cayce during the Egyptian period, and if so what was the relation?

A-9. This has been given.

Q-10. Is there any message of encouragement or advice to the group as a whole at this time?

A-10. Keep that which has been committed into the care and keeping of each, as individuals, as related to one another, as a group, in a service to that ideal which has been set before the group, as a group, as the individuals; for he that has promised, he that has vowed and vowed, must keep same—or else it becomes sin!

We are through.

This psychic reading was given by Edgar Cayce at his home on Arctic Crescent, Virginia Beach, Va., on July 24, 1932, at 4:00 P.M., in accordance with a request made by those present: Edgar Cayce; Gertrude Cayce, conductor; Gladys Davis, steno; C. A. Barrett, Minnie Barrett, M. L. Black, Mildred Davis, Edith Edmonds, Florence Edmonds, F. M. Freeman, Sarah Hesson, Douglas Johnston, Gladys Johnston, Lucille Kahn, Ruth LeNoir, Hannah Miller, F. Y. Morrow, Eloise Potter, C. W. Rosborough, M. L. Rosborough, Helen Storey, and Esther Wynne.

৯ 262-24 ৶

Mrs. Cayce: You will have before you the members of the Norfolk Study Group #1, present in this room, and their work on the lessons which they are preparing. We present the lesson on Fellowship, *a copy of which I hold in my hand. As I call the number of each paragraph, you will suggest any changes or additions that would be advisable. You will answer the questions which will be asked.*

Mr. Cayce: Yes, we have the group as gathered here, as a group, as individuals, and the work of preparing lessons.

Ready for questions.

Q-1. A-1. [The lesson on *Fellowship,* consisting of 29 paragraphs, was read; to each paragraph Mr. Cayce answered "Good" or "Very good." To paragraph 12, he added, "There may be some change in the presentation of same, in the personal application. This very good."]

Q-2. Any suggestions regarding this lesson?

A-2. Very good.

Q-3. Please give us the meditation for our daily prayer on patience.

A-3. HOW GRACIOUS IS THY PRESENCE IN THE EARTH, O LORD. BE THOU THE GUIDE, THAT WE WITH PATIENCE, MAY RUN THE RACE WHICH IS SET BEFORE US, LOOKING TO THEE, THE AUTHOR, THE GIVER OF LIGHT[LIFE?].

In the preparation of selves, as individuals, for presenting patience in the experience, this—as other lessons—must be experienced by the individuals. Would we have that love, that patience of the Maker of the worlds, we must show patience to our brother, and—as was asked of Him, how oft shall I forgive?

Seven times? Yea, seventy times seven, that ye may know that which is builded in self. Through patience does the understanding come. Knowledge of itself is nothing. Understanding in the Lord becomes that of love, in patience, that maketh for the glorifying of that which is the gift of the Father in the material, the mental, the spiritual world. Stand *still*, will ye see the glory of the Lord. In patience possess ye your souls. As there is gained more and more those understandings in cooperation, self, activities in self, and the more there is gained a knowledge of the presence of Him in the experience, greater does patience work in the life, the experience, the heart, and the soul grows in understanding of His presence; for as these gifts—that are attributes of His consciousness in the lives of individuals, as entities, in a material life—become the greater manifestations of individuals' activities, so will there be in the experience that as would be the next lesson— *The Open Door.* Would ye enter in the joys of thy Lord?

Ready for questions.

Q-4. Please outline the central thoughts and basis upon which we should begin our meditations and questions on Patience.

A-4. As given, in patience possess ye thy presence before the throne. Seek oft, then, to gain an audience with thine inner self which bears witness before that throne. With patience may this be reached; for as one loses their hold on self in the lack of patience, so does that give the opportunity for the entering in of those things that would make afraid. Not that one should remain unactive, or inactive, but in patience run the race that is set before thee, looking to Him, the Author, the Giver of light, truth and immortality. That should be the central theme in every individual. Not in submissiveness alone, but in righteous wrath serve ye the living God.

Q-5. [69]: When does patience cease to be a virtue?

A-5. When thou art satisfied with thy own surroundings or conditions.

Q-6. [560]: In learning the lesson of patience, *please advise how we may overcome the little harassing annoyances that come in our daily lives.*

A-6. As was given of Him, as ye seek, know there is that Comforter present that will speak for thee under *every* condition; for, as He gave, "I will not leave thee comfortless. Be *not* afraid." Be *mad,* but sin not! In thine *understanding* gain the presence of Him ever as thy companion, in every act, in every word; for every thought must be accounted for, and in grace— His grace is sufficient—will there be that constant, prayerful attitude for a purposeful life; forgetting self, preferring another above self. Lose self in Him. *These* will answer. Not as an outward, but an *inward* growth—that makes for the beauty of the soul that has patience *shining* through. [See 262–25, A-3.]

Q-7. [*993*]: *When we reach the development of ceasing to see faults in those we contact, is it then we can say we have patience?*

A-7. When we see rather Him that we worship even in the faults of others, *then* we are at the *beginning* of patience.

Q-8. [*69's husband*]: *Explain my shortcomings in connection with patience, and furnish the remedy thereto.*

A-8. Remove self far from criticisms or fault-findings in others, and there comes then patience in word, deed and act. These are the *beginnings,* as it were, of wisdom. Knowest thou that which has brought about the activities of another? Rather, then, find the fault in self, and this will be that path that will lead to *lightening* the way of thine own patience. [Do] there arise those periods when little petty disturbances call for the quick retort, find rather the fault in self, if there be one; then, if there is not, according to thy standard that is set in thine ideal, open not thy mouth—even as He did not when railed upon.

Q-9. [*295*]: *What is the Master's definition of patience?*

A-9. Know ye that, in patience possess ye your souls! In interpreting, then, how one possesses their souls, that in the *loss* of patience there is the entering—as He gave—of those influences that would separate the real self, the soul, from the Maker. Hence in patience *possess* ye your souls!

Q-10. Please comment on the following statements: Epictetus said there were two faults far graver and fouler than any others, inability to bear and inability to forbear.

A-10. In these we have the variations that would come from the experiences of individuals giving the expression of *their* experience in *meeting* the conditions that arise in one's daily experience. An expression, then, of an inactivity on the part of one, and an overanxiety on the part of another.

Q-11. "All great things are slow of growth."

A-11. Just true! For, as has been given oft, the soul grows upon that it is fed. The soul of man is the greatest, then, of all creation, for it may be one with the Father. Little by little, line upon line, here a little, there a little—these are the manners of growth, that this may be one with Him. Lose not that as was given by Him, the greater of all those who gave the truths, that not only one *with* Him but individual in self! Not the whole, but equal *with* the whole—for one with Him. Ye, then, are not aliens—rather the *Sons* of the Holy One.

Q-12. "Content but not satisfied."

A-12. Content in that "Have Thy way, Lord. Use me as a channel. Not my will but Thine be done!" That is content. Satisfied means gratified, and is the beginning of the falling away, for *self* is to be then glorified.

Q-13. "The offenses committed through desire are more blamable than those which are committed through anger."

A-13. Be angry, but sin not. Means there has been lost rather the desire of exaltation, that the anger is as of the Giver of light that disperses the darkness as it falls upon same. These would depend, as a statement, upon the experience of the one so stating; for in this *some* would find the excuse for self. Rather that, in the desire that may be lost in Him may there come the knowledge of Him, in that there is found the light which comes from patience with self, with thine neighbor, seeking ever that He, the Lord, shall lead.

Q-14. [2125]: Could I develop automatic handwriting?

A-14. Anyone could. [See also 262-25, A-12, -13.]

Q-15. Is there any message for the group as a whole at this time?

A-15. Prepare self in this, as thou studiest thyself approved unto Him, for the door is to be opened.

We are through.

≈ 262-25 ≼

This psychic reading was given by Edgar Cayce at his home on Arctic Crescent, Virginia Beach, Va., on August 7, 1932, at 4:10 P.M., in accordance with a request made by those present: Edgar Cayce; Gertrude Cayce, conductor; Gladys Davis, steno; C. A. Barrett, Minnie Barrett, Annie Cayce, Mildred Davis, Edith Edmonds, Florence Edmonds, Helen Ellington, Sarah Hesson, Ruth LeNoir, F. Y. Morrow, Helen Storey, and Esther Wynne.

Mrs. Cayce: You will have before you members of the study group present in this room, and their work on the lesson of Patience, *an outline of which I hold in my hand. You will please give us that information which we will need in expanding this outline, and suggest any changes or additions that would be advisable in the approach to this subject. You will answer questions which various members will ask.*

Mr. Cayce: Yes, we have the group as gathered here, as a group and as individuals. Also the work on preparing the lessons—the lesson in *Patience.*

As is seen in this outline, this is very good. The expansions should be rather in this direction, that the activity of patience is meekness in action, pureness in heart, that makes for those forces enabling one to become aware and conscious of their soul's expansion with the Creative Energies in the activities of the spiritual life. As there is the expansion of the spiritual forces of the material body, the reflections from same are those attributes that make for the expressing of the Christ-life in the daily walks of the body. So that love in its essence is manifested in every word, act, thought and experience of the body, even as it was in Him. Patience is that necessary activity of the mind, mentally, physically, spiritually, that makes for expansion of and acquaintance with the activities of that that may be known in self, as to whether there *is* the proper attitude with that which is held as the ideal, as to whether the faith is in faith or by works, whether the virtue is as with understanding or is as a set rule, whether self is in possession of the ideal, and with cooperative measures activating in the experience of individuals. Hence, as we find, this lesson must be the summing up of all that has been experienced by individuals through that they have given to others, that they now must live themselves in their daily activities—that they may enter in.

Ready for questions.

Q-1. [307]: *How may I more perfectly live the life, that I may through patience gain the understanding?*

A-1. In the application of that known day by day. The spirit does not call on anyone to live that it does not already know and understand. In the doing does there come the knowledge, the understanding for the next step. Today, now, is the accepted time! Those that will enter in will trust in that they have through faith and with patience wait for that necessary activity for the next step. Use that in hand.

Q-2. [303]: *Is there a message for me that will help me in the practice of more perfect patience?*

A-2. As the trust, the hope, the faith is manifested by the patience day by day does there become the more awareness in self's own inner consciousness that all is well with Him; knowing that if the Lord is on thy side, who may be against you? Trust, and do that thou knowest to do, acting as the spirit moves within—and look not back; remember Lot's wife. [See 262-28, A-1.]

Q-3. [560]: *In reading of July 24, 1932, [262-24, A-6], what was meant by "Be mad but sin not"? Please explain.*

A-3. One that may control self in anger is beginning the first lessons or laws of experience. One that may control self in anger, that must come as resentment in the speech of individuals, may make for that which disregards the words said; disliking that which would produce such a feeling within self, yet able to love the soul of one that causes or produces such a state of feeling. This is patience, and love, and hope, and meekness, and pureness of heart. The meek shall inherit the earth, said He—the pure in heart shall see God. They are promises! Believest thou Him? Then "be angry and sin not" is to know that these are thine *own* promises—to thee—to thee!

Q-4. *In patience am I expressing "Possess ye your soul"? If not, please simplify how I may do so.*

A-4. All make that expression in whatever their activity may be; for that is as a truth that one becomes conscious of, aware of, that possession that makes them one with, a child of, the living God; for flesh and blood does not inherit the possessions with Him, but the spirit makes alive that soul that is aware of His consciousness in a material, a mental, or a spiritual plane. Hence all express this in whatever their actions be. As to whether this or that individual is doing this in the manner another would do so, this is to judge. Who is the judge? He that giveth judgment! The individual's soul, that would be one with Him.

Q-5. [413]: What has really happened to an individual when they think their patience has completely worn out?

A-5. They have lost patience with themselves.

Q-6. [379]: Is there any message for me that will help me to more perfectly practice patience in all my work and under all conditions?

A-6. Be faithful to that which is given in thy charge day by day, for he that is faithful over the little things will be made the ruler over the many. Those who have gained that consciousness of the indwelling of that spirit, that is abiding with those who seek to know His face, have the consciousness that this *is* the day, the time, when all men must seek to be patient one with another, under all conditions and circumstances, that they may be one with Him who in patience endured all that we might have the access to the Father, through the patience, the love, the consciousness, shown in a material plane. Be faithful to that thou *knowest* to do. Question not what nor whether another has chosen. Rather do that *thou* knowest to do.

Q-7. What time is referred to in James 5:8, "Be ye patient; stablish your hearts, for the coming of the Lord draweth nigh"?

A-7. As just given, this is the time—today—when the time draweth nigh for each soul to become more aware of the necessity of magnifying *His* presence through the patience borne one to, one with, one of, another, that He may be glorified in us, through the promise of the Father that such will be to those that love His coming. Let each live, then, as though they *expected* their concept of the Master Christ to *dine* with them today. What *would* ye have to offer as the fruits of thine own life, thine thoughts, thine acts, thine deeds? For, "Inasmuch as ye have done it unto the least of these my little ones ye have done it unto me."

Q-8. [585]: Is it the lack of patience that causes me to find my problems so hard to overcome? If so, how may I gain the necessary patience to overcome these problems?

A-8. As has been given, first: Is thine ideal only in Him? Is thine self in accord with thine ideal? Is thine virtue and understanding in accord with these? Then with patience wait for that awakening which will make for an understanding of that necessary to overcome—even as He. Taking stock, then, with self, one may know whether it is patience, faith, virtue, knowledge, brotherly love, or what, lacking in self. Do not find the fault in the other, but rather cleanse thine *own* mind, heart and soul, and the proper attitude toward whatever problem that presents itself will be in that manner of understanding love that knows no fear, but being content in *His* praise, His love, His understanding.

Q-9. From time to time I have had to come into my room a friend who has passed on. Is this contact harmful or beneficial?

A-9. In this, there are always those seeking that we may help, that may help us; for as we help another does help come to us. Pray for that friend, that the way through the shadows may be easier for them. It becomes easier for you.

Q-10. [993]: Is there a message for me that will help me to practice patience?

A-10. Use that thou knowest, and with patience wait for the light that comes with the knowledge of "I am using that Thou gavest me."

Q-11. [69]: When one has gotten the understanding of the oneness with the Father-Mother-God, why is it one does not experience the joy and bliss, and overcome all inharmony, which is their divine birthright? May I have the answer from Master Jesus, if possible?

A-11. Then, with patience wait for that. Is that attained in thine self so that the consciousness of the Master comes to thee in all thine hours, then with patience wait ye on the Lord; for as one finds that in the understanding of the Oneness, when *He* has *found* that the vessel is worthy of acceptation it is *kept* full.

Q-12. [*2125*]: *You told me* [*262-24, A-14*] *that anyone could do automatic writing. Will you please tell me how I may develop it?*

A-12. By practice. Sit alone with pencil and paper, and let that guide that may be sought — or may come in — direct. It will come. Anyone may; but is it the better may oft be the question. This may only be the better when surrounding self with those influences that may bring those of the *constructive* forces alone.

Q-13. Who is giving me this message?

A-13. That one sought from.

Q-14. Compilers: Is there any message to the compilers?

A-14. Take that given, in how the expansion should be, and weave it into that which has been given in, in such a manner that it may become a blessing to those who seek.

We are through for the present.

≱ 262-26 ≰

This psychic reading was given by Edgar Cayce at his home on Arctic Crescent, Virginia Beach, Va., on August 21, 1932, at 4:00 P.M., in accordance with a request made by those present: Edgar Cayce; Gertrude Cayce, conductor; Gladys Davis, steno; C. A. Barrett, Minnie Barrett, M. L. Black, Hugh Lynn Cayce, Mildred Davis, Edith Edmonds, Florence Edmonds, Helen Ellington, Elizabeth E. Evans, Lu Hesson, Sarah Hesson, Lucille Kahn, Ruth LeNoir, Hannah Miller, Noah Miller, F. Y. Morrow, Chester Robinson, C. W. Rosborough, M. L. Rosborough, and Esther Wynne.

Mrs. Cayce: You will have before you the group gathered here and their work on the lesson of Patience. *You will give to each, as I call their names, a personal message on patience which will enable them to complete the lesson within themselves. You will also answer the questions which will be asked.*

Mr. Cayce: Yes, we have the group as gathered here; the work, the experiences through which each pass in the attempt to apply that which has been gained in the study of patience.

Each should take this as a basis for the application of patience in their experience:

Patience is active rather than passive, and is that by which, through which, one may judge their *own* reaction as to the attributes they have set towards that of an ideal in their individual lives; whether that attribute be virtue, purity, hope, faith, understanding, cooperation, brotherly love, loving-kindness, or patience itself; for, as given, these are attributes of the soul, and are spiritual in their essence. So does the activating force of patience make aware in the consciousness of the individual who has named the Name, or who has set an ideal of any nature in reference to any phase of its experience; whether it be of the mental, material or spiritual nature. With patience do ye seek, and through patience do ye accomplish; for whom the Lord loveth He chasteneth. Should one find themselves in that position where patience is not necessary in their experience, they are no longer then on a road to that kingdom—and are no longer sons of light.

In the activating forces, then, these should be the experiences that each should apply in their own experience, as to whether ye be worthy to enter in.

Ready for questions.

Q-1. Regarding personal message on patience. First, [115].

A-1. Let that mind be in thee as was in Him, that in patience will ye possess—or be aware, or understand the development of thine own relationship to the Creative Forces that may manifest in material forces in the earth.

Q-2. [404]:

A-2. Keep that as is set before thee as thine ideal, whether in relationships to individuals, home or abroad, and know that no temptation or trial is not accompanied with the way or manner of escape in thine ideal—else thine ideal is below the mark of the higher calling set in Him.

Q-3. [341]:

A-3. In patience comes understanding of the relationships of ideals, and those that make for that unworthy of being tried are unworthy of being trusted for the entering in; for who goeth to war without first counting the cost? So, in thine ideals, as in relationships to the attributes of the Father, count the cost through the patience that may be had in thine own experience.

Q-4. [288]:

A-4. Count not that day as an ideal that something has not been overcome in the experience of patience; for as ye sow ye reap—and the reward is in Him.

Q-5. [307]:

A-5. In using day by day that as is known, in Him does the growth come; for ye grow in grace, in knowledge, in understanding, in Him. Through patience does there come the abilities of application of that gained day by day, line upon line, here a little, there a little. As ye overcome is strength gained.

Q-6. [2124]:

A-6. Keep in the way that leads to the spiritual awakenings of the abilities in Him that may be manifest in thee. Thou art the keeper of that entrusted in thy care, that is of Him. What will ye return for that as has been given thee?

Q-7. [295]:

A-7. In patience does the ability come to manifest His attributes in the relationships with others; for the kingdom is within. With patience does the knowledge and understanding of its attributes come to be known in thee. Let thine acts day by day be in keeping with that He has given.

Q-8. [303]:

A-8. Watch, that ye be not overcome. Watch and pray, for as the Father giveth so does the understanding come as to what may be accomplished in the efforts of the self in relationships to others; and ye are the light-bearers for Him. [See 262-28, A-2.]

Q-9. [993]:

A-9. Ye know in whom ye have believed. Keep that as is committed in thy care, that the returns may be in keeping with that trust as given in thy care.

Q-10. [69's husband]:

A-10. Day by day showeth forth the love of the Father. In patience do we become aware of same in our own experience, and as to how same adds to the spiritual man. In hope, in faith, in charity, in love, in patience, does the understanding—and knowledge—and intellect—and integrity—come.

Q-11. [294]:

A-11. Keep the way open that patience may have its course in thee, knowing that the crown comes to him that overcomes self.

Q-12. [560]:

A-12. The way is set before thee. In patience vary not from same. In the glory of the Father may all be accomplished. Follow in His way.

Q-13. [379]:

A-13. By the works of self, through the faith in that thou believest, does patience exercise itself in thine experience. Know, as ye are known, that the answers to thy problems are set in Him.

Q-14. [538]:

A-14. Through patience and endurance does the crown of joy, happiness, as the peace of His presence, give those blessings that are from His throne. His presence, with peace, is the promise of those who with patience endure the crosses that are set before thee day by day.

Q-15. [2125]:

A-15. Keep the faith, and in patience know in what thy faith is placed; for it is as the crucible and the test of all attributes as related to the forces in the earth to the Father in glory.

Q-16. [69]:

A-16. In patience does the knowledge of the peace and understanding of His presence come. An active force, not a passive one. Necessary that patience be exercised that ye know the hope, the faith, the knowledge, the understanding of His ways in the earth.

Q-17. [413]:

A-17. In knowledge and power comes responsibility, that in patience may be tested in self. Be not overcome by either trials or by those joys that may make forgetfulness of the source from which the power comes. In patience is the race of life run, that the joys may be the greater in Him.

Q-18. [585]:

A-18. As patience magnifies His presence in thy experience, so does the glory of "well done" come with the activities of the attributes of love, hope, charity, patience, that ye know the way —and He is the guide. In patience possess ye your soul.

Q-19. [462]: *Is there a message for me today?*

A-19. In those understandings that bring the knowledge of the Father, in the relationships of individuals day by day, may there with patience be gained the understanding of the crosses that may be borne, the attaining of that as may gain the greater knowledge of His will. He that is without those crosses has ceased to be of notice, and is no longer among the sons. In patience, then, comes the knowledge and the abilities to apply same in the relationships of men among men, for, "All power is given me in heaven and in earth," and in patience may ye receive the promise of, "My presence will be thy guide, my peace will be thy reward."

Q-20. [404]: *How does tribulation work patience, as given in Romans 5:3?*

A-20. As has been indicated in that, "Whom the Lord loveth He chasteneth," and purgeth every one; for corruption may *not* inherit eternal life, and must be burned up. Know that thy God is a consuming fire, and must purge every one, that ye may enter in. In patience does one overcome.

Q-21. *Is there a message on patience for me today?*

A-21. As given, keep the promise. They are thine, who are faithful in the little things—and ye will be ruler over many.

Q-22. [295]: *Of what significance in this lesson was my experience during meditation recently, in which a voice asked, "[295], can you reach?" and then stopped suddenly. Did I hear all of the question which stopped so suddenly?*

A-22. Compare with that as has been given, in that ye purge yourselves through patience of that that would hinder from entering in.

Q-23. *Compilers: What should we do regarding the paper on "Present World Conditions" which we sent to* The Westerner, *Calgary, Alberta, Canada?*

A-23. Patience; for this is on its way.

Q-24. *What is their attitude regarding this paper?*

A-24. With patience wait, that ye may know—for it worketh as the leaven.

Q-25. [69's husband]: *Furnish the information concerning the disaster which has been predicted to happen around the last of this month, the results and location.*

A-25. As *we* find, from those various channels through which such information has come, know rather that as was given by Him—"The hour ye know not, and the time ye know not. Not even the Son, but the Father." These are then rather those that shall be of the spiritual awakening, than material disasters in the present; for the time has not *yet* come—saith the oracle—for it is not yet fulfilled.

Q-26. *Is there any message for the group as a whole at this time?*

A-26. Ye have taken upon yourselves that as is worthy of the calling as set in Him. "Ye have chosen me, even as I have chosen you." Be faithful and patient, that ye may enter in.

We are through.

This psychic reading was given by Edgar Cayce at his home on Arctic Crescent, Virginia Beach, Va., on September 4, 1932, at 3:50 P.M., in accordance with a request made by those present: Edgar Cayce; Gertrude Cayce, conductor; Gladys Davis, steno; C. A. Barrett, Minnie Barrett, Mrs. Bryant, Annie Cayce, Hugh Lynn Cayce, Mildred Davis, Edith Edmonds, Florence Edmonds, Helen Ellington, Lu Hesson, Sarah Hesson, David Kahn, Lucille Kahn, Ruth LeNoir, F. Y. Morrow, Dr. and Mrs. Sewell, Esther Wynne, and others.

⊱ 262-27 ⊰

Mrs. Cayce: You will have before you the group gathered here, and their work on the lesson Patience, *a copy of which I hold in my hand. As I call each paragraph you will go over it and suggest any changes or additions which should be made before this lesson receives its final preparation for publication. You will also answer the questions which will be asked.*

Mr. Cayce: Yes, we have the group as gathered here, as a group, as individuals, and the work in preparation of the lesson. In this there is the preparation for the understandings that have come to each. Ready for questions. [Twenty-five paragraphs from the lesson on *Patience* were read. Mr. Cayce answered "Good" or "Very good" to each, except to paragraph 7 he added, "The illustrations as used here may be made more personal, or expanded upon in that manner."]

Q-1. Please give a meditation for the lesson on The Open Door.

A-1. AS THE FATHER KNOWETH ME, SO MAY I KNOW THE FATHER, THROUGH THE CHRIST SPIRIT, THE DOOR TO THE KINGDOM OF THE FATHER. SHOW THOU ME THE WAY. [See 262-28, A-6.]

In the preparations, then, for the lessons that may be gained by each that have dedicated themselves and their efforts in the preparation of the way, the door is through the Life, the Spirit of the Life—*not* the man, but the spirit as manifest in the Christ Consciousness in the material world. So, as each do manifest in their daily walks in and before men with that consciousness as the standard, so may the door be opened for that entity, that soul, to so grow and magnify that spirit to the glorifying of the Father, losing self in the service to others, that in the earth His name may be established forever.

BE STILL, MY CHILDREN! BOW THINE HEADS, THAT THE LORD OF

THE WAY MAY MAKE KNOWN UNTO YOU THAT HAVE BEEN CHOSEN
FOR A SERVICE IN THIS PERIOD WHEN THERE IS THE NEED OF THAT
SPIRIT BEING MADE MANIFEST IN THE EARTH, THAT THE WAY MAY
BE KNOWN TO THOSE THAT SEEK THE LIGHT! FOR THE GLORY OF THE
FATHER WILL BE MADE MANIFEST THROUGH YOU THAT ARE FAITH-
FUL UNTO THE CALLING WHEREIN THOU HAST BEEN CALLED! YE
THAT HAVE NAMED THE NAME MAKE KNOWN IN THY DAILY WALKS
OF LIFE, IN THE LITTLE ACTS OF THE LESSONS THAT HAVE BEEN
BUILDED IN THINE OWN EXPERIENCE, THROUGH THOSE ASSOCIA-
TIONS OF SELF IN MEDITATION AND PRAYER, THAT HIS WAY MAY
BE KNOWN AMONG MEN: FOR HE CALLS ALL—WHOSOEVER WILL
MAY COME—AND HE STANDS AT THE DOOR OF THINE OWN CON-
SCIENCE, THAT YE MAY BE AWARE THAT THE SCEPTER HAS NOT
DEPARTED FROM ISRAEL, NOR HAVE HIS WAYS BEEN IN VAIN: FOR
TODAY, WILL YE HARKEN, THE WAY IS OPEN—I, MICHAEL, CALL
ON THEE! [See also 262-28, A-5, -11, and -12.]

*Q-2. What should be the basis and fundamental thoughts to
be presented in the lesson on* The Open Door?

A-2. The Christ Spirit is the door, the truth, the way; *not* the
man—for, as the Father knoweth thee, so may ye know the
Father through the exemplifying of His attributes in the earth.
Little by little, line upon line, precept upon precept, here a
little, there a little, for the glory of the Father—not the exaltation of thine own self; for with the exaltation of self—or the
gratifying of the desires of flesh—the door closes. [See also
262-28, A-10 and 262-29, A-3.]

We are through.

⧖ 262-28 ⧗

This psychic reading was given by Edgar Cayce at his home on Arctic Crescent, Virginia Beach, Va., on September 18, 1932, at 4:00 P.M., in accordance with a request made by those present: Edgar Cayce; Gertrude Cayce, conductor; Gladys Davis, steno; C. A. Barrett, Minnie Barrett, Annie Cayce, Hugh Lynn Cayce, Mildred Davis, Edith Edmonds, Florence Edmonds, Helen Ellington, Lu Hesson, Sarah Hesson, Ruth LeNoir, Hannah Miller, F. Y. Morrow, Helen Storey, and Esther Wynne.

Mrs. Cayce: You will have before you the group gathered here, and their work on the lesson The Open Door, *also the outline of this lesson which I hold in my hand. You will give any advice and counsel which will be helpful at this time, and answer the questions various members will ask.*

Mr. Cayce: We have the group as gathered here, as a group, as individuals, and their work in preparation of the lesson, *The Open Door.*

As to the preparation of selves, the application of that as has been given is the manner in which the individuals become the door for the entering in of that consciousness of the Master that presents the way, the manner of approach to the kingdom.

Then, as He has given, "I stand before the door and knock." Who will open? Who, then, will become the door that will lead others to that knowledge, that appreciation of the oneness of the Son with the Father, which may be made manifest in the material world through the application of those attributes of the Son, of the Father, in the activities of the individual?

Who, then, has learned to be truly cooperative one with another? Who has discerned self sufficient to know wherein self stands as in relationship with its fellow man? Who has set the ideal wholly in Him? Who magnifies the faith in the Father, in the Son, that it may be counted to them for righteousness? Who hath virtue and understanding, that they may magnify in their lives that fellowship which brings patience in the knowing of self to be growing in grace, in nurture and admonition of the Lord day by day?

He, then, it is that opens the door that He may come in and sup with him!

The outline that is presented is well, so that it is made to be

-114-

an individual act that opens the way, that the door may come to mean the access of the Son of man, the Savior, and the consciousness of the at-oneness with the Creative Forces that manifest in a material world.

James. [James 1:1? James 5:9?]

Ready for questions.

Q-1. [303]: In the reading of August 7th [262-25, A-2], please explain what is meant by "Look not back. Remember Lot's wife."

A-1. Looking to the front ever, for as one looks towards the light the shadows fall behind and do not become stumbling blocks to individual development. Thoughts are things, and while the past that is passed may be used as stepping-stones to higher things, looking back causes one to stumble, even as Lot's wife looked upon that left as longing for those satisfying elements that made for the carnal, rather than the spiritual life.

Q-2. In the reading of August 21st [262-26, A-8], I was told, "Watch that ye be not overcome." Is there any specific thing of which I should be watchful?

A-2. That there is not the looking back upon associations, relations, or conditions that make for the tendencies to dwell upon the past.

Q-3. [413]: Is there a special message that will help me in contributing to the lesson on The Open Door?

A-3. In learning the application of those lessons that have been given may the individual know how and the manner in which self may contribute to that lesson, in the application of *The Open Door*. Self must open the door that He may enter in. Self will work at that job of bringing that consciousness, that awareness of His presence in the material and mental affairs of life, knowing that lesson must ever be that the spirit is the life, the mental is the builder, and the physical or material results are the effects of the application of the knowledge or understanding toward life, light, or the spirit of *any* effort. So, then, measure self and self's efforts by that standard in Him who went about doing good. Do thou likewise.

Q-4. [69]: I would like to have a message on The Open Door.

A-4. As the application of self to those attributes that have made for the awareness of that consciousness of His presence in the material activities is put into actual actions of self, so does there become the ability to open the way for others to become aware of that necessary in their experience to enter into that kingdom through that open door.

Q-5. [307]: *Please explain to me, "the way is open," given in the reading of September 4th* [262-27, A-1, par. 3].

A-5. That there has been given in those lessons of preparation that which makes the consciousness of the mental forces of individuals the way, the manner that they, the individual, may open the door, and the way is ready for activity through the opening thereof.

Q-6. *Please explain "The kingdom of the Father."* [See 262-27, A-1, par. 1.]

A-6. The consciousness of His force, power, activity, in every element of action on the part of those who without thought of self have opened the way for the activity of the Christ Consciousness in the material world; for only those of material thought or material activities may demonstrate or bring to the consciousness of the individuals in material life as to what is the activity, the spiritual essence in the life. Let's illustrate, then, in an everyday act of an individual:

As is known of all, water is a necessary element in the material forces for the sustaining of life in the material plane; hence this element often is called the mother of creation. *How* does water, then, supply that which nourishes in this material plane? Being made up of elements in itself that are the essence of that which may truly be called spiritual in itself, it gives that association or connection between the spiritual forces acting in the material elements of the earth, or material forces; hence in entering in the kingdom of the Father is knowing and following and *being* those elements that supply the needs of that which builds in the material plane towards the continuity of the spiritual forces manifest in the earth. So, one enters, then, through that door with the Savior, that brings that necessary force in the life of others, and in saving others saves self. How came the Son of man the way that leads to perfection in heaven and in earth? In overcoming the forces in nature and in earth, by giving of self for others; hence becoming the Savior of others becomes the Son and one with the Father.

Q-7. [560]: *In meditation I had a consciousness of the Christ walking with a shepherd's rod in His hand, and beside Him was one lone sheep. Again in consciousness I saw Him, and there were many sheep beside Him. Is this in any way connected with the lesson on* The Open Door? *Please explain.*

A-7. As He is the way, and stands at the door, and those who hear His voice are His sheep and He the good shepherd, so may *many* become His sheep through the seeking to be one with Him. This is an illustration of that which has been given, as to how one who has, does, will apply those things given in the lessons may now open the door that many sheep may enter the fold, for they hear His voice and answer by name even as He calls, and "There are other sheep I have that are not of this fold," gave He, "they also will I bring and they will be one fold." That as applied in self, in self's seeking with Him, through Him, through the door opened by self to Him; for, even as He gave, "I do nothing of myself." So may we in opening the door with Him be one with Him in the Father, that we all may be one in Him.

Q-8. [993]: Would appreciate a message on The Open Door.

A-8. Take that thou hast in hand, that thou hast builded day by day, and without fear *open* the door that He may come in and abide with thee; for "He that takes my yoke upon him and learns of me, with *him* will I abide day by day, and all things will be brought to remembrance that I have given thee since the foundations of the world, for thou wert with me in the beginning and thou may abide with me in that day when the earth will be rolled as the scroll; for the heavens and the earth will pass away, but my word shall *not* pass away." The promises in Him are sure—the way ye know!

Q-9. [404]: Can lost opportunities be redeemed?

A-9. Nothing is lost. Nothing is lost; we have used or abused our opportunities and there abide by them. In Him, through Him may they be blotted out, for "Though your sins be as scarlet, in Him they shall be as wool." "He that heareth my voice and abideth in me shall *know* no lost opportunity!"

Q-10. Please enlarge on the statement: "Through gratifying of the desires of flesh the door closes." [See 262-27, A-2.]

A-10. As self is a free-willed agent in a material world, with the birthright of the attributes of the sons of God, then gratifying of the earthly desires through the gratifying of the flesh *does* close the door to the spiritual life; for the closing is in self.

He is ever ready. The spirit is ever willing; and one needs then to rely upon those promises, not in the passive, but the positive, active manner, that there be kept the door open that He may enter in.

Q-11. What should be understood by the statement, "The scepter has not departed from Israel"? [See 262-27, A-1, par. 3.]

A-11. Israel is the chosen of the Lord, and that His promises, His care, His love, has not departed from those that seek to know His way, that seek to see His face, that would draw nigh unto Him. *This* is the meaning, this should be the understanding to all. Those that seek are Israel. Those that seek not, have ye not heard, "Think not to call thyselves the promise in Abraham. Know ye not that the Lord is able to raise up children of Abraham from the very stones?" So Abraham means call; so Israel means those who seek. How obtained the supplanter the name Israel? For he wrestled with the angel, and he was face to face with the seeking to know His way. So it is with us that are called and seek His face; we are the Israel. Know, then, the scepter, the promise, the love, the glory of the Lord has not departed from them that seek His face!

Q-12. What is the relationship between Michael, the lord of the way, and Christ, the way? [See 262-27, A-1, par. 3.]

A-12. Michael is an archangel that stands before the throne of the Father. The Christ is the Son, the way *to* the Father, and One that came into the earth as man, the Son of man, that man might have the access to the Father; hence the way. Michael is the lord or the guard of the change that comes in every soul that seeks the way, even as in those periods when His manifestations came in the earth.

Bow thine heads, O ye sons of men, would ye know the way; for I, Michael, the lord of the way, would warn thee that thou standest not in the way of thy brother nor in the seats of the scornful, but rather make known that love, that glory, that power in His name, that none be afraid; for I, Michael, have spoken!

We are through.

[According to Gladys Davis the above reading was so powerfully given that "many of us were moved to tears; all were touched deeply.]

This psychic reading was given by Edgar Cayce at his home on Arctic Crescent, Virginia Beach, Va., on October 2, 1932, at 3:45 P.M., in accordance with a request made by those present: Edgar Cayce; Gertrude Cayce, conductor; Gladys Davis, steno; C. A. Barrett, Minnie Barrett, Annie Cayce, Hugh Lynn Cayce, L. B. Cayce, Mildred Davis, Edith Edmonds, Florence Edmonds, Helen Ellington, Sarah Hesson, Ruth LeNoir, Hannah Miller, F. Y. Morrow, Evelyn D. Ott and husband, Helen Storey, Esther Wynne, Katherine Zvirin, and others.

ᘏ 262-29 ᘏ

Mrs. Cayce: You will have before you the group gathered here and their work on the lesson The Open Door, *a copy of which I hold in my hand. You will please give any suggestions as to changes or expansions in this data, and continue any further information on this subject which will aid us in preparing this lesson. You will answer the questions which individuals will ask.*

Mr. Cayce: Yes, we have the group as gathered here, and their work in the preparation of the lesson *The Open Door.*

In that which has been so far prepared, it would be very well that this be continued in the same vein or manner but expressed or given in the terms for the individual, or the individual interpretations, that this may reach in its entirety the greater numbers which has been indicated is necessary for the greater good to be accomplished through the distribution of such data, that is presented in such lessons.

For those who have as yet not become contributors to this lesson, begin rather in the manner that has been indicated for each. How does cooperation make for an attribute to *The Open Door?* Cooperation, as has been indicated, is making self selfless in the way that the ideal of the body may be in that phase of experience as to be led by the ideal; thus, when properly considered, becoming the opening of the door that He who stands and knocks may enter in. In making self selfless selfishness is obliterated, that there may be the activity of the ideal, and being led then by the spirit of truth gains the understanding of the ideal in its operation upon the lives and activities of individuals; thus becoming a practical application in a material world through the spirit of truth that makes not afraid, but through faith leads on to the opening of the ways in virtue, understanding and patience, in which all become the more conscious of that oneness with the Father, so that as we are known of the Father so may we know the Father, thus making in the material activities of the mental and the conscious mind those channels that we as individuals, thus applying these necessary forces or activities in our own experience, become channels that the way may be known to others; thus entering into the kingdom of heaven.

This variation differentiates the kingdom of heaven from the kingdom of the Father: One is the experiences of the finite. The other is the glory with the oneness in the infinite.

Thus, as individuals become aware of these activities, the kingdom of heaven is within. Even as He gave, not that this is to be attained only through transition; but through the consciousness, the awareness of the activity of the spirit of truth in and through us, as individuals, with that birthright of the sons of the Father; one with Him as the way, the truth, the light, that is shed abroad in the world, the earth, that we may have that advocate with the Father in light.

Ready for questions.

Q-1. What is meant by the throne of the Father?

A-1. The approach to being wholly in the at-oneness with the Father, reached only through the abilities to leave the carnal forces and be one in spirit with the Father.

Q-2. Please explain clearly the difference between the Christ Consciousness [and] the Christ Spirit.

A-2. As the difference might be given in that which makes for the birth in the flower, and the flower. The consciousness of the spirit and the abilities to apply same are the differences in the Christ Consciousness [and] the Christ Spirit.

As has been given, the devils believe, the devils know, individuals that may be conscious of an activity. Those with the abilities to call upon, to be so unselfish as to allow the spirit to operate in self's stead, are aware of the spirit's activity, while those that may be conscious or aware of a truth may not wholly make it their own without that which has been given, "He that would have life must give life"; for *He* thought it not robbery to be equal with the Father, yet of Himself did nothing, "but the Father that worketh in me, through me."

Do thou likewise, that thou may know the consciousness of the Christ Spirit, and experience the operation of that witness, that "My Spirit beareth witness with thy spirit, that the Father may be glorified in you, even as *I* am glorified in the Father through you. If ye love me keep my commandments, and I will abide with you. I will *not* leave thee comfortless; I will make thee aware of that glory I possessed with the Father before the world was."

In such a manner may individuals become aware of the Christ Consciousness and become one with the operative forces of the Christ Spirit abroad in the earth; for He shall come again, even as ye have seen Him go. *Then* shall the Christ Spirit be manifest in the world, even as the Christ Consciousness may make thee aware of that promised as the Comforter in this material world.

Then, the Christ Consciousness is the Holy Spirit, or that as the promise of His presence made aware of His activity in the earth. The spirit is as the Christ in action with the Spirit of the Father.

Q-3. Explain and expand fully the thought that the Christ Spirit, not the man, should be the door, the truth, the way. [See 262-27, A-2.]

A-3. That which has been given may be used to illustrate the difference that may be felt by a soul that has become aware of itself, as the Christ, or as Jesus the man became aware of the Spirit of the Father through those experiences of the man as He "went about doing good," and at those periods when there was received those acknowledgements of the Father that He *was* the one who could, *would,* through those activities, become the Savior of man. First, as "in whom I am well pleased"; then as "This is my Son; hear ye Him!"

In the overcoming, then, He *is* the way, the manner in which individuals may become aware of their souls that are in accord with that as may be one with the spirit of truth; for corruption inherits not eternal life. The spirit is the true life. Then, as individuals become aware of that ability *in Him* to be the way, so they become the door, as representatives, as agents, as those that present the way; and the door is thus opened; and not to the man but the spirit of self that bears witness with the spirit of truth through Him that overcame the world, thus putting the world under His feet.

So we, as heirs of the kingdom, as brothers one with Him, may enjoy that privilege as He has given to those that hear His voice and put on the whole armor; that we may run the race that is set before us, looking to Him, the Author, the Giver of Light; for in Him ye live and move and *have* your being. Do ye become rebels? Do ye find fault one with another, that are as self heirs to that kingdom? Rather be in that humbleness of spirit, that His will "be done in earth as it is in heaven." Thus do we become the children of the Father, the door to the way, and joint heirs with Him in glory.

Let thy yeas be yea, thy nays be nay. "Let others do as they may, but for me I will serve a *living* God," who has shown in man—*all* men, everywhere—that image of the Creator, in that the soul may grow in grace, in knowledge, in peace, in harmony, in understanding.

Be ye doers of the word; not hearers only. Thus ye become the door that the WAY, the Christ, the Savior, may enter in; for *He* IS the way, the truth, and the light.

Q-4. As it was given in the last reading, "Let none be afraid," clarify and explain the cause of fear and tell us how one seeking to awaken the soul forces may conquer same.

A-4. *Self*-awareness, *selfishness,* is that that makes men afraid. The awareness of the necessities of the carnal forces in a material world seeking their gratification. Know ye not that whether ye live or die ye live or die in the Lord? As He gave, "If thine eye offend, pluck it out. If thine hand lead thee in error, cut it off."

When one has set the ideal, and knows what the ideal represents, and then knows self measured by the ideal, one sees, is aware of that lacking or that overdone in self, and plucks it out, and beholds *not* the mote that is in his brother's eye but considers rather the beam that is in his own eye.

Then, when one is set in the manners that there is fear cast aside by the wholly relying upon His promise, one may demand that to be fulfilled in that He said, "He knoweth what ye have need of before ye have asked," and he that trusteth in Him, though the heavens may fall, though the earth may pass away, His word faileth not; yet *men* act rather as if all depended upon whether tomorrow was the day of reckoning. Know ye not that he that watches lest his own feet stumble is in the way that the Father, the Son, may guide day by day? Not that ye would sit and wait for the morrow, but use that opportunity, that privilege, that birthright, that promise, *today!* Be joyous in the labor that is before thee! Be the *best* of whatever position thou doth occupy; as a wife, the *best* wife in the whole community; as a friend, the *best* friend; and there is the friend that sticketh closer than the brother; yea, the friend that gives rather his life for a friend. Ever gave ye the truths that thine brother might enjoy even a moment's rest in the Lord?

Peace be to him, peace *is* with them, contentment is in thine hand, that becomes not afraid, but trusts rather in Him.

Q-5. [*295*]: *Please give me a message on* The Open Door, *that I may contribute to the lesson.*

A-5. Learn first that lesson of cooperation. Become less and less selfish, and more and more selfless in Him. Be not afraid to be made fun of to become aware of His presence, that self may be a channel through which the glory of the Father may come unto men in a manner that all may know there is a glory, even an Israel, of the Lord.

Q-6. Is there any message for the group as a whole at this time?

A-6. Be patient, long-suffering, bearing one another's burdens. Be joyous in the Lord. Be not tempestuous in manner, thought, act or deed; rather *serving* in humbleness of spirit. Enjoy the labors. Enjoy those things that make for the unison of thought in Him, knowing ye have been called, and that "By *His* power I, as a member of such a group, called to give myself first, called that self may become a channel, called that I as an individual may cooperate with my brother *everywhere* in making known the joyous words of the Lord"; for the Lord is in His holy temple, let all the earth keep silent. Who *is* this Lord? Where is His temple? Know ye not that your bodies are the living temple, holy and acceptable unto Him, would ye walk in His ways?

HARK! O YE CHILDREN OF MEN! BOW THINE HEADS, YE SONS OF MEN: FOR THE GLORY OF THE LORD IS THINE, WILL YE BE FAITHFUL TO THE TRUST THAT IS PUT IN EACH OF YOU!

KNOW IN WHOM YE HAVE BELIEVED! KNOW THAT HE IS LORD OF *ALL*, AND HIS WORD FAILETH NOT TO THEM THAT ARE FAITHFUL DAY BY DAY: FOR I, MICHAEL, WOULD PROTECT THOSE THAT SEEK TO KNOW HIS FACE!

We are through.

[Gladys Davis made the following note regarding the above reading, "Tears, silence and beautiful attunement followed above reading. Edgar Cayce had a vision during the reading, had to leave the room a while; said he saw each of us as we should be and as we are."]

☆ 262-30 ☆

This psychic reading was given by Edgar Cayce at his home on Arctic Crescent, Virginia Beach, Va., on October 16, 1932, at 3:45 P.M., in accordance with a request made by those present: Edgar Cayce; Gertrude Cayce, conductor; Gladys Davis, steno; C. A. Barrett, Minnie Barrett, Annie Cayce, Hugh Lynn Cayce, L. B. Cayce, Mildred Davis, Edith Edmonds, Florence Edmonds, Helen Ellington, Lu Hesson, Sarah Hesson, Margaret K. Kahn, Ruth LeNoir, Hannah Miller, F. Y. Morrow, Evelyn D. Ott, Helen Storey, Esther Wynne, and others.

Mrs. Cayce: You will have before you the group gathered here and their work on the lesson The Open Door. *As I call each individual's name, you will give them an individual message on* The Open Door, *and will then answer the general questions which will be asked.*

Mr. Cayce: Yes, we have the group as gathered here, and their work as individuals, as a group, in preparing the lesson on *The Open Door*.

Q-1. [585]:

A-1. In the preparation of self for this lesson, there are many material and mental conditions that the body must correlate, that there be the proper understanding of *The Open Door* being a positive activity for self; something to do, something to be done, that there be those activities in accord with the lessons that have prepared self for the same.

Q-2. [413]:

A-2. The visions of self's meditations *do* draw to the consciousness of self *The Open Door* to the understanding, and interpretation of, activities in the lives of those whom the body contacts day by day. In the actions of self, be not afraid to declare His walks with thee in thy meditation.

Q-3. [303]:

A-3. As there is put into activity that gained, and as self looks onward, upward, there comes the clarifying of the way in the consciousness of self. There *is* the growth in self. Be not weary in well-doing.

Q-4. [295]:

A-4. As those determinations in self are set in Him, as the door is opened that He may walk with thee, so will that promise

-125-

as given come to mean more in the experience of self; for "My yoke *is* easy, my burden is light. If ye love me, keep my commandments, that I may abide *with* thee, that the way may not be shadowed by doubts or fears that make for faltering steps." Keep in the light, that the promises may be fulfilled in thee, that there may be that closer communion with those that seek to know Him face to face.

Q-5. [*341*]:

A-5. As there is the experiencing of the varied temperaments of associations with the truth that is in Him, so may the self come to know the full answer as from old, "Is this not he of whom the prophets spoke?" Keep in that understanding that makes for seeking to bring thy brethren close in that way, through *The Open Door.*

Q-6. [*379*]:

A-6. In the application does the knowledge come of what *is* to be accomplished by self, in the step by step, line by line, that others may know of that promise that *is* to each individual that may be one with Him. Be not unmindful that those met in the way are seekers also, and are the Israel of the Lord.

Q-7. [*560*]:

A-7. As there is given those presentations from day to day, in the steps that are taken, in thy *own* way does the knowledge, the understanding come of "Well done, enter into the joys of Him who shows the way," for him that is called is also predestined for the activities of *His* kingdom.

Q-8. [*993*]:

A-8. In seeking, in doing, in the meeting day by day, let self be as naught that *He,* the leader, the guide, may be the better understood by those that look to thy activities; for in Him is the light, and as there is the closer walk with Him the way becomes brighter to all that would follow in the light.

Q-9. [*404*]:

A-9. In opening the door there are those responsibilities, as well as those joys, in following in the light. Be *thou* the guide to many, that no stumbling block of condemnation be placed in the way of any. *Well* hast thou chosen in thine choosing, for *He* is the guide.

Q-10. [*288*]:

A-10. In the understanding of *The Open Door,* be mindful that *His* way is pointed out to all. "Not my will but Thine be done," even as He gave, "For this purpose came I into the world"; the greater service, then, being that *He* would have you be.

Q-11. [*538*]:

A-11. In the application of those tenets, those precepts gained, keep the knowledge that *He* is the guide, "upon him may I lean." Though at times the way be heavy, or the storms such as to cause doubts and fears, He stills the tempest, He brings harmony to those that are weary, and tired.

Q-12. [*294*]:

A-12. Keep the faith that opens the door to Him. That which is given as the next lesson must be *In His Presence,* for "If His presence go not *with* thee, [ye] be not lifted up," and the meditation for all shall be with this lesson:

OUR FATHER, WHO ART IN HEAVEN, MAY THY KINGDOM COME IN EARTH THROUGH THY PRESENCE IN ME, THAT THE LIGHT OF THY WORD MAY SHINE UNTO THOSE THAT I MEET DAY BY DAY. MAY THY PRESENCE IN MY BROTHER BE SUCH THAT I MAY GLORIFY THEE. MAY I SO CONDUCT MINE OWN LIFE THAT OTHERS MAY KNOW THY PRESENCE ABIDES WITH ME, AND THUS GLORIFY THEE.

Q-13. [*307*]:

A-13. Keep the faith of the fathers burning bright along the way, for many will follow where thou leadest. Open the door of thine heart, that He may abide with thee.

Q-14. [*69's husband*]:

A-14. Know in whom thou hast believed, that He is able to keep that way, that door thou openest, that thy brother may see the glory of thy God in thy walks daily among men.

Q-15. [*69*]:

A-15. In keeping the way be joyous in the glory of the birthright in Him; for as thou hast *obtained* mercy be merciful to those who falter or seek to know the variableness of those conditions that cause fear and trembling in the minds, in the hearts, of many. Peace—be still, that *thy* efforts be in the way as *He* doth guide.

Q-16. [*379*]: *Please explain what is meant by "the secret place of the Most High."*

A-16. In understanding "the secret place of the Most High,"

let's determine what in the seeker is being sought; whether the knowledge of the interpretation of the Most High's manifestations to men, or that as determines the relationships of that manifested *to* the Most High; for as in the secret chambers of one's own heart are stored that that makes for the real activities of that soul-consciousness, so is the holy of holies where one meets with that they worship as their God.

Q-17. [307]: Please explain the words of the Master as recorded in twenty-first chapter of Luke, "Many shall come in my name, saying I am Christ."

A-17. As has been given, many have arisen; for as He gave in the same connection, there were many false prophets, even those that would lead the very elect away. There be those who, finding something of the power that is in the material activities of those that would walk in the light, turn same into their own selfish purposes; hence become false prophets, false Christs, and lead many astray. Let's remember, there has been given the manner, the way to determine as to whether such a prophet is of the Spirit of God or not. They that deny the call of the prophets of old, or the burdens of the world upon the Son or His death, His resurrection, are not of the spirit; for "As ye have *seen* Him go, so *shall* He come." As He overcame the world through the birth as one born in due season, through those varied periods when necessity and the *demand* of the Sons of God brought forth those leaders in their proper places, so He is that one that is given power over death, hell and the grave, and in Him is the power made manifest in the consciousness of Him and His power in the earth; hence we may see how the consciousness of His presence may be misconstrued, when turned to selfish motives. Know that even as the powers of evil are loosed for the correcting of many, so are the glories of Him made manifest in the hearts and lives of many.

Q-18. Is there a message for [462]?

A-18. In that thou hast seen a light, be not dismayed nor frustrated by those things that would hinder from pressing on to the mark of the higher calling that is set in Him. Fill each day with the love of Him, that may be manifested among those that self contacts day by day. "As ye are faithful over the few things, so will ye be made lord over many." Know in *all* things the *glory* is in the manifesting of His power in the earth. [See also 262-31, A-4.]

Q-19. *Compilers: We would appreciate some advice in regard to the paper, "Present World Conditions," which we sent to Calgary, Canada, for publication.*

A-19. As there has been given, *patience* endureth unto the end; for in same recognize ye your souls. Prepare, then, and send on in the way that has been given.

We are through for the present.

This psychic reading was given by Edgar Cayce at his home on Arctic Crescent, Virginia Beach, Va., on October 30, 1932, at 3:50 P.M., in accordance with a request made by those present: Edgar Cayce; Gertrude Cayce, conductor; Gladys Davis, steno; C. A. Barrett, Minnie Barrett, Annie Cayce, Hugh Lynn Cayce, L. B. Cayce, Mildred Davis, Edith Edmonds, Florence Edmonds, Lu Hesson, Sarah Hesson, Hannah Miller, F. Y. Morrow, C. W. Rosborough, M. L. Rosborough, Helen Storey, and Esther Wynne.

⨭ 262-31 ⨴

Mrs. Cayce: You will have before you the individuals gathered here and their work on the lesson of The Open Door, *a copy of which I hold in my hand. You will go over this and as I call each paragraph make any suggestions as to change, or addition of material. You will answer the questions which will be asked.*

Mr. Cayce: Yes, we have the group as gathered here, as a group and as individuals, and their work and preparation on the lesson *The Open Door.*

Ready for questions. [Paragraphs 1 through 33 were called, to each of which Mr. Cayce answered "Very good."]

Mr. Cayce: Now, in connecting the thoughts as presented in paragraphs eight and nine, there should be an expansion that makes for a closer association of carrying the idea one to another. The rest is good; very good.

Q-1. You will please suggest outlines, the central thoughts and ideas around which we should build the forthcoming lesson on In His Presence.

A-1. In building the thoughts upon which the mind of each individual should center, in preparing self for the realization of practical application of lessons, and the lesson *In His Presence*, taking all that has been presented in the manner in which each individual has put to use that gained by the meditation upon the thought and application of each lesson, one comes to the realization of now *being* in His presence; for each has gained (that have applied the lessons) that innate expression of being in His presence. The motivative forces in life itself are the composition or composite activity of the spirit of life; hence, as individuals first, we recognize that each activity, each expression of self in its relationships to that from without and that

-130-

from within, is the expression of that we have done about—or with—the knowledge and the consciousness of His presence abiding with each.

As we look upon our fellow man we find his activities, in whatever sphere of activity they may be, but an expression motivated by that same concept of what *that* individual has done about that he worships, or would present as that force the individual would use to manifest the spirit that abides in life.

Then, the central thought is: Would we be forgiven, we must forgive; would we see good in our fellow man, we must reflect that which is well-pleasing in His presence, knowing that all power, all force, emanates from Him. He, the Lord thy God, is *one!* All power emanates, then, from Him. What would *you*, as an activating force for manifesting that power in the earth, do respecting same?

Q-2. Are there any suggestions which may be given at this time that will aid the various members and the group as a whole in carrying on the work which it has set out to perform?

A-2. This answer would depend upon whether this is in reference to preparation for the lessons to be given out, or in disseminating that gained.

In the preparation, let each individual—in his own imaginative self—set himself as in that position of giving forth *from* His presence that which would make known to those he meets or contacts day by day the more awareness of that presence, first in their *own* lives; and how gently one (or self) would look upon the shortcomings of his brother! Judge not that ye be not judged, for with what measure ye mete it shall be measured to *you* again; for He hath made man a little lower than the angels, with the ability through his (man's) will to make himself equal with the Father, that *man* may even judge angels!

Q-3. Any advice in disseminating the lessons already given?

A-3. There has been given oft, first must it come to the individual consciousness that there is that worthy and acceptable *to* be given to others. Then, with that same might and power that comes from that One Source will it be given, through the study of that *given,* as to how such goes to the groups, the classes, the masses. How has it been set that cooperation is to be sought in self, in the group, in association? How has it been given ye shall know self, how ye shall know even as ye are known? How hast there been set that faith must come by the hearing of that which is building in the lives and experiences of others? How judgest thou thy neighbor? How has thine patience made known thy understanding and thy activity in opening the door for those that seek His presence? Apply that thou hast in thine own experience, for the activities of life are practical, in the material, the mental, the spiritual life; for it *must* be one, even as He is one.

Q-4. [462]: *Please explain more fully to me the statement given in the reading October 16th [262-30, A-18], "In that thou hast seen a light, be not dismayed . . ."*

A-4. This as given, seen in thine own experiences that there is a way opened before thee. With fear and with trembling hast thou put forth efforts in uncertain manners at times; hence the injunction "Be not dismayed"; remembering that He hath given His angels charge concerning thee, that thine guide, thine guard, is ever in His presence, even as He gave, "And I, *if* I be lifted up, will draw all men unto me. I will *not* leave thee comfortless, I will *come* and abide with thee." Then be not afraid to declare thyself at any and *all* experiences.

We are through.

𝄃 262-32 𝄁

This psychic reading was given by Edgar Cayce at his home on Arctic Crescent, Virginia Beach, Va., on November 13, 1932, at 4:00 P.M., in accordance with a request made by those present: Edgar Cayce; Gertrude Cayce, conductor; Gladys Davis, steno; C. A. Barrett, Minnie Barrett, Annie Cayce, Hugh Lynn Cayce, L. B. Cayce, Mildred Davis, Edith Edmonds, Florence Edmonds, Helen Ellington, Ruth LeNoir, F. Y. Morrow, C. W. Rosborough, M. L. Rosborough, and Esther Wynne.

Mrs. Cayce: You will have before you members of the study group, some of whom are present in this room, and the outline on the lesson In His Presence *which I hold in my hand. Advise us regarding the completion and expansion of the outline, and give the group that which it needs in continuing the preparation of this lesson. You will answer the questions which will be asked.*

Mr. Cayce: We have the group as gathered here, and the work and the outline *In His Presence.* As each contribute to the lesson there should be that continued thought of self being one in His presence, one that would have self and that as expressed in keeping with that He would have each one be, knowing that as others view the expressions of self in the lessons there is gained by them a concept of what His presence means to those that would walk with Him day by day. Let each in the light of their understanding so live that they bespeak that they profess with their lips to believe, that others may know that that individual is keeping that presence they hold as their ideal in such a direct consciousness as to be a living example of that they profess. In such ways and manners do the truths gained in meditation and thought become living truths and acceptable truths in His sight. So do we show forth that we would crucify the flesh, that the spirit of Him may be made manifest in this material world. Each recognize that the world, the country, the nation, the people, are passing through a period of seeking, a period of adjustments in the spiritual thought, the spiritual intent. The mental world is looking to the spiritual-minded for hope, to those who are in their material walks representatives of the spiritual forces in the thinking people, for that thought that will guide all men closer to His presence. So may this group as a group, so may each individual as their contribution to the work of the group, so may each individual as their contribution to their Maker and their Elder Brother in the Christ, bring soon that day when all may know they stand in His presence. If the country, the nation, the land, is to be lifted up as a light to the world, they must be lifted in Him and His presence abiding in them day by day.

Ready for questions.

Q-1. Will the Forces please select a secretary to take the place of Mrs. Miller while she is in Florida?

A-1. Not as one to take a place, but one to fill a place while another is absent. One that may be chosen by the group. As we would give, Mrs. Morrow or Mrs. Ellington.

Q-2. [413]: Have I applied the past lessons sufficiently to entitle me to a place in His presence?

A-2. Each should recognize that heritage that all are entitled to a place in His presence, for He wills that none should perish but that all should come to the acceptable understanding of His Spirit bearing witness with thy spirit. As to the application of that gained, or that may be gained from the study of those things given, each must answer for themselves; for as given, "My Spirit beareth witness with thy spirit whether ye be acceptable in His presence or not"; remembering, then, as He gave, "Inasmuch as ye have done it unto the least of these my little ones ye have done it unto me." Have the activities of thine heart and mind led thee to act towards thy neighbor, thy brother, thine enemy, in the manners that have been presented in approaching this thought, those understandings that come from being conscious of His presence abiding with those that would seek His face? Then know He, the Father, is ever ready to hear; for He wills not that any should fall short of that grace which comes with the acknowledging of, the thoughtfulness of, the living of, the communion with Him.

Q-3. Is there a message to help me to help others find a place in His presence?

A-3. Study to show thyself approved unto Him day by day. So does the light of His presence shine unto others in precept and example. Not by faith alone, but "by my word, by my works," show ye forth the love of keeping in His understanding and in the consciousness of being in His presence. With the *living of* that given all will come to the knowledge, to the understanding of, we are all *in* His presence whether we acknowledge it in the present or not; for, as has been given, it is in Him we live and move and have our being; hence to induce, to persuade, to give that which will bring others, take their positions, their place, *see* as by the light of *His* presence the needs of the inner man, and so present that He gives thee day by day. Thus, as He has given, may we find ourselves happily [haply? See Acts 17:27.] in His presence; for, "I will not leave thee comfortless but will come to thee, and bring to remembrance that necessary of my strength to meet the needs of the hour, of the day."

Q-4. [*303*]: *I would appreciate a message that will help me to more fully realize* In His Presence.

A-4. As self is less and less put forth, and more and more faith, hope, reliance, sought in His word, each as individuals may become aware of His presence abiding with each; for those that would know Him must believe that He is, and *if* He *is* He abides ever with those that seek His face.

Q-5. [*2124*]: *Please give the significance of the dream I had the morning of November 3rd, in which I saw an incline, three houses tied together, a man drowning, bubbles, etc.*

A-5. As the varied stages of developments in the consciousness of the soul forces find in the various planes that which to the body-consciousness represents the various stages of activity and development, so that experienced in the vision represents to the self the necessary understanding of the various planes or stages of the mental visions of that which represents either the sliding into the consciousness of the material things or that as in the bubbles, which represents the life even in the spheres that to man's own understanding is incapable of being the dwelling place of man alone, that in these spheres come the various stages of development as to meet that *necessary* for the gaining of the presence of that power from which all spiritual force emanates.

Q-6. What is the significance of the dream immediately follow-ing, in which I was discerning the spirits, getting messages and giving them to people?

A-6. The continuation of that just given, that in the various planes of development there *are* those abilities to reach only that to which that influence, that entity, that represented in the presentation of the spirit *to* give out—see?

Q-7. What is the connection between the first and second dream?

A-7. A continuation, just as the house, the water, the rope, the manner in which the tying of one. It is one. O, that all men would know, "Know, O ye children of men, the Lord thy God is ONE!" Each spirit, each manifestation of *Life* is ONE, and a manifestation either in this, that or the other sphere, or scope, or space of development *towards* the knowledge, the under-standing, the conception of that ONE—HIM—I AM—God—Jehovah—Yah [?]—ALL ONE!

Q-8. You will give an individual message on the lesson to each of the following as I call their names: [404]:

A-8. In Him is the light; hence in His presence does light shed abroad that which prevents stumbling feet from faltering.

Q-9. [462]:

A-9. In His presence all stand, and as that we see reflected in the mirror of life shows what manner of shadows are cast, so does keeping in the consciousness of the indwelling of the spirit of the Master keep all in the way of truth and light.

Q-10. [993]:

A-10. As the reflections of self come through the awareness of His presence through the activities, whether in fact, in thought, or in deed, so does the consciousness make aware the presence of His forces in a manifested manner in the lives of others, as well as to self; for as in water the face answereth to face, so in His presence must our deeds, our thoughts, be reflec-tions of Him. Not in that of long-faced or in mourning, or in sorrow, but in gladness of purpose, of service, worshipfulness in Him.

Q-11. [560]:

A-11. In the activities of the body so reflect the strength of the physical man; so in the activities of the mind reflect the strength of the mental body as directed by the presence of His spirit as may be sought, as may be found, as is ever present with each that seeks to abide in Him.

Q-12. [*69*]:

A-12. Keep that patience of faith, that oneness of purpose in His presence, that as many bless thee in their thoughts so may self hold that glorious oneness of purpose in Him; for all are witnesses unto the effect of His presence in our lives. So do the expressions in word, in thought, in deed, reflect whether we are conscious of His presence abiding in us.

Q-13. [*69's husband*]:

A-13. Keep in the way of understanding, so that there may be more and more that glorious consciousness of His presence abiding in us; for as one conquers in self that which makes for hindrances, the souls of men pass from glory to glory until the glorious knowledge of His abiding presence is ever before us.

Q-14. [*307*]:

A-14. Unto him that hath shall be given; unto him that seeketh shall he find; and as we grow in grace, in knowledge, in understanding, we come into the presence with that desire of the mind, of the heart, that opens the way for the greater understanding in Him.

Q-15. [*538*]:

A-15. Keep in the way that leads to the higher planes of light, for though the way may be heavy and His presence as of shadows, yet the shadows are only of thine own misunderstandings, and His glory will make for the glorifying of self in a service that brings more and more the knowledge of entering into the joys of thy Lord; for His presence abides with those that love Him. "If ye love me keep my commandments. Learn of me, for my yoke is easy, my burden is light" to those who come to the knowledge that His presence abides with those that seek His face.

Q-16. [*294*]:

A-16. Know in whom thou hast believed, that He may call thee by name as ye enter into His presence day by day. Even in laying aside those things that so easily beset may the consciousness of His abiding peace be in thee, bringing harmony to the mental, the physical body, that ye may go on in that way

that leads to the closer walk with Him. Minister to those who
seek, but minister in *His* name.

Q-17. [*379*]:

A-17. Glory in the Lord, not in self; not in the wisdom of the
earth, knowing that those things that partake of the earth are
earthy, those that partake alone of the mental may easily
become stumbling stones in the way of many. Let the spirit of
truth separate the chaff from the wheat, and enter in with the
full knowledge of His presence, shutteth out all those things
that would beset to him that believes and acts in that manner.

Q-18. [*341*]:

A-18. Keep in the knowledge, in the understanding that His
ways are to many past finding out; for to those that are called
does He give the power to become the Sons of God by dwelling
in the consciousness of His presence abiding in the steps of self
day by day. Study to show self approved rather unto God than
man, rightly dividing the words of truth, that thy ways, thy
thoughts, thy deeds, may bear witness of *His* glory being manifest in the earth; for "Lo, I am with thee always, even unto the
end of the earth." Day by day show forth that thou hast seen,
hast known, the glory of His presence in thine *own* understanding.

Q-19. [*295*]:

A-19. As self has been chosen, as self may make self a channel
of blessings to many that He may speak face to face with His
own, so let thy yeas and thy nays be such that His presence
abides with thee in thy daily walks of life; for His strength, His
power, may cleanse the world of sin through the glorifying of
Him in the life of those that seek to do His biddings. Keep the
faith. Keep in His presence day by day.

Q-20. [*585*]:

A-20. As self finds the spirit of truth, keeping the way open
for a more perfect understanding in Him, so may we pass step
by step into the consciousness of His presence abiding with us.
In the light of His presence do we measure our own shortcomings, leaving those things behind that are not in accord with
His ways, and taking on more and more that love that He
showed forth in His walks among men. So do we become conscious of that abiding faith that may make for the consciousness

of His presence abiding with us through every trial, every temptation, that arises in our experience. *Give* the *glory* when glory arises. Give the praise when the praise is near. Seek at all times to be conscious of *His* being near.

Q-21. [*288*]:

A-21. As self finds the mirrors of life showing forth those lights of the thoughts of the inner man, whether directed to His ways or to the shadows of life, so may we in reflecting upon the glory of His presence in our lives come to measure those steps that we must take in our journeys of meditation and prayer. Seek, then, to show self approved unto Him; for in Him is the light. The light may be reflected in us through those mirrorings in our own selves of His glory, for that as was given Him of the Father abides in those that seek through His name to know the Father's presence in their own life.

We are through.

This psychic reading was given by Edgar Cayce at his home on Arctic Crescent, Virginia Beach, Va., on December 4, 1932, at 3:45 P.M., in accordance with a request made by those present: Edgar Cayce; Gertrude Cayce, conductor; Gladys Davis, steno; C. A. Barrett, Minnie Barrett, Annie Cayce, Hugh Lynn Cayce, L. B. Cayce, Mildred Davis, Edith Edmonds, Florence Edmonds, Helen Ellington, Lu Hesson, Sarah Hesson, Ruth LeNoir, F. Y. Morrow, Helen Storey, Esther Wynne, and a visitor.

≫ 262-33 ≪

Mrs. Cayce: You will have before you the Norfolk Study Group #1, members of which are present in this room; and the work on the lesson In His Presence. *You will please give a discourse on this subject which will aid us in completing this lesson. Answer questions.*

Mr. Cayce: Yes, we have the group as gathered here and their work in preparation of the lesson *In His Presence.*

With that which has been given each for their own individual interpretation there is seen, as in general, few have applied same in their everyday experience; for each keeps His presence as a thing apart, something to be experienced, something only made aware of when one is disturbed in some manner or form, when it should be the experience, knowledge and understanding of all that His presence abides with those *as* they seek to do His biddings. Not with that outward show which may be experienced by attempting to solve some problem that there may be the enjoying of the reward for same, but rather that there may be the experiencing of the joy, the happiness, the harmony, the love, that fruit which comes from recognizing and using the privileges that are for those who—in their simplicity of manner—recognize, know, experience His presence; which abides with thee, wilt thou but recognize, understand its own closeness to thee in thine daily experiences. In this manner, then:

In putting into practice that thou knowest to do, in the *little* things, being led by that which has been *given* to each, thy contributions may be such from this as to aid others who may seek to know His presence, the joy of His presence, the harmony, the peace that comes with abiding in Him.

Q-1. Please explain how we may distinguish between the terms, especially pronouns, referring to the personality Jesus and God as used in this information, and how we may clarify this in terms we use in our lessons.

A-1. As their activities and personalities are one, in the activities of men often the pronoun used becomes confusing. Follow rather closely in that which has been given. It is used the same as *He* gave. Him refers to the Father, He to the Son. In the preparation of the lessons these may in the general be referred to in that manner; for, as it is generally understood by the critics—or those that would prefer good English, Him is rather inclusive while He is definite—or the one Son.

Q-2. Please expand on how we may come into the realization of His presence.

A-2. As we have given above, the greater fault from the realization is that it—His presence—is kept as a thing apart. *He* wills that all should come to the knowledge of His presence abiding with all. We come to this knowledge and consciousness by doing those things that are conducive to bringing into every atom of our being that which gives the attributes *of* His presence in the earth; and in *doing* this do we come to know His presence.

Q-3. Please expand on how we may prepare ourselves that we may abide in His presence.

A-3. This would refer rather to the individual experience; for in the preparations of self there are varied consciousnesses, and what to one might be necessary to another would be secondary, and to that which may be the attribute of good judgment, clean living, without thought of same being a command or a law of universal nature; yet as we, as individuals, become more and more conscious—through meditation and prayer, and *application* of that we seek in the way of preparation—of that which keeps or holds, or preserves us as individuals in the consciousness of His presence, we become more conscious of His presence abiding with us, as we let that mind—through meditation and prayer—be in us during and at *all* periods.

Whether in joy, in sorrow, in trouble or in pain, let that mind be in you as was in He that gave, "*I* am with you *always*, even unto the end of the world."

Will that consciousness of the Christ love make our joys the more joyous, our sorrows the more in accord with the manner in which He met sorrow, or disturbances in the material affairs more in accord with the manner in which *He* met the material conditions?

As individuals we oft find that that as He gave, in the "thought of the morrow," or "wherewithal shall ye be clothed" was meant for someone else, *not* us. That consciousness as He gave, "In patience possess ye your souls"; *what* becomes aware of His presence, the physical-carnal body or the spirit of life that impels the soul in its development?

Then, as His love is shed on us, as we muse and meditate and pray to that we hold as our door to His presence, do we become aware of, do we enter in, do we find ourselves abiding in His presence.

As we may experience by that abiding presence, what are the fruits of same? *Worries* pass away, joys take their place; for as He looked upon Peter in the hour of trial and of denial by him, who had been declared to be—that spoken by Him—as the foundations of that He was to leave in the earth, did He frown or did He smile? What broke the heart of the man, the frown or the smile?

Then, when ye abide in His presence, though there may come the trials of every kind, though the tears may flow from the breaking up of the carnal forces within self, the spirit is made glad; even as He in the hour of trial, the hour of denial, *smiled* upon him and brought to remembrance—even as He has said to each that has named the name, "I will bring to remembrance the promises I have made, if ye will abide in my presence." The promises, then, are sure; and not a thing apart from those that abide in His presence, but are ever remembered in the hour not only of sorrow; not only is He the resurrection, not only is He to come in the hour of trial, but He supped also in the hours of joy with those in Cana, He enjoyed even the feast with Zaccheus, laughed and joked. "Yea, though I walk through the valley of the shadow of death—thou art with me; though I fly to the utmost parts of the heavens thou art with me." Will we, as individuals, then, know His presence? How? "If ye love me, keep my commandments." Are they then so burdensome, those commandments? What are His commandments? How may we abide—how may we show the love? "Inasmuch as ye have done it unto the least of these my little ones, ye have done it unto me."

Q-4. The group feels the need of strength and power. May we have instructions as were given to the disciples, as to what we should do that we may receive this power?

A-4. It is in Him. Do not allow self to become cold, even as the church, but rather let the simplicity of the service be done day by day through the knowledge that His love, His promises abide; for there is power in the name, there is strength and glory to those that are faithful, there is the abiding hope to all that come in *humbleness* seeking even as He, "Not my will but Thine, O God, be done in me." There is no power, no strength, save in Him. That puny strength man may assert in the power of his own manhood is but the *shadow* of that shown by Him, in the ways that lead to the thoughts of everyday action.

Then, the *power* as needed by all is the realization of abiding in His presence; even as may be seen in the next lesson—which is to be *The Cross and the Crown,* but gain that strength in the cross ye bear day by day; for He is *willing,* the flesh *is* weak. Humble thyself, that the glory and the power may come from Him, from the Father, from the Son, in the consciousness of "We love Him, He loves us. We abide in Him, He abides in us."

Q-5. [69's husband]: What is the meaning of my experience during meditation?

A-5. That the strength of the spirit arouses every atom of the physical and mental body, even as the experience is the shadow of the fire and the strength to do that as is *known* to be in *His* way.

Q-6. Would it be advisable to send the article on "Present World Conditions" to the East-West Magazine published in Los Angeles, California?

A-6. No.

Q-7. Please give the address of the publishers of the magazines the Blue Goose and the Argosy which were suggested as magazines to which the paper "Present World Conditions" should be sent.

A-7. *Argosy,* Argosy Building, Pennsylvania Avenue, Washington, D.C.; *Blue Goose,* 57th Street, New York City.

Q-8. What might one who reaches the point of realization of His presence expect as a result in their daily life and activity?

A-8. As given, the consciousness that He often walks and talks with thee, that His promises are ever present; not retroactive, but *very* active in the causes of the actions in the daily life; that there is the abiding hope, and not the doubts nor the fears that make men afraid; not that that makes for faltering steps, but rather the joys, the *pleasures* in service, even though it require that there be yet greater and greater sacrifices of the carnal forces within our own experiences—rather, the all, "that I may know more and more of the joys of His service." The service may not be rendered to self, only to another; and he that serves—either in the kindly word, the kindly thought, the kindly deed—is lending to the Lord, is giving of himself even as He.

Q-9. Is there a message for the group at this time as a whole?

A-9. BOW THINE HEADS, O YE MEN THAT WOULD SEEK HIS PRESENCE! BE STRONG IN HIS MIGHT! FALTER NOT AT THINE OWN WEAK SELF! KNOW THAT THY REDEEMER LIVETH AND MAY THIS DAY MAKE KNOWN IN THINE OWN HEART HIS PRESENCE ABIDING WITH THEE! ROOT FROM THINE BODY, THINE CONSCIOUSNESS, AUGHT THAT WOULD HINDER HIS ENTERING IN; FOR HE WOULD SUP WITH THEE! WILT THOU, THEN, O MAN, MAKE KNOWN THINE OWN DECISIONS? WILL YE BE ONE WITH HIM? THE WAY WHICH I GUARD LEADS TO THAT OF GLORY IN THE MIGHT OF THE LORD. I, MICHAEL, WOULD GUIDE THEE. DO NOT DISOBEY. DO NOT FALTER. THOU KNOWEST THE WAY.

We are through.

This psychic reading was given by Edgar Cayce at his home on Arctic Crescent, Virginia Beach, Va., on December 18, 1932, at 4:00 P.M., in accordance with a request made by those present: Edgar Cayce; Gertrude Cayce, conductor; Gladys Davis, steno; C. A. Barrett, Minnie Barrett, Annie Cayce, Hugh Lynn Cayce, L. B. Cayce, Mildred Davis, Edith Edmonds, Florence Edmonds, Lu Hesson, Sarah Hesson, F. Y. Morrow, and Esther Wynne.

➤ 262-34 ➤

Mrs. Cayce: You will have before you the individuals gathered here and their work on the lesson In His Presence, *a copy of which I hold in my hand. You will go over this and as I call each paragraph make any suggestions as to change, or addition of material. You will answer the questions which will be asked.*

Mr. Cayce: We have the group, as a group, as individuals, gathered here, and their work on the lesson *In His Presence.*

Ready for questions.

[Mr. Cayce answered "Very good" to each paragraph.]

Q-1. Is the interpretation of He *and* Him *correct, as given on the paper which I hold in my hand?*

A-1. Very good.

Q-2. Compilers: Please give a more complete address for the Argosy *magazine, as the paper ["Present World Conditions"] sent to the address given was returned.*

A-2. Argosy Publishing House, Argosy Bldg., Pennsylvania Avenue, Washington, D.C.

Q-3. Please give street number and complete address of the Blue Goose *magazine publishing house.*

A-3. As given, 57th Street, New York City.

Q-4. [993]: Please interpret the message I received on December 13th about 6:30 A.M., when a voice said, "It is time for you to take the Holy Grail."

A-4. With the study that has been going on, in the activities of the body, the reading of the quest of the Holy Grail at the present time would bring to the body the proper interpretation of how and what the vision should mean to the body in the present; for it will be seen in the story of the quest how that it becomes necessary for the individual to partake of that which

-145-

was meant by Him who gave, "Ye must eat of my body, drink of my blood."

Q-5. For [1929], who is contemplating Study Group work: Please interpret her dream of November 19, 1932, a copy of which I hold in my hand. [Mrs. 1929 was the first member of Group #2, who met weekly with Esther Wynne as the teacher.]

A-5. As we have given for [1929], there are those interpretations that come to self in the development of self, through the experiences and activities of the entity in the material application of the spiritual elements of the entity. So, in the vision, as the application of self is to those things seen, in their essence or elements represent the developments of varied experiences and activities through others; and these may be brought to a better interpretation by study along the lines as visioned.

Q-6. What should be the basis and fundamental thoughts to be presented in the lesson on The Cross and the Crown?

A-6. As there has been presented in the lessons that which may be applicable in the thought and study through any activity of an entity, so in the lesson The Cross, the Crown, there is made the definite stand of the activities of an entity, that must come to stand as that which is first and foremost in the minds mentally, the minds spiritually, of each entity. As given, "I am determined to know nothing among men save Jesus, the Christ, and Him crucified." So, He, with the cross, represents something in the experience of every entity in their activities through the earth, and has led in all of the experiences of thought in any of the presented forms of truth in the earth, and comes at last to the cross. So, this should be the central thought, the reason of the cross, the crown; for, as ye may be known by the name that He has given, so must the central theme, the basis of each individual's approach be: Not "What is my cross?" which is the usual first question in every material mind, but rather "How may I with His aid best meet my cross, in my approach to the crown of righteousness?" and not as of a temporal or even a mental kingdom, but the cross of glory, the crown of glory, in, through and by His name.

Q-7. Please give affirmation for this lesson.

A-7. OUR FATHER, OUR GOD, AS WE APPROACH THAT THAT MAY GIVE US A BETTER INSIGHT OF WHAT HE BORE IN THE CROSS, WHAT

HIS GLORY MAY BE IN THE CROWN, MAY THY BLESSINGS—AS
PROMISED *THROUGH HIM*—BE WITH US AS WE STUDY TOGETHER
IN HIS NAME.

We are through for the present.

This psychic reading was given by Edgar Cayce at his home on Arctic Crescent, Virginia Beach, Va., on January 8, 1933, at 4:00 P.M., in accordance with a request made by those present: Edgar Cayce; Gertrude Cayce, conductor; Gladys Davis, steno; C. A. Barrett, Minnie Barrett, Hugh Lynn Cayce, L. B. Cayce, Mildred Davis, Edith Edmonds, Florence Edmonds, Ruth LeNoir, Dr. Jas. R. Parker (during latter portion), and Esther Wynne.

⊁ 262-35 ⊀

Mrs. Cayce: You will have before you the group gathered here and their work on the lesson The Cross and the Crown. *You will please give further material on this subject which will aid us in developing this lesson. You will answer the following general and individual questions, as I ask them.*

Mr. Cayce: Yes, we have the group as gathered here, as a group, as individuals, and their work on the lesson *The Cross and the Crown.*

As indicated by the outline, or the basis of thought, as well as the meditation and the questions that each should ask themselves, the group, the individuals, have reached then that place in their study, their work, where—as it were—they are, as individuals, to apply that in their experience, in giving out to others in the lessons that are being and are to be prepared, that they have experienced in preparing themselves for the various channels of blessings each are to be in the service as of furnishing data in lessons for others. Much in this manner:

Why has the way of the cross been chosen by the group?

Why is it necessary that each must bear a cross? Just because the cross was borne for us by Another?

Why was it necessary that He, the Maker of heaven and earth, bear a cross as a man?

Why did He come into the world as a man, that He might *as* a man bear a cross?

Why do we as individuals necessarily bear much that He did, yet we say taking His yoke upon us the cross becomes easy?

These and similar questions must be answered by each individual, and give in their own hearts an answer that will satisfy them in the light of that which has been their experience through the living of the lessons that have been given to others.

Does the life, do the lives, lived in accordance with thine own faith, thine own virtue and understanding, thine own walking in the Presence, make for the explanation of why each soul must bear a cross?

Why has the cross been chosen, rather than many of the other philosophies of thought that make for a unison of conditions in the experience—and make for the correlation of the material and spiritual life?

Why is the cross the emblem of shame yet necessary, for the crown that is to be in the experience of those that bear same? For we have reached that place in the experience where *we,* as individuals, will walk no more with this thought or else say as Peter, "Thou alone hast the words of eternal life, to whom shall we go?"

These, then, are the questions that each individual should ask *self,* and put into the lesson; as: "Why *I* as a soul, in the development through this material plane, must bear a cross."

Then, when this portion has been received by selves, and the answer written, we may give "Why the crown."

We are through for the present.

This psychic reading was given by Edgar Cayce at the Edmonds' home on Pennsylvania Avenue, Norfolk, Va., on January 22, 1933, at 4:00 P.M., in accordance with a request made by those present: Edgar Cayce; Gertrude Cayce, conductor; Gladys Davis, steno; C. A. Barrett, Minnie Barrett, Hugh Lynn Cayce, Mildred Davis, Edith Edmonds, Florence Edmonds, Ruth LeNoir, F. Y. Morrow, Helen Storey, and Esther Wynne.

ⵣ **262-36** ⵥ

Mrs. Cayce: You will have before you the group gathered here, and their work on the lesson of The Cross and the Crown. As the questions suggested in the last reading have been answered, will you please continue the counsel as "Why the crown," giving that which will be strengthening and helpful to each in their daily life. You will answer the questions as I ask them.

Mr. Cayce: Yes, we have the group as gathered here, as a group, as individuals, and the work of each that have contributed to this present understanding.

In the study, in the thought, this is found to be experienced by all—that there was the necessity, for man's understanding, for the entering in of the Son of man, and that the cross becomes the emblem of Him who offered Himself, of Himself. For that cause, for that purpose came He into the world, that He, Himself—in overcoming the world—might gain the crown.

So, each in their respective lives, their own experiences, find their cross overcoming the world, overcoming those things, those conditions, those experiences, that would not only enable them to meet the issues of life but to become heirs with Him of the crown of glory.

What, then, is this crown of glory? Does this bespeak only of those things, those conditions, that have to do with the spiritual life? Did the overcoming give the authority? Did the overcoming make this Son of man the Lord, the glory, the crown of life?

So He, as the pattern for each, makes the way clear, the way open that each soul—as it meets the crosses, endures the temptations and overcomes them—may become an heir, *joint* heir with Him to the crown of glory; with power temporal, power mental, power spiritual to become the sons and daughters of

God, as many as are called—and all that fulfill that purpose for which they, as individuals, are called—and carry on in that manner, overcoming, meeting, bearing within themselves. Not in sorrow, not in wailing, but in the joy of the Lord.

Then, the first of the signs that may be given—to as many as have met the cross, as have endured, is given that which enables them—in whatsoever state they find themselves in meeting their crosses—to do so in the *joy* of the Lord. Happiness and joy go hand in hand.

He that overcomes, then, is joyous in the knowledge that power to meet, power to use, power to overcome is given in his understanding.

With joy, then, do such individuals enter into the service that may be their part, their portion, as the channels, the ways in which they may serve in the making known to others the way of the cross and the crown of glory that comes with the same, in the knowledge of the life being spent in a way that He would have one go; for His presence then abides ever. The door is open. The virtue and understanding finds activity. The faith is renewed day by day, for self is understood in the relationships of each and every condition that arises—either from the mental, the material or the spiritual forces; for the access of the Father is held as a cooperative force in whatsoever sphere of activity an individual is engaged in this service.

Then, let each know that in enduring the cross the patience —that makes for the awareness of the soul—finds its kinship with the Father in the manner of service that may be rendered day by day.

As He has given, and as has been presented again and again, not in times nor seasons, not in new moons nor in any place, but *every* day, *every* hour we show forth His love in a manner that makes for the knowledge of all contacting us that He walks with us, that He is our friend.

With the cross comes the crown to those that are faithful in the few things, and their joys shall be many in the service that each are called to do; for His ways are made known to those that seek. As He has given, he that seeks shall find, to him that knocks shall it be opened.

Ye shall enter into the joys of thy Lord, *enjoying* that crown that brings joy, happiness, harmony, peace; for *He* is the Prince of Peace.

Ready for questions.

Q-1. The paper, "Present World Conditions," which we sent to the Argosy Publishing House, Pennsylvania Avenue, Washington, D.C., has been returned to us, unclaimed. Is there any further advice to us concerning this address or the paper?

A-1. That is the address, that is the building. If these are rejected, then send on to the others.

Q-2. Upon what is His glory in the crown conditioned?

A-2. Faith-ful-ness.

Q-3. Please explain, "He, with the cross, represents something in the experience of every entity in their activities through the earth, and has led in all the experiences of thought in any of the presented forms of truth in the earth, and comes at last to the cross." [See 262-34, A-6.]

A-3. As we have given, and as was given by Him, in the beginning He was the Son — *made* the Son — those of the sons that went astray; and through the varying activities overcame the world through the *experiences, bearing* the cross in each and every experience, reaching the *final* cross with *all* power, *all* knowledge in having overcome the world — and of Himself *accepted* the cross. Hence doing away with that often termed karma, that must be met by all. The immutable law of cause and effect is, as evidenced in the world today, in the material, the mental and the spiritual world; but He — in overcoming the world, the law — became the law. The law, then, becomes as the schoolmaster, or the school of training — and we who have *named* the name, then, are no longer *under* the law as law, but under mercy as in Him; for in Him — and with the desires — may there be made the *coordination* of all things.

Remember the pattern in the mount, in self, in the physical body, in the mental body, in the spiritual body. *That* is the mount! So long as there is perfect coordination in the mount, all things work together for the *good* of the mount. When there is the rebellion in the mount, then there is disconnection, destruction, disconcerted effort, and the coordination — the cooperation of activity — is made awry. Hence death in the physical ensues, by the disintegration, through the disconcerted action, through the *incoordinated* action—and this mental, and physical, and spiritual.

So, in overcoming all He set that as the throne, or the mercy seat, that is within the temple, as the pattern, as in the mount —and in the mount, "I *will* arise and go to my Father, in Him, through Him. I *will!* I *will!*"

Q-4. *What is to be understood by the definite stand we all must now take?*

A-4. As the reason, *materially*, that the cross—rather than the mental, or any other phase of experience—is accepted as the ideal.

We are through for the present.

≫ 262-37 ≪ *This psychic reading was given by Edgar Cayce at the Edmonds' home on Pennsylvania Avenue, Norfolk, Va., on February 5, 1933, at 4:10 P.M., in accordance with a request made by those present: Edgar Cayce; Gertrude Cayce, conductor; Gladys Davis, steno; C. A. Barrett, Minnie Barrett, Annie Cayce, Hugh Lynn Cayce, Mildred Davis, Edith Edmonds, Florence Edmonds, Ruth LeNoir, Frances Morrow, Helen Storey, and Esther Wynne.*

Mrs. Cayce: You will have before you the group gathered here and their work on the lesson, The Cross and the Crown. *You will answer the questions which they will ask as individuals and as a group.*

Mr. Cayce: Yes, we have the group as gathered here, as a group, as individuals, and their work on the preparation of the lesson, *The Cross, the Crown.*

In the preparation of selves, in the study—as there may be given through each that which may enable others to comprehend and understand the lessons, the causes for the selection of this means of approach to that as should come in the next lesson, *The Lord Thy God Is One,* so does each individual find the necessity for analyzing themselves as to that which is, which has been, which may be, the impelling influence in their lives. And there must be put out of same that as would bespeak of selfishness, or the magnifying of those desires that are gratifying only to the carnal influences in lives.

Ready for questions.

Q-1. Please explain, ". . . ye may be known by the name [that] He has given . . ." [*See 262-35, A-6.*]

A-1. As He gave, there is no other name given among men whereby they may be saved. Saved from what? For what purpose? So, in the expression given, this name which has been chosen should stand for the answering of those questions in the experience of each individual. For, as has been given, to those whom He has called gives He the power to become the sons of God. And called for a service in some specific direction or channel, that each may be a channel of blessing to someone.

Q-2. Please explain more fully what is meant by the mount as patterned in the physical body. [*See 262-36, A-3.*]

A-2. A whole volume might be written on this subject! The

-154-

reference is given as to the pattern given in the mount as for those under that particular dispensation, for *their* edification in the approach to that they worshiped through that period. And the pattern in the mount is represented in the body through that shown in the glorification in the mount, as seen upon transfiguration, showing the specific reference as to the cross and the crown. For, as the pattern in the first approach of man that came to the outer court (the physical body), the inner court (the spiritual man) is approached through the mental body (to the holy of holies), where the Father may speak as face to face. So, in the vision—or the representation in the mount, the law and the prophets were represented in the physical, the mental, the spiritual; in Moses, Elijah, and the Christ.

So, in selves do we find the physical, the mental, the spiritual (in self) as the patterns that must find the counterpart in the experiences of others, the application of the many, and the direct application of self in this *present* experience.

Q-3. As I call the name of each individual in the group, you will please give an individual message of guidance. First, [993]:

A-3. As has been given, the way is set before self—and to remain faithful in that which is undertaken, leaving Him as the guide from day to day.

Q-4. [560]:

A-4. As the reasoning of self leads the way, in the experiences of the awakening in self of those activities from day to day, so keep self in the way of following in *His* guiding ways.

Q-5. [69]:

A-5. Unto him that hath been given much is much required, and as there is seen the necessity of meeting those conditions that must answer for the hope that is within self, renew same only in the strength of that as must be the guide through *all* phases of the experience.

Q-6. Please tell me the condition.

A-6. That in self that would make for the *renewing* of the hopes within self.

Q-7. [69's husband]:

A-7. Keep in the way that is open before thee, in giving to those that self contacts the concept of the vision held by self that lies ahead. [See 262-40, A-5.]

Q-8. [585]:

A-8. As those conditions arise that make for the testing of self's own hold upon the promise, know these are efficient and sufficient unto thee; that these will guide in those periods when there is the need of same. Faint not, for the crown is ahead.

Q-9. [538]:

A-9. Keep self close to that mental and spiritual awakening that comes with the communion with Him in thine inner self, for He is able to guide through all shadows that may arise.

Q-10. [294]:

A-10. Keep the faith, for he that endures will wear the crown of life.

Q-11. [341]:

A-11. As the way is opened for the giving out of that gained through the activities of the mental *and* material in the spiritual relationships, be ever ready—as He gave, "Go call thy brother."

Q-12. [288]:

A-12. As the awakenings come in the varied experiences, through the study of those hardships that come to self or to others, so may the cheering hand bring that of peace and harmony to thy fellow man.

Q-13. [295]:

A-13. In the promise that in thee may come the blessings to many, make thyself—then—as a perfect channel, that the glory may come to those that seek His face.

Q-14. [413]:

A-14. Keep the way open and the heart attuned to those calls from within, that His glory—through the activities in the mental self—may gain the more of the peace and harmony from contentment in His service.

Q-15. [303]:

A-15. In keeping thy face to the light the shadows fall far behind. His strength will sustain, His love is sufficient, His power does not abate—to those who are faithful in His service. Spend *self* in the love for His ways.

Q-16. [462]:

A-16. Keep the way that brings for gladness in the strength of the power of *His* might in thy life.

Q-17. [404]:

A-17. The door is open, the way is before thee. Let that as makes for a closer walk with Him guide thy every footstep in the choosing of the way before thee.

Q-18. [*379*]:

A-18. In the way of the cross is light. Though it may have its crown of thorns, it has also its glory that passeth understanding in the finite mind. Yet, as the infinite opens the way the thorns become less and the way the brighter.

Q-19. [*307*]:

A-19. The glory of the Lord is in the service of self day by day, in *His* ways being made known unto others through the life that self shows in the experiences that may be given to others as signposts along the way. For, he that endures will bear the cross and the crown.

Q-20. [*234*]:

A-20. The way before thee is in His keeping. Trust ye in Him.

Q-21. Is there any message for the group as a whole?

A-21. Be joyous in thy service day by day. Let not trouble bar thee from knowing the peace, the happiness, the joy in the Lord.

Q-22. Any other message at this time?

A-22. Keep the heart singing. Keep the glory of Him before thee. Amen!

Mrs. Cayce: That is all.

Mr. Cayce: We are through for the present.

≥ 262-38 ≤ *This psychic reading was given by Edgar Cayce at the Edmonds' home on Pennsylvania Avenue, Norfolk, Va., on February 19, 1933, at 4:25 P.M., in accordance with a request made by those present: Edgar Cayce; Gertrude Cayce, conductor; Gladys Davis, steno; C. A. Barrett, Minnie Barrett, Hugh Lynn Cayce, Mildred Davis, Edith Edmonds, Florence Edmonds, Ruth LeNoir, Frances Y. Morrow, Helen Storey, and Esther Wynne.*

Mrs. Cayce: You will have before you the group gathered here and their work on the lesson, The Cross and the Crown, *a copy of which I hold in my hand. As I call each paragraph you will comment on it and make such suggestions for corrections or additions that will make this lesson a more complete expression of the truth we are trying to convey. You will answer the questions which will be asked by the group or by individuals in the group.*

Mr. Cayce: Yes, we have the group as gathered here, as a group, as individuals, and their work on the lesson.

Q-1. [Please comment on] paragraph one [of the lesson].

A-1. This is very good. There may be the addition showing, in the introduction, just why the group as a group chooses the way of the cross as *their* way; for, as is set forth, *if* ye know the truth the truth shall set you free. In the cross, then, there must be more freedom than is ordinarily termed or considered in a way of the cross. [Mr. Cayce answered "Very good" to each paragraph from 2 through 39.]

In considering additions to the reasons, as suggested in the preamble or introduction, it will be found that some minor changes will be necessary in the presentation of that given in paragraph twelve.

As we begin with the next lesson, then, presented in *Know He, the Lord Thy God, Is One,* the affirmation should be:

AS MY BODY, MIND AND SOUL ARE ONE, THOU, O LORD, IN THE MANIFESTATIONS IN THE EARTH, IN POWER, IN MIGHT, IN GLORY, ART ONE. MAY I SEE IN THAT I DO, DAY BY DAY, MORE OF THAT REALIZATION, AND MANIFEST THE MORE.

Then, the culmination of this series of lessons will be *Love;* for He so loved the world as to give His Son, His Self, that man

-158-

should come to the realization of the oneness of the Father in the earth.

As this group, as a group, as individuals, have been chosen that they may manifest the power, the might, the glory of the love of the Father, so may each come step by step to the realization of that wonderful experience in themselves of being a channel through which many may come to know the mercifulness of God, the loving-kindness of His love, the power in His name.

And all may be on fire with the powers that may manifest through them; becoming less and less self-centered, less and less selfish; and more and more at peace and in harmony with those experiences that are theirs in the going about to show forth His love, through the application of that each are gaining through their walks with Him in prayer, in meditation.

So, their coming together may mean more and more the shedding abroad those truths that make *them* free in their abilities to become lights, helpers for, through and by, His power.

As ye seek, then, my children, to know His way, so does He glorify in thee that whereunto thou hast been appointed.

Keep thine heart open, that the voice of Him who has called may quicken each thought, each act, in thy daily walks.

For, little by little, line by line, do ye grow in grace, in knowledge, in understanding of His ways. They are not hidden, nor afar off; for *all* is manifest to those that will hear, will see, the glory of the oneness in the Father.

We are through. [See 262-39, A-5 and A-9, regarding a vision Mr. Cayce had during this reading.]

This psychic reading was given by Edgar Cayce at his home on Arctic Crescent, Virginia Beach, Va., on February 21, 1933, at 4:30 P.M., in accordance with a request made by those present: Edgar Cayce; Gertrude Cayce, conductor; Gladys Davis, steno; Hugh Lynn Cayce, L. B. Cayce, and Mildred Davis.

≳ 262-39 ≲

Mrs. Cayce: You will have before you the enquiring minds of those present in this room and you will answer the questions which they will submit.

Mr. Cayce: Yes, we have the enquiring minds and those conditions that prompt the questions in the minds of each.

Ready for questions.

Q-1. The Norfolk Study Group #1 wishes to hold an open meeting to which each individual will invite individuals whom they feel are seeking light. They have selected March 13, 1933, as the date for this meeting. Is their idea to present a reading at that time the correct step in their efforts to help others through the expansion of this work? Are any of the subjects listed below the best subject for such a reading? If not, please suggest a subject that will be the most helpful to those present.

1. Interpretation of Luke 21

2. Conditions in [the] United States through 1938

3. Lemuria

4. Unemployment

5. Revelation

A-1. The date chosen, through the astrological influence, comes at a period when such a reading (through the channels chosen by Norfolk Study Group) would be well. And *any* subject which might be chosen would be enlightening to *any* that might be present, *provided* there is the presentation and questioning in line with constructive thought.

As to which would be chosen of the subjects given here, this would vary according to the character of individuals present.

The interpretation of Luke 17 would be rather for those that have questioned within their inner selves, either through correlating of thought from various channels or from thoughts that may have arisen from the various associations of their own mental developments, and would be rather a controversial subject for those who are considering—or do consider themselves of—an orthodox trend of mind.

That relating to conditions in the United States through 1938 would be rather the gratifying of those that are looking for, feeling for, the sensational in their own imaginations, or for the verification of that which has been the imagination of others or individual minds.

That related to Revelation and its basis would be rather for those seeking an interpretation of spiritual influences in the inner life of individuals.

The group should be able to choose. *Any* question may be answered, provided they are as given—and made helpful, and of a constructive nature.

Do not begin before a quarter to nine, nor let it last longer than eleven, without some harmful effects.

Q-2. *Do you refer to the reading itself, or to the meeting as a whole?*

A-2. Reading! That's what they asked for! Didn't ask about the meeting!

Q-3. [295]: *What is the meaning of, "He that findeth his life shall lose it; and he that loseth his life for my sake shall find it," as recorded in Matthew 10:39?*

A-3. The *literal* application is as given by Paul in Colossians, as to how the body perisheth that the renewed life may be made manifest in material things. So, as given in the text referred to here, he that loseth his life shall find it in the service of Him that IS life! What, then, *is* life? How is it found? How is it obtained?

Life is the manifestation of *Creative* forces in a material world, in whatever form we may become conscious of it in. For, there are within the material experience of man many forms of life; even matter, even in the various strata of activity about the individual that man is not conscious of. And in *obtaining* the consciousness of it, through the applications of individuals, how many lives have been lost? In *accomplishing* that, in the use of that as it is manifest, in any particular plane or sphere, how many lives have been lost and gained? Applied; making application, then, materially—see?

Q-4. What is meant by, "The first shall be last and the last shall be first"?

A-4. As illustrated, when life ends it begins. The end is the beginning of the transposition, or the change. The first is last, the last is first. Transposition.

Q-5. Was the Master speaking to us in our group reading [262-38] of Sunday, February 19th, on the finishing up of the lesson, The Cross and the Crown?

A-5. No.

Q-6. Could we of this group at this time have a message from the Master to guide us on our way?

A-6. When each has shown self, as He has given, as being able or capable of receiving or vibrating to that which may make the consciousness for each in that realm.

Q-7. Should he [294] accept invitation to address group next Sunday in Norfolk?

A-7. If there is that which is worthwhile being given to others, then do not fail in an opportunity to present same. Is there not that injunction, "Always be ready to respond to that which is as evidence of the faith that is within"?

Q-8. What should be the subject?

A-8. As the spirit moves. He hasn't accepted yet!

Q-9. Please explain [the] vision experienced [by Mr. Cayce] last Sunday during reading [262-38] suggesting how this may be accomplished.

A-9. As there is evidence of that being awakened in many of the group of the presence of the Creative Forces in the activities of many in the group, would it not be worth the while then to prepare self in such a manner that the Master—as He spoke *with* thee—might, through thee, speak the lesson of Love that He so well represented and presented in His experience as the man of Galilee?

Is it not worthwhile, then, *cleansing* the body, in thought, in all manners as *necessary,* to raise the flesh vibrations to such an extent that there may be no harm to same in the experiences that may be had by all during the periods of preparation on such a lesson?

Has not there been the promise that through thee, in part, may come one that may be a blessing to many, that *many* may speak with those higher forces, higher sources, as face to face? Is it not well, then, that the body be cleansed, be purified, be renewed, that there may be that power, that vigor necessary, that there may come that *in* power, in might, as *representing* that influence as comes in the life with the union of the expressions that may bring same to pass?

Then, how may this be accomplished? Thou knowest that as is well with thine soul. Thou knowest that as is well to be accomplished in the body, in the flesh, that there may be the power, the might, the glory that may come to others.

Be faithful, as given, to the trust which has been given into thine hands; for the glory that comes with faithfulness is as but short to the *crowns* of glory that will be with *His* presence in this—even this—material world!

Q-10. Is there any advice or counsel for me [Gertrude Cayce] as conductor of readings?

A-10. As has been oft given, the conductor should be *passive;* that there may be the more positive reaction from that which is given. While the questions as directed should always be positive, the transmission as by directress should be in the passive; that the answer may be the positive.

In this, then, this attitude should the body always approach such service to the fellow man, or the seeker after truth or light: Never with a grudge, a hard feeling, an indecisive manner; but as being *used* as a handmaid of Him thou would worship in the Creative Forces, that may be made manifest by the acts, voice and speech of self through such an experience for any.

Q-11. Please explain to me what it means by being passive.

A-11. Passive, as the word itself indicates; not being one-sided. As indicated, not in a mood or manner where a hard feeling, a resentment is held, or grudge; but rather as being used—a channel, a door, an outlet for that as may be presented.

Q-12. Should any change be made in either of the suggestions I use at beginning or end of reading, or in obtaining readings?

A-12. These have been given. When they are to be changed, we'll change 'em for you!

Q-13. Please advise me [Hugh Lynn Cayce] regarding the preparation and presentation of the article or story which I am preparing on the great congress held during the age of the de-

*struction of the enormous animals that once roamed the earth.
[See 5748-3.]*

A-13. In the period when this became necessary, there was the consciousness raised in the minds of the groups, in various portions of the earth, much in the manner as would be illustrated by an all-world broadcast in the present day of a menace in any one particular point, or in many particular points. And the gathering of those that heeded, as would be the scientific minds of the present day, in devising ways and means of doing away with that particular kind or class of menace.

As to the manner in which these gathered, it was very much as would be were the Graf [Graf Zeppelin?] to start to the various portions for those that represented, or were to gather those that were to counsel, or were to cooperate in that effort. And, as this, then, was in that particular plane or sphere that then was in the land which has long since lost its identity, except in the inner thought or visions of those that have returned or are returning in the present sphere, the ways and means devised were as those that would alter or change the *environs* for which those beasts were needed, or that necessary for their sustenance in the particular portions of the sphere, or earth, that they occupied at the time. And this was administered much in the same way or manner as were there sent out from various central plants that which is termed in the present the death ray, or the super-cosmic ray, that which many are seeking into which will give their lives much, from the stratosphere, or cosmic rays, that will be found in the next twenty-five years.

This presented, then, in such a manner, and drawing upon the varied conditions that existed in the various portions of the land then occupied by man.

Q-14. What was the date B. C. of this gathering?

A-14. 50,722.

Q-15. Were there any outstanding methods of destruction developed which I have not mentioned?

A-15. Draw on these that we have given here.

Q-16. Were any countries represented which I have not named?

A-16. Og.

Q-17. Who was the general leader for this congress?

A-17. One with the nomenclature Tim.

Q-18. *Of what land or country?*

A-18. Poseidia, from Atlantis.

Q-19. *To what magazines should I send this for publication?*

A-19. Many of them should have the opportunity. It will be more acceptable to either the *Liberty, Weird, Amazing* or *Astounding Stories.*

Q-20. *Any special ones that should have the opportunity?*

A-20. Any of those that present this character of phenomena.

Q-21. [288]: *What was meant by, "through carnal influences are there to be brought changes in material associations, mental understandings, for the* spiritual *uplift of the many"?* [*See 288-31, A-3.*]

A-21. The rebirth into the earth of a representative, to those who will listen. Not the Christ, no; for He will appear as He is—but *as* a forerunner.

Q-22. *How will this come about? And through whom?*

A-22. To those to whom same has been promised in their activities, or their abilities to keep themselves in the manner in which they may bring about such conditions in the earth.

Q-23. *How should I govern myself, in regard to the great responsibility I feel in this direction?*

A-23. Act as if in the manner of being a channel for that, which to self must represent that which is held as the ideal.

Q-24. *Is there a message for any individual present, or for the group as a whole?*

A-24. Study to dwell together in unity of thought. Cooperate in every way as to show forth His love, that may be manifest in thee in thine own particular phase of endeavor or activity. Faint not.

We are through.

This psychic reading was given by Edgar Cayce at the Edmonds' home on Pennsylvania Avenue, Norfolk, Va., on March 5, 1933, at 4:00 P.M., in accordance with a request made by those present: Edgar Cayce; Gertrude Cayce, conductor; Gladys Davis, steno; C. A. Barrett, Minnie Barrett, Hugh Lynn Cayce, Mildred Davis, Edith Edmonds, Florence Edmonds, Helen Ellington, Mrs. Foster, Ruth LeNoir, Frances Y. Morrow, Helen Storey, and Esther Wynne.

⋊ 262-40 ⋉

Mrs. Cayce: You will have before you Norfolk Study Group #1, members of which are present in this room. You will give at this time a discourse on the basic thoughts upon which we should base the lesson, The Lord Thy God Is One. *You will answer the questions which will be asked by members of the group.*

Mr. Cayce: Yes, we have the group as gathered here, as a group and as individuals.

In the study of the lesson, in the preparation for selves, there should be—as indicated in the more recent lessons—the preparation rather in self than in discourse; for you each are learning, you each are becoming conscious that there is an activity to take place within self, and self is to become the more conscious—as indicated—of that oneness that may manifest through the activities of the individual, in making the application in their lives, that there may be given that which will be an aid, in study from or of another of such experiences.

Then, those conditions that may arise in the experience of each, there may be enlightenment to self in those manners that will enable each to expand in words and in act, and indeed become the more aware, the more conscious.

For, as is and should be recognized in each, the contending forces that are within man as his individuality and personality (for a name) are that as self has builded, or that builded and the spirit of the living influence of life itself.

And these, then, made more and more aware that, "My life, my activities, my thoughts, my meditation, must be more and more in accord with the will of the Father." For in such, through such, does the individual, the entity, the soul, the in-

-166-

dividuality of an entity, become more godlike, less of self, less of the carnal influence may bear upon the activities of an individual, an entity, in this material plane.

Then, the activities of the will, the consciousness, the various terms that have been and are applied to the manner of expression in consciousness, are the basic thoughts, the basic activities through which each should prepare themselves for the abilities, for the activating forces that may assist them in giving that they must experience in their individual consciousnesses, as to how they may be expressed that others may gain a greater concept of the oneness of the Father in the material plane.

Ready for questions.

Q-1. [585]: *On March 2nd, whose voice did I hear speak to me, and what was the message?*

A-1. As is felt within self that there is a manifestation of a force, a power from without, this then is builded into that as the self through its experience gives such an influence and power concerning the consciousness of self. To be sure, this was a manifestation—but rather than being specific, rather than being an entity activity from without, it is rather the awakening within of the abilities to so associate and so connect and communicate with those influences from without. Then, as given of old, if there will be held and magnified within the consciousness of self that that desired, that voice, that presence that would aid in bringing the various consciousnesses to self, must be from the universal influences, or from His messenger, then may this be magnified in self and for self. Be mindful that it is not clothed in some other power.

Q-2. [69]: *Please tell me to whom was I talking the morning of February 3rd and just why am I getting this experience?*

A-2. As given, be not afraid when it is said, "It is I." Rather, then, the experiences that are necessary for making aware within the consciousness of self how the inner self may be controlled by those powers, those influences, that an entity, an individual, entertains. Be not unmindful that ye entertain strangers that come to thee in thine consciousness, that reaches to the inner self and to the cosmic spheres; for angels are often entertained. Then, clothe and feed them only upon the words and the activities of the spirit of truth, and through same may come those experiences that have been long sought; for the time is near at hand. [See 262-41, A-3.]

Q-3. Is this information that I have been receiving the past four nights coming from some source other than my subconscious?

A-3. To be sure, and these are worth entertaining.

Q-4. Please tell me who is doing the talking?

A-4. Who would the body have? Who would the inner forces entertain? For, "Seek and ye shall find" is spoken of the soul, spoken of those that would be the guides, the influences in the experiences, and is bound close with that which is being the study in the present, *The Lord Thy God Is One*. Do not accredit it to lower forces than His emissaries.

Q-5. [69's husband]: Please explain in a manner that I may correctly interpret, "Keep in the way that is open before thee, in giving to those that self contacts the concept of the vision held by self that lies ahead." What is the vision? [See 262-37, A-7.]

A-5. The vision is that that is held as the approach to the throne, of the consciousness of the divine that is within each individual. That self is oft in the position of being in a quandary, and fearful of being lightly spoken of for giving the experiences of self as contacting the various influences, is that referred to. Being, then, this: Be not loath nor unmindful to bear witness, in word, in act, to thine associates from day to day, of the manifestations of the power, the influence, that comes in thine experience; and thus may each soul, each entity, become more and more aware of the oneness of the Father in the world.

Q-6. [303]: One night some weeks ago I saw floating above my head in space an exceedingly bright sphere or planet. It seemed to be moving within itself as well as through space. Please interpret this to me.

A-6. As given, this group, these individuals, varied individuals, are reaching that period, that place in their experience, where signs, where activities within self, the consciousnesses within self, become more and more aware of the very lessons,. the very truths that are being given out, that are to be made manifest in the experiences of selves and in the lives and experiences of others.

So, in the vision seen, it is the world without and the world within—their movements as one coordinating with the other, the brightness of the orb itself as reflecting that which is the movement within self, that makes for the shedding abroad of the light, the understanding, the enlightenment that is obtained from within.

Well was it said by Him, "Ye do not light a light to put it under a bushel."

In this same manner that is experienced in self, when there is that consciousness within of being more and more in accord with the light that shineth even unto the darkness, though there may come strifes, though there may come disappointments, though there may come turmoils from without and from within, yet His peace maketh for a harmony—with that cooperation of the personality, the individuality; or self and thy God.

Q-7. *Please explain how I may spend self in the love for His ways.*

A-7. By that even as visioned. Let the light that shines without be lighted by that light which is created from within, making the activities of the inner self and the outer self in accord; or let that seen of others be impelled by the light from the love of the Giver of life, light, immortality.

Q-8. *Compilers: "There is no other Name given among men whereby they may be saved." Saved from what? Please explain.*

A-8. From what may *anyone* be saved? Only from themselves! That is, their individual hell; they dig it with their own desires!

We are through.

This psychic reading was given by Edgar Cayce at the Edmonds' home on Pennsylvania Avenue, Norfolk, Va., on March 19, 1933, at 4:10 P.M., in accordance with a request made by those present: Edgar Cayce; Gertrude Cayce, conductor; Gladys Davis, steno; C. A. Barrett, Minnie Barrett, Hugh Lynn Cayce, Mildred Mary Davis, Edith Mildred Edmonds, Florence Edmonds, Helen Ellington, Ruth LeNoir, Frances Y. Morrow, and Helen Storey.

⋊ 262-41 ⋉

Mrs. Cayce: You will have before you the Norfolk Study Group #1, members of which are present in this room. You will give at this time such counsel as will aid them as individuals and as a group to make the present lesson, The Lord Thy God Is One, *a complete expression of truth. You will answer the questions which will be asked by the group and individuals in same.*

Mr. Cayce: Yes, we have the group as gathered here, as a group, as individuals.

As has been given, to make the lesson complete it must be lived, experienced by each individual, and interpreted in their lives. And such activities that enable them to be nearer in accord with those truths, those lessons that are gained by such experiences, are those that must make the lesson complete for the lives, the experiences of others.

Well, then, that each — in their own way and manner — correlate that which has been gained from time to time, that there may be the better understanding. For, the tenets, the truths, the lessons are before thee day by day. Only self shuts out the glories that may be thine own experience, in the application of the lessons that are before thee.

Ready for questions.

Q-1. I hold in my hand a copy of an outline on this lesson.

A-1. [Interrupting] Which is very good, but there's some of it that needs changing very badly! And we would change it! For, there are some portions that have been set as the outline which would be impossible to be filled in by individuals' experience; but would only be tentative experience!

Q-2. Which part?

A-2. The second part!

Q-3. [69]: Please explain what was meant by "It is I" and "the

-170-

*time is near at hand" as given in answer to my question in the
last reading [262-40, A-2].*

A-3. It has been given for some time past as to what is to
happen and who is to speak. Has the body reached the state that
such has been forgotten, or not looked for nor expected, nor
understood? and as to what the message is to be, or who it is
to be from? If so, then it is falling away!

*Q-4. [379]: How may I become more conscious of the oneness
of the Father, and apply same in my daily activities?*

A-4. The consciousness becomes the portion of self as the
application of that known is made in the experience of self; as
pertaining to the fact that all force, all power, all glory, comes
from the one source. In the activities, then, in the application
to self respecting same, does this become more and more the
experience of self as it is applied in thine own experience.

*Q-5. [303]: How may I better apply personally the affirmation
on this lesson?*

A-5. Just do it!

*Q-6. [560]: Seeing an arm, was told to touch it. And after
touching it, it seemed to become an arm of flesh. Is my interpretation correct? If not, please give the interpretation.*

A-6. As we have given respecting visions or experiences of
individuals, they in themselves may be the better interpreters
of their experiences; provided, to be sure, there is the attempt,
the desire in each to know, and the willingness to be guided or
directed by those influences.

As interpreted by self, in the greater portion do we find this
correct; that variation being as to the relationships to particular individuals, for this is rather more universal.

Q-7. May I receive a message on The Lord Thy God Is One?

A-7. Study to show self approved unto that that would make
for little vain-glorying in any. Know whereunto thou hast been
called; for His glory is sufficient, His mercy is far-reaching; His
understanding maketh known those things that would prevent
individuals from becoming afraid, in the knowledge of the glory
of the Lord.

Keep thy paths straight. Avoid the appearance of evil. Find
fault in no man.

Q-8. Should any changes or additions be made in the paper,

"Present World Conditions," before sending it to any other magazine?

A-8. If it seems well to those who are preparing such, change it!

Q-9. It has been sent to those that were suggested. To whom should we now send this paper?

A-9. *Sunset Magazine* in Dallas.

Q-10. What should the group as a whole do regarding this paper?

A-10. What they choose!

Q-11. Please give the address of the magazine in Dallas.

A-11. Just to Dallas.

Q-12. Dallas, Texas?

A-12. Dallas, Texas. Not many Dallases worthwhile for the *Sunset Magazine* to be published in; there's only three in the United States!

Q-13. Any message for the group as a whole at this time?

A-13. It's time for all to get started doing some work! We are through.

≈ 262-42 ≼

This psychic reading was given by Edgar Cayce at the Edmonds' home on Pennsylvania Avenue, Norfolk, Va., on April 2, 1933, at 4:15 P.M., in accordance with a request made by those present: Edgar Cayce; Gertrude Cayce, conductor; Gladys Davis, steno; C. A. Barrett, Minnie Barrett, Hugh Lynn Cayce, Mildred Mary Davis, Edith Mildred Edmonds, Florence Edmonds, Frances Y. Morrow, and Esther Wynne.

Mrs. Cayce: You will have before you the Norfolk Study Group #1, members of which are present in this room, and their work on the lesson, The Lord Thy God Is One, *a copy of which I hold in my hand. You will give such counsel and further treatment of the lesson as the group needs at this time to continue the work on this lesson. You will answer the questions which will be asked by individuals and by the group as a whole.*

Mr. Cayce: Yes, we have the group as gathered here, as a group, as individuals, and the work of the group on the lesson.

In giving that as may be helpful, beneficial to the various members of the group in preparing data, as given, it is well that the lesson, the preparation be in self rather than in advice or counsel.

But, that there may be the impulse for further consideration, for application in the experience of each, there should be the sincere attempt on the part of each to put into practice or application that that is known.

Does each individual understand that as was given, one must give account of every idle word spoken? that this is in reference to the oneness of purpose in an individual? that the mind, the body, the aptitude of the soul is under surveillance through such activity?

And, as given, as the body, the mind, the soul is one, so is God in the manifestations in power, might and glory in the earth.

That, then, should illustrate as to why there should be joyousness, gladness in the heart, in the speech, in the magnifying of the activities of each individual.

For, if the hate, grudge or selfishness has created such an influence as to separate self from a friend, a foe, any activity that has made for the loss of self's own respect of its abilities

-173-

or its relationship to its Maker, how *can* such a soul be one in Him?

Then, let each test self; and it will be found that the ability to so illustrate in or from self's own experience will aid in lighting the way for others that seek to know the Lord, thy God, is one.

How sincere *is* the *desire* on the part of each *to* know the Lord, thy God, is one? Sufficient to be active rather than just passive in the statement?

For, he that would gain the concept must believe that He is; and that He rewards those who seek to do His biddings.

Then, let each be active; up and doing, with a heart that is singing the joyous message that the kingdom of heaven is at hand. It *is* within! I AM the brother! I AM the associate with the Son, in the relationships to the Father!

And the life will mean more! For, has it not been given that the earth *is* the Lord's and the fullness thereof? True, many within themselves stumble over that which, even, has not been comprehended; in that there is the mental body, the physical body, the spiritual body. They are one!

In analyzing, then, do not let the analysis become the object; but the body in the Lord, the oneness in *purpose,* that is gained through the knowledge that the mental—the consciousness, *is* the builder. And that the oneness of purpose is in Him *as* one doth clarify the conditions that are to be met.

When there is seemingly the slighting on the part of another, evidences in the material mind that conditions or activities are as stumbling blocks not compatible with thine *own* ideal, then know that all activity is a manifestation of *One* power—and *is* the *attempt* of the individual to assert either the power and glory of *God,* or of self!

Where is thine *own* will? One with *His,* or to the glorifying of thine own desires—thine own selfish interests?

The way is not long, nor is the cross more grievous than ye may bear—if the trust will be in Him, that "I will not leave thee comfortless, I will come and abide with thee."

But we are so constituted, by that builded within ourselves, that He does not come without the invitation that He abide with us.

For, with that power of will are we the sons of God—capable of being equal *with* Him in the glory that He would share with us. As He gave, "I and the Father are one, and ye in me, I in the Father—"

These, then, should aid all in making that contribution that enables all to *want,* to *desire,* to be on fire with that desire, to *manifest* the oneness of the Father in life.

For, as He is life—we in life may make manifest that our desires, our hearts, our minds, our souls, are *one* with Him in bringing to the knowledge of one—*anyone*—*everyone*—that the power of God, through the Christ, is able to save; even unto the utmost.

We are through.

≫ 262-43 ≪ *This psychic reading was given by Edgar Cayce at the Edmonds' home on Pennsylvania Avenue, Norfolk, Va., on April 16, 1933, at 4:10 P.M., in accordance with a request made by those present: Edgar Cayce; Gertrude Cayce, conductor; Gladys Davis, steno; Alf Butler, Hugh Lynn Cayce, Mildred Davis, Edith Edmonds, Florence Edmonds, Ruth LeNoir, Frances Y. Morrow, Helen Storey, and Esther Wynne.*

Mrs. Cayce: You will have before you the Norfolk Study Group #1, members of which are present in this room; also a copy of the lesson, The Lord Thy God Is One, *which I hold in my hand. You will go over this lesson as I call each paragraph, making such suggestions for change or additions that would more completely express the truth we are trying to convey. You will answer the questions which will be asked.*

Mr. Cayce: Yes, we have the group as gathered here, as a group, as individuals. Also the work, the lesson that has been prepared by members of the group.

Ready for questions.

[Mr. Cayce answered "Very good" to each paragraph, 1 through 32.]

Q-1. Please give us the affirmation for the lesson on Love.

A-1. OUR FATHER, THROUGH THE LOVE THAT THOU HAST MANIFESTED IN THE WORLD THROUGH THY SON, THE CHRIST, MAKE US MORE AWARE OF GOD IS LOVE.

In the preparation, then, for the study of self that each has manifested in their lives, through the varied experiences that have been theirs in the preparation of the lessons, there has been brought to each a better concept of the Father, of the Son, and of why He, the Son, came into the earth that we as sons of God might have the access to the throne of mercy, grace, peace and pardon through the Son; and through His life in the experiences of each manifesting these in our own lives.

For, he that would expect mercy must show mercy to his fellow man; he that would find peace and harmony in the love of God must show love, peace, harmony, with his fellow man.

And, as each individual has had its own problems, its own experiences, in reaching this understanding in the study and preparation of self in giving truth, light, the words of life even, for others, so may each in the preparation of this present lesson find love that passeth understanding; peace, as He gives peace; love, as He gave love.

For, if each will prepare themselves they may in *this* lesson find Him as a brother that would speak with them.

For His promises are sure; even as He gave, "I will not leave thee comfortless, but will come to you."

"If ye love me, *keep* my commandments—that I may abide with you," and through *you* shed abroad the light, the love of God, unto the sons of men!

We are through.

This psychic reading was given by Edgar Cayce at the Edmonds' home on Pennsylvania Avenue, Norfolk, Va., on April 30, 1933, at 4:30 P.M., in accordance with a request made by those present: Edgar Cayce; Gertrude Cayce, conductor; Gladys Davis, steno; C. A. Barrett, Minnie Barrett, Hugh Lynn Cayce, Mildred Davis, Edith Edmonds, Florence Edmonds, Ruth LeNoir, Frances Y. Morrow, and Helen Storey.

☆ 262-44 ☆

Mrs. Cayce: You will have before you the Norfolk Study Group #1, members of which are present in this room. You will please give at this time that which will aid them in preparing the lesson on Love. *You will answer the questions which will be asked by the group and by individuals.*

Mr. Cayce: Yes, we have the group as a group; and those of that group as gathered here, and their work in preparing the lesson on *Love.*

In the preparation, as given, they each have prepared themselves in this or that way and manner.

They each have become expectant for that which may be in their own consciousness to become aware of, that that may make manifest in their experience more as respecting Him who was love made manifest in the earth.

In this preparation, here, there, those that have attempted oft the harder have fallen short of that as should be accomplished in their experience.

The first lesson that each must learn: Love is the giving out of that within self.

Then, where slights, slurs, or even suspicions, have been allowed to enter in as respecting the fellow man, there cannot be all of what love should be, should mean, in the experience of such an one.

For, "He so loved the world as to give His own son." And it has been asked of everyone, "Love me, keep my commandments, that I may abide in thee even as I abide in the Father."

All believe, yes; all know, yes; all understand that those things that hinder each and every soul are only self-centeredness, selfishness in self, that prevent even the dawn of that concept of what love means in their experience.

All see in various activities in the earth that of maternal love, that of love in friendship, that of love for an ideal, for self, for the varied experiences that are seen in everyone's experience.

Yet, to know the whole truth that makes one free indeed; that love that prevents slurs, slights, unkind remarks, falterings here, disappointments there—in things, in people, in conditions; to not shake faith, the foundation of manifesting in the material experience; few have found this.

Has anyone in the group, then, wholly prepared self?

For, in His presence has anyone opened the door and been satisfied, or not even dismayed at times, at that seen within self?

Has He entered with thee in thy daily conversation one with another?

Purpose, yes; aims high, desires mounting; yet that of self not left in the background, rather taking the place—even as he when he answered as to who the Son of man was, when there was the presentation of that that must suffer in body, in the mental mind, was needed to be upbraided for that, that such things must not be when God Himself walked in the earth. Yet love, as *He* gave, was able even then to say, "Get thee from me, for thou savorest rather the things that be of the earth than the things of life."

Then, come ye, my children! Harken unto that thou hast attained in thine self, that ye may put on the whole armor and be fruitful in the love of Him that calls that *everyone* should hear, should know, should understand, that God is in His heavens and that His love endureth even to those who harden their hearts—and wills that no one should perish; rather that in the love as may be manifested in the daily walks, the daily activities of every soul, each may show through that manifested the love which impels the giving of everything within self as a manifestation of He, the Master, having spoken with thee!

Faint not. Be not overcome. Be not impatient with thine brother, with thine neighbor, and—most of all—with thine self.

For, as given, "In patience possess ye your souls," that may know Him as thine Elder Brother, who is at the right hand of

God to make intercession for you day by day; and who calls unto all that will harken, "Inasmuch as ye do it unto the least of these, my brethren, ye do it unto me."

As we show forth, then, in our speech, in our actions day by day, do we make manifest that which will make for the awareness within our own consciousness of the love, that love, His love, that passeth all understanding in man's life—as man; yet is a practical, personal love that makes for joy in the services that one may render, even in toil, in pain, in misunderstandings that shape the activities of the lives of so many that would walk with Him!

In the deed, in the act, do we see that promised come to each, that "I will come and abide with thee—if ye love me, keep my commandments." For, these are neither grievous nor hard to bear when self is not sought to be exalted in the day or in the hour.

But, "Ye that have known me knoweth my Father also, for I am in Him, and ye in me"—may know that love that maketh the life burn as an ember in a darkened and unregenerated world. "For unto me must come all that would find the way. I AM the way. Ye are my brethren. Ye have been begotten in the flesh through the love made manifest in the earth."

Then, in the spirit and in the mind that hast brought thee to that understanding and consciousness of His love made manifest, abide ye day by day.

We are through.

ꙮ 262-45 ꙮ   *This psychic reading was given by Edgar Cayce at the Edmonds' home on Pennsylvania Avenue, Norfolk, Va., on May 14, 1933 at 4:15 P.M., in accordance with a request made by those present: Edgar Cayce; Gertrude Cayce, conductor; Gladys Davis, steno; C. A. Barrett, Minnie Barrett, Hugh Lynn Cayce, Mildred Davis, Edith Edmonds, Florence Edmonds, Ruth LeNoir, Frances Y. Morrow, and Esther Wynne.*

Mrs. Cayce: You will have before you the Norfolk Study Group #1, members of which are present in this room and their work on the lesson Love. *You will answer the questions which will be asked by members and the group as a whole.*

Mr. Cayce: Yes, we have the group as gathered here, as a group and as individuals—and their work in preparation of the lesson *Love.*

Each may find in this that which is being sought by each, in the study of the lesson and that which each seeks to manifest in the lesson. As each goes forth to make manifest, each may find that sought.

The first, in that expressed in a baby's smile; in the hope, the light, the seeking, the manifestation of that which is love undefiled.

The next may see it in the rose, as it seeks—with that it has to do with—to make manifest that beauty in expression that may *glorify* its Maker.

The next may find it in friendship, in that which speaks without thought of self, that which makes for the expressions of love *glorified* through the friendliness that comes with friendship.

The next may find it in that as reasons for the beauty of a song, in the harmony that shows forth in the expression of the soul within; whether in instruments or the soul raised in praise to the Giver of light.

The next may find it in the expressions of the duty that may be the lot of one that, without thought of self, shows forth in the acts of life that first thought of the duty from a material standpoint, yet the *love* made manifest from wholly showing forth His life, His love, till He come again!

The next may find it in the manner of speech under the

-181-

varied circumstances that arise in the experience of all, through that association which comes in the daily walks of life, and in the encouragement that may be given through the kind word spoken; the giving of the cup of water to anyone seeking, to those that thirst. This may show to such an one the love that is manifest in "God is love."

The next may find it in whatever the hands find to do, that done well, in all phases of one's experience, that lends self in the daily walks of life, doing the best with that which presents itself, in the glorying of the expressions, "As ye do it unto the least of these, my little ones, ye do it unto me."

The next will find it in the glory that comes in the satisfaction of a contented heart, in knowing that each day has brought an opportunity that has been taken advantage of by self in showing the kindness here, going out of the way in self's own life to make the lot of a neighbor more joyous, brighter, in the activities of the daily life.

The next may find it in looking forward to those days that may come, for the filling of those places that may be made or given in the lives spent in the service of Him who may call that thy face be that which may bring the knowledge of thine life, thine heart, spent in His service day by day.

Ready for questions.

Q-1. Please give a definition on at-one-ment.

A-1. At-onement may be given even as atonement. At-one-ment, then, is making self's will one with the Creative Forces that may become the impelling influence in thought, in mind, that is the builder to every act of a physical, mental or material body.

Then, in making at-onement, the will of an entity, an individual, is made one with the Creative Influences in the experience.

Q-2. [Please give an explanation] on "the blood of Jesus Christ cleanses from all sin."

A-2. As given, without the shedding of blood there was no remission of sin. As given in the beginning of man's concept of making atonement for the wrongs done self in relationship to the Creative Forces.

For, the error that man makes is the more oft against himself than making for the breaking of law as related to divine influence in the experience. For, love is law—law is love, in its essence. And with the breaking of the law is the making of the necessity for atonement and forgiveness, in that which may take away error to or what has been brought in the experience of the individual.

Hence the shedding of the blood in the *man* Jesus made for the atoning for *all* men, through making Himself in at-onement with the law and with love. For, through *love* was brought the desire to make self and His brother in at-onement. Hence in the atoning or shedding of the blood comes the redemption to man, through that which may make for *his*—man's—at-onement with Him.

Q-3. *Is there any advice on the paper, "Present World Conditions," which we have sent to Dallas, Texas?*

A-3. This should be re-sent to that of Holland's, in Dallas, Texas.

Q-4. *Please give an individual message on love for each member of the group, calling the name of each as the message is given.*

A-4. To each has been given that which it may apply in the individual personality and individuality of its experience.

Q-5. *Were the messages for each to choose?*

A-5. Each knows self better than you may tell 'em!

Q-6. *There were two more present than messages were given.*

A-6. They didn't ask!

Q-7. *Any message for the group as a whole?*

A-7. Seek and ye shall find; knock and it shall be opened unto you.

Study in the lessons that He gave, as He presented Himself in the expectant way in the entry before the crowning of the glory that He had before the world was, that there is in each experience that even as He gave. If the life is so lived that it makes manifest His love, the very rocks and stones will cry out in praise should man keep his mouth.

Yet these lessons will bring in the experience of all that which is sought, in showing forth the love as He gave—even in that, "Though one may possess all things and have not love, his life is nothing."

We are through.

This psychic reading was given by Edgar Cayce at the Edmonds' home on Pennsylvania Avenue, Norfolk, Va., on May 28, 1933, at 4:25 P.M., in accordance with a request made by those present: Edgar Cayce; Gertrude Cayce, conductor; Gladys Davis, steno; C. A. Barrett, Minnie Barrett, Hugh Lynn Cayce, Mildred Davis, Edith Edmonds, Florence Edmonds, Ruth LeNoir, Frances Y. Morrow, and Esther Wynne.

⇾ 262-46 ↰

Mrs. Cayce: You will have before you the Norfolk Study Group #1, members of which are present in this room; also their work on the lesson Love. *We present a copy of the preparation so far, a copy of which I hold in my hand, and seek guidance in completing this lesson. You will answer the questions that may be asked.*

Mr. Cayce: Yes, we have the group as gathered here, as a group and as individuals; also their work and that presented on the lesson *Love*. Much of that is good.

Rather than presenting so many illustrations of that which may be termed as applied by seeing in others, or things, the expressions or manifestations, present more of that which may come from within.

Give as this in the experience, that each may find within self the truth, the love, the life. Life is, in all its manifestations in every animate force, creative force in action; and is the love of expression — or expressing that life; truth becoming a result of life's love expressed. For, these are but names — unless experienced in the consciousness of each soul.

Then, commune the more often in the inner shrine, in the holy of holies. Meet the presence of the Father there; *know* the love of the Christ in action; experience and see truth and the Holy Spirit in the results that come from such consecration of the ideals of self.

For, each may have the experience of speaking with Him through such a consecration; for His promises are true, "I will not leave thee comfortless, but will come and abide with thee."

In such experiences in self, then, may there be added to the lesson on love that which will awaken in the hearts, the souls, the minds of others that desire to know *His* ways better.

Each has been chosen as a channel, and each in its own way

—and not alone of self, but manifesting life through love will
bring the Spirit's reaction in the daily experiences of every soul.
For, they are one—*all* believe, all have heard. Then, let them
that have eyes see, and ears hear, what the Spirit saith unto
them in such meditation in the *inner* self.

For, from the abundance of the heart the mouth speaketh;
and the love of the Father through the Son constraineth all,
if each will be less selfish, less self-centered, more desirous of
showing forth *His* love, His abundant mercy, His peace, His
harmony, that comes from being quiet in the Lord, being joyous
in service, being happy in whatsoever state ye find self; knowing that he whom the Lord loveth, him doth He call into service,
if each soul will but seek to know *His* way rather than "my way
or thy way." Let thy yeas be yea in the Lord. Let thine understanding take hold on the things of the spirit, for they are alone
eternal.

For, the children of light are called—even now—into service, that His day may be hastened, lest many faint.

Ready for questions.

*Q-1. Please give a definition for, "God so loved the world as
to give his only begotten son."*

A-1. A beautiful lesson has just been given, and definition.
This may suit those seeking this the better.

God, the Father, the first cause, seeking—in the manifestations of self—brought the world, as we (as individuals) observe
it about us, into being—*through* love; giving to man, His creation, His creatures, that ability to become one with Him. That
Son *we* have called the Son of man, the Christ Spirit, the love
made manifest in bringing the creature into material being in
a plane we have called earth. That Son was shown, then, the
way, through the love of the Father, and He made manifest that
love in giving His earthly, material life for a cause, an ensample, a mediation, a contact with the Father, a mediator for man.
Hence in love, through love, God *is* love, in the Christ Consciousness, the Christ Spirit; the Son of man made same manifest in all the experiences through the earth. Hence, as given
by the beloved disciple, "God so loved the world as to give His
only begotten son," that we, *through* Him, might have life—
God—more abundant. He, though He were the Son, learned

obedience through the things which He suffered. He that climbs up any other way than accepting those things that are to be met day by day, even as He, seeks through some other channel. The servant may never be greater than the master. He has given that we may be equal and one with Him, yet through Him, His manifestations, in Him, we live in the earth, we move and have our being.

Q-2. What is meant by the children of light, as just given?

A-2. They that choose to be guided by His will and do not, through themselves, attempt to manifest self rather than the will of the Father.

In the beginning was the word, and the word was God. He said, let there be *light*—and there was light. Like begets like. It *is* both cause and effect, and they that choose some other way become the children of darkness; and they are these: Envying, strife, hate; and the children of these are sedition, rebellion, and the like.

The children of light first love, for "Though I may have the gift of prophecy, though I may speak in unknown tongues, though I give my body to be burned and have not the spirit of the Son of man, the Christ Consciousness, the Christ Spirit, I am nothing." For, the children of light *know* Him; He calleth each by name.

Q-3. [404 and 462]: Please give us a message in regard to our experiences.

A-3. Be ye patient in well-doing. Count not the time long, for in so doing ye give the forces of doubt a place in thine own experience; and he that doubteth, or looketh back, is worse than an infidel. For, unto thee has come much, in joy, much in peace; and the little discouragements that make for faltering, if the heart will be kept singing, will make for the brighter joys, the greater appreciations, and the glories of the Son may be made the brighter in thy experience. For, live each day as if ye were to meet Him the next; in that expectancy, in that glory, and let not those things that would hinder have a place in thy consciousness. Thus do *His* children, His brethren, manifest that faith that removes mountains.

Q-4. [69]: When may I expect the promise given me to be fulfilled?

A-4. In waiting, in being overanxious, oft does one delay the appearing. Open rather thine self, and know that He will speak with thee. "Be not afraid, it is I." Then, when self is open, there will come—not one, but many—such experiences.

Q-5. *How may I open self more than I am doing?*

A-5. By entering more into the holy of holies, into the inner self.

Q-6. [*295*]: *May I have a message on the lesson?*

A-6. In self may there be manifested that love, even as He showed in thee, in the experiences in the ministering with and for Him; and the promises that were made thee *are* true, if self will be kept in that way in which that spirit of love, of faith, of hope, of charity, may be kept in His way. "If ye love me, keep my commandments" is ever the call of Him.

Q-7. [*993*]: *Why do records entities are making come constantly to me, and a desire to know more about them?*

A-7. As has been given thee, there were those experiences in which those that consecrated and set themselves as individual souls to accomplish definite conditions in the experiences and the affairs of the sons of men, were the records kept by self. Then, this experience of seeing, feeling—visioning, even, at times—the records made by entities, by groups, is just a portion of self's development towards those marks of higher calling as may be set only in Him. For, through the glorying in Him, and not in self, do we become conscious of that He would accomplish *through* us. So keep, even as was said of her of old, "She pondered these and kept them in her heart," knowing that there would be revealed—even as they may be put to service for others—that as each soul may need for the stimulation of *its* soul in a broader, better service in His name. For, there be no other name given under heaven whereby men may be saved.

Q-8. *Please explain what was meant in the life reading given* [*329*] *that he would be offered work on the 15th of May.*

A-8. The way was opened; and ye may assist him in understanding what is to be done in the material and mental self, for the carrying on is to only give the understanding in the relationships to time, space, conditions, relations, and individuals.

Q-9. *Any message for the group as a whole at this time?*

A-9. Take that as has been given, that ye—each soul—enter

into the quietness of self and seek to know His bidding with thee at this time. For, as it has been given, there is a cause—a purpose—for which the group was called, and enjoined, that each study to show self approved unto Him, avoiding the appearances of evil, *rightly* dividing the words of truth, life, light, and love; and by thy conversations, by thy deeds day by day, make manifest that love He has given, He has shown, in the earth.

We are through.

≫ 262-47 ≪ This psychic reading was given by Edgar Cayce at his home on Arctic Crescent, Virginia Beach, Va., on June 11, 1933, at 4:35 P.M., in accordance with a request made by those present: Edgar Cayce; Gertrude Cayce, conductor; Gladys Davis, steno; C. A. Barrett, Minnie Barrett, Hugh Lynn Cayce, L. B. Cayce, Mildred Davis, Edith Edmonds, Florence Edmonds, Helen Ellington, Ruth LeNoir, Frances Y. Morrow, Helen Storey, and Esther Wynne.

Mrs. Cayce: You will have before you the Norfolk Study Group #1, members of which are present in this room, and their work on the lesson Love. *You will give to each member of the group, as I call the names, a personal message which will aid in their own experience. You will then answer the general questions which I will ask.*

Mr. Cayce: Yes, we have the group as gathered here, as a group and as individuals; and their work on the lesson *Love.*

In the preparation, as we have given, each must so examine self that there be that in the heart, the soul of each, that each would present as a manifestation of that each would have Him present in the relationships with self.

For, as each seeks in its own way, there is given that which will enable each to gain a better concept of the Christ Consciousness in activity.

Ready for questions.

Q-1. [379]:

A-1. In thine own experience comes the answer to that which shows forth the love which is manifested in those that seek to know His way. Be not weary in well-doing.

Q-2. [295]:

A-2. Seek to show forth that which has been given, in that there may be presented through the activities of self that glory in Him. For, as much may be forgiven as there is love shown. Keep that as He gave, that all present themselves in that way which keepeth in the light.

Q-3. [585]:

A-3. In the presenting of that which is found in self's own experience, study to show self approved unto Him. For, as given, he that seeketh to know He will in no wise cast out. For, love exalteth. Love manifested in the daily life, then, gives more and more those expressions of His grace in a material world.

Q-4. [413]:

A-4. In showing forth that which is manifest in thine experience, let the love that was manifested in forgiveness be in thee, that there be no envy, no strife, no knowledge of other than good works through the activities of self. For, in glorying in the knowledge of the Father comes more and more the manifestations of the spirit of the Christ. "Inasmuch as ye do it unto the least of these, my little ones, ye do it unto me."

Q-5. [307]:

A-5. In the power of the name is there glory and love shown to all those who seek to know, to do His biddings. For, unto him that is faithful in the few things is there given the ruling of many. Then, keep the way that thou hast set before thee; knowing that His presence abides ever.

Q-6. [303]:

A-6. In the presenting of self's love for the ways He would have thee go, look not back upon that which would make afraid; for they who turn their faces to the light show forth in their speech, their actions, their lives, that love even as He has given, "If ye love me keep my commandments." For, they are not grievous to those that seek to know His way.

Q-7. [294]:

A-7. Study to show self approved unto Him, rightly dividing the words of truth, avoiding the appearance of evil, that thy love, thy goodness, be not evilspoken of. Glory in the Lord, in His promises, day by day, that in thee, through thee, may come many that call Him blessed.

Q-8. [538]:

A-8. "Let not thine heart be troubled; ye believe in God, believe also in me," knowing that unto every good work is the love of the Father shown through the Son to those that would bless His holy name. Not in envy, not in strife; rather in the little kindnesses, even in the ways that present themselves in every manner, whether in the home, in the street, in the associations one with another. Keep thy paths clear.

Q-9. [560]:

A-9. In thine presentation of the love as manifested through those that would know His way, seek from the inner self to know that He would have thee do; for in the promises in Him does the love of the Father made manifest through Him become expressive in the acts of the mind, the body, the ways. For, His ways are not past finding out; neither are they hard to those that would show forth His love till He come again. For, He will not tarry, if those that love Him will but manifest His love in the earth.

Q-10. [993]:

A-10. That that is set before thee in measuring the ways that He would have thee go; for, as the love of the Father was shown in the life of the Master, so may His love in thee be shown in the hearts, the minds, the souls, of those whom ye contact day by day. For, unto him to whom much is given much is required; yet who would turn back that they may not press on to the ways that His love passes all understanding and is shown forth in the life day by day?

Q-11. [69]:

A-11. As thy ways are His ways, glory in the love that is shed on thee. Pass it on. For, in giving does one receive that glory that He gave; so did the glory of the Father shine on the earth. Even though there be trials, disappointments, His love enables all to know, to understand, to comprehend, that He would have each do day by day, here a little, there a little.

Q-12. [69's husband]:

A-12. In thy daily walks let His light so shine in thine own self that those ye contact may know that the love of the Father is being shown in thy daily conversation, thy daily activities. For, as He gave, he that would show forth the love of the Father will keep His ways day by day. For, glorying in self is as the activities of self-exaltation, but glorying in the Father, in the Son, is showing forth that He bids thee do day by day. What, then, are His biddings? "Love the Lord thy God with all thine heart, thine soul, and thy neighbor as thyself!"

Q-13. [341]:

A-13. In showing forth the love that He manifested, study thy ways, thy going in, thy coming out. Know that, he that seeks shall find; to him that knocketh will He open the door, and—as He has given—"My ways are not thy ways" unless ye keep the way of the Lord. In thy glorying, let self be as naught; that His glory may be manifested in thy acts day by day.

Q-14. [*288*]:

A-14. In showing forth His love, know "As ye would that men should do to you, do ye even so to them." For, as self manifests to thy brother, so is the Father glorified in thee. The manifestation in any act is the reflection of that purpose in the heart. Keep the heart clean. Keep the purposes in Him; for He is the way and the light.

Q-15. [*404*]:

A-15. Glory in the Lord, that the ways that He would guide are the ways in which the soul may know Him better. In the love of the Father He gave the Son. In the love that self would show, in keeping His ways day by day. For, His ways are not grievous; nor are they hid from any that would seek to know His face.

Q-16. [*462*]:

A-16. In manifesting that love as He has shown, just be kind one to another; not in vainglorying, not in hardness of heart. Rather in the little things that bespeak of a mind that oft speaks with Him. Not in that which would make for vainglory, but rather that takes hold on the things that are oft despised of men yet shows forth the love of the Father for His children. For, as the father pitieth the children, so does the heavenly Father have mercy on those that would glory in Him.

COME YE, MY CHILDREN, IN THAT YE HAVE ALL BEEN CALLED UNTO THAT WAY WHICH WOULD SHOW FORTH TO THY NEIGHBOR, THY BRETHREN, THAT THE FATHER LOVETH HIS CHILDREN. WHO *ARE* HIS CHILDREN? THEY THAT KEEP HIS COMMANDMENTS DAY BY DAY. FOR, UNTO HIM THAT IS FAITHFUL AND TRUE IS GIVEN THE CROWN OF LIFE. THE HARVEST IS RIPE, THE LABORERS ARE FEW. BE NOT WEARY BECAUSE THERE HAS BEEN THAT WHICH HAS *SEEMED* TO TROUBLE THEE, FOR THE WAYS ARE BEING OPENED TO THOSE THAT SHOW THEMSELVES FAITHFUL AND TRUE. FAINT NOT, FOR THE DAY OF THE LORD IS NEAR AT HAND. [See 262-49, A-3.]

We are through.

This psychic reading was given by Edgar Cayce at his home on Arctic Crescent, Virginia Beach, Va., on June 25, 1933, at 4:10 P.M., in accordance with a request made by those present: Edgar Cayce; Gertrude Cayce, conductor; Gladys Davis, steno; C. A. Barrett, Minnie Barrett, Annie Cayce, Hugh Lynn Cayce, L. B. Cayce, Mildred Davis, Edith Edmonds, Florence Edmonds, Walter Krulewitch, Douglas McPherson, Edgar McPherson, Frances Y. Morrow, Esther Wynne, and another visitor.

⊁ 262-48 ⊀

Mrs. Cayce: You will have before you the Norfolk Study Group #1, members of which are present in this room, and their work on the lesson Love. *You will give that which they need at this time to enable them to complete their work on this lesson. You will answer the questions which will be asked.*

Mr. Cayce: Yes, we have the group as gathered here, as a group, as individuals, and their work on the lessons, their work on the lesson *Love.*

There needs be only that compiled that is contributed by the members, in such a way and manner that may be made practical in the experience of those who study and apply same in their experience.

In the completing of same, there should be those contributions from all who will of themselves contribute to same.

In considering, then, that there has come the completion of those lessons that may form the basis of study by those who are interested in seeking truth, that may be applicable in their experience, now those that are called realize that in the greater part that compiled is as but knowledge *unless* applied in their daily lives.

Then, begin with that study, that application of that which has been gathered here, and with same begin with the compilation of that which may be the parallel with the truth as given.

Hence, the next lesson, the next application of self in the group, would be upon *Opportunity;* the next on *Day and Night;* the next on *God, the Father, and His Manifestations in the Earth.*

Then, these—as will be seen—may become more of living truths, as each of the group applies self in its daily experience to that which has been set.

Ready for questions.

Q-1. Is there any advice to the compilers in regard to the paper, "Present World Conditions," which has been returned from Dallas, Texas?

A-1. We would edit same to the present conditions and then present to *Collier's.*

Q-2. Should that editing be done on the basis of another reading?

A-2. This has been asked for by compilers. Let the compilers seek that as may be necessary to meet conditions.

Q-3. What was the significance of the group being called to the home of Miss [993] *on the morning of June 15th by Mrs.* [585]?

A-3. The activity of influences in the experience of the one calling same.

Q-4. Was it a good influence?

A-4. "By their fruits ye shall know them."

Q-5. Any message to the group as a whole at this time? [*Long pause.*] *If there is no message, that is all the questions.* [Gave suggestion to wake up.] [See 254-67, A-2, for explanation as to why no answer was given to this question.]

This psychic reading was given by Edgar Cayce at his home on Arctic Crescent, Virginia Beach, Va., on July 9, 1933, at 4:10 P.M., in accordance with a request made by those present: Edgar Cayce; Gertrude Cayce, conductor; Gladys Davis, steno; C. A. Barrett, Minnie Barrett, L. B. Cayce, Mildred Davis, Helen Ellington, Ruth Le-Noir, Frances Y. Morrow, Helen Storey, and Esther Wynne.

⊰ 262-49 ⊱

Mrs. Cayce: You will have before you the Norfolk Study Group #1, members of which are present in this room; also a copy of the lesson on Love, *which I hold in my hand. You will go over this lesson as I call each paragraph, making such suggestions for change or additions that would more completely express the truth we are trying to convey. You will answer the questions which will be asked.*

Mr. Cayce: Yes, we have the group as gathered here, as a group, as individuals, and their work on the lesson *Love.*

Ready for questions.

[Mr. Cayce answered "Very good" to each paragraph, 1 through 40.]

Q-1. Please give the affirmation for our next lesson, Opportunity.

A-1. IN SEEKING TO MAGNIFY THY NAME, THY GLORY, THROUGH THAT THOU DOST MAKE MANIFEST IN ME, O LORD, BE THOU THE GUIDE, AND—DAY BY DAY, AS THE OPPORTUNITY IS GIVEN—LET MY HANDS, MY MIND, MY BODY, DO THAT THOU WOULDST HAVE ME DO AS THINE OWN IN THE EARTH; FOR, AS I MANIFEST, MAY THY GLORY BECOME KNOWN TO THOSE THROUGH THE LOVE, THE PROMISES THOU HAST MADE IN THY SON.

Q-2. What should be the basis and fundamental thoughts to be presented on this lesson?

A-2. First, as opportunity in making, in the life, that of filling each of the thoughts that are presented in the lessons that have been given, each in their respective place, time, and in a manner befitting those that call on His name.

Q-3. What is meant by "the day of the Lord is near at hand"? [See 262-47, A-16.]

A-3. That as has been promised through the prophets and the sages of old, the time—and half time—has been and is being

-195-

fulfilled in this day and generation, and that soon there will again appear in the earth that one through whom many will be called to meet those that are preparing the way for His day in the earth. The Lord, then, will come, "even as ye have seen him go."

Q-4. How soon?

A-4. When those that are His have made the way clear, *passable,* for Him to come.

Q-5. [303]: What is the significance of my dream about two weeks ago, in which Mr. Cayce was watching clouds come together, expecting something unusual—and when they met, crystals came down like fireworks?

A-5. This is a vision that will come to the body again, and with same will come an awakening as to the import of the vision.

Q-6. Will you give us some outline upon which we may base the lesson?

A-6. First that as the material definition. Then the introduction in each of the lessons that have been presented, and how that the individuals in preparing themselves step by step through that presented in the lessons, and applying same in the life, may gain the knowledge and understanding in love.

Q-7. Is there a message for the group as a whole at this time?

A-7. So let thine own light shine in such a manner as may hasten the day of the Lord.

We are through.

This psychic reading was given by Edgar Cayce at his home on Arctic Crescent, Virginia Beach, Va., on July 30, 1933, at 4:10 P.M., in accordance with a request made by those present: Edgar Cayce; Gertrude Cayce, conductor; Gladys Davis, steno; L. B. Cayce, Mildred Davis, Edith Edmonds, Florence Edmonds, Frances Y. Morrow, Esther Wynne, and the Misses Barclay and Wisman, visitors.

⇾ 262-50 ⇽

Mrs. Cayce: You will have before you the Norfolk Study Group #1, members of which are present in this room, and their work on the lesson Opportunity. *You will answer the questions which will be asked by individuals and the group as a whole.*

Mr. Cayce: Yes, we have the group as a group, and individuals as members of the group; and their work in preparation of the lesson *Opportunity.*

In making the outline, and in the definitions that have been presented, rather should there also be given that, while opportunity is in the sense as presented, yet it must ever be considered as the material manifestation of a thought or spiritual ideal; as it is sometimes quoted, that "Man's extremity is God's opportunity."

In man's advent into a material world is an opportunity for the material manifestation of that which is builded by the individual soul through its activity in the various spheres of consciousness, and in the material becomes the opportunity of parallelling, correlating, cooperating, making for that which brings into existence the effects of using that which is presented in opportunity for the developing of the soul.

Hence opportunity, primarily, is a material manifestation of spiritual actions in conscious forces of the material plane.

Ready for questions.

Q-1. Any other corrections or suggestions that may be necessary in the outlines for the lesson, a copy of which I hold in my hand?

A-1. Do these, and then we can progress.

Q-2. [585]: What is my definite part or work in this group?

A-2. First, as given, finding self and self's relationship to the creative forces.

Each and every soul must come to the consciousness of being

-197-

a service in the activities of that it, the soul, worships in the infinite sphere or spiritual force.

If the forces or influences are in the creative energies that arise through the love manifested through the Son in the activity in the earth, then it is shown thee day by day that thou shouldst do.

Do with a might what the hands find to do, in the service of the Lord; not in self, not in gratification of self, not in magnifying any of the material influences or forces.

The fruits of the spirit are rather as we have shown: Brotherly love, kindness, mercy, patience, love, long-suffering. Against such there is no law, for they *are* the law of love.

Q-3. As I call each individual to you, you will give the name by which He will call each; also telling each that special opportunity which each is called upon individually to take advantage of at this time.

A-3. Rather than as individuals seeking the name, when the individual is called each shall be called by name, even as He called Mary, Martha and Peter.

In seeking to know that opportunity that is given each in the present, it is one thing to live that there may be presented to another that which will open another's opportunity; and it is for *self* to recognize and use the opportunity in self's own development.

But know, as each has been called, that there will come the *greater* opportunity in self's development, self's understanding, in preparing that which is for the enlightenment of thine neighbor. For, as He gave, let him know that has saved a soul from perdition that he has covered a multitude of sins in self.

Study then, *each,* to show self approved unto God, *rightly* dividing the words of truth. Let the meditations of the heart, let those activities of the body, bespeak that thou wouldst offer in self as an opportunity or channel for another to seek, to know, thy God. For, if thine God, thine service, doeth not thee good day by day, how wilt thou present Him to another? For, the life of self bespeaks the thoughts of the heart; and each shall so live that He, the Christ, becomes the opportunity for all who meet thee—whether at the table, in sleep, or walking in the street. For, where the treasure is the heart is also.

We are through for the present.

This psychic reading was given by Edgar Cayce at his home on Arctic Crescent, Virginia Beach, Va., on August 20, 1933, at 4:15 P.M., in accordance with a request made by those present: Edgar Cayce; Gertrude Cayce, conductor; Gladys Davis, steno; C. A. Barrett, Minnie Barrett, Dr. S. A. Bisey, Hugh Lynn Cayce, L. B. Cayce, Mildred Mary Davis, Edith Mildred Edmonds, Florence Edmonds, Mr. and Mrs. H. B. Harrell, Jr., Mrs. H. B. Harrell, Sr., and Esther Wynne.

⋊ 262-51 ⋉

Mrs. Cayce: You will have before you Norfolk Study Group #1, members of which are present in this room; also their work on the lesson Opportunity. *We present a copy of the preparation so far, a copy of which I hold in my hand, and seek guidance in completing this lesson. You will answer the questions that may be asked.*

Mr. Cayce: Yes, we have the group as gathered here, as a group, as individuals, and their work thus far on the lesson *Opportunity.*

In that which has been thus far presented, each individual in its own way is finding the consciousness of opportunity. And the lessons that may be presented from such individuals may be made worthwhile in the experience of those who seek to understand opportunity from the view that has been presented, in that opportunity itself—of the spiritual activity in the experience of individuals—comes to materialization in what the individual does respecting that the individual holds as the spiritual activity of such an experience as related to *its* ideal.

Hence all should study more and more the experiences, in a manner analyzing the experience that each—as an individual cooperating with the group—may present for others that may be helpful in *their* experience or presenting and acting upon opportunity.

For, as given, each may believe—but the activity of each soul should be, as respecting the faith within self, to show forth in its actions that it *professes* to believe.

For, from the abundance of the heart the mouth speaketh truth. While, that which may be found as a tinkling cymbal may come only from that held as a tenet or as an ideal. But that which becomes ideal is the heart's seeking for the knowing and doing the will of Him that giveth light, life and understanding in all the experiences of those that seek to know His way.

Ready for questions.

Q-1. [69]: As was given in the reading by John [5749-4], how may I make my will more in accord with His will, that He will speak with me?

A-1. As He has given to those to whom He spoke, to those to whom He will speak: "If ye love me, keep my commandments. If ye love me, feed my sheep. If ye love me, feed my lambs."

So, in the experience of all that seek to know His biddings, do with the might that the opportunity presents to thee in each day's activity.

Be not impatient, but know that He will not tarry—to those who love Him and keep His biddings.

Q-2. Where am I falling short?

A-2. Who am I that would speak against any fault in any soul? Seek rather to find the fault from thine own inner self, and He will guide thee aright. So spake He to those that asked of Him, and so speaks He to those that seek. For, "My Spirit beareth witness with thy spirit" to all that love His coming.

Q-3. [288]: Why do I have such a feeling of loneliness and uselessness, especially with this lesson?

A-3. As the activities of self are expressed in that done unto others, so is the abundance of love, companionship, expressions of His closeness, found in thine experience.

For, as given, *holy* is he or she that has the love of the Father expressed in the acts of thine hands, and thine mind, day by day. For, with the love of the Father to those about thee manifest in the life day by day, so is the fullness of the life filled with the joy of the Lord.

Q-4. [341]: Is there any symbolical difference, or practical difference, between "feed my sheep" and "feed my lambs" as just given? Please explain.

A-4. Symbolical; in that one represents that of the fold and the other that seeking the fold. The sheep represent those that know of, and know, the way. The lambs represent those that seek, that would know, that would find the way, that would come if shown the tenderness expressed in, "The good shepherd feedeth the sheep; he tendeth the lambs."

Q-5. Is there a message for [341] on opportunity?

A-5. Keep in the way that may be shown to those who seek to know His biddings, and to know the spiritual and material advantages in opportunity that has been presented to those — as self.

Q-6. [307]: Please give me a message that may encourage me at this time.

A-6. Faint not in well-doing; for there is being opened the door for the greater opportunities in the lives of those the body contacts through its labors, in the activities of the study of the truths presented; there is being opened glory in the spirit of truth, that convinceth and convicteth man unto the acknowledging of his relationship to the Father.

Q-7. Is there a message for [295] on opportunity?

A-7. Study to show thyself approved in meeting all those opportunities that come in the activities of the study of the lessons and the truths that have been and are being presented in the meditations day by day. Be not faint-hearted in those things, conditions, experiences that would appear to hinder; either in judgments or in activities; for whom the Lord loveth and calleth into service, him He testeth — even to the cleansing as by fire.

Q-8. [993]: Why am I called to read Revelation and the prophets during this lesson?

A-8. For, as has been presented, opportunity is of the spirit presented or manifesting itself in the activity of individual souls. As is shown in the prophets, *these* were also called to present truths that came into the experience of those to whom the prophets spoke.

So, in Revelation is there seen, in the activities of those that name the name, those that are called, those that would harken — hence, as in water the face answereth to the face, so in thine consciousness does the spirit of truth in the prophets, in the Revelation, answer to the consciousness in self. Know that those who spoke there spoke even as is spoken to thee in thine experiences, in meeting the spirits of truth in revealed activity in thy meditation.

Q-9. [560]: May I have a message on opportunity?

A-9. As there is being shown thee in the material way, in the thinking or heart way, in the spiritual experiences, the opportunities that are both lost and grasped by many, so—as the parallels are drawn for thee—know that thou art being lifted up, being drawn more and more into the abilities in the *material* ways to strengthen those that falter here and there.

To all may it be as this, upon the opportunities that have been given, from the purposes in the beginning of the group, that:

The time draweth near, the time is at hand, when there is more and more seeking for the light and understanding.

Let each, then, in your own way, in that which seemeth good in the light of that which has been presented thee, from day to day, so manifest that love that has been showered on thee —in thy studies, in the preparation for truths to thy fellow man, so live thine own life that it may be an ensample unto those that study.

For, as ye call on Him, the Lord guide Thou Thy servants in the ways they should go.

"Let my going in, mine coming out, be wholly within the ways Thou would have me go. Direct my steps, direct my mind. Let Thy will be done in me. For, as the heart panteth after Thy own will, may my spirit bear witness in the things my body does day by day, that—the Lord is in His holy temple, and the rod has not passed from those that call on His name; for the *glory* of the Father to the sons of men may be expressed in those that would guide, guard and keep the holy ways."

We are through for the present.

≈ 262-52 ⱪ *This psychic reading was given by Edgar Cayce at his home on Arctic Crescent, Virginia Beach, Va., on August 25, 1933, at 11:50 A.M., in accordance with a request made by Esther Wynne and Hugh Lynn Cayce. Present were: Edgar Cayce; Gertrude Cayce, conductor; Gladys Davis, steno; Hugh Lynn Cayce, L. B. Cayce, Mildred Davis, and Esther Wynne.*

Mrs. Cayce: You will give at this time a discourse which will sum up and correlate the data already given through this channel on the fundamental truths regarding the oneness of all force, and will furnish us with some basic, logical, systematically arranged statements which can be given out as fundamental truths to students of this work. You will answer the questions on this subject which will be asked.

Mr. Cayce: Yes. In giving that which may be given out as basic truth, and correlating the statements that have been made from time to time, it would have been better to have gathered from that given the basis for expansion through these channels. Yet, we may give that which may be the basis or the foundation of truth that may be gathered here and there.

As to the correlation and the setting out of paragraphs, at *least* you should do something!

The basis, then: "Know, O Israel, (Know, O People) the Lord thy God is one!"

From this premise we would reason that: In the manifestation of all power, force, motion, vibration, that which impels, that which detracts, is in its essence of *one* force, one source, in its elemental form. As to what has been done or accomplished by or through the activity of entities that have been delegated powers in activity is another story.

As to the one source or one force, then, are the questions presented in the present.

God, the first cause, the first principle, the first movement, *is!* That's the beginning! That is, that was, that ever shall be!

The following of those sources, forces, activities that are in accord with the creative force or first cause—its laws, then— is to be one with the source, or equal with yet separate from that first cause. When, then, may man—as an element, an

-203-

entity, a separate being manifested in material life and form
—be aware or conscious of the moving of that first cause within
his own environ? Or, taking man in his present position or
consciousness, how or when may he be aware of that first cause
moving within his realm of consciousness?

In the beginning there was the force of attraction and the
force that repelled. Hence, in man's consciousness he becomes
aware of what is known as the atomic or cellular form of movement about which there becomes nebulous activity. And this
is the lowest form (as man would designate) that's in active
forces in his experience. Yet this very movement that separates
the forces in atomic influence *is* the first cause, or the manifestation of that called God in the material plane!

Then, as it gathers of positive-negative forces in their activity, whether it be of one element or realm or another, it
becomes magnified in its force or sources through the universe.
Hence we find worlds, suns, stars, nebulae, and whole solar
systems, *moving* from a first cause.

When this first cause comes into man's experience in the
present realm he becomes confused, in that he appears to have
an influence upon this force or power in directing same. Certainly! Much, though, in the manner as the reflection of light
in a mirror. For, it is only reflected force that man may have
upon those forces that show themselves in the activities, in
whatever realm into which man may be delving in the moment
—whether of the nebulae, the gaseous, or the elements that
have gathered together in their activity throughout that man
has chosen to call time or space. And becomes, in its very movement, of that of which the first cause takes thought *in* a finite
existence or consciousness.

Hence, as man applies himself—or uses that of which he
becomes conscious in the realm of activity, and gives or places
the credit (as would be called) in man's consciousness in the
correct sphere or realm he becomes conscious of that union of
force with the infinite with the finite force.

Hence, in the fruits of that—as is given oft, as the fruits of
the spirit—does man become aware of the infinite penetrating,
or inter-penetrating the activities of all forces of matter, or that
which is a manifestation of the realm of the infinite into the
finite—and the finite becomes conscious of same.

As to the application of these as truths, then:

It may be said that, as the man makes in self—through the ability given for man in his activity in a material plane—the will one with the laws of creative influence, we begin with: "Like begets like; as he sows, so shall he reap; as the man thinketh in the heart, so is he."

These are all but trite sayings to most of us, even the thinking man; but should the mind of an individual (the finite mind) turn within his own being for the law pertaining to these trite sayings, until the understanding arises, then there is the consciousness in the finite of the infinite moving upon and in the inner self.

So does life in all its force begin in the earth. The moving of the infinite upon the negative force of the finite in the material, or to become a manifested force.

Ready for questions.

Q-1. Explain how so-called good and evil forces are one.

A-1. This has just been explained. When there is delegated power to a body that has separated itself from the spirit (or coming from the unseen into the seen, or from the unconscious into the physical consciousness, or from God's other door—or opening from the infinite to the finite), then the activity is life; with the will of the source of that which has come into being. As to what it does with or about its associations of itself to the source of its activity, as to how far it may go afield, depends upon how high it has attained in its ability to throw off both negative and positive forces.

Hence, we say, "The higher he flies, the harder the fall." It's true!

Then, that which has been separated into the influence to become a body, whether celestial, terrestrial, or plain clay manifested into activity as man, becomes good or bad. The results to the body so acting are dependent and independent [interdependent?] (inter-between, see) upon what he does with the knowledge of—or that source of—activity.

Q-2. In relation to the oneness of all force, explain the popular concept of the Devil, seemingly substantiated in the Bible by many passages of Scripture.

A-2. In the beginning, celestial beings. We have first the Son, then the other sons or celestial beings that are given their force and power. Hence that force which rebelled in the unseen forces (or in spirit), that came into activity, was that influence which has been called Satan, the Devil, the Serpent; they are one. That of *rebellion!*

Hence, when man in any activity rebels against the influences of good he harkens to the influence of evil rather than the influence of good.

Hence, will is given to man as he comes into this manifested form that we see in material forces, for the choice. As given, "There is set before thee (man) good and evil."

Evil is rebellion. Good is the Son of life, of light, of truth; and the Son of light, of life, of truth, came into physical being to demonstrate and show and lead the way for man's ascent to the power of good over evil in a material world.

As there is, then, a personal savior, there is the personal devil.

We are through.

≫ 262-53 ≪

This psychic reading was given by Edgar Cayce at the Edmonds' home, Pennsylvania Avenue, Norfolk, Va., on September 3, 1933, at 4:30 P.M., in accordance with a request made by those present: Edgar Cayce; Gertrude Cayce, conductor; Gladys Davis, steno; C. A. Barrett, Minnie Barrett, Hugh Lynn Cayce, Mildred Mary Davis, Edith Mildred Edmonds, Florence Edmonds, Frances Y. Morrow, Helen Storey, and Esther Wynne.

Mrs. Cayce: You will have before you the Norfolk Study Group #1, members of which are present in this room, and their work on the lesson Opportunity, *a copy of which material I hold in my hand. You will give such suggestions as will aid them in filling out and completing this lesson. You will answer the questions that may be asked.*

Mr. Cayce: Yes, we have the group as a group; and the members of same as individuals.

That prepared is very good, in the greater portion. There needs be all compilations in order, each contributing its portion to same.

As to that presented itself, this is very good so far as the completed portions have gone, save in the third portion where there needs be some more enlightenment as to the references to experiences of individuals as they apply the thought in their experience.

Ready for questions.

Q-1. Are we as individuals submitting the type of material which will be the most helpful for those studying the lessons? Please tell us how we can improve our work on these lessons in any way.

A-1. As given respecting the manner in which each individual presents that received through its periods of meditation, and the experiences that have been applied in its own experience; not as theory, not as feeling or understanding only, but as the experience of the body itself as related to that obtained through the meditation on the lessons in the various periods. *This* should be presented, and—as we have given—each has been called to present that of self for the enabling of others to find, in their study, meditation and experience, that which will be helpful to those seeking. This is the manner in which the lessons should be prepared.

The responses that have come regarding the experiences of others, in their study of that presented, should make for evidence that that being presented *is* worthwhile in the experience of those to whom the lessons may be presented as a line—or an outline—for thought and study.

Let each, then, keep first and foremost its application to the various experiences; for presenting that obtained is not presenting self, but rather that self is made a channel through which there may be received that which will be helpful to those that seek through these channels for a better understanding.

In this manner, in this way, will there ever be presented that which *will* be helpful, so long as each individual presents that it has received of those experiences through the meditation on that presented.

If self is presented, this becomes weakening; but rather—as given—make self a channel. How? As ye would be a channel, as there is the willingness and the desire to be used by those forces or influences sought, there will be given that which will be of aid to others. For, has it not been given, "Ye that would speak in my name take no thought of what ye shall say, for in the selfsame hour it will be given thee"? This is often referred to in regard to those periods when the disciples were to speak or defend themselves before those in authority. *Who* is in authority in the earth as related to self? There is the continual war between "There is set before thee good and evil." That whom ye serve is the master, according to thine *own* activity. Then, speak and act in *His* name; He that is the Savior in the earth.

Q-2. Please give a message of help to [462].

A-2. In those periods when there are the doubts and the fears that arise, these are as the testing times in each soul's experience. He that endureth, he that looketh to the promises—and believes and acts in that manner, to him it is counted as righteousness.

Then, *know* in whom, in what, thou hast believed—and keep the faith.

Q-3. Please give a message of help to [404].

A-3. Trust and obey, for there's no other way to be happy in Him in whom thou claimest to be in accord with that He would have thee do. Know that His ways are not past finding out. Be not in the shadow of doubt or fear, but keep the heart singing; knowing that in His own good time and way He will bring the desires of thine heart to pass—that are in accord with His will —in thine experience.

Q-4. [993]: *Please explain my recent experiences of waking and being conscious of praying that "God have mercy on us all."*

A-4. As the consciousness of the position of the world and those about the body is made more and more in accord with His will, the experiences even as He had—as He wept over Jerusalem—become the experiences of His children. Read there, then, that which caused this feeling of the Master to give forth those expressions even as He did in the presence of His disciples. And there will come to self, through this meditation, through this concentrating in self, and consecration of self to His service, that understanding.

Then, to all, we would give this: Consecrate yourselves, your bodies, your minds, your abilities in *every* direction, to the opportunities to be of service to those ye meet and contact day by day.

For, as well as in meditating and prayer, make—through the promises that self may make in consecration of self—that position in the attunement of self that thy promises and His promises may be one; and fulfill all thou dost promise.

Know that He will keep those that keep His ways, and— "Seek and ye shall find."

For, those periods for the studies of that presented in *Day and Night* draw near!

We are through for the present.

≫ 262-54 ≪

This psychic reading was given by Edgar Cayce at the Edmonds' home on Pennsylvania Avenue, Norfolk, Va., on September 17, 1933, at 4:25 P.M., in accordance with a request made by those present: Edgar Cayce; Gertrude Cayce, conductor; Gladys Davis, steno; C. A. Barrett, Minnie Barrett, Hugh Lynn Cayce, Edith Edmonds, Florence Edmonds, Ruth LeNoir, Frances Y. Morrow, Helen Storey, and Esther Wynne.

Mrs. Cayce: You will have before you the work of the Norfolk Study Group #1, especially that phase of it represented by the lesson Opportunity, *a copy of which I hold in my hand. As I call the number of each paragraph you will make such suggestions or comments as will enable us to make this lesson of real value to those who may study it. You will then answer such other questions as may be asked regarding this group's activities.*

Mr. Cayce: Yes, we have the group as gathered here, as a group and as individuals; the work in preparation of the lesson *Opportunity,* and that in that prepared which may be helpful to those who study same.

As to the varied paragraphs that are presented here, we find these are very good in the manner of presentation.

In reference to that which has been suggested as to the experience, this should be changed even yet in the way of presenting same. While, that [paragraph 30] presented in the ideal and the effect of the activity in the mental experience of one so stating same is good, the manner, the wording in presenting of same would become confusing to many as to whether this is an influence from without or the raising of the self in the activities of the mental and spiritual forces from within. Hence this should be clarified.

Ready for questions.

Q-1. Is there any need of going over each paragraph by number for correction?

A-1. Only in this, as we find, would there be changes in the present draft, other than some little variation in the punctuation.

Q-2. Any special paragraph besides 30?

A-2. Only what has been given.

-210-

Q-3. Please give the meditation for the next lesson Day and Night.

A-3. In Thy mercies, O heavenly Father, wilt Thou be the guide in the study of the manifestations of Thy love, even as in "Day unto day uttereth speech and night unto night sheweth knowledge." So may the activities of my life, as a representative of Thy love, be a manifestation in the earth.

Then, in the study of the thoughts, of the ideas, and along the ideals that have been presented in the lessons that have gone before, and in presenting this lesson, this thought—that there may be grounded in the heart and soul of each that which may offer for every soul, ever, the answer within self for that it believes.

Knowest thou what thou believest? Dost thou present in thine own life day by day that thou professest to believe concerning the manifestation of God's activities in a material world?

As recorded in the beginning, "The evening and the morning were the first day." What transpired in the first day? What transpired in the first night? When began the morning stars to sing together? When gathered first the sons of God to produce, or to bring about, the manifestations that man calls day? Is the day significant of the life that is a span experience or existence in a sphere of activity when an entity, a soul, becomes conscious of that activity in or about self, or self's own associations during such an experience? Is night the rest from such an activity? Or, as manifested in the material world, is night only a change from one realm of a source of consciousness to another?

Such questions have been sought since the foundations of the world.

Or, does day and night present that experience sought in every soul that is given expression to as in days of yore, when it was said, "If a man die, shall he live again?" Live, or give expression, or manifest? From whence came man into the consciousness of day and night? What makes for the awareness, in the experience of each soul, of a change?

Are such questions merely answered in the heart of each, as "the sun goes up, the sun goes down, and there will be a big night tonight"?

These are questions. These are basic truths. What thinkest thou? What wilt *ye* do with presenting these and all phases of that through which man, and the soul of man, passes in his experience of a consciousness in a material world?

We are through for the present.

This psychic reading was given by Edgar Cayce at the Edmonds' home on Pennsylvania Avenue, Norfolk, Va., on October 1, 1933, at 4:10 P.M., in accordance with a request made by those present: Edgar Cayce; Gertrude Cayce, conductor; Gladys Davis, steno; C. A. Barrett, Minnie Barrett, Hugh Lynn Cayce, Mildred Mary Davis, Edith Edmonds, Florence Edmonds, Helen Ellington, Ruth LeNoir, Frances Y. Morrow, Helen Storey, and Esther Wynne.

⊀ 262-55 ⊁

Mrs. Cayce: You will have before you the Norfolk Study Group #1, members of which are present in this room, and their studies on Day and Night. *You will give at this time such guidance as will aid them in understanding this subject that it may be adequately presented for those who may study it. You will answer the questions which will be asked relating to it.*

Mr. Cayce: Yes, we have the group as gathered here, as a group, as individuals.

As to the study of that being considered by the group at this time, it is the time or period—as given—when there should be a self-analysis of that each holds not only as an individual ideal and as a group ideal, but as to what is the belief upon the varied subjects that may be now presented from time to time. And when this decision is reached, how does each react to that each professes to believe?

For, as presented, what one believes alone is not sufficient; but what one does about that one believes either makes for advancement or growth, or retardment. For, in acting in the material plane may one do in all good conscience that one may develop in the line of thought set in motion by activities.

The first questions or subjects presented begin with the Beginning, as recorded in the accepted text or word of faith in the accepted Christian world. Then, the subject is *Night and Day,* or *Day and Night.*

In or from the material standpoint, night and day in the material world are only relative. For, were one to view the earth from an outer sphere there would be only varied shades; or *relatively* there would be night and day, from the position of the earth in its journey about the source of light. And, as

-213-

given, these conditions that exist in the material plane are but shadows of the truths in the mental and spiritual plane.

Hence we find, as given, that first there was for matter, that gathered in a directed plane of activity called the earth, the separation of light and darkness.

Hence these, then, are figures of that from the spiritual plane termed in the mental world as the good and evil; or in the spiritual as facing the light and the dark, or facing the source of light—which, to the mind of those that seek to know His biddings, is the voice, the word, the life, the light, that comes in the hearts, minds, souls, of each to awaken them, as individuals, to their relationships with the source of light.

Again, in the figurative sense, we find that light and darkness, day and night, are represented by that termed as periods of growth and the periods of rest or recuperation, through the activities of other influences in those forces or sources of activity condensed in form to be called matter, no matter what plane this may be acting from or upon.

This would be the line of thought then, with each individual in the group answering to self that presented for consideration in this study.

Ready for questions.

Q-1. [585]: *Was it the Master's touch, the Master's voice, which I felt and heard one afternoon two winters ago?*

A-1. As has been given.

Q-2. [288]: *Is night the shadow of the original sin, or significant of man's seeking after knowledge which separated him from the light? And is that why children instinctively fear the dark?*

A-2. It is both! Now this is leaving self to study some! For, it *is* both; but figure it out!

Q-3. [993]: *Please explain why during the study of day and night, Eve has stood out so plainly and also Mark 14, [and] Daniel 12.*

A-3. Each here in their respective sphere of activity, Eve in hers. Daniel in recording the vision, or with the viewing of the wrestling between the forces of darkness and the forces of light. And that referred to in Mark as the source of light, the source of night. Each in his respective sphere presenting to a seeking mind a phase of the study. Hence each may be used as their shadow, or as their contribution to the study of the thought or lesson being presented.

Q-4. [560]: *Was Jesus, the Christ, ever Job in the physical body? May this information be given?*

A-4. No. Not ever in the physical body the Jesus. For, as the sons of God came together to reason as recorded by Job, *who* recorded same? The Son of man! Melchizedek wrote Job!

Q-5. *Was the experience I had in meditation in connection with the study of night and day? The words, "alpha and omega, the beginning and the ending. Thus saith the Lord." Please explain.*

A-5. Compare this with that written in Isaiah, as to how the Lord, the God, is the beginning and the end of that brought into material manifestation, or into that known by man as the plane or dimension from which man reasons in the finite. Then there will be to the body the correct conception of that meant. "I am alpha and omega, beginning and the end." That God, the Father, the Spirit, the Ohm, is the influencing force of every activity is not wholly sufficient unto man's salvation, in that he is a free-will being. As intimated that alpha, beginning; omega, ending. For, the confirmation, the segregation, the separation, the building, the adding to it, is necessary—in relation to those activities that lie between—for man's building to the beginning and the end.

Q-6. [303]: *Please explain to me the affirmation given in this lesson, that I may be able to apply it in my activities better.*

A-6. As in the material life there is the day, in which the activities of the body are put in motion to supply the material things of the earth, and—as shown—such materials add to the abilities of the body to carry on in its daily activities, through the sustenance gained by the attitudes of self in the daily activity; so it is seen in the same association and connection that the night becomes the period of meditation, rest, associations of those ideas through the activities of the day; which are the gift not of self, not of self's abilities, but from the source from which mercies, truth, love, knowledge, understanding, arise. So is given, "May Thy mercies guide" in the understanding, that the concepts of that presented in *Day and Night, Night and*

Day, may be builded in self in such a manner as to make for the glorifying *in* the activities of self day *and* night to the glory of Him that *is* the Maker, the Giver, the Father of light.

Q-7. [*413*]: *Please give me the significance of the dream I had the night of September 26th at which time I saw the Master.*

A-7. As there has been in self that seeking more and more for the material confirmation of the thought, the intent and the purpose of self's activities, so in that given, that seen, is a confirmation of that purpose, that thought, that activity.

Hence, rather than bring fears on the part of self, or anxiety as respecting those visioned in same, rather know that self is being led by Him who *is* the guide, the giver, the promise to all mankind.

Q-8. Compilers: Please give some suggestions for outlines.

A-8. In the beginning, as presented, first the approach will be in the introduction from the *material* basis of presentation. Then, in the latter portion of introduction, both the mental and spiritual presentation. Then, that which may be given under each heading as the contribution from those that study this as given.

Q-9. Please explain the part of the affirmation, "Day unto day uttereth speech, night unto night sheweth knowledge."

A-9. *This* is to be applied in each *individual* experience. For, day unto day uttereth speech, whether from the material, the mental or the spiritual aspect; as does night show forth in the varied applications the same as given of life; for it *is* alpha and omega. For, this must be determined, as to the basis of the hope that is within each.

Did, is, was, God, the Father, worshiped by each, honored by those that love His name; dishonored by those who seek their own rather than His biddings? Is He, was He, the Creator of all things? Or came it, the earth, the heavens, the day, the night, into being by chance?

We are through for the present.

This psychic reading was given by Edgar Cayce at his home on Arctic Crescent, Virginia Beach, Va., on October 15, 1933, at 4:25 P.M., in accordance with a request made by those present: Edgar Cayce; Gertrude Cayce, conductor; Gladys Davis, steno; C. A. Barrett, Minnie Barrett, Hugh Lynn Cayce, Mildred Mary Davis, Edith Mildred Edmonds, Florence Edmonds, Ruth LeNoir, Frances Y. Morrow, and Esther Wynne.

≈ 262-56 ≈

Mrs. Cayce: You will have before you the Norfolk Study Group #1, members of which are present in this room, together with their preparation of the lesson Day and Night. *You will give at this time such information and counsel as they may need as individuals or as a group in continuing their work on this lesson. You will answer questions.*

Mr. Cayce: Yes, we have the group gathered here, as a group, as individuals; and their work on preparation of the lessons, and that in the present, *Day and Night, Night and Day.*

As considered by many, in the meditation and the study on the subject, in the preparation, each should get fixed in self— as it were—as to what is the first cause as related to bringing that into existence by the Creator of all; and as to how there is the necessary material preparation through the activity of mind in and on that each individual sees manifested in a world today.

Know that all is of a one source in its power, and that changed or altered from the purpose is only the change in activity of that force that may be manifested in man. Yet, with the setting of those alterations there came good and that opposite from good (to know good) into the material manifestations. And man, through the will, makes for his development or retardment through what he does about that he sees manifested in the material world. This is a law that is applicable, whether we are speaking of purely material, mental or spiritual things. Consider the conveniences in man's activity today. The laws that govern them have existed from the beginning. Only the mind and the application of self respecting the laws has brought such conveniences into the experience of the individual, then groups, then masses, then the populace.

It is this same thought, then, that must be the activity in the

-217-

study of that presented. Then each in preparing that which
may be helpful in the experience of those to whom self would
pass it on, makes that presentation of self's own experience in
the spiritual, the mental and the material plane; thus showing
to self what one believes concerning the developing of the consciousness which in the beginning made the awareness of that
about the individual activity.

Each then asks the question: How is this to be paralleled with
that which has been given respecting the influences in the
experience of each individual? What *is* day in the spiritual
light? What *is* night in the spiritual darkness? What is darkness and its relations to the light which brought into being that
the individual sees about self in the present? The ability for the
spiritual to manifest in that today called matter, and brings
with same both good and evil.

Then, in the mental plane, what becomes day and night?
That which separates the one from the other. Or, as illustrated,
the day becomes the first day of the consciousness of separation
from the forces which the power, or the activity, is in action.
And there is set then in the materiality, or in the plane in
which the physical activity begins, those that represent time
or space. So we have the *rulers* of the light, or day, and the
rulers of the night.

Hence we have that basis from which each is to present that
which may be given out.

Ready for questions.

Q-1. [*993*]: *Please interpret fully my experience of about ten
days ago regarding the Master walking with someone in the
garden.*

A-1. In the meditation were the experiences of the awareness
of that which separated itself. (This, to be sure, is given in light
of the lesson here, you see.) The separation of light from the
source of light, that manifested itself in the material, the mental and the spiritual world. The walking in the garden represents the figure of the oneness of light, the oneness of purpose,
the closeness of that source of light, to those that seek to know
the way as He would have each one go.

Hence more and more there may come to those that seek the
experiences that to them represent or give the better interpre-

tation and understanding of that they seek in the study of the way He, the Master, would have them go.

Q-2. [69]: What is the best time of day for me to seek greater attunement with the Infinite in obtaining something for the lesson?

A-2. It is the material experience of the entity that this is changeable. At some periods it may be in the quietness even of the nighttime, and at others even when the hands are the busiest—or the mind—there comes the awareness of the activity in the direction of the mental being, to the studies of this lesson or this thought.

Hence, as He has given, be constant in prayer, be watchful, and be mindful of that which may be obtained when the self is in attune, when there is felt, seen, heard the expressions of that which may come over, in, or through the mental being.

Q-3. [288]: Is it true that day and night are condensed or miniature copies of incarnations into the earth and into planetary or spiritual sojourns; they in turn being miniature copies of what took place in the beginning?

A-3. Very good, if you understood just what all this means! It's a very good illustration of that which has just been given; as to how there is the evolution of the soul, evolution of the mind, but not evolution of matter—save *through* mind, and that which builds same.

Q-4. [585]: Please explain what was meant by a passing shadow of the Christ, as given in one of our readings in answer to a question on one of my experiences.

A-4. This has been explained. Then, let's interpret it from another angle. As one is passing there may be a flash of a shadow from a plane, a cloud, a bird, or that which makes one more aware of the light; though one may itself be wholly in the light. Hence, as given, the thought, the intent of the mental mind of self at the experience was made aware of the Master's passing by the shadow—as explained, see? One becomes aware by comparison in the material plane. One may be in the brightness of the noonday sun and scarce aware that this is true, save by that which makes the awareness of same in the material-mental consciousness.

Q-5. [*307*]: *Please give me the significance of my dreaming so often of being in strange places, with strange people.*

A-5. The body is going into strange places, among strange people, in presenting the ideas, expressions and experiences of those that are making themselves channels that others may become more aware of the usefulness of that obtained in and through that being presented; and thus gain development through that channel for themselves.

Q-6. Are we to understand that evil existed before the creation of the world, and that it (the devil) was sent into the world?

A-6. How readest thou? As given from the beginning, by becoming aware in a material world *is*—or was—the only manner or way through which spiritual forces might become aware of their separation from the spiritual atmosphere, the spiritual surroundings, of the Maker.

What has been given as the truest of all that has ever been written in Scripture? "God does not will that any soul should perish!" But man, in his headstrongness, harkens oft to that which would separate him from his Maker!

Q-7. [*295*]: *May I have a message on day and night that will help me in my contribution to the lesson?*

A-7. *Think* on the experiences of self, as self has passed from darkness unto light, from day unto night, in the *mental* associations of that which makes the awareness of that which would make of thee a channel of blessings to many. And then there may be seen in self's experience the meaning of what is day, and what is night. The ability to become aware; or, to put into other words, to become *conscious* is day and night.

Q-8. [*560*]: *May I have a message that will help me in my contribution to the lesson?*

A-8. Again may the experiences of self be given, as to how self has become aware step by step—in a portion of life in this experience—of how one may be used in His service, in aiding others to become aware of their obligation, their duty, yea—above all—their privilege, their birthright, to become the sons and daughters of the Creator. For, with this awareness in self has there grown the ability, the opportunity, the privilege for self to become the more often such a channel. And as we know, as we believe, He made Himself a channel by taking on mortality, that He would experience day and night in the material world, in the *mental* world, and hence become the lord of all in the spiritual world! Who, having named the name of the Christ, has become conscious of that He represented or presented in the world? As the records have been handed down that Abraham represents the faithful; Moses meekness; David, the warrior, yet humility; so the Christ represents love, that all may know that He hath paid the price for all.

Q-9. [*379*]: *May I have a message that will help me in contributing to the lesson?*

A-9. In self's own physical self there may be the illustration of day and night. Each element, each corpuscle of the body is a universe in itself, or a universe on the beginning of power and force. When there is that called dis-ease, there becomes the unawareness—or the darkness—of the light that may become life in its manifested form. So, from day and night gain this lesson: Only in the experiencing of that which is the awareness of same may we know what *is* day and night.

Q-10. [*General*]: *Please explain the existence of darkness before the existence of light.*

A-10. This has just been explained, to those who will read that given! That man, or war, or sin, or separation in glory of those that were heedless. Then, that there might be the way for those—What has been given as the most meaning of all that written? *He* has not willed that any soul should perish, but from the beginning has prepared a way of escape! What, then, is the meaning of the separation? Bringing into being the various phases that the soul may find in its manifested forms the consciousness and awareness of its separation, and itself, by that through which it passes in all the various spheres of its awareness. Hence the separation, and light and darkness. Darkness, that it had separated—that a soul had separated itself from the light. Hence He called into being light, that the awareness began. Hence we look out and see the heavens, the stars; and, as the psalmist has said: "The heavens declare the glory of God and the firmament sheweth his handiwork, as day unto day uttereth speech and night unto night sheweth knowledge."

Q-11. *Comment upon the following. Is it worthy of expansion; that is, does it carry any light of truth?*

The Creator, in seeking to find or create a being worthy of companionship, realized that such a being would result only from a free will exercising its divine inheritance and through its own efforts find its Maker. Thus, to make the choice really a divine one caused the existence of states of consciousness, that would indeed tax the free will of a soul; thus light and darkness. Truly, only those tried so as by fire can enter in.

A-11. The only variation that we would make is that all souls in the beginning were one with the Father. The separation, or turning away, brought evil. Then there became the necessity of the awareness of self's being out of accord with, or out of the realm of blessedness; and, as given of the Son, "yet learned He obedience through the things which He suffered."

Come, my children! Ye no doubt have gained from the comment this day that a new initiate has spoken in or through this channel; Halaliel [?], that was with those in the beginning who warred with those that separated themselves and became as naught.

We are through.

This psychic reading was given by Edgar Cayce at the Edmonds' home, 611 Pennsylvania Avenue, Norfolk, Va., on January 7, 1934, at 4:00 P.M., in accordance with a request made by those present: Edgar Cayce; Gertrude Cayce, conductor; Gladys Davis, steno; C. A. Barrett, Minnie Barrett, Hugh Lynn Cayce, Mildred Davis, Myrtle Demaio, Rosario Demaio, Edith Edmonds, Florence Edmonds, Helen Ellington, Ruth LeNoir, Frances Y. Morrow, Helen Storey, and Esther Wynne.

≽ 262-57 ≼

Mrs. Cayce: You will have before you the Norfolk Study Group #1, members of which are present in this room, together with their work on the lesson Day and Night. *As I call each paragraph you will comment on same and give such suggestions for improvement as will be of help in making this lesson more valuable for those who will study it. You will answer the questions which may be asked.*

Mr. Cayce: Yes, we have the Norfolk Study Group #1, as a group, as individuals, and their work on the lesson *Day and Night.*

Ready for questions.

[Mr. Cayce answered "Very good" to each paragraph, 1 through 47. To paragraph 20, he added: "We will comment on this later," and to paragraph 46, he put great emphasis on " *Very* good."]

In reference to that presented in paragraph twenty, the idea should be expanded upon; not merely that the loss makes aware but rather the lacking of the associations *with* the light. For, the illustration here would, in its essence, appear to indicate that to become aware is to lose. To become aware is also to gain. For those that have lost their way, even as the Master gave with the ninety and nine, all might be left to seek the one. And the joyousness in the finding, not in the loss, should be expressed in this paragraph. Just add about four more lines.

Q-1. Give the fundamental thoughts and the principles back of the next lesson.

A-1. It will appear to some that the fundamentals back of the next lesson have been expressed in words in the present lesson. That the manifestations in the earth that are good (and there are some that call *all* good) are of God, and the variations in the manifestations, and the ability to discern that which will lead to the light or to God and that away from the knowledge of the Father, are the fundamentals in the next lesson.

Hence an outline would be first on the questionings that may be by all, in the varied studies.

God is an all-wise, all-inclusive, all-manifesting force in the experience of man. The Father is that loving *influence* in the experience of those that seek Him. God is a fact. The Father— those that seek may know. The manifestations—how and what they are.

Q-2. *What is the affirmation for this lesson?*

A-2. MAY THE DESIRE OF MY HEART BE SUCH THAT I MAY BECOME MORE AND MORE AWARE OF THE SPIRIT OF THE FATHER, THROUGH THE CHRIST, MANIFESTING IN ME.

Q-3. *Please explain the statement given in Genesis, "In six days God made the heaven and the earth and rested the seventh day."*

A-3. That each may interpret this to his own comprehension is rather that each becomes aware of the power of the Father in His manifestations in the earth.

When it is considered (as was later given, or *written* even before this was written) that "a thousand years is as but a day and a day as but a thousand years in the sight of the Lord," then it may be comprehended that this was colored by the writer in his desire to express to the people the power of the living God—rather than a statement of six days as man comprehends days in the present. Not that it was an impossibility —but rather that men under the environ should be impressed by the omnipotence of that they were called on to worship as God.

Q-4. *Who is Halaliel, the one who gave us a message on October 15th [262-56, A-11]?*

A-4. One in and with whose courts Ariel fought when there was the rebellion in heaven. Now, where is heaven? Where is Ariel, and who was he? A companion of Lucifer or Satan, and one that made for the disputing of the influences in the experiences of Adam in the Garden.

Q-5. *Does the truth "By becoming aware in a material world was the only manner through which spiritual forces might*

become aware of their separation from spiritual surroundings"
show that the reincarnation of those who die in childhood is
necessary?

A-5. As the awareness comes by separation (which is being
manifested in materiality as we know it in the present), there
is the necessity of the sojourning in *each* experience for the
developments of the influences necessary in each soul's environ, each soul's attributes, to become again aware of being in
the *presence* of the Father. Hence the reincarnation into this
or that influence, and those that are only aware of material or
carnal influences for a moment may be as *greatly* impressed as
were a finite mind for a moment in the presence of infinity. How
long was the experience of Saul in the way to Damascus? How
long was the experience of Stephen as he saw the Master standing—not sitting, *standing?* How long was the experience of
those that saw the vision that beckoned to them, or any such
experience?

When one considers the birth of a soul into the earth, the
more often is the body and the body-mind considered than the
soul—that is full-grown in a breath. For, did the Father (or
Infinity) bring the earth, the worlds into existence, how much
greater is a day in the house of the Lord—or a moment in His
presence—than a thousand years in carnal forces?

Hence a soul even for a flash, or for a breath, has perhaps
experienced even as much as Saul in the way.

Q-6. What is the explanation of "The Lamb slain before *the
foundation of the world"?*

A-6. If this is taken in conjunction with many another expression of the Master, it may be the more easily comprehended in
the intellectual activities of those who would seek to experience
same.

As the Master gave, "Before Abraham was I AM—before the
worlds were I AM." Hence, when there came the necessity in
the realm of the spiritual home for the coming of the Lamb into
the earth for its redemption, the truth, the light, the offering
was made. Hence the expression as given. For, as has been
given, the thought, the mind, is the builder.

Then, as each soul builds for that it as a soul is to act, whether
in spirit, in mind or in body, the *soul*-mind is already in the

throes of the influences necessary. Then, when we comprehend we realize there is no time, no space, and that the divinity of the man Jesus was perfect in his *own* activity in the earth. For, it was offered even from the first.

So, as ye gathered here—ye each have your duties, your obligations, in materiality. Ye each have your promises in your material things, if ye will but follow in the way that has been opened—that has been shown thee—that each in your own experience may be the channel for the greater blessing to thy fellow man. And, as has been given you, ye have been chosen; each one that *chooses* to *do* His biddings.

Then, pray ye the Father that through His Son, the Christ, ye may be shown more of the light, that ye may in *this* day, in *this* opportunity He has given thee in thy experience in the material world *now*, fulfill that whereunto ye have been called.

For, as the Master gave, "Think ye not that ye have a promise through Abraham? Or that ye are children of promise through him? For I say He may raise unto Himself of these stones children unto Abraham."

Ye are children of the promise, in Christ. Ye have—of all people—the greater right for glorying in that promise; but if ye allow selfishness, unkindness, evil thoughts, evil communications, or little worries of the day to separate you, then ye have rejected being His children—and must one day, one time, suffer that of being offered on the altar.

Then, make much of this opportunity. This, as He gave: "Love ye one another—prefer one another instead of self." *Know* the truth, for only truth is of God.

Your next lesson will be *Desire.*

We are through.

࿂ 262-58 ࿃

This psychic reading was given by Edgar Cayce at the Edmonds' home, 611 Pennsylvania Avenue, Norfolk, Va., on February 11, 1934, at 4:30 P.M., in accordance with a request made by those present: Edgar Cayce; Gertrude Cayce, conductor; Gladys Davis, steno; C. A. Barrett, Minnie Barrett, Hugh Lynn Cayce, Mildred Mary Davis, Edith Mildred Edmonds, Florence Edmonds, Helen Ellington, Ruth LeNoir, Frances Y. Morrow, Helen Storey, and Esther Wynne.

Mrs. Cayce: You will have before you the work of Norfolk Study Group #1 on the lesson God and His Manifestations in the Earth. *You will give the members of this group, present here, such material as we need on this lesson to continue our work. You will answer questions.*

Mr. Cayce: Yes, we have the group gathered here, as a group and as individuals, and their work in preparation of the lesson.

It has been given respecting how the individuals should in themselves, in their meditation, in their study, in their observation of that being presented in the lesson *God and His Manifestations in the Earth,* each make the application of that which is conscious in their individual experience. For, as He has given, ye may call "Lord, Lord," even may heal the sick, cast out demons even in His name, and yet not be accepted in His sight; for by the fruits ye shall know them that are called of the Lord, in the ways and manners that His manifestations are through the lives of the individuals that make profession in their life *of* their associations; but if their life and the fruits of their lives bring not forth greater manifestations, and those things that are of the spirit, the fruits of the spirit, then they are none of His. Not everyone that saith "Lord, Lord," but he that doeth the will of the Father, the same is acceptable in His sight.

What, then, are the manifestations of the Father in the earth? That ye do good unto all peoples, and that the fruits of the spirit are manifested in thy thoughts, in thy acts day by day as ye meet thy fellow men in their own conditions where troubles, doubts, fears, distresses arise. And as there is given those things into their experience from thine own desire to be the channel through which the manifestations of the spirit of the Christ, of the Christ Consciousness, may be in the experience of such individuals, thy words and thy acts are in keeping with that He, the Father, makes manifest in the earth through the Son — as He in His life made manifest in His walks in the earth, doing good to those whether they were of His fold or those that even rejected that He had done rather as an experience in their lives.

Then, as they each may manifest in the thought, in the application of those truths as He gave, they may come to those experiences wherein they oft may be as a lamp to the feet of the wayward, as an aid to those who seek, as a light to those that have gone astray, as a guiding hand to those that would know more and more of the love of the Father as it manifests in the acts, the thoughts, the lives of His followers.

Ready for questions.

Q-1. [560]: May there be expanded upon the protection of the Father and His goodness in manifestation in the earth?

A-1. As He has given from the beginning, "If ye will be my children, I will be your God." So, as individuals, in the application of that known in their experience as to what the will of the Father is, go about *thinking*—and *thinking* it in such a manner that the words of the mouth and the activity of the hand bespeak the will of the Father; then this activity, this thought, makes the individual the channel through which the manifestations are in the earth.

For, who may know in the earth the heart of the mother save a mother? Who may know the will of the Father, God, save those that put into the acts of their hands, in the thoughts of their minds, those things that He has given and as He shows forth in the experience of all men from day to day?

So simple, then, is it to know the Father that all stumble in that they *think* of themselves more highly than they ought to think. Be rather as a channel through which the Father may make His love, His glory, manifest in the earth. *Listen* to the voice from within. For, He is very nigh unto each of you, if ye will but look *within*. And that thou experienceth with the desire that thy self be nothing, that the Father, the Christ, may be glorified in the earth, brings to the experience of all the consciousness of being a manifestation of the love of the Father to the sons of men.

Q-2. [993]: For some time I have been thinking continually about the coming of the kingdom on earth and His coming. Has it any bearing upon the lesson? Please give me more light upon the kingdom and His coming.

A-2. How long has been the cry of those that have manifested in the earth the glory of the Father through the Son, "Hasten, O Lord, the day of thy kingdom in the earth!" How have the promises read that the Son has given? "I go to prepare a place that where I am there ye may be also. I will come again and receive you unto myself." Then, as the individual heart attunes its mind and its body-activity into that consciousness of the desire for the hastening of that day. Yet the merciful kindness of the Father has, in the eyes of many, delayed the coming, and many have cried even as the parable He gave, "We know not what has become of this man. Show us other gods that may lead us in this day." Yet the cry in the heart and the soul of those that seek His way is to hasten that day. Yet, as He has given, in patience, in listening, in being still, may ye know that the Lord doeth all things well. Be not weary that He apparently prolongs His time, for—as the Master has given, "As to the day, no man knoweth, not even the son, but the Father and they to whom the Father may reveal the son prepareth the way that all men may know the love of the Father." And as ye would be the channel to hasten that glorious day of the coming of the Lord, then do with a might that thy hands find to do to make for the greater manifestations of the love of the Father in the earth. For, into thy keeping, and to His children and to His sons, has He committed the keeping of the saving of the world, of the souls of men; for, as He has given, "Who is my mother? Who is my brother? Who is my sister? They that do the will of my Father who is in heaven, the same is my mother, my brother, my sister." So, as He gave, "I leave thee, but I will come again and receive as many as ye have quickened through the manifesting in thy life the will of the Father in the earth." Hence know that, as thine mind, thine activities, long more and more for the glorifying of the Son in the earth, for the coming of the day of the Lord, He draws very nigh unto thee.

Q-3. Please discuss, "How and what are the manifestations of the Father?"

A-3. The fruits of the spirit. Gentleness, kindness, the loving word, patience, hope, persistence, and—above all—consistency in thy acts and in thy speech. Be ye glorious in thine activity. Be ye joyous in thy words. For, *happy* is the man that knoweth that his life bespeaks that the Son and the spirit of truth directs the words and the activities of his body!

Q-4. You will give a personal message on this lesson for each individual as I call the names. [413]:

A-4. Let that that is in thine heart be manifest in the acts of thine hands and in the speech of thy mouth day by day. For the *abundance* of the heart the mouth speaketh, and in the acts of the body they show forth the meditations of the heart.

Q-5. [303]:

A-5. Keep in the glory of that thou hast purposed in thine heart. For, in the gentleness of the speech, in the kindness of the activity, thou showest forth the love of the Father. Be not overcome of those things that would hinder, but overcome the evil with the good, and give the glory—*always*—to the Father.

Q-6. [307]:

A-6. Keep thine heart and thine mind *singing* in the glory of the manifestations, of the beauty and of the glory of the Father in the earth, as thou hast seen manifest among men. Look not on those things that appear as stumbling blocks in the lives of others, for—as he has given of old—"I am persuaded that there is nothing in heaven nor in earth, nor in hell, that may separate man from the love of the Father and the manifestations of that love save man's own self." [See 262-60, A-3.]

Q-7. [379]:

A-7. In the glory of the Lord and His manifestations in the earth, be thou the channel through which some blessings may come day by day. For in so doing may thou come to know more and more how *great* is the glory of the Father, through the Son. For, as He has given, "What ye ask in my name, *believing*, that I will give unto thee, that the *Father* may be *glorified* in me and in thee."

Q-8. [69]:

A-8. Keep in the way thou hast set before thee, in the love of the consciousness of the Christ in thine activities day by day. Doubt not. Faint not in thine activities, for—as He has given

—"If ye will draw nigh unto me, I will draw nigh unto thee."
And through *thee* may there be the manifestations of God's love
in the earth, through the Father, through the hope, through
the activity of the fruits of the spirit in the earth.

Q-9. [*69's husband*]:

A-9. Let thy going in and thy coming out be acceptable in the
sight of Him who has promised to come and abide with those
that love His coming, love His glorifying in the earth through
those promises He has given into the keeping of the sons of
men; that ye be kind, ye be gentle, ye be in keeping with those
things that thou knowest in thine heart are well pleasing in
the sight of the Father. For, thus may the manifestations of
that promised from the beginning be in *thine* experience. For,
those that seek God and to know Him must believe that He is,
and He is a rewarder of those that diligently seek Him.

Q-10. [*560*]:

A-10. Let thine heart be glad in the things thou hast seen in
thine experience of the glories of the Father, through the Son,
in the lives of those that thou hast contacted day by day. For,
these are but naught, wilt thou keep thine heart singing, keep
thine life pure, keep thy ways as His ways. For, He loveth and
protecteth, and guideth and directeth those that call on Him
in faith—and *not* for themselves alone, but rather that self
shall be effaced that the face of the Christ may shine more and
more in the lives of others.

Q-11. [*993*]:

A-11. Keep the heart singing for the glories of the Christ
child, in the lives of the children, in the lives of the grown-ups,
that thou meetest day by day. For, in His ways are the ways
of the Father. For, as He gave, no man may do anything of
himself, save as the Father in His mercy has granted that
through the love and through the manifestations of His love
in the earth may that increase of His manifestations come into
the experience and in the lives of those that seek to do His
biddings.

Q-12. [*585*]:

A-12. Let thine life, in mind, in body, in soul, cry unto the
Lord in weakness, and in strength He will raise thee up. For,
as He has given, "They that seek in my name shall in no wise

be cast out, and he that giveth a cup of cold water in my name shall in no wise lose his reward." Be not impatient that some glorious mighty thing has not been in thine experience, for the experiences that thou has been awakened to the abilities that may be made manifest through the love of the Father, through the Christ, *without* the thought of self, without the desire for self-exaltation, only in such ways and manners may His glory be wholly shown in thee.

Q-13. [288]:

A-13. Keep in the way that thou knowest to do, for He requires not other than that ye be true to that thou knowest in thine heart to do. For, He calleth those by name that have named the name of the Christ and that keep His ways, and through such may the love of the Father through the Son be manifest in the earth.

Q-14. [295]:

A-14. In thine understanding and in thine closeness in the love of the Master, as He has called unto all that would know His ways, there may come in thine experience those manifestations that make known unto thine soul that thou hast been called to be a channel of blessing to many. For, as the love of the Father is manifested in the earth through the Son, so may self—becoming selfless in thy associations with those that would bespeak of self-exaltation or self-glorification, for of such is it said, "Though ye may do wonders in the earth in my name, self may be abased." But those that glory in the love of the Father through the Son, in *selflessness,* may be exalted in the manifestations in the earth.

Q-15. [341]:

A-15. Let the words of thy mouth and the meditation of thine heart be acceptable in the sight of Him that thou hast heard give, "Though I go away, I will come again and receive you unto myself, that where I am there ye may be also." And the greater love as was shown, "and Lo, I am with thee always, even unto the end of the world." What greater manifestations could there be in the inner soul of anyone in a material plane than bespeak those things of the Son of the Father in such a way and manner that those that hear may know that thou hast indwelling in thine inmost soul the knowledge of the Father, in the Son, and the *love* of the Father to the sons of men!

Q-16. [*294*]:

A-16. Keep the heart true to those things thou hast declared in thine life. For, as there is seen in thine walks in and before man, so are the judgments of what thou thinkest of the promises of the Son. For, as the Son would be glorified in thee, as the Son would glorify the Father in the love as He has shown in the earth, abuse not those gifts that are showered upon thee through the love of Him who has said, "If ye will keep my commandments I will come and abide with thee, and will guide thy footsteps lest thou stumblest."

Q-17. [*538*]:

A-17. Let the love of the Father in the Son guide thee. Be not impatient, nor be thou longing for those things that are other than the love of the Father in the Son that may be manifested in the glories that thou hast had in knowing that thou hast been a channel, thou art a channel, through which many approach the throne of grace. And they, as He has promised, that have saved a soul from sin, from perdition, have covered a multitude of sins, and their robes are washed in the blood of the Lamb; and He knoweth thee by name, and He calleth thee that thou wouldst keep the way that many may know that the Father through the Son will come to those that seek to know His face.

To all would this be given:

Love God. Eschew evil. Love thy neighbor as thyself. For, as He gave, "A new commandment I give unto you, that ye love one another," even as the *Father* hath loved you in giving His Son that ye through faith, that ye through the love that He has shown, may know the love of the Father and thus be the greater channel of blessings to those ye meet day by day. For ye have been called unto a purpose, as into the service of the Son of man. Make known to Him thy desire, in *His* will, and—thy will one with His—there will come to thee many blessings, physically, mentally, spiritually.

We are through.

This psychic reading was given by Edgar Cayce at his home on Arctic Crescent, Virginia Beach, Va., on April 8, 1934, at 4:20 P.M., in accordance with a request made by those present: Edgar Cayce; Mildred Mary Davis, conductor; Gladys Davis, steno; C. A. Barrett, Minnie Barrett, L. B. Cayce, Edith Edmonds, Florence Edmonds, Helen Ellington, Jeanne LeNoir, Ruth LeNoir, Frances Y. Morrow, Helen Storey, Alvin Kirk Wheeler, Jr., and Esther Wynne.

◁ 262-59 ◁

Mildred Davis: You will have before you Norfolk Study Group #1, members of which are present in this room, together with their work on the lesson God, the Father, and His Manifestations in the Earth. *Please give us further help that will enable us to complete the lesson so as to be of the best service to others. You will then answer the questions which may be asked.*

Mr. Cayce: Yes, we have the group gathered here, as a group and as individuals, and their work on the lessons; also that which may be helpful to others.

If there is applied in the experience of each that which has been given respecting the present subject, you each will find there may be given by each of you that which will be your contribution to that as is helpful to others.

For, unless we use that we know, we may not comprehend or use that which may lead for the next step.

For, as has been shown, it should be line upon line, precept upon precept, here a little, there a little. We each must apply ourselves in that which we know to be a manifestation of the love of the Father to the sons, the children of men, in our daily experience.

Ready for questions.

Q-1. Please explain, "Be glorious in thine activity, be joyous in thy words."

A-1. Be glorious in thy activity. If the activities of a soul-mind are in that direction of manifesting the love of the Father to others, then it—the activity—must be glorious in the essence of that causing, producing or making for such an activity.

So, in such an activity there will indeed be that joy which

comes with every soul doing that it knows or has been shown is the acceptable service unto a living God.

Hence, be glorious in thine activity—joyous in thy service.

Q-2. What is meant by "The soul must feed upon dead patience that it may grow into an abundant life"?

A-2. For, as given by Him that is the light, the life, we become aware of our souls through patience. Then, patience that is crucified of self in service to another is as dead in the sense of the earth's activity, and alive in the knowledge of the Father dwelling *in* thine service or thine activity through such experience.

So, if these be put into practice in the experience of each, they each know well what it means: Be angry and sin not. Be patient. Seven times forgive; yea, seventy times seven. And, being dead, being crucified to the things that pertain to the earth, looking for that *acceptable* day of the Lord.

This makes a question in the minds of some, as to when is the acceptable day of the Lord. When ye love God better than yourself! Then is it the day, the hour, of the awakening in thine self! to do His service, to do His biddings, to be—as it were—a *sacrifice* in all those things that make for *burnings,* for *longings* for those things that make for the weakening of the flesh; that ye may know that He will have His way with thee. Becoming selfless, becoming conscious of His Spirit, His love, moving in and through thee, prompting thee in thy words, thy activities, thy service.

Q-3. Please explain Luke 1:35.

A-3. [In undertone:] (The Holy Ghost shall make that within thee alive.) This is the body of the mother becoming aware of the spirit of truth being made manifest into materiality, or the spirit of the Father making aware through conscious forces active in material body that the *body* is then moved or acted upon by the Spirit of the Father—or the Holy Spirit active in material force.

Q-4. Please explain the statement given in II Cor. 5:21, "For he hath made Him to be made sin who knew no sin," etc. Was His sin of His own choosing?

A-4. This may be given in that which follows near, that

though He were *without* sin yet He thought it not robbery to make Himself equal with God in *making* Himself manifest through the power of God; for, as He gave, "I do *nothing* of myself save that *given* me by the Father."

But, as given respecting this same reference, when the spirit brought *in* spirit that of condemnation or sin in manifested form in the earth, then the Son came *in* manifested form—or in sin—that through Him the earth, or the spirit of man, might have the advocate with the Father and through Him once for all be made free from sin through that activity of the Christ Spirit in the earth. Hence that given, He became sin—or *in* sin, rather should be the translation—that those in sin, or in the earth, or in materiality, might know the light and have life, and having life have it more abundantly—or more often—in Him.

Q-5. [462]: Please give me a message that will help me at this time.

A-5. Be not overcome of thine self, nor of those things that would make thee weak in those that are the besetting influences in thy experience. Know that the strength to overcome is in Him. Conform thine mind and thine body to the things of the spirit, rather than to the things of the flesh. While in flesh we may make manifested those forces in spirit. But abide in His time. Listen to the voice within thee.

For, His Spirit will bear witness with thy spirit and guide thee in the way that thou shouldst go.

Q-6. [404]: I would appreciate a message that will enable me to better understand my relationship to the work and my family.

A-6. Study to show thyself approved unto *God*, rather than to any work, any family, *any* relationships. For, oft do personalities and those things that partake of same become stumbling blocks. But know that thy Redeemer has made the way clear, that if ye will follow in not only His precepts but His example thy *life* will become as joyous as He has promised in the service for Him and His activities in the earth. For, though the heavens may pass away, though the earth may fail, His promises shall *not* fail. For, all that was made, all that is active in the influences in the earth, are His. What wilt thou do with thine abilities in the present?

We are through.

The psychic reading was given by Edgar Cayce at the Edmonds' home, 611 Pennsylvania Avenue, Norfolk, Va., on April 22, 1934, at 4:15 P.M., in accordance with a request made by those present: Edgar Cayce; Gertrude Cayce, conductor; Gladys Davis, steno; C. A. Barrett, Minnie Barrett, Hugh Lynn Cayce, Mildred Mary Davis, Edith Edmonds, Florence Edmonds, Helen Ellington, Margaret Joyner, Ruth LeNoir, Helen Storey, and Esther Wynne.

➢ 262-60 ↙

Mrs. Cayce: You will have before you the Norfolk Study Group #1, members of which are present—and their work on the lesson, God, the Father, and His Manifestations in the Earth. *You will give at this time that which will clarify for us the proper presentation of this lesson, and such counsel as will direct and guide us in completing it. You will answer the questions that may be asked.*

Mr. Cayce: Yes, we have the group gathered here, as a group, as individuals, and their work on the lesson, *God, the Father, and His Manifestations in the Earth.*

In the compilation of that which has been presented, much has been given as to how this should be set forth. All have not contributed to the lesson, and much that has been presented is rather in a disconnected state at present. Then, much clarification may be necessary before that which is presented should be presented. For, all should contribute. Each that fails, fails in its portion of a service, a calling that has been assumed by each individual in the group. For, as given, the cooperation of each gives that impetus to the work of the compilers, of the thought, of the spirit of that which is sent forth with the power and the blessings of those influences that direct each soul in its labors.

Then, how may this be clarified? First, let each contribute a word, an act, an expression of its experience, with the thought, the purpose, the message that has been received through the study, the preparation of itself for being a contributor to this message.

Then, as given, compile as to that thought, that line first given as to how the outline should be; the stating of the purpose, the contributions and those that coordinate one with another,

-237-

the experience and the application of that which may be the experience of all that would be a channel through which there may be a manifestation of the Father's love, the Father's mercy, the Father's long-suffering, the Father's patience with a stiff-necked people.

These should be the manners in which this preparation should be for this lesson.

What is the purpose of this particular lesson? Has it not been pointed out to those as they have followed that presented, that in this there may be seen or known to each as to how, when and in what manner they as individuals may be conscious of the spirit manifesting through them in material things?

Ready for questions.

Q-1. Please explain Matthew 24:34, "Verily I say unto you, this generation shall not pass, till all these things be fulfilled."

A-1. Those individuals that were in hearing and in keeping of those things presented by the Master in that experience would be in the manifested form in the earth during the periods of fulfillments in the earth of the prophecies spoken of. Not in what is termed as generation of four score and ten years, but the experiences of those souls in the earth during those periods when there must shortly come the completing or fulfilling of those things spoken of.

Q-2. [303]: Please give me a message that will give me some consolation at this time.

A-2. That which has been given should be worked upon. In this: Thou hast found in thine experience that, though the burdens of material things may weigh heavily upon thee in the present, that thou hast manifested in the gentleness, in the kindliness, in the patience thou hast shown with thine self, with thine neighbor, with thine household, has brought and does bring those contentments that make for the greater peace and harmony that may be had in the experience of a soul in the earth's environs.

Then, be thou ready to be used as He sees fit. Let thy supplication be from day to day:

"Lead me, O Father, just for today, that I may be used as a channel of blessing, that I may today manifest Thy love through my association with those I contact; for as I show forth

Thy love in the earth to my fellow man, the promise comes to
me that thou wilt guide, guard, protect and comfort me in the
ways that I go."

These will bring to thine consciousness that presence of the
Christ Spirit abiding with thee. No greater consolation can be
in the experience of any than, "He walks and talks with me day
by day."

Q-3. [307]: In reading of Feb. 11th [262-58, A-6] I was told,
"Look not on the things that appear to be stumbling blocks in
the lives of others." How may I so conduct myself in this particular instance as to be of help and bring into the lives of others
a more perfect understanding of the love of the Father, through
the Son?

A-3. Condemn not in word, in thought or activity, that ye be
not condemned. See in every expression of activity the attempt
of that soul to express or manifest that soul's concept of divine
reality. For, each soul, as it gives expression in thought, in act,
shows by the fruits of that done as to what is the impelling
influence in that soul's experience. Then, not as a judge, not as
a faultfinder, but rather as He gave, be merciful to those that
err, for they know not what they do—unless they be guided by
the spirit of truth that cleanseth all from that of selfishness and
makes of them as one with the influence of the Christ Consciousness in their lives. Seeing such, sending forth the same
prayer as He in those words over Jerusalem—"thou that ston-
est the prophets, how oft would I—and ye would not!" Yet those
very things, those very souls are today seeking to know the
meaning of those words of His in their own experiences in the
present. Let thy light so shine among those that they may take
thought of those things as He gave, in those blessings He gave
even to those that crucified; who gave Himself that others
might know the way, the light, the truth.

Q-4. [585]: Please explain the Master's statement to Nicodemus, "Ye must be born again."

A-4. In its whole setting, rather, should this word be understood. Nicodemus was among those of the Sanhedrin, those of
the teachers, those of the elders, with that privilege of being
in access to all that had been given from the time there was
delivered to Moses on the mount the ordinances, the relation-

ships of individuals to individuals, the relationship of the individual soul to its Maker. Much had come now to be rather as hearsay, as omens, rather than the ordinances of old. And when Nicodemus asked, "How can such things be?" the rebuke came in His answer, "Art thou a teacher in Israel and knoweth not these things?" Ye must be born of water and of blood. Or, of the spirit and through the flesh. Or, that *all* must pass under the rod, even as was given by those teachers that as Moses and the children passed through the sea they were baptized in the cloud and in the sea; as an example, as an omen, as a physical activity of a spiritual, a physical separation from that which had been builded in their experience as the sojourn in Egypt. As the Master gave to Nicodemus, ye must be born of the spirit where ye may make manifest the fruits of the spirit. Where? In the earth! Not that these come in their order as indicated in the question by Nicodemus, but in their relative position as to *their* development, their necessities, their needs for their soul growth, their soul understanding. O that all would gather more of that understanding that the soul is a body and the physical is the mere temple, the mere shell, the mere material manifestation of that which may not be touched by hands! For, it appears that we must be born again that we may dwell in those mansions not made with hands—but are prepared for those that have washed their robes, their bodies, their souls in the blood. For, ye are ones that may know the truth, if ye will but manifest in thine own experiences that ye have learned in thine meditations with thine God. Ye must be born in flesh, in spirit again, that ye may make manifest that ye have experienced in thine own soul!

Q-5. *Please explain II Corinthians 5:1, "For we know that if our earthly house of this tabernacle were dissolved, we have a building of God, an house not made with hands, eternal in the heavens."*

A-5. Just given. Would that each soul might grasp that truth that, though the soul may not be seen, that it doeth, that growth it makes, that body, must dwell in that house not made with hands, eternal with the Father. For the life *is* the spirit of the soul, it is God eternal, however it may manifest itself in that we know as materiality or matter. Why, why, has not the man, the scientist, been able to find in the brain words? or be able to tell what has made for a *developed* brain and an *un*developed brain, when he says it is the seat from which emotions and activities emanate? For, was it not given, would ye have life ye must give life? Would ye be that as would be one with Him, then live it! For those things are not made with hands, rather by the deeds done, that expended; and it, the deed, as the light itself, shineth on and on—and though the source from which it may visibly emanate may be destroyed or extinguished, the light shines on—that has passed into what? The realm through which, of which, are those mansions where the body that is indestructible is to preside.

What is thy light? What *is* thy guide? That thou mayest see how it operates, or that in the experience of thine neighbor, thine brother, thou hast just been kind? For, as has been said, the smile raised hope in that one upon which it was given; that hope made possible activity; that activity made possible a haven for some discouraged, some disheartened soul! Be thou, each of you, one that may smile though the heavens fall; though thou may be ground to dust upon the altars of thine own selfishness thou may *shine* even in *His* light that He has set before you for thine own redemption! Let Him, the Christ, be the guide. Let Him build for thee the mansion, rather than with thine own puny hands where moth and rust doth corrupt and where those that unconsciously in their stumbling manners oft make the road rough for thee. Forgive them, if ye would be forgiven. Hold not a grudge, for that which is thine may not be taken from thee lest *thou alone* cast it aside by envy, strife, unkind thoughts, unkind acts, and thus destroy that thou lovest most— *life!*

Q-6. In canonizing the Bible, why was the life of Zan [Zend] left out? [See 993-3, A-2, -3; 364-9, A-2, -3.]

A-6. Called in other names. For, much might be given respecting that ye have that ye call the Bible. This has passed through many hands. Many that would turn that which was written into the meanings that would suit their own purposes, as *ye* yourselves often do. But if ye will get the spirit of that written there ye may find it will lead thee to the gates of heaven. For, it tells of God, of your home, of His dealings with His peoples in many environs, in many lands. Read it to be wise. Study it to understand. *Live* it to know that the Christ walks through same with thee. For, as He gave, in righteousness may ye know those things that have been preserved from the foundations of the worlds in thine own experience. For, these are told there in the manners of those that recorded same in their own environ. What wilt *thou* write today that will be as the words of life to thy brothers in the ages to come? For, He has given, ye have been called—and ye have a work to do.

Then, in the next lesson ye shall have, shall much be given concerning how that which is carnal and that which is mental and that which is spiritual may be found—in *Desire*. For, it builds—and is that which is the basis of evolution, and of life, and of truth. It also takes hold on hell and paves the way for many that find themselves oft therein. In spirit, in body, in mind.

The message, then, that ye would study in this, should be:

"FATHER, LET THY DESIRES BE MY DESIRES. LET MY DESIRES, GOD, BE THY DESIRES, IN SPIRIT AND IN TRUTH."

We are through for the present.

This psychic reading was given by Edgar Cayce at his home on Arctic Crescent, Virginia Beach, Va., on May 5, 1934, at 3:40 P.M., in accordance with a request made by Miss Esther Wynne. Those present were: Edgar Cayce; Gertrude Cayce, conductor; Gladys Davis, steno; Hugh Lynn Cayce, L. B. Cayce, Mildred Davis, and Esther Wynne.

⩔ 262-61 ⩗

Mrs. Cayce: You will have before you the place of group work in the Association for Research and Enlightenment, Inc., considering each group as a unit and also the whole program and purpose of group activity, also the various group leaders and teachers, especially Esther Wynne, present in this room. You will give at this time information which will help in better organizing and carrying on this work. You will answer the questions which will be asked on this subject, as I ask them.

Mr. Cayce: Yes, we have the work that is to be filled by the activities of the group in the study lessons.

Much has been given as to the place of such lessons in an association organized for the work research and enlightenment. That there has not wholly been the comprehension of what is to be accomplished by such groups is evidenced by the manner in which these activities have proceeded.

Not that there is fault to be found, or any condition that could under the existent circumstances be altered. But those that function in the capacity of the research and enlightenment should set forth more the purposes and the place that each study group has in such a work.

For, as is seen, unless there is a more definite outline, there will continue to be thought and expressed that the purpose of such is to propagate some kind of special cult or tenet or thought, that to some must eventually—or from the beginning—take the ideas of a cult. And this should be the farthest from the thought of any leader or teacher of such lessons.

For, they are founded rather in the ideal set in the manner each of the meditations for each lesson is presented; that the individual development is sought, or enlightenment respecting the approach of individuals to a thought or a fact that exists

-243-

in the character of the lessons that may be presented through such channels.

To some at present, as we find, this presentation thus far is rather hazy, rather indefinite as to what is being given; but there should be considered more of that given in the beginnings, as to how, why and when these should be presented, and how this should be the basis and the purpose of the research—then from such research the natural arising of the presentations found applicable in the experiences of all seeking to make of themselves channels through which the activities of those influences or forces that direct that given from period to period may be presented.

That's a little more clarification. Now we'll approach it from a different angle:

As should be understood by all leaders, students or those interested in the lessons presented, the *lessons* are only a portion of the work of a research organization. This research organization has presented those things that are from or through psychic sources, though *psychic* does not appear in the words —and this itself makes confusion. But psychic, as given, should be considered rather as of the soul; and if the information is of that nature then those that are in attune (as given in the direction about attunement) will be influenced in their study and application of this character of information. For, no stream of thought may be greater than the source from which it rises. If it arises from superstition, or from the purposes of an individual as for the presentation of some peculiar thought or pet idea or ideal of an individual as related to any circumstance or condition in the experience of human affairs, it will never be larger than the individual. If it arises from the higher sources from which it emanates, it must increase the perspective of the consciousness of those that make application of same. As tenets, never. For, such as presented in the lessons —and that may be presented from time to time—may never be called tenets, but should *ever* as outlined; that which has been applied in the experience of individuals as *producing* something in their experience. And when so used, so presented, so used in the presenting of same from period to period, these may then become those very things that have had their influence in the earth in the ages throughout.

For a moment, review that which most of you have considered as the basis of thought pertaining to the ideals of the spiritual life in thine own experience.

From whence arose the purpose or idea or ideal that ye hold so close in thine experience. *Ye* say that there were those periods when for four hundred years little or nothing had happened in the experience of man as a revelation from the Father, or from God, or from the sources of light. *What* was it, then, that made the setting for the place and for the entering in of that consciousness into the earth that *ye* know as the Son of man, the Jesus of Nazareth, the Christ on the cross? Did the darkness bring the light? Did the wandering away from the thought of such bring the Christ into the earth? Is this idea not rather refuting the common law that is present in spirit, mind and body that "Like begets like"? As was asked oft, "Can any good thing come out of Nazareth?" Isn't it rather that there were those, that ye hear little or nothing of in thine studies of same, that dedicated their lives, their minds, their bodies, to a purpose, to a *seeking* for that which had been to them a promise of old? Were there not individuals, men and women, who dedicated their bodies that they might be channels through which such an influence, such a *body* might come? Is it not rather that which ye seek? For, that is what ye look for in this; that ye present in those lessons, that they may build in the hearts, minds, bodies and lives of those that *apply* them—not learn, not simply have knowledge of, but *apply* them—that which may be presented from lesson to lesson in their daily experience—that there may again come the greater influences in the activity of individuals that may save a world, may save a nation, may save the peoples. And be truly said of that service, that work ye do, that it fills this place, that there is being builded in the hearts, minds and bodies of individuals that longing for—yea, that activity such as will bring into the earth, into the environs of people—such as has been and is the saving influence in the lives, hearts and minds of thy people. Such should be the place, first. In such a way and manner should this being given in thy lessons be presented.

Then, necessity demands that there be rather first the school of teachers, for the preparation of individuals in various groups. Not chosen because they may be popular, well spoken of, or ones of influence in their individual groups—or of affluence, or the like—but rather those in such groups that have been moved to dedicate, consecrate their lives to such a service. In this way and manner may the groups and the *lessons* in same be presented.

The first principles, then, are these:

Are the lessons as presented things worthwhile in the experience of individuals, sufficient to carry forward that thought, that idea? That is what is required. Art thou meeting same? Answer in thine own selves. Is thy life, thy activity, such as that, though it took from thee all that is near and dear to thy *earthly* environ, ye would present rather that as the Father would present to a waiting world?

So live, then, each of *you,* in such a manner. Thinkest thou rather of what others will say? Thinkest thou as to whether it will be popular here or popular there? Was He? In no land in which *Jesus* presented Himself was He accepted; for was it not said, truly He came unto His own and His own received Him not? Have ye received Him? Know ye Him, day by day?

This is the manner of the approach, then.

Ready for questions.

Q-1. Questions on Group #2: Please give suggestions for the leaders and members in becoming more helpful and efficient.

A-1. Applying. Do not the truths presented in the lessons, when lived, fulfill the same in their experience? If they do not, they are *not* for those individuals.

Q-2. How can this group best meet the conditions that have arisen in relation to the Church?

A-2. Do the lessons not make the individuals that are members of individual churches *better* Christians, better or nearer Christ-like; thus filling their lives with such love that dogmatic principles (as in some churches) must be taboo? But present them to those that are weak, *living* them before those that *stumble*—but do not cram them down anyone's throat! Neither argue with them! Did thy Master ever argue, even when there were the greater railings or abuses? He presented that which each *has* found, did find, convicted them. What said He respecting that? "I do not condemn thee, for thou art condemned already in thine own self." So, in the approach to those influences, the truths and lessons as presented—and *lived* by individuals—should fill the needs, even in the greater or higher places in any individual organization; and may fill some with awe—and they may speak evil. So did the high priest condemn thine Lord! So did those of the Sanhedrin wreak their own purposes upon Him. Yea, art thou willing to live that which has proved and does prove in thine experience that which makes thee closer with thy God? If these lessons are not founded in such, have nothing to do with them.

Q-3. What was the meaning of the dream had by [540] regarding seeing the Sunday school teacher, Mrs. Bell, teaching lessons on the Pyramid?

A-3. This is rather confusing, but we may find it from this source here. [Pause] Yes. The consciousness in [540] of the tenets held by some, and the truths that are experienced in her own understanding. It becomes necessary that those truths are only applicable in the experience of those that have experienced same. So will these eventually become as truths to that one seen teaching, see?

Q-4. Should she be invited to group meetings and how should she be approached?

A-4. She may be told of them, and let her seek herself to know more of what is being presented.

Q-5. Questions on Group #3: [See 473-1 and 473-2.]

A-5. Here we have many sincere individuals seeking from many varied angles, and here almost the great necessity (as in and among those who prepare, present and experience the lessons) for the basis as to why and where the lessons are founded. And if those members do not find in the *application* of same in their experience the answering for the faith that is within, then move on.

Q-6. Any special advice for this group, considering their individual situation?

A-6. As just given, the purposes and desires should be presented; not as tenets, but as living experiences that may be applied in the daily lives of those that use same. And the individual presentation by those that present same as teachers or as exhorters from time to time should be ever: Take this idea presented in this, that or the other lesson and give the invitation, "Will ye apply this in thine experience today and give that reaction it makes, irrespective of what thy thought or connection has been or is?" Then we'll get somewhere!

Q-7. How can Mr. [478] better serve this group as a leader?

A-7. In offering such a manner of presenting, and in *applying* first in his own experience.

Q-8. Was this group properly organized and is it being conducted correctly?

A-8. The fruits will tell. *Not* from the purpose (get that given first). Not any group should be organized for any special purpose for the *Association*. The Association presents that it has found worthwhile, asking individuals to apply same in their experience from day to day. And what is the purpose and ideal? That again there may be that saving grace that comes from the Father, the Maker of the universe, in the experiences of those individuals in such groups that may be a channel of blessings to their neighbor today. In such a way and manner may they always be organized and always presented.

Q-9. Question on Group #4: Considering this group's individual situation, give such counsel and advice for carrying it on that will aid its members at this time.

A-9. Here we see rather a confusion of tongues rather than ideas. The more and more of the first lesson, that may be made applicable in the experiences of those that may present the lessons or those truths found in same; and more and more may the invitation be given that the individuals will apply that lesson they may gain from a paragraph, a line, a word as the experience of another in their experience. What taught thy Master? Any new tenet? "Love the Lord thy God with all thine heart, and thine mind, and thine body, and thy neighbor as thyself." *Older* than man himself, for this thought in its inception brought the world and man into being. So, in the group and its lessons, let them each in their expressions of themselves find first some one thing as a standard, and no better may be found than: Does this thought make for constructive influence in the experience of the presenter, and is it applicable in the experience of thy neighbor? And this will bring a more *unified* purpose and ideal.

Q-10. Questions on Group #5: Please advise [333] as to the proper way to develop and handle this group.

A-10. It has been experienced by this leader, rather than teacher, that it behooves him to first find himself, and as to how and in what manner he may present same in his experience to those questions and tenets that arise in the minds of those that have been or may be interested in the thought or presentation of such lessons. Then, let him live the lines, the ideas, the thoughts in his *own* experience. And it will not only attract, but will build on a *sure* foundation.

Q-11. What are the causes of its inactivity and how can he meet the seeming lack of interest?

A-11. In first preparing self.

Q-12. Question on Group #6: Advise [642] as to the proper manner to develop and handle this group.

A-12. By the unifying of the thought, the ideas that are presented; in making them as practical lessons in the experiences of those that are studying or seeking for an understanding. Knowledge of itself is worth little. Unless it is applicable or is a practical thing in the experience of any seeker, it goes very, very little way. But apply it; it will build and grow and serve its purpose. This is rather the scientific group, but added in a manner as to how, why, the sources, the natures of those that present same, are applicable and worthwhile.

Q-13. Question on Group #7: Should the meeting place for Group #7 be in Fairmont Park or in Colonial Place?

A-13. As we find, the better would be in Fairmont Park; for the surroundings and the natural tenons of environs would be the better.

Q-14. General questions on group work: Any suggestions for organizing a group in Virginia Beach, and who would be a proper teacher?

A-14. There are many in Virginia Beach that are known, through one channel or another, to be interested in various phases of psychic phenomena. It would be well that there be an invitation by any one of a group, or member of a group, that is well grounded in the purposes and aims, to meet at some particular place, and the purposes and desires and the aims of the presenting of the lessons be presented. And you'll have a group! It'll surprise you, too!

Q-15. Who would be the proper teacher for this group?

A-15. Mrs. Edgar Cayce would be a very good teacher! [4/13/38 Virginia Beach Group #8 was formed.]

Q-16. Please give Esther Wynne advice regarding her future activities in this department.

A-16. Keep that thou hast purposed in thine self, to be used as a channel of blessings to thy fellow man. Be not discouraged, nor be afraid; for art thou basing thine activities on the promises He has made from the beginning, that as ye sow so shall ye reap? Though the harvest at present seems scant, though many discouraging things come into thine experience, with work and labor and prayer the harvest will be great.

We are through for the present.

This psychic reading was given by Edgar Cayce at the Barretts' home, 301 42nd Street, Norfolk, Va., on May 6, 1934, at 4:00 P.M., in accordance with a request made by those present: Edgar Cayce; Gertrude Cayce, conductor; Gladys Davis, steno; C. A. Barrett, Minnie Barrett, Hugh Lynn Cayce, Mildred Mary Davis, Ruth LeNoir, Frances Y. Morrow, Helen Storey, and Esther Wynne.

≈ 262-62 ⋊

Mrs. Cayce: You will have before you the Norfolk Study Group #1, members of which are present in this room, and their work on the lesson, God, the Father, and His Manifestations in the Earth, *a copy of which I hold in my hand. You will go over this lesson as I call the number of each paragraph and suggest such changes or additions as will make this lesson a more complete expression of the truths we are attempting to convey. You will then asnwer the questions on our work which we will present.*

Mr. Cayce: Yes, we have the group gathered here, as a group, as individuals; and their work on the lesson, *God, the Father, and His Manifestations in the Earth.*

Ready for questions.

[Answer, "Very good" to each paragraph, and in addition on 8 and 9, "Some things to be changed here."]

Q-1. What should be our approach to the lesson on Desire?

A-1. First the outline of that which is physical desire. Then an outline of that which is mental desire. And divide the questions in the various groups that may make for the presenting of this so that all may be a part of this lesson.

Q-2. Where does desire originate?

A-2. Will.

Q-3. Define spiritual, mental and physical desires.

A-3. Let's commence at the first! Make the questions first! We will get to the spiritual part when we know what is spiritual and what is material!

Q-4. What should comprise the highest spiritual desire of a soul-entity?

A-4. Let's get to the first things first. Either begin at the beginning or commence backwards, if you choose, and then know how to put them together! Begin with the questions—first make a list of the questions respecting the outlines on physical, and then on mental. Then the next approach will be the difference, or how these are spiritualized.

Q-5. How long should the group spend in preparing each lesson?

A-5. How long is it necessary for giving that which is worthwhile of themselves? Whether it's a week, month or a year! Have something to give!

Q-6. Why should one develop organic trouble while praying for his fellow man?

A-6. A natural consequence of being in organic matter. There are laws in organic influences that are seen through the natural chemical reaction, and those that pertain to the natural forces or environs; for under whatever environ an individual is, it is subject to the laws of that!

Q-7. How does that fit in with the promise of Jesus that whatsoever we desire shall be given to us?

A-7. In their proper time, in their proper place. He was not unreasonable. We are!

Q-8. Will you help [560] overcome this physical inharmony?

A-8. In Him is strength, if the self will be made in accord with that which will produce harmonious coordination in the physical, the mental well-being of this body.

Q-9. Is Mary, the mother of Jesus, on the earth plane?

A-9. No.

Q-10. Please give the group a spiritual message at this time.

A-10. Let that mind be in each of you that was in Him, who went about doing good to those that were seeking to know the manifestations and whose desires were that His will be manifested in the earth.

For, as you each make your lives a channel of blessing to someone, so may those promises, those influences of the spiritual life affect and produce that in our material world that will make for the glorifying of Him ye would name as thine ideal.

Q-11. Anything else on the lesson on Desire *that could or should be given the group at this time?*

A-11. Ye have asked how to approach. Approach it through that way. Then we may give as ye really desire.

We are through for the present.

≫ 262-63 ≪ *This psychic reading was given by Edgar Cayce at the Edmonds' home, 611 Pennsylvania Avenue, Norfolk, Va., on May 20, 1934, at 4:25 P.M., in accordance with a request made by those present: Edgar Cayce; Gertrude Cayce, conductor; Gladys Davis, steno; C. A. Barrett, Minnie Barrett, Mr. and Mrs. Brooks, Hugh Lynn Cayce, Mildred Mary Davis, Edith Edmonds, Florence Edmonds, Helen Ellington, Ruth LeNoir, Frances Y. Morrow, Mrs. Edgar Parry, Helen Storey, and Esther Wynne.*

Mrs. Cayce: You will have before you the Norfolk Study Group #1, members of which are present in this room, and their work on the lessons, God, the Father, and His Manifestations in the Earth, *and* Desire. *Before taking up the second of these, please tell us what changes should be made in paragraphs 8 and 9 of the copy I hold in my hand. You will answer the questions which may be asked.*

Mr. Cayce: Yes, we have the group as gathered here, as a group, as individuals, and their work on the lessons.

In the paragraph as referred to for alterations, this experience should be worded not as different from the experience of the individual, but as an experience or as a question.

In the preparation for the lesson on *Desire,* as has been given, there should be the outline as to the nature of physical desire, mental desire, and how these may be spiritualized.

As to that which may be helpful at this time for those that have (in a way) drawn some questions, consider these and see how they rate. First, we would give this:

In creation we find a difference in that recorded in the Word and that which is nature and that which is the experience of all that have given thought; for when man was brought into being there was a variation in the creation. For it was to him, it is to him, it will be in him, that the changes are wrought as to the manifestations of the Father, the Creator, in material plane. How?

Consider that in the beginning of the earth, that has been shown in information given that may be illustrated in the experiences of those that study any phase of the biological or pathological aspects of nature. Man has either drawn away from the first creation or has been endowed with that which is of a different stage or condition, the ability to react in more than one plane. Through what?

As given in the Scripture, there was breathed into man the soul. Biologically, man makes himself as an animal of the physical; with the desires that are as the instinct in animal for the preservation of life, for the development of species, and for food. These three are those forces that are instinct in the animal and in man. If by that force of will man uses these within self for the aggrandizement of such elements in his nature, these then become the material desires—or are the basis of carnal influences, and belittle the spiritual or soul body of such an individual.

So, the basis of physical desire is adding to, contributing to, or gathering together in forces that which makes for the abilities for such a soul, such an individual, to revel in those forces that are of the animal nature of that individual. Hence he becomes, through carnal or physical desire, one who has no recourse through other than spirit; though he is given the soul that it may be everlasting, that it may be a companion with the Creator, that it may be aware of itself yet one with those influences that make for the spiritualizing of that force which is creative in itself—that makes for god-likeness in the individual soul or activity.

Then, what is the basis of mental desire? The mental as an attribute is also of the animal, yet in man—with his intellect —the ability to make comparisons, to reason, to have the reactions through the senses; that are raised to the forces of activity such that they create for man the environs about him and make for change in hereditary influences in the experience of such a soul. These are the gifts with that free-will agent, or attributes of same; or mind is a development of the application of will respecting desire that has become—in its essence—used as a grace, the gift to give praise for that which it has applied in its experience.

Then, the mental desire that is to laud self, to appraise self above its fellows, or to use that gift in its application to the various activities in the experiences of self or others, makes for that channel through which the carnal desires only become the stumbling blocks in the experiences of those who dwell on same.

For, as has been given as one of the immutable laws, that which the mind of a *soul*—a SOUL—dwells upon it becomes; for mind is the builder. And if the mind is in attune with the law of the force that brought the soul into being, it becomes spiritualized in its activity. If the mind is dwelling upon or directed in that desire towards the activities of the carnal influences, then it becomes destructive in such a force.

Hence, as it has been given, "Let Thy will, O God, be my desire! Let the desire of my heart, my body, my mind, be Thy will, O Father, in the experiences that I may have in the earth!"

When there is the consideration within self, through the self-analysis of self in the light *truly* of that which has been given, how oft must thine own acts condemn thee! And, as the Master has given, "I do not condemn, for thou are condemned already" in the manner thou hast applied thyself, thy abilities, thy birthrights, in the light of that thou knowest, that thou seest manifested in thy life day by day!

And when ye consider what disappointments ye have had in individual associations, think how thy God must have been disappointed in thee when thou hast spoken lightly of thy brother, when thou hast condemned him in thine own conscience, when thou has questioned as to the purpose of those hearts that sought in the light of the best that *they* understood —or that even used their abilities for the aggrandizing of their own selfish motives. Hast thou prayed with them? Hast thou spoken kindly with them? Might not their path have been shown in *thine* life that desire as He manifested when He thought it not robbery to be equal with God and to offer Himself, His life, His body, His desires, as a sacrifice for thee that thou in thine own self-glory, in thine own understanding, might come to a knowledge that the desires of the heart—if they are spiritualized in that thou livest the life He has shown thee— thou may have in thine experience that He has promised, "What ye ask in my name, believing, that may the Father give thee"? Why art thou impatient? For the carnal forces are soon given over to the lusts thereof, but the spirit is alive through eternity! Be not impatient, but love ye the Lord!

We are through.

COME, YE CHILDREN THAT SEEK THE LIGHT! BOW THINE HEADS IN PRAISE TO THE SON. FOR, THE WAY FOR EACH OF YOU THAT WOULD SEEK HIS FACE IS BEING OPENED BEFORE THEE. THE SON OF MAN, THE CHRIST, THY LORD, IS AMONG THEE, EVEN IN THINE HEART—IF YE WILL BUT OPEN THE DOOR TO HIM!

≍ 262-64 ≍

This psychic reading was given by Edgar Cayce at the Edmonds' home, 611 Pennsylvania Avenue, Norfolk, Va., on June 3, 1934, at 4:25 P.M., in accordance with a request made by those present: Edgar Cayce; Gertrude Cayce, conductor; Gladys Davis, steno; C. A. Barrett, Minnie Barrett, Effie Brooks, Hugh Lynn Cayce, Mildred Mary Davis, Myrtle Demaio, R. L. Demaio, Edith Mildred Edmonds, Florence Edmonds, Helen Ellington, Ruth LeNoir, Frances Y. Morrow, Ethel Parry, Edgar Parry, Helen Storey, Margaret Wilkins, and Esther Wynne.

Mrs. Cayce: You will have before you the Norfolk Study Group #1, members of which are present in this room, and its work on the lesson, Desire. *You will give that which will aid the members of the group in continuing their work on this lesson and answer the questions which will be asked.*

Mr. Cayce: Yes, we have the group as gathered here, as a group and as individuals; their work on the lesson *Desire.*

In continuing that given respecting the principles or basic factors in the activity of desire in human experience, those of the group that desire to assist others in their study by the application of the truths that have been presented, *should* apply same in their daily life and thus—as given—make known that which has been and is found that applies in their *own* experience.

For, desire—as has been given—is of the earth earthy and also of the spirit spiritually, but is activative in the realm in which it is directed by that which is the motivating force through the will and the mental abilities and faculties of the individual.

Hence it is a growth, as knowledge, to know in material things what to desire. For, thou hast been given that thine heavenly Father knoweth what ye have need of before ye ask. Then the weak or the pessimist may say, "Why do I have need to ask, if it is known?" The very act shows what the desire is. The very expression shows—if the self will analyze same in the light of that given—as to what is the motivative force in the experience of such a mind, soul or body.

But seek ye, for he that seeketh findeth. To him that

knocketh it shall be opened. Apply, then, that thou hast received. Know ye within yourselves as to how, in what manner and as to what fruit it will bring in thine own experience.

For, as has been given, "We believed for the word of the woman, but now we believe for we have seen and heard ourselves." Apply ye that ye know, for in the application comes understanding. For, as the Master gave, "Ye *are* gods," if ye will use His force of desire and will in His kingdom, but *not* thine own.

Ready for questions.

Q-1. [379]: *Please interpret the dream I had the night of May 1st or 2nd in which a member of Group #1 and I were climbing a mountain and later I was separated from her and could not find her.*

A-1. As there has been given, dreams are of different natures, and have their inception from influences either in the body, in the mind, or from the realm of activity *without* the body through the desires and purposes of the soul itself. Hence there are the various applications of such experiences in the individuals, as visions, dreams or nightmares may affect the body.

In this it arises from seeking and, as is understood, it is an emblematical experience in the mental development or application of experiences in the body-mind. Through that vision it may be seen that the mountain represents the reaching higher and higher in the mental development of self and those associated with self, that in climbing these heights of mental or spiritual experience there come separations; which is not to be wondered at, but rather as experienced. For the body will find that in the studies there will come at times separations as to the purpose or application of that found.

Then, in making use of same, know in what ye have believed; for there has been set a standard through Him, and *in* Him, that ye may measure thine self without condemning thy brother.

Q-2. *How can we discriminate between selfish and unselfish desires?*

A-2. As to what has motivated and does motivate the desire. If it is for the self, or for the glorification of the Christ Consciousness in thine experience. That this or that may appear to self as being well, if such and such an experience were thine own. But, as has been given, each soul may find in self an answer to that it seeks or desires to *know* from what source it (the desire) *has* originated, or is in its impelling force. First ask self in the physical consciousness, and answer—and find an answer—yes or no. Then enter into the inner self through meditation and prayer, and seek the answer there; for "My Spirit beareth witness with thy spirit as to whether thou art the sons of God or not," in thine activity, thine desire, thine purposes, thine aims.

Q-3. [*303*]: *What should I do in order to bring into material manifestation my desires? Are not physical needs in life spiritual in essence?*

A-3. If the desires for the physical things in life are *spiritualized,* they are indeed then as necessary as the higher motivative force in spiritual things. But who is the judge? He that is the Giver of all good and perfect gifts. Even as He prayed, "Father, let this cup pass from me, but *Thy* will—not mine—be done." Again and again do we see in this the manifestation of the flesh warring with the spiritual life itself. And we are to be in that position in our desires that His pattern, His life, is the pattern for our lives. Seek ye ever, but "Thy will, O God, be done in me, through me, as Thou seest; for the desire of my heart is that I may be the channel of blessings to others in the ways and manners Thou seest; not my way, O Lord, but *Thy* way."

Q-4. [*585*]: *I saw the Christ again—early in the morning of May 24th. This time it was a radiant Christ and the morning seemed to be breaking just above His head. What does this mean?*

A-4. What indeed should it mean to each soul, to any soul, to thy soul, that thou hast been through thine experience granted a privilege of such a vision! It should make thee the more humble, the more self-sacrificing, the more glorious in the praises that thou art even in the way of being shown *many* things—if ye will but live the life. What did He give as thy standard? "Inasmuch as ye do it unto the least of these, my brethren, ye do it unto me." Then, see rather in that thou wouldst give in word of mouth, in deed, in act of body, that thou art ministering unto thy Lord. For of such He said, "I will come again to you, and comfort you—I will receive you unto myself —I *will* abide with you." Art thou living in such an atmosphere? It is being opened before thee. Turn it not aside.

Q-5. Please explain Haggai 2:7, "And I will shake all nations and the desire of all nations shall come; and I will fill this house with glory, saith the Lord of host [hosts]."

A-5. In the interpretation of that spoken by Haggai or any of the prophets, take into consideration first to whom the message was being given. Yet know that any message that bespeaks of God's dwelling in the heart or in the temple of man is to the individual a lesson now, today. Here we find, however, from the literal interpretation, that a wayward people had forsaken their temple worship, where they had been appointed to meet with the living God. For there alone they had heard the words, and there alone they had received the instruction as of old. And the interpretation was that these should be turned again, as they were only a few years later, in how that even those that were called the heathen were shaken to the core and *granted* the peoples again to establish the desire of their heart in rebuilding the temple. As ye have received from Him, "The day cometh when neither in Jerusalem nor in this mountain shall ye seek or desire to know the Lord, for ye will find Him in thine own heart, in thine own conscience"; and if the desire of thy heart will be that the temple of thy soul (the image of thy Maker; the soul, not the body, the image of thy Maker) shall be renewed in Him, thou shalt be able in self to know that— and the *way* that thou shouldst go.

Q-6. What is the difference between the desire of the heart and the desire of the will? And is it not possible for harmonious coordination of these? How may it be attained?

A-6. Only in Him. In speaking of the heart and of the will, analyze for the moment as to what they represent in thine own experience. The heart is ordinarily considered the seat of life in the physical, while the will as a motivative factor in the mental and spiritual realm. To be sure, these may be made one. But how? In that the will of self and the desire of the heart are selfless in the Christ Consciousness. Even as He gave in the shadow of the day when the cross loomed before Him on Calvary, when the desire of the heart and the will of self were made one. Indeed, as He gave, the flesh is weak—the spirit is willing. If the spirit and the will of the inner self will be made in accord with the spirit of truth, in the desire of the heart to be one in and with and through Him. For, the soul is in Him; yet, as the promise in the Christ is, the soul shall be free in Him through that love, through that manner of making the desire and the will one in the Father as did He in Gethsemane.

Q-7. *What is desire? How does it build physically?*

A-7. This has been given. And how does it build physically? Desire, as first given, was in the motivating force that may separate or make the soul one with or separate from the Whole, through the manifestations in the will. And it builds in that the spirit moves in the direction in which it is motivated by will and desire.

Q-8. *Is it necessary to give up physical desires for spiritual development?*

A-8. Rather spiritualize the physical desires as He did in the garden. What there is shown thee as to how the physical, the spiritual, fought—as it were—one with another? "Father, let this cup pass from me." This is as every experience in the physical man when there is the fear of the loss in this or that direction. There is the constant, "Father, save me from this—from this." Yet, even as He, if there has been builded in thine experience as was in His experience—offering Himself for the world—then thou must pass through same, in making the physical desire and the will of the Father as one, that there may be the cleansing in the soul of those things that may bring the consciousness of the oneness with the Father in whatever realm.

Q-9. *What should we hold in mind when we hold the affirmation in the present lesson, "Let thy desire be my desire," etc.?*

A-9. What to hold in mind? Hold the Christ before thee, ever. For, He has promised to take His own self and to take thy burden upon Himself, as he bore same. Rather would thy prayer be, *"I cannot bear this alone, my Savior, my Christ. I seek Thy aid."* And such a cry has never, no never, been denied—the believing and *acting* heart.

We are through.

This psychic reading was given by Edgar Cayce at his home on Arctic Crescent, Virginia Beach, Va., on June 24, 1934, at 4:40 P.M., in accordance with a request made by those present: Edgar Cayce; Gertrude Cayce, conductor; Gladys Davis, steno; Hugh Lynn Cayce, Mildred Mary Davis, Edith Mildred Edmonds, Florence Edmonds, Frances Y. Morrow, Helen Storey, and Esther Wynne.

≫ 262-65 ≪

Mrs. Cayce: You will have before you the Norfolk Study Group #1, members of which are present in this room, and their work on the lesson, Desire. *You will give such information as will be of assistance in completing this lesson, treating the subject of the spiritualization of desire. You will answer the questions that will be asked.*

Mr. Cayce: Yes, we have the group as gathered here, as a group, as individuals, and their work on the lesson *Desire*.

In giving that which will aid those studying, contemplating or meditating upon the meanings of desire and the spiritualizing of same, there may be an illustration of same as drawn from that the Master gave in the Sermon on the Mount. "He that would smite thee on the one cheek, turn the other also." To another it has been said, "Vengeance is mine, saith the Lord." To those whose desire has ever been in that of being and doing the will of the Master, *this* would be sufficient. To him who has felt antagonistic to those that have spoken unkindly, or have made accusations that would hurt the inner self, then that as He gave, "He that would smite thee, turn the other cheek," is spiritualizing the desire for vengeance. "He that would sue thee and take away thy coat, give him thy cloak also." Because others would use thee, or take advantage of thee, if thy desire is in the Lord, in the Creative Forces, should not cause thee to speak harshly nor to desire that calamitous things or conditions come upon others for their unkindness. For they, as He gave, who would even destroy thy body are nothing. Think rather on him that may destroy thy soul also. Who may separate you from the love of the Father? Only thyself. For, an injury that may be done thee—or done thy body—is as being done unto the Maker, and the *Lord* is the avenger of those that love Him.

Thus may you spiritualize desire, whether for those things

-262-

that bring the comforts or the necessities or the activities in thine experience in the earth. What is spiritualizing desire? Desire that the Lord may use thee as a channel of blessings to all whom ye may contact day by day; that there may come in thine experience whatever is necessary that thou be cleansed every whit. For, when the soul shines forth in thine daily walks, in thine conversation, in thine thoughts, in thine meditation, and it is in that realm where the spirit of truth and life may commune with same day by day, *then* indeed do ye spiritualize desire in the earth.

For, as He has given, "It must indeed be that offenses *come,* but woe unto him by whom they come."

Let the desire ever be, then, that thou may never sin against thy fellow man; for God is the avenger. And from Him we may in mercy find mercy, as we show mercy, patience, truth, justice, loving-kindness, to our fellow man. For, "As ye do it unto these, my brethren, ye do it unto me." Preferring one above another? No. Preferring *others* above thyself! that thou may be the arm, the shoulder, the one upon whom someone may lean in coming to know the knowledge of the love of the Christ in their experience.

Ready for questions.

Q-1. As I call each name you will give that which will be applicable in the individual life in relation to this lesson:

A-1. [Interrupting] Well, first, that you each make that move necessary to give expression of your *own* experience as in reference to that which has brought to you a knowledge of desire towards the Christ Consciousness moving in and through the efforts of the body in your own experience. Then may there be *truly* given that which may aid you in *understanding* your approach the better. For, each soul is a free-will agent in a material world, with the choice before it in its own experience. This you each will recognize as you meditate upon putting it into *activity*. To *know* to do good and to do it not, is what? He that had experienced same gave that it is sin. Listen to that which convicts you that *activity* is necessary in your experience, in order to come to the knowledge and understanding of what an approach should be—through such an activity. Why, say ye, activity? For the Lord thy God is a *living* God; not of stone, but a *living* God. And the Christ, thy Mediator, thy brother, is a *living* Christ, that may be known of all that would seek to have His consciousness. For He has come to those among you; He will guide and protect you. He is in sorrow when ye speak unkindly; when ye forsake even for the moment that thou hast purposed—thou *hast* purposed—in thy heart to do.

Make thy purpose, thy desire, one with Him. "Here am I, Lord, use me—send me."

We are through.

This psychic reading was given by Edgar Cayce at his home on Arctic Crescent, Virginia Beach, Va., on July 11, 1934, at 11:30 A.M. This reading was voluntarily given by Mr. Cayce after the suggestion had been given for obtaining reading number 608-7. Those present were: Edgar Cayce; Gertrude Cayce, conductor; Gladys Davis, steno; L. B. Cayce and Mildred Davis.

⊁ 262-66 ⊀

Mr. Cayce: This might be interesting to those who are compiling things.

Each state, country or town makes its own vibrations by or through the activities of those that comprise same; hence creates for itself a realm in which the activities of each city, town, state—or city, state and town—may be in the realm of those forces where the activities bring the associations through relativity of influence in the material plane. Hence why astrological influences, and why in the various activities or centers may there be born or brought into the earth the various influences, even though their realm or place of activity may be very foreign to that place wherein they entered.

Those activities make for such an impression upon the realm of data, or between time and space, as to make for what men have called *Destiny* (which will be your next lesson) in the material affairs of individuals.

[Here the reading 608-7 started for an 8-year-old girl who had been born in Florida.]

This psychic reading was given by Edgar Cayce at the Edmonds' home, 611 Pennsylvania Avenue, Norfolk, Va., on July 15, 1934, at 4:15 P.M., in accordance with a request made by those present: Edgar Cayce; Gertrude Cayce, conductor; Gladys Davis, steno; C. A. Barrett, Minnie Barrett, Mildred Davis, Edith Edmonds, Florence Edmonds, Helen Ellington, Ruth LeNoir, Frances Y. Morrow, Helen Storey, and Esther Wynne.

⊱ 262-67 ⊰

Mrs. Cayce: You will have before you the Norfolk Study Group #1, members of which are present in this room, and their work on the lesson, Desire. *You will please give to each, as I call the names, a personal message that will help them at this time as individuals to better perform their part in the work of the lesson. You will answer the questions that will be asked.*

Mr. Cayce: Yes, we have the group as gathered here, as a group, as individuals, and their work on the lesson on *Desire.*

In that which has been given may they each become more and more aware of the spirit of truth working in and through them, as they apply in their daily experiences that which has been pointed out; as to how the desires of the body, of the mind, may be spiritualized in those things that may make for the oneness of purpose in self to the will of the Father.

Ready for questions.

Q-1. [413]:

A-1. Let thy purposes, thy aims, thy desires, ever be in the light of that which has been given, "Inasmuch as ye do it unto the least of these, my brethren, ye do it unto me," whether in desire, in the purposes of the heart, or in the aims of the activities in the body.

Q-2. [307]:

A-2. Glory in those things that bespeak of the activities of the spirit of truth as it convicts the hearts, the minds, the desires of those that seek to know His ways; for he that would know the Father, that would know His will, His desire as toward him, must believe that He is. That, then, which moves in the hearts and minds of those who seek to know Him, is *of* Him. *Glory* thou in same.

Q-3. [379]:

A-3. As the purposes and desires of the body, the mind, are

made more and more in accord with that thou seest to praise in thy fellow man, more and more will the consciousness of the Christ Spirit working in and through men be manifest in thine own heart.

Q-4. [*993*]:

A-4. Keep the way as thou hast purposed in thine heart, for His ways are not past finding out to those that seek to know Him. And they that walk in the light shall have no darkness at all in their heart. For He giveth life, light, hope and eternal life to those that seek His ways.

Q-5. [*560*]:

A-5. Let praise and honor ever be in thine purposes, in thine desires towards those things that make thee aware of His presence abiding with thee. For His promises are sure that they who walk with Him shall *know* Him even as He is. Let thy light so shine that others may know thou walkest, thou talkest with Him, and that thy desire is towards those that seek His way.

Q-6. [303]:

A-6. In the Father's house are many mansions. As thine desires are towards the knowledge of the Father's ways, of the Father's purposes with thee as concerning thine fellow man, put *into practice* that thou knowest and give praise and honor and be joyous in the service that thou renderest to thy neighbor. For they that do good unto their neighbor lendeth to the Lord, and *He* will repay in those ways that bring peace, harmony and understanding in thine conscience; for ye know that ye are His, for He calleth His own by name.

Q-7. [*69*]:

A-7. That thou purposeth has brought—and purpose in thine inner self—that consciousness of the purposefulness in being one with that spirit of truth that maketh every soul alive in Him. Let thine praises be, then, to the Father of light in whom there is no variableness, and He will walk with thee as thou goest about doing good.

Q-8. [*69's husband*]:

A-8. Let thine inner self, thine consciousness of the desires and purposes of thine heart, be more and more one with Him; leaving with Him—that is within self—that knowledge that He will be thy guide, wilt thou but let the Christ have His way with thee. Let thy yeas be yea and thy nays be nay in the purposes of the Lord.

Q-9. [295]:

A-9. Keep that which has been purposed in thine self and the desire of thine heart towards Him shall be made manifest in thine life. Let the Father have His way with thee. For His word has gone out to those that seek to make the desires of their hearts, of their minds, one with Him, and it shall not return to Him void. Let thy light, then, shine in praise, in glory to Him.

Q-10. [585]:

A-10. The ways that the Father maketh known His praises, His glory unto the sons and daughters of men, are through the purposes and desires that are builded by the sons and daughters of men towards the *Lord's* way in the earth. *Thou* knowest the way. Walk therein, and His light and His ways shall guide thee as thou goest; for His promises are sure and may be thine as ye fulfill that ye have purposed in thine heart to *do* towards those things thou knowest to be the Lord's way with man.

Q-11. [294]:

A-11. Let thine desires, of the mind, of the body, be one with Him; for He will guide thee and direct thee, if ye will but put thy trust *wholly* in Him. And He will walk and talk with thee, even as He has promised to those that let the inner desire be one with thy Lord, thy God.

Q-12. [538]:

A-12. As the ways are opening before thee, as to how the desires of the heart, of the mind, may make for the pathway being bright or dim, so let the light of truth in the promises in the Christ *be* in thine life, that thy words, thine acts, may be in keeping with that thou desirest toward thy Lord. For, as ye do it unto the least of thy brethren, ye do it unto thy God. For He is in the life, He *is* the life, of thy brethren.

Q-13. [288]:

A-13. Walk in the light, even as He is in the light. Let less and less of self enter into the desires of thy mind, of thy body, but that thy desire may be, "Have Thy way with me, O Lord. Be *Thou* the guide. Let that Thou *would* have me do be the purpose of my life, the *desire* of my heart, and let me give the praise to Him that leads the way."

Q-14. [*341*]:

A-14. Glory in the Lord. As thou hast seen, as thou hast heard from within how the desires of the self make for the opening or closing of the door to the heart of God, so let thy purposes, thy desires in self, be more and more aware of the fact that the Lord is in His holy temple in thine self, if ye will but let *Him* be the guide. For thine body is the temple of thy soul, the image of thy God. Let Him have His way with thee. Be up and doing with that thou art given to do day by day.

Q-15. [*404*]:

A-15. Faint not in trial nor tribulation. Let thy purposes and thy desires be in Him. Let the ways of the Lord be known in thine inner self, "Not my will but *Thine,* O Lord, be done *in* me, through me. Let me be the channel of blessing to someone day by day, that Thou hast purposed in the inner man, that which is needed for my soul awakening in Thee to its greatest abilities be in the desire of my heart towards the will of the Father in me."

Q-16. [*462*]:

A-16. Glory and praise to him who purposes in his heart to seek the Lord while He may be found in thine own self. For He is not far away, but even in thine inner self. Open the door of desire towards Him in such measures, in such manners, as to bring in thine own experience the ways of the Lord being manifest in thine daily life. For His promise has been, ye that seek in the name of the Lord thy God, thy Christ, thy Savior, *shall* receive according to the desire of the heart unto the Christ *having* His way with thee. What hast thou purposed? That ye may know the way in the light of thine own desire, or that the Lord would have thee do?

Q-17. [*288*]: *What is meant by, "the desire remaining in the One, for which the Oneness was created"?* [*See 288-6, p. 1, par. 3.*]

A-17. The desire remaining in the purposes of the Creative Force, or God, in thee, as to those things necessary to purge the soul that it may be a companion with the first purposes, the first desires, in the *one,* in God. For flesh is weak, the spirit is willing. Let the *spirit* be the motivating force in thy desire, rather than the exaltation of the flesh in any individual experience. For God giveth the increase, whether in the flesh or in the mental forces, *as* thou hast purposed or desired from within. For thou *art* gods in the making. What wilt thou be to thy fellow man if the desire is for exaltation of self? For thus sin entered in the flesh.

Q-18. Is it possible to be selfless while seeking fulfillment in the flesh of the heart's desire?

A-18. If the heart's desire is one with the purposes of the spirit force in self, and not of the fulfillment of flesh desire alone. Let Him have His way with thee. As thou meetest those things of the flesh, of the body, as related to the spirit of truth, so does the desire come to be one with, one of, those forces that makes for *unifying* of self in body, in mind, in soul, to the purposes of thine indwelling in the flesh.

Q-19. Explain, "He desires truth in the inward parts."

A-19. He that giveth his soul to the purposes of the Lord, he that loveth his enemies, he that loveth those that speak harshly to thine inner self, *desires* the Lord in the inner self. Thus the answers for all come in the love that He gave, that He left His glory with the Father that He might know the desires of the flesh as related to all those things pertaining to the waywardness of man; yet the desire that arose from the inner self that life was given by Him, life must be maintained in the *desire of* Him towards those to whom He had given the power to become the sons of God through *their* experience in the earth. So is the inner desire one with the Father-God. So is the soul made one with the soul of thy Savior. For, "If ye love me ye will keep my commandments, and a new commandment I give, Love ye one another, even as I have loved you."

Q-20. [413]: Please give interpretation of foreign [apparently Greek] letters I saw in meditation on July 5th.

A-20. As these were as mysteries to thine consciousness, yet knowing that they bear a message to those that are aware of their meaning, so have the purposes, the desires in thine heart been such that ye might know that that man has made a mystery of God's purposes with man, and they—those mysteries, as those letters—may be known to thee, if ye will but put into practice, into active service in thine inner self, that thou knowest to do step by step. For all the words that may be said are combined in the twenty-six letters in thine own language, yet there is the necessity of thine using thine own self and the faculties of thine mind to combine them in such manners and measures as to make known that thou desirest to give to thine fellow man as to that thou purposeth in thine inner self. So with the characters as seen. This may be as foreign to thine consciousness as those characters, lest ye put them to *work* in thine own experience.

COME, MY CHILDREN, YE THAT SEEK THE LORD. HE IS NIGH UNTO THEE. THOU HAST PURPOSED WELL IN THINE STUDIES, IN THINE PREPARATION FOR THOSE THAT WOULD SEEK THROUGH THESE CHANNELS TO KNOW MORE OF WHAT THY LORD, THY GOD, WOULD HAVE THEM TO DO. BE NOT SATISFIED, BUT RATHER CONTENT IN THAT YE ARE BEING A CHANNEL OF BLESSING TO THY FELLOW MAN. THOU ART AS THE LEAVEN THAT WILL LEAVEN THE WHOLE, FOR SOME THERE BE AMONG YOU THAT WILL HEAR HIS VOICE—AND HE WILL WALK AND TALK WITH THOSE THAT ARE WILLING, JOYOUSLY, THAT HE, THY BROTHER, THY CHRIST, THY SAVIOR, WOULD DIRECT THY WAYS. KEEP THE FAITH.

We are through.

This psychic reading was given by Edgar Cayce at the Edmonds' home, 611 Pennsylvania Avenue, Norfolk, Va., on July 29, 1934, at 4:10 P.M., in accordance with a request made by those present: Edgar Cayce; Gertrude Cayce, conductor; Gladys Davis, steno; Mildred Davis, Edith Edmonds, Florence Edmonds, Ruth LeNoir, Frances Y. Morrow, Helen Storey, and Esther Wynne.

⋊ 262-68 ⋉

[Background: Emergency call caused members to give over the period originally set for Group #1 lesson on *Desire,* to seek physical counsel for acute condition of a member of another group. Many seemed "let down" to have to give up the reading. Diagnosis and treatment was given rather fast; when finished, Edgar Cayce said: "We are through with this reading," at which time Gertrude Cayce gave the suggestion for the Group #1 reading which had previously been planned. The following 262-68 was the result. All seemed elated over it.]

Mrs. Cayce: You will have before you Study Group #1, members of which are present in this room. We seek, from the sources through which we have been called, a "checking up," as it were, as to just where we stand. Also if it be in keeping at this time, we desire information, advice and guidance as to our individual and group calling.

Mr. Cayce: Yes, we have the group as gathered here, as a group, as individuals, and those influences in the experience of each; also that whereunto the group as a group and as individuals have been called.

In giving that which may be helpful at this time to the group, let each take that given as applying to their individual selves. For if there is the cooperation, if there is the understanding, if there is the enlightening to the minds and hearts and souls of those that seek to be a channel of blessing, their purposes, their object, are one.

That there is through the natural tend or bent of individual activity the negative influence, or that which may be termed as egotistical activity in the actions of some, this is not as a fault; rather as the warning. Let the object of the activities of the group in service for others, in the preparation of that which may be applied in the experience of others that may study

-272-

same, that may read same, that may apply the information which is supplied by the activities of the group, be rather that there may be presented the love of the Father that is manifested in the lives and the hearts of all through the Son and *His* advent into the earth, and His promises that are sure in the lives of those who may so apply themselves from their own selfish interests or motives as to make of themselves an object for *service* in His name.

For, all that have been called in this service, in these activities as a group, as individuals, have responded with their very souls. Some have been discouraged. Some have been faint-hearted. These are not faults. Rather use that which *thou* knowest has been thine individual weakness in the service, in the light, in the understanding that thou hast had in thine activities as individuals, as a group; the stepping-stones for those things that may make for a greater service, a greater activity in behalf of thy fellow man, without thought of self, without thought of satisfying, of glorifying, other than that desire which is in the spiritual activity of the soul that seeks to magnify Christ in the lives, the hearts of all. Not desiring to give a law, to give a precept as to how this, that or the other individual may use or as to what they should do with their lives. Rather, as the calling has been, present that thou hast tested in thine own experience and hast been found in thine lives to be that which has answered for those troubled periods, those times when darkness or shadow, doubt or fear assailed thee. For, each soul must know Him as He is. Then, let each soul, each individual, rededicate their lives, their hearts, their bodies, to the service of thy brother, thy neighbor, that there may come in the earth that which will make for, "That Thou gavest me, Lord, have I used to the best of my ability. Thou, O Lord, must give the increase."

Faint not when there are discouraging activities in the hearts, in the souls even of those that may falter here and there; for *God* looketh on the heart, thou only seest the outward appearances. Look to thine own self that thine own skirts, thine own mind, thine own body, are kept wholly in the way that He has called thee. When there comes fear or doubt, look to Him; arouse in thyself that consciousness of His presence abiding

with thee, and He will quell the storm within thine own life.
He abides with thee, wilt thou keep Him, His precepts, "Love
ye one another."

Ready for questions.

We are through.

This psychic reading was given by Edgar Cayce at the Edmonds' home, 611 Pennsylvania Avenue, Norfolk, Va., on August 12, 1934, at 4:30 P.M., in accordance with a request made by those present: Edgar Cayce; Gertrude Cayce, conductor; Gladys Davis, steno; Mildred Davis, Edith Edmonds, Florence Edmonds, Abbie Kemp, Ruth LeNoir, Frances Y. Morrow, Helen Storey, and Esther Wynne.

~ 262-69 ⟨

Mrs. Cayce: You will have before you the Norfolk Study Group #1, members of which are present in this room, and their work on the lesson Desire, *a copy of which I hold in my hand. Please give us that needed for completing this lesson, and for living it in our daily lives. You will answer the questions that may be asked.*

Mr. Cayce: Yes, we have the Norfolk Study Group #1, members of which are present in this room. We have them as a group and as individuals, and their work on the lesson *Desire.*

As seen from that given again and again, if ye will apply that *known* of self then there may be given the next step in thine self making application of that thou knowest to do. Yet, if there is held doubt, fear, trembling, these only make for confusion in thine own experience. For it has been given that the desires of the heart that are of the spiritual forces in application are spiritual desires; while those that are for the comforts, or ease, or gratification of self's own interest, are born of the earth and do bring confusion to those that seek even the clarification in their own minds when meeting, contemplating those things that pertain to the spirit. For man looketh on the outward appearance, God looketh on the heart. What *is* thy desire towards thy brethren? Let each of you gathered here meditate before Him, opening thy mind, thy heart, to the influences from without, surrounding thyself with the thought, the purpose of the Christ life, the Christ Spirit as manifested in the earth among His brethren; and ask self: "What do I desire? What are the motivating purposes that prompt me to speak thus and so respecting my brother, respecting the activities in the life of an individual?" And then, "What is the desire of my heart as to the manner of life that I would live, as a channel of blessing, as one who has been called to a purpose?" in giving to thy brother those things that bespeak of the glories of a Christ-like life, who thought it not robbery to make Himself equal with God. Think it not robbery of thyself to make thyself equal to a god among thy brethren, but look upon the heart of self. Is it for the satisfying of the ego in self? Is it that self may be lauded, praised? Is it that self has been taken advantage of, and there is the desire that there be a reckoning in thine own heart and conscience and purposes? Or hast thou put on the whole armor of Christ? Hast thou looked into the face of the Christ, that thou surroundest thyself with, and said—as it has been given—"Here am I, Lord, use me, send me!" For the day of the Lord draweth nigh, and eternity is long with thy soul! [See 262-70, A-1.] If ye will purpose in your hearts and seek out *these* things, my children, ye may know the truth that sets men free indeed! Ye may know how ye may live that which has been given thee! Ye may know to give to others that thou hast experienced; for His promises are sure, "If ye will keep my commandments, if ye will love one another, if ye will prefer thy neighbor, thy brother, thy friend before thyself, then ye may indeed know the Lord liveth and *will* guide, guard and keep thee!"

Ready for questions.

Q-1. [993]: Please interpret and enlarge on the dream I had in July, regarding the marriage ceremony in which a big red apple was outstanding and had to be placed on the altar.

A-1. As fruit is emblematical, as the marriage is emblematical in the experience, then the vision is rather the change that will come to pass in the sacrifice that is to be made in much of those judgments, feelings prompted in the inner self, respecting individuals and groups and associations. So may there come through same the greater vision, as the purifying of the offering brings to the hearts, the souls of those that seek to make their calling and election sure in Him.

Q-2. [585]: Please explain the vision I saw early Friday morning, July 20th, when I saw the sky open and the figures treading earthward, bowing as if before a king.

A-2. A vision whereunto there will be again opened to thee thine own interpretation through the experiences that thou wilt have in thine own self. For as the heavens, to the heart, the mind of man, declare the glory of the Infinite, and as the heart of man has been trained in and throughout the ages to look *up* and *out* to those sources for the aid, for the strength, for the power, and for the unseen forces that may move in and through the hearts and minds and bodies of individuals, so — as the heavens open before thee, through thine own meditation and thine seeking — it is as that thine prayers have been heard, thine supplications have come before the throne. Be not weary in thy turmoil or thy strife, for He has heard and will answer speedily.

Q-3. [303]: *Give me a message that will help me at this time.*

A-3. As has been given thee, be not weary in thine doing; for *thou* hast purposed in thine heart to know thy Savior, and He draws near to thee oft in thine walks with thy fellow man. Be not unmindful, be not boastful, yet know, "As ye have done unto the least of these, my brethren, ye have done it unto me." Just being kind, just being patient, is the whole duty of man. Let God have *His* way with thee. Rail not on circumstance, that seems to make body and soul even shiver in those things that tread upon thine conscience at times, for God is not mocked — and whatsoever a man soweth, that must he also reap. But ye have been called. Keep ye faithful. In patience will ye know that ye possess the soul that may be given, in the hours of trial, in the periods of testing, that He thy Savior would have thee do. Open the door of thy heart to Him. In thy prayer, in thy meditation, call on Him; for He is near. Hath He not chosen thy body for one of His companions in the earth? Then know that He will not leave thee comfortless, but will come to thee.

Q-4. *Is there a message for the group as a whole at this time?*

A-4. Come! Sing and make a joyful noise unto the Lord, thy King; for thy Elder Brother, even Jesus the Christ, has a mission for each of you in the earth. Fulfill that *thou* KNOWEST to do in thine mind, in thine heart, in thine body; for the *Lord* loveth whom He testeth, and will purge every one — that you may be His companions with Him. What *is* a day of joy in the earth compared to an eternity of glory with thy Brother, the Christ? For by Him all things were made, and even as He has loved you, so may ye love Him — if ye will do His biddings.

We are through.

This psychic reading was given by Edgar Cayce at the Edmonds' home, 611 Pennsylvania Avenue, Norfolk, Va., on August 26, 1934, at 4:00 P.M., in accordance with a request made by those present: Edgar Cayce; Gertrude Cayce, conductor; Gladys Davis, steno; Hugh Lynn Cayce, Mildred Davis, Edith Edmonds, Florence Edmonds, Helen Ellington, Ruth LeNoir, Frances Y. Morrow, Helen Storey, and Esther Wynne.

⊱ 262-70 ⊰

[Background: A period of "drought" was being experienced by the group; contributions to and work on the lesson seemed at a standstill.]

Mrs. Cayce: You will have before you Group #1, members of which are present in this room; as a group and as individuals we seek at this time further counsel and guidance in carrying forward our work. Questions.

Mr. Cayce: Yes, we have the group as gathered here, as individuals, as a group, and their work in the preparation for that which may be helpful to those of their fellows who seek through such channels for aid.

In the applications, as has so oft been given, does the individual find that which to it, as an individual, is the experience.

In this present dilemma in which they each find themselves it would be well that ye harken to that which has been given, that ye counsel one with another in the experiences and applications of that thou—as an individual—hast gained from the experience in *Desire,* and ye may analyze what is desire in thine own experience. Many have condemned that in their own consciousness that has been given, without insight into the purposes and desires of their own inner self. Where is the meeting place with thy Maker? In the holy of holies in thine own self! Raise the Christ Consciousness within self to thine own judgments, that there may be shown thee as He has given: "Take no thought, for—if thou art in accord—it will be given thee in the selfsame hour." Laud not thyself, but rather let the purposes, the desires of thy heart be, "Thy will be done in and through me, and Lord be Thou the guide in the time of temptation." For it must needs be that those come in thine experience, but not of self nor in the exercising of thine strength that thou

-278-

wilt meet same—rather in thy weakness may He strengthen thee in thy desires, in thy purposes. *Empty* thyself of physical desires, that the spiritual aptitude of self may be glorified through thee in thy walks before thy fellow man.

Condemn not others; condemn not self. Let thy yeas be yea and thy nays nay, lest ye enter into temptation without His being near.

Ready for questions.

Q-1. *[560]*: *May this be explained, in reading of Aug. 12, 1934: "For the day of the Lord draweth nigh, and eternity is long with thy soul!" [See 262-69, p. 2, par. 1.]*

A-1. The day of the Lord draweth nigh. Each soul has been called in this group for a service unto the Lord. Hence the day draweth nigh, for the night cometh when no man labors. Eternity is long with thy soul. As eternity to the finite mind indicates that without beginning, without end, so is the soul of man that has made his desire as one with the Lord. For as eternity so the soul, and it is *long* with thy soul. So, keep the paths straight. Walk in the light, even as He is in the light. Be joyous in thy service in that thou hast to meet day by day, for the day of the Lord draweth nigh when *ye* who have been called must give an account unto the keeper of thy Lord's vineyard. *Each* soul *is* writing His gospel day by day, and others read whether it is faithless or true. What is the gospel of thy Lord, according to you?

Q-2. *Each soul is a free-will agent in a material world, with the choice before it in its own experience. Are there not times when the will is overruled by higher forces? May this information be given?*

A-2. Yes. It is overruled. Through the destiny, that ye must learn—but take the first steps first. Learn that thou hast to learn, then it may be given.

Q-3. *[295]*: *Will you give me a message that will help me to apply the lesson and contribute something toward the lesson?*

A-3. As thou hast known, and *do* know in thine experience as to how desire in the material may be spiritualized by making the desire as "Thy will, Thy purpose, Thy way be done in and through me; as the Father seeth fit, use me," so give expression of same in such a manner that it may be helpful to thy fellow man. "Not my will, not my desire, save that desire be in accord with Thy purpose of the god that manifests itself in and through me as *to* my attitude, my purpose, my desire, towards my fellow man." So may the application of thy experience aid others in knowing this.

Q-4. Is there a message for the group as a whole?

A-4. Let that desire, that thought, that purpose, be in each of you that was in the *man* Jesus that, though He were in the world yet not of the world, neither was He strange nor curious, neither did He fain [refrain?] from partaking of those things that were about Him in the social, in the home life of His fellow man. Yet His desire ever, "Not my will but Thine, O Lord, be done in me." As He has given ye, ye have all been called unto a service in Him; some to sacrifice here, others to toil and to disappointments there, yet He has promised and is able to keep that He has committed unto thy keeping against any obstacle, whether of the earth or of the unseen activities, against *thou* fulfilling that whereunto thou hast been called, if— *if*—thy *desire* is in Him.

We are through.

This psychic reading was given by Edgar Cayce at the Edmonds' home, 611 Pennsylvania Avenue, Norfolk, Va., on September 9, 1934, at 4:00 P.M., in accordance with a request made by those present: Edgar Cayce; Gertrude Cayce, conductor; Mildred Mary Davis, steno; Hugh Lynn Cayce, Edith Mildred Edmonds, Florence Edmonds, Helen Ellington, Ruth LeNoir, and Frances Y. Morrow.

⊰ 262-71 ⊱

[Background: Edgar Cayce said often he almost had to force himself to give readings but he was eager to give this one.]

Mrs. Cayce: You will have before you Norfolk Study Group #1, members of which are present here, and their work on the lesson Desire, *a copy of which I hold in my hand. You will go over this material and make such suggestions as to arrangement, statement of facts, additions, or changes that will aid us in completing this lesson. You will answer the questions that may be asked.*

Mr. Cayce: Yes, we have the group as gathered here, and their work on the lesson *Desire,* and those who are not gathered, whose desire is towards those activities as related to the data as presented here.

In giving that as may be helpful to those that would correlate those experiences and those thoughts and lessons as presented by others, this would be the most helpful:

Consider, first, that as was given as to how the outline should be divided, for, the dealings are with that as partakes of the spiritual in its highest sense and of material in its most destructive or degrading sense. For, as is presented, the presentation to an active force of *desire* is to set in motion those things that become miracles or crimes in the experiences of individuals.

As to the data itself, then: Separate same into such, and in making those separations, make the headings under these varied presentations of that as is the experience of the individual presenting same. The thought or the truths as presented there are *evolutionary* and *revolutionary* in the minds of some, yet are basic truths in the experience of individuals that have lived or experienced or visioned them, and will bear fruit.

To ALL we would give: Be patient. That part thou hast chosen in such a work is born of truth. Let it come in and be a part of thy daily life. Look in upon the experiences, for, as will be seen, my children, there has been appointed one that may aid thee in thy future lessons, and he will be thy teacher, thy guide, one sent through the power of thine own desires. Thine own selves, then, may prevent his being, meeting, living, dwelling, with thee. Not the Christ, but His messenger, with the Christ from the beginning, and is to other worlds what the Christ is to this earth.

As many of you ask now, "Why should the realm of spirit be mindful of this group, of the work of these gathered here?" The sincerity of thy purpose has merited, has destined, that such can be thy experience. "What, then," ye ask, "is the way, the manner?"

That no one mention *who,* though the name and the activities of any desire may be given thee, but when thou speakest outside thine own group, thou hast cut thyself aloof. [See 262-77, A-5.] Art thou willing to accept such a charge? [Pause, of about a minute's duration.] The answers are slow. Some accepted; some know not. Some ask themselves, "What is this?" "In what manner am I approached?"

Ye would enter the garden with Him and watch while He, as thy Savior, makes intercession for thee. Wilt thou watch? Ye must answer in thine own heart.

Accept, then, that presented here, and arrange same; for thine presentations must, from here, take a turn, for thou that hast made thy purposes, thy desires, thy aims thy Lord's, are to be honored with His guest, with His presence. Accept ye? [See 262-73 and -74 re the choice made.]

Ready for questions. [Loudly.]

Q-1. Is the definition of mind on page 2, paragraph 3, "Mind is a development of the application of will respecting desire used as a grace" correct?

A-1. Correct. As ye analyze grace, which is a gift of the Creator to the creature that ([aside] "Pay attention to what you are doing here!") [Later in discussing this in the group, several said they thought Edgar Cayce was talking to them, as did Gertrude Cayce as conductor.] the mind is acted upon by the grace, through the grace, and not of self alone, but the gift of the

Creator that *that* mind, *that* soul, may be the companion with, one with, that mind of the Maker.

Q-2. Should any further explanation be made of "the pattern in the mount" as mentioned on page 5, paragraph 2?

A-2. This sufficient, that it is seen that this must be an individual experience, calling even as He to those that would vision same, even as those came as messengers to those shown the pattern. So may there come to thee a messenger to show thee the way.

Q-3. Will it be necessary to present this lesson again, paragraph by paragraph, or simply correct and fit in the contributions not yet in?

A-3. This would be, then, in accord, much as many of those that were altered or outlined according to those where changes were suggested. Not necessary, then.

Q-4. [585]: Is the experience which I had about a year ago in which I felt that I spiritualized certain desires about those who had been in my home, the proper material for my contribution to this lesson?

A-4. Proper contribution, *provided* it is presented in the experiences that it, the desire and the activity on the part of self, has brought into thine own self life's activity or work.

Q-5. [307]: Please give me a message of promise and consolation at this time.

A-5. As He has promised thee to meet thee in thine inner self, trust in that as is shown thee, as ye turn within, for thou hast been given charge concerning those things that become as living water in the minds and the hearts of many erring children, even, that seek the light, and as He has given, "He that turns an erring one from the way of darkness has saved a soul and covered a multitude of weaknesses in self."

Be not overcome in thy anxiety or thy overzealousness, for the harvest is in the hands of those that give the increase, and this is under the law of mercy. Hence, ever may thy prayer be, "Mercy, Lord—not sacrifice" [262-72, A-3], and it will break a light in thine heart and mind that will bring peace, harmony and joy in the service that thou art rendering thyself and thy fellow man.

Though the body be weak, though the way may be rough and fraught with those things that would distract and destroy thee from thine own purpose, even, His mercy is sufficient, His strength will sustain thee, His arm will be about thee, His voice will speak to thee; for the light breaketh, and the day is at hand for the fruits of thy labors in His mercies to His children.

Q-6. [993]: *Please interpret the vision that I had on Sept. 2, 1934, which I have in my hand.*

A-6. As the pattern thou hast seen in thine visions of the realms of the faithful are builded as in those of the materials that in the earth or physical, are precious, so do the lives of the saints become precious in His sight as they take their place, even as thou visioned in the part—are—by looking upon same.

For, as He has given by His prophets, "The days when these shall be so simple, he that runs may read." So is it given thee as thou heard the teacher give that thy prayers, thy deeds, thy acts, thy thoughts, even, are ever a memorial before His throne.

So should ye all live, so should ye all think; for, what would be thy thought, O ye children of men, to see the statue, the figure, of that thou hast thought of thy brother, of thy neighbor, of thy sister, even *Maker,* for, what are ye building, or are ye giving thy Maker to build for thee? What are thy thoughts? What are thy deeds? What are thy prayers? These be that which thy Maker, thy Savior, may place in the balance for thee. Vision thou that someone has spoken evil or chooses rather to call thee by an uncomely name—what does this look like in thy soul's vision?

Now, ye come to that change that must be wrought in thine experiences, would ye give to this seeking, this waiting world that as thou hast, as a group, been prepared for. What is thy destiny, then? What wilt thou give to thy friend, thy neighbor, thy brother, everywhere? Think not that because *that* thou hast given has not received praise and promise and glory from the life, that it has not been heralded abroad as yet, is thine own completing in this lesson that ye must learn. Who of the whole peoples of that city that His temple of Jehovah had been sat in, looked upon the King on the cross and thought or felt that there would come the day when His words, even, "My peace I give unto you," would change the whole world, and that *time*, even, would be counted from that death, that birth?

So we give, though in [the year] 2034, thy lessons, if they are given in His name, will still be living in the hearts and the souls, even, of those that before the throne of grace will be calling thee by name.

Think ye well, then, on that which has been given thee and choose ye!

We are through.

This psychic reading was given by Edgar Cayce at the Edmonds' home, 611 Pennsylvania Avenue, Norfolk, Va., on September 23, 1934, at 4:00 P.M., in accordance with a request made by those present: Edgar Cayce; Gertrude Cayce, conductor; Gladys Davis, steno; Hugh Lynn Cayce, Mildred Davis, Edith Edmonds, Florence Edmonds, Helen Ellington, Ruth LeNoir, Frances Y. Morrow, Helen Storey, and Esther Wynne.

⋊ 262-72 ⋉

Mrs. Cayce: You will have before you the Norfolk Study Group #1, members of which are present here, and their work on the lesson, Desire. *You will advise us in completing this lesson and answer the questions which will be asked.*

Mr. Cayce: Yes, we have the group as gathered here, as a group, as individuals; and their work on the lesson, *Desire.*

In the completing of same, we find the greater portion of that which has been given has been well selected. The contributions from individuals as to their study, their application, their meditation and their experiences respecting same are very good.

Well chosen in the manner of separation. Only necessary, then, here and there, as it is re-edited, that some words, some phrases, be altered to better make the terminology in keeping with each phase of that being presented.

Ready for questions.

Q-1. We present the lesson as a whole, a copy of which I hold in my hand. Any suggestions as to changes or additions that will make this lesson more effective?

A-1. Use it as given.

Q-2. Please explain, so that we may all understand, just what was meant in the last reading, as to the help to be given on the lessons, what we should do, what our approach should be. [See 262-71 in re Halaliel.]

A-2. Whether that which has been given as lessons to others is to be lived and exemplified in the lives of the members of the group or not, individually, is a choice in the individual—not as a group. This first, as given, must be determined to the best of *their* ability. They, as individuals, as members of the group seeking to be a channel of blessing to someone else, will—with the help of those sources through which they have received inspiration, help, aid—live their own lives in that way and manner as they have asked others to do. Not of themselves; for, as given of old, no soul can say that Christ is come of God *save* the Holy Spirit convict him of that statement. And should one say such and not live the *life* that would exemplify that, then such an one is condemning self already.

So, in the experiences that have been given by the varied members of such a study group, have given that they as individuals *will* accord their fellow members and their fellow man day by day.

This chosen, this desired, as has been manifested on the part of those—some, to be sure, have been shirkers, some have been jerkers; yet all have manifested that which is their *own* state, phase or period of development. And now, as the lessons may change to a more informative nature, the help may be that— with the living of that they as individuals have given or have accepted. Say not, "I didn't contribute that, so I don't have to live it!" Thou art a portion of the whole, and what is thy first lesson? What is thine last lesson? Do these not work one with another? Has not a full cycle been completed? Be not as those that seek farther as curious, or as wantonly. Remember Er [?], Uzzah and Malchus[?], how their curiosity brought to them that period of night when that they had builded must be accounted for.

Then, when ye are ready, *say* so!

Q-3. [307]: Please explain more fully what was meant in the last reading by "and this is under the law of mercy; hence ever may thy prayer be, Mercy, Lord, not sacrifice."[See 262-71, A-5.]

A-3. This is plain to thee. For as the law of sacrifice as committed unto men bespoke the coming of the law of mercy that was and is demonstrated in the life of the man Jesus, thy Christ, who offered Himself as the sacrifice once for all, entering into the holy of holies where He may meet thee day by day, thou art then indeed—as many as have named the name—come under the law of mercy, *not* of sacrifice. That is not in the term that no man offers sacrifice, for the life of every soul that seeks in the material world to demonstrate the spiritual life is a life of sacrifice *from* the material angle; but to such that have passed from death unto life, in that law of mercy in naming Him as thine God, thine Brother, thine Savior, who has paid,

who has offered Himself, thou art passed from death unto life
—and the sacrifice is as *mercy* from thy God to thy brother.
Hence he that would despitefully use thee, a kind word is as
mercy. As ye would have mercy, show mercy. *Thou* knowest in
thine heart.

Q-4. [560]: *May I have a message from the highest forces that
I can reach that will help me at this time?*

A-4. Let thine mind, thine heart and thine purposes be as
upon the altar of love to Him whom ye would serve, thy Master,
thy God. For He is mindful ever of those that seek to know His
ways; for His ways are not past finding out. For to those that
have put on Christ, who have named the name of Him that
promised, "If ye love me, keep my commandments, and I will
come and abide with thee; my yoke is easy, my burden is *light*
to *those* that *love* the Lord." Let not those things that would
trouble thee interfere; for yet a little while and thou should see
face to face—even as thou hast been called unto a service to
thy fellow man, even as He; for He will not leave thee comfortless, but will come and abide with thee, and thou shalt *know*
Him as He is.

Q-5. *Do we understand correctly that we, each member of the
group, must decide that we as individuals will live the lessons
already completed before going on to the next lesson?*

A-5. They must decide within themselves. Promise themselves—not thy brother, not thy neighbor, not thine friend, but
promise the God within thee that with His help, with His
mercy, with His aid, "I will do my best." Then say so.

Then may ye go on, as individuals, as a group.

Q-6. *As individuals, we have tried. Tell us how to do this
better.*

A-6. Meet thy Maker face to face, in the holy of holies—and
make thy promise there.

Q-7. *May we have the affirmation for our next meditation?*

A-7. Let's choose first; but pray ye as this, when ye meet thy
Maker and thyself face to face, as ye choose the way:

MY FATHER AND MY GOD, AS I (NAME THINE OWN NAME) AP-
PROACH THE THRONE OF GRACE AND MERCY, SEEKING TO BE A
BETTER CHANNEL THROUGH WHICH THE BLESSINGS AND THE
KNOWLEDGE OF MY LORD AND MY SAVIOR, AS MANIFESTED

THROUGH THY SON, JESUS, THE CHRIST, MAY NOW BE MANIFESTED
IN THE EARTH, MAY I, AS THY SERVANT, CHOOSE THE WAY I SHOULD
GO.

Q-8. [295]: What about the teacher as promised in the last reading?

A-8. Be not overanxious; for he that is overanxious, even, is as Uzzah.

Q-9. [993] desires a message:

A-9. Grace, mercy and truth be with thee as ye seek to bring the glad tidings of truth to others in His name. For there be no other name under heaven whereby *men* in the earth may be saved.

Let His love, His grace, His mercy be sufficient unto thee. Be not anxious of the morrow, for *He,* thy Lord, thy God, doth provide. *Know* thy Redeemer liveth, and is in and with thee. Amen.

Q-10. [585] desires a message:

A-10. What seekest thou *here?* Ye know the way, and in whom ye have believed; for He is ever with thee as ye seek to bring a message of cheer and comfort and hope to others. "Inasmuch as ye do it unto the least of my brethren, ye do it unto me."

What *mercy,* what graciousness ye wilt find if ye will but *know* that as ye do in His name ye lend unto thy Maker—and *He* WILL repay! Be not impatient. Be slow in thy judgment; for as ye would have mercy shown, so be merciful.

Q-11. [303]: May I have a message that will strengthen me at this time?

A-11. Come! Sing a joyful song unto thy Lord and thy Redeemer, who hath *strengthened* thee in the hours of trial, of test, of tribulation; for they that meet their troubles, their sorrows, with *joy* in the name of the Lord shall not be troubled again. They that kick against the pricks find that they but entangle their own mental minds, their own consciousnesses in the turmoils of the flesh. Ye *live* in the flesh, yet be as He —in the world yet not *of* the world; for all strength, all power, all glory, all joy is given unto Him—for *He* has overcome, and ye may in Him overcome also. Count it rather as a blessing, rather as that thou art *chosen* that ye may in the name of thy

Lord speak a kind word to those that are abrupt or cross with thee, and in so doing ye will heap the coals of judgment upon their consciousnesses; for ye are His and He is thine, if ye will hold to that thou hast chosen.

Q-12. Are the other groups excluded from this one in the readings, last given?

A-12. How readest thou, in thine own conscience?

Q-13. [379] desires a message:

A-13. As others look to thee for strength, for guidance in Him, in thine home, in thine life, in thine meetings day by day, so be ye strong in Him. For to him whom much is given, from him is much required; yet him that hath, to him it *shall* be given —and thou hast known His ways. Keep thine way perfect, then, in thine walks, in thine talks with those that trust in thee. For as thou dost represent the home, the way, the light to many, so will *He* give His strength, His power, His grace, that *ye* may bear those burdens in the flesh in the way that He would have ye go. For He will not leave thee comfortless, for He will guide thee as ye walk day by day.

Q-14. [538]: May I have a message that will help me at this time?

A-14. Keep thy ways in the light of Him that has promised to guide, guard and direct. Be not impatient. Be not other than that thou wouldst have thy fellow man be unto thee. For as ye speak of another, as ye speak *to* another, so will ye be spoken to; for the seed ye sow will be *given* the increase by the power of His word. So, sow the seed of joy, of love, of life, in the minds, in the hearts of those thou meetest day by day. Let thy love for thy Maker constrain thee in thy daily activities, for to thee hast been entrusted that which may wreck, may make, thine own understanding.

Q-15. [404]:

A-15. Let the law of love, of mercy, of justice, that is shown in the law of love and mercy, be thy guide day by day. For the Lord is not slack in counting His mercy as men count slackness. And be patient and be trustworthy, even to thine own soul. For the brighter day dawns, and the star of hope to thee rises in those that ye show the way and the light. *Mercy, mercy,* for those that err; even as ye would have mercy shown to thee!

Q-16. [*462*]:

A-16. Up to the throne of grace hath gone thy words of commendation and of love, yet ye trust in the power of those things that are within thine own self. *He* is able through thee to make thee strong in the ways that thou shouldst go! Eschew evil, *love* justice and mercy, and put those things *from* thy heart that would cause thee to doubt.

Q-17. [*295*] *desires a message:*

A-17. Let those things that would cause thee to fear, to doubt, become the stepping-stones for those things that have been promised in and through thee if thou wilt keep His ways. Let justice and mercy, let *joy* and harmony, let thine self be the way; for "He that would be the greatest among you, he is servant of all." Grace, mercy, peace, the love of the Father through the Son abide with those that love His coming. Be patient, be *kind,* be *just* in thine commentations, in thine activities to thy fellow man; for only in such will ye find peace and harmony. For some cry Peace when they themselves become, through the condemnation of self in others, that which is the stumbling block to many. Make a joyful noise unto the Lord for the mercies, the promises, the glories that may be thine in the earth through the love thou may show unto thy fellow man.

Q-18. [*413*]: *Is there a special message for me?*

A-18. As thou hast been strong in thine weakness, strength and grace and power is given thee. For many are they (and the number grows) who seek through thee to know more of the light and the way. Be thou strong, then, in His power, that the blessings that He has prepared for those that love His ways may be thy very own. Let not doubt nor fear turn thee aside, for in *His* ways are the peace and harmony and love that will bring this to come in thine own *experience.* They that love the Lord shall *prosper* in the earth.

We are through.

This psychic reading was given by Edgar Cayce at the Edmonds' home, 611 Pennsylvania Avenue, Norfolk, Va., on October 28, 1934, at 4:35 P.M., in accordance with a request made by those present: Edgar Cayce; Gertrude Cayce, conductor; Gladys Davis, steno; Louvenia Benthall, O. J. Benthall, Hugh Lynn Cayce, Mildred Davis, Edith Edmonds, Florence Edmonds, Helen Ellington, Alice Harris, Abbie Kemp (and her two grandsons), Ruth LeNoir, Frances Y. Morrow, Elizabeth Perry, Helen Storey, Nellie Twiddy, and Esther Wynne.

⊰ 262-73 ⊱

[Background: See 262-72 on 9/23/34 stressing individual choice and dedication to the Christ, in preparing the Search for God lessons, before the subject of the next lesson, and affirmation for it, would be given.

Discussion preceded 262-73 on 10/28/34, led by Hugh Lynn Cayce, in order to help those visitors present from other groups understand why Group #1 could not continue to include visitors in the reading period. He pointed out that the purpose of Group #1 is to compile lessons; those coming in as visitors might not understand and, therefore, cause friction; lack of room to include all members of other groups in the average home, therefore giving opportunity for some to feel hurt at not being invited. A turning point is now being reached in the affairs of Group #1; members must make decisions, a cycle having been completed and a change imminent. Hugh Lynn Cayce stated that we as Group #1 members have nothing to hide; we are merely feeling ourselves out.

Edgar Cayce was in good spirits. He also made a short talk to the members present preceding the reading. Later a copy of 262-73 was sent to all those who were present for the reading, even though some were visitors.]

Mrs. Cayce: You will have before you the members of the Norfolk Study Groups gathered here. You will give a mental and spiritual message that will aid them in carrying on, with any special advice for the further work of Group #1 that will be helpful at this time.

Mr. Cayce: Yes, we have the group, members of groups that are gathered here, as a group and as individuals.

As to that which has been given, that has been presented to others, to groups, for serious consideration, for application in their own experiences, ye have found these lessons not merely tenets; neither are they theories. Rather, as ye have applied them they have brought to each of you in thine own particular, peculiar sphere of activity, an experience. Hence, as ye seek to become that channel through which there may come to others those blessings, those experiences that are *thy* very own, know that—if ye have chosen that which is the foundation of those lessons, the Christ, the consciousness of His presence abiding in thee—there is that strength, that grace sufficient for ye in every trial, in every blessing, in every shadow, in every light.

For He *is* the way; He is the life; He is the vine and ye are the branches. Bear ye fruit, then, worthy of that thou hast chosen; and He will keep that thou hast committed unto Him against every experience that may be required, that may be needed, that may come in thine attempts to show forth the Lord's death till He come again; death meaning that transition, that decision, that change in every experience. For if ye die not daily to the things of the world ye are none of His.

Then, lift up thine hearts, thine minds, in praise to Him who has *given* thee the opportunity that ye may be as lights showing the way; reconsecrating thyself, thy service, thy joys, thy sorrows, to His service, that ye may have the greater joy, the greater blessings in Him.

How readest thou as to what shall be thine own judgments and the judgment before the throne of grace, the throne of might? "As ye did it unto the least of these, my brethren, ye did it unto me."

So, let His ways be thy ways. Let thy sorrows be His sorrows. Let thy joys be His joys, and *He* will abide with thee.

To those that seek to prepare the lessons: How hast thou chosen? [See 262-71, 262-72 re Halaliel.] Have ye rededicated thy lives? Have ye chosen through what channel ye would seek? The Master has called, and His love will protect thee if thou wilt in thy daily life live that thou hast given thy brother, thy friend, as a guide, as an example!

So, as ye choose, know that lesson thou hast been given becomes a part of thee—thy destiny! For ye as souls, as individuals, are *building* same. What will the manner of the structure be?

Let thy prayer, thy meditation in preparation, then, be:
LORD, THOU ART MY DWELLING PLACE! IN THEE, O FATHER, DO
I TRUST! LET ME SEE IN MYSELF, IN MY BROTHER, THAT THOU
WOULD BLESS IN THY SON, THY GIFT TO ME THAT I MIGHT KNOW
THY WAYS! THOU HAST PROMISED, O FATHER, TO HEAR WHEN THY
CHILDREN CALL! HARKEN, THAT I MAY BE KEPT IN THE WAY THAT
I MAY KNOW THE GLORY OF THY SON AS THOU HAST PROMISED IN
HIM, THAT WE THROUGH HIM MIGHT HAVE ACCESS TO THEE!
THOU, O GOD, ALONE, CAN SAVE! THOU ALONE CAN KEEP MY
WAYS!

As ye choose, then, my children, as ye know that ye are being
given a work to do, know that His blessings will guide thee day
by day. Be ye not stiff-necked; be ye not seekers after vainglo-
ries. For the day of the Lord is at hand, and many of ye shall
see His glory in the experiences of thy life here among thy
fellow man. Are ye willing to drink the cup even as He drank,
or that thou may receive even the praise of thy brethren for
a day? Let His ways be thy ways. Let there be that as He gave,
"Love ye one another and thus fulfill the law of God."

Ready for questions.

*Q-1. Is it well for Group #1 to invite members from other
groups to join them in the preparations of the future lessons?*

A-1. When others of other groups, of any group, feel called
to service, ask—and then they may be chosen; for, "Whosoever
will, let him come and partake of the water of *life.*" For when
ye take His yoke upon thee thy burdens become light. Be ye
messengers, be ye light-bearers, then, for the Christ-child.

Q-2. Any other advice or guidance at this time?

A-2. Much might be given thee. This: Keep, preserve ye in
thine inmost self:
LET THE LIGHT OF THE LOVE OF THE CHRIST BE MY GUIDE. MY
BROTHER, MY FRIEND, MY NEIGHBOR, MINE ENEMY EVEN, ARE
CHILDREN OF GOD—MY BRETHREN, MY LOVED ONES. LET ME,
THEN, SEE THAT I DO NOT CAUSE ONE OF THESE TO ERR, NOR TO
PUT A STUMBLING BLOCK IN THE WAY OF ANY.

We are through.

[See 262-74 commending Group #1 for its choice of the
Christ.]

This psychic reading was given by Edgar Cayce at the Edmonds' home, 611 Pennsylvania Avenue, Norfolk, Va., on December 23, 1934, at 3:20 P.M., in accordance with a request made by those present: Edgar Cayce; Gertrude Cayce, conductor; Gladys Davis, steno; Hugh Lynn Cayce, Mildred Davis, Edith Edmonds, Florence Edmonds, Helen Ellington (late arriving), Ruth LeNoir (late arriving), Frances Y. Morrow, Helen Storey, and Esther Wynne.

⊁ 262-74 ⊀

[Background: See 262-73 urging that the Christ (not Halaliel) be the guide. Sense of haste pervaded room, due to holding the reading earlier so [295] could participate in a church Christmas program and not have to miss the reading. Some resented this change in usual procedure; two came late because they weren't notified of the change. See also 262-56 Supplement in re Halaliel.]

Mrs. Cayce: You will have before you Group #1, members of which are present, and their work on the lesson Destiny. *As individuals and as a group we seek that approach which will be most in accord with our ideal of service in His name.*

Mr. Cayce: Yes, we have the group as gathered here, and their work on the lesson *Destiny*. As a group and as individuals there has not been the choice as to how there would be the activities in the preparation of the lessons. This, as has been given, should first be determined, and an amicable expression and a meeting that would make for a clarifying of that purpose *with* those that would prepare same.

Rather, then, at this time would there be given ye as this:

As ye seek in the name of Him who came in due season, that ye through His name might have the access to the Father, then will ye not in His name strive to be the greater channels of blessings to those that look to thee in His name for guidance, for direction, for sustainment during those periods of anxiety, of doubt and of fear?

Then, quit [Biblical expression as in I Sam. 4:9 and I Cor. 16:13, meaning acquit?] yourselves as the children of the Most High—and *know* whereunto thou hast chosen that which would be thy direction in this matter.

Some among you are fearful; some are weak; some are doubt-

-295-

ing; some are seeking more and more. What will ye do with that
thou hast chosen? Be strong in Him, for His promises are sure
—and ye may walk with Him if ye will choose to be channels
of blessings in His name.

Let thy yeas be yea and thy nays be nay in His name, for thou
hast chosen the better part—He has chosen thee as thou hast
chosen Him. Go ye, then, into the field that is ripe unto the
harvest; for His ways are those that lead to eternal life.

Ready for questions.

Q-1. Please explain so that we may all understand just—

A-1. [Interrupting] All understand much better than they
will acknowledge in themselves! Quit ye thyselves like ye believe that thou hast given to thy brother for the directions.

We are through for the present. [Gladys Davis's note: Two
or three in the group were still not convinced that we were right
in rejecting Halaliel's help in preparing the lessons.]

This psychic reading was given by Edgar Cayce at the Edmonds' home, 611 Pennsylvania Avenue, Norfolk, Va., on January 6, 1935, at 4:30 P.M., in accordance with a request made by those present: Edgar Cayce; Gertrude Cayce, conductor; Gladys Davis, steno; Hugh Lynn Cayce, Mildred Davis, Edith Edmonds, Florence Edmonds, Helen Ellington, Ruth LeNoir, Frances Y. Morrow, Helen Storey, and Esther Wynne.

≈ 262-75 ≤

[Meeting was held to discuss decision as to procedure; differences of attitude yet friendliness expressed. Some still felt we could follow Christ and Halaliel, too. See background of 262-71 through 262-74.]

Mrs. Cayce: You will have before you the Norfolk Study Group #1, members of which are present here, and their desire as individuals to continue work on the lessons in fulfilling the purpose of the group as a unit. To each individual heart has been left the decision to make a new and earnest effort to apply the lessons already given to others. As we stumble at times, blinded by selfishness, ignorance, doubt and fear, we can only turn to the promises of our Christ that He will guide and direct if we will seek His face. In the name of Jesus, the Christ, we seek the light that will guide us along the path He would have us go.

Mr. Cayce: We have the members of the group as gathered here, and their work, and the various decisions that have been made by the individuals respecting the information that may be given as a basis for the preparation of lessons.

In the approach, then, may they each hear in their own language and apply that which has been given others in their own lives to such measures that it, *their* work, may bring that as the loving Father has destined that such labors, such efforts, may bring to the experience of each soul.

Then, in the approach to the lesson that has been assigned or given, let's first approach in the manner which has been indicated; that a cycle has been reached, a turn has come — in informative information, or that which will be found by many to be at variance to much that has been presented by men, or man, here and there.

First, then, to define destiny — that is in accord with truth:

Destiny is of the next three lessons that would be given through here. Then, destiny is of what? *Mind, body, soul.* The next three lessons. Mind, body, soul.

Destiny is, then, a law—an immutable law, that is as lasting as that which brought all into being that is manifested in all the varied spheres of materialization, or manifestation; and that of which man has seen the signs here, there, written in those experiences of the travelers along the varied spheres of experience. Man in the interpretation of those signs has often mistaken the sign for the law.

Hence to those that hold to this or that theory, then, this group would present—in reference to the destiny of mind, of body, of soul—that which may become as a light to many who have stumbled upon those signs in their activities, in their efforts here and there. [See 262-77, A-1.]

Then, in giving that from which and upon which ye as individuals have applied and may apply as a group in giving an aid to others, in making their paths straight, look ye to the *law* that is destiny—destined—in the word of Him. For He gave that though the heavens and the earth pass away, His word shall *not* pass away. What is the gospel? What *is* the truth? What is the judgment? What is the law?

"As a man thinketh in his heart, so is he"? ye ask. "As ye do it unto the least of these, my little ones, ye do it unto me"? another asks. "As ye would that men should do unto you, do ye even so to them" says another.

What gave He as the last command? "A new commandment I give unto you, love one another." What is thy lesson on *Love?* How many live same in their daily experience?

But ye ask again, What of destiny? He hath not willed that any soul should perish but that *every* soul shall know the will of God to DO it!

Then, ye wonder—can such be possible in threescore and ten years in the earth? Also ye wonder—doth the time of birth, the place of the environment, make or have a part in destiny? Do the days or the years, or the numbers, all have their part? Yea, more than that! Yet, as has been given, all these are but signs along the way; they are but omens; they are but the marks that have indicated—for, as given, He has set His mark, and these are *signs,* not the destinies! For the destiny of the mind, of the body, of the soul, is with Him. For naught that man may do maketh for the righteousness, but the mercy of the Father as exemplified in the Son makes for the destinies of that trinity of the mind, the body, the soul, in its effort, in its endeavor, in any environ, in any experience, to mark the way; yea, even so clearly that there may not be longer the stumbling, the wandering—for the day of the Lord draweth nigh for many. While ye wander, search thine own heart and *know* as of old that faith is counted as righteousness to those that love the Lord. Those of ye study that ye show yourselves approved unto Him that giveth life; that would direct the mind, that manifests in the body, that would have thy soul as a *companion* with Him—thy Elder Brother! Who hath *opened* the gates of heaven, who hath closed—to you that manifest love—the gates of hell! For He hath given. And he that confesseth that Jesus is the Christ, the Son of the living God, hath *life* eternal—and the gates of hell shall *not* prevail against him!

What, then, is thy destiny? It is made in that thou pervertest not that thou *knowest* to do in thine heart respecting thy fellow man! For ye look to Him who is the author and the finisher of faith. He *is* faith, *and* truth, *and* light— *and* in no other is there comeliness at all. For He is the rock of salvation; the bright, the morning star; the rose of Sharon; the *wonderful* counselor. In Him *is* thy destiny. Turn ye not away from Him. [Gladys Davis's note: Again warning not to accept Halaliel or any other.]

As to those things that are marks, signs, omens along the way — *understand* them for what they *are!* Put *not* thy trust in *them!* For He has given (and remember He gave, "Heavens and the earth may pass, but my word shall not!"); he that seeks shall find; he that knocketh, to *him* shall be opened. For He hath spoken, and His word is; that "Though ye wander far afield, though ye become beset by the doubts and the fears, though ye even turn thy back upon *me,* if ye will remember the promises and *turn,* I *will* HEAR—*speedily*—and will forgive thy trespasses, even as *you* forgive those that trespass against you."

Let love be without dissimulation. Look not upon that which may bring only joy to thee, yet even peace to thee; for *He* is thy light and thy guide. Put rather thy life, thy *experiences,* thy associations, even thine own self, into His keeping; knowing He is able to keep that thou hast committed unto Him—and may save thee, for He alone hath the words of life. And no matter what ye make or mark, or mar, He is *still* with thee, ready to harken when ye call.

Let thine heart be raised, then, in praise that thou hast *named* the name above every other name; for He alone can save —and He alone can *forgive*—He alone can answer prayer; to the same measure that *thou, in* thine own experience, *answereth* the prayer of thy fellow man.

Ready for questions.

Q-1. [*303*]: *Please give me a message that will help me.*

A-1. It *has* been given, but—in thine heart—let not your heart be troubled, and be not afraid. Fear rather him who may destroy thy soul, thine mind. Keep the faith. Look only upon that which brings peace, harmony, joy, in the lives of those that thou may serve from day to day. Think not upon those fearful things about thine self, for *He* (in faith) will care for these. "As ye do it unto these, ye do it unto me." Art thou, then, mindful of what the Master would say, as He would walk with thee? Listen to the voice within; for He is nearer even than thine own body!

Q-2. [*307*]: *Please give me a message of help at this time.*

A-2. Thou hast had it, but—know, let the love of God and not of man constrain thee at *all* times. *Love* the Lord, eschew evil. Think not of the glories other than that thou may create in the hearts and minds and bodies of thy fellow man. For thus may thine own soul learn the lessons that thou hast given.

Q-3. [*560*]: *May the dream I had this morning—*

A-3. No dreams. Rather, this: Glory and peace and honor is thine, in that thou—as He has given—looketh on those things that bestir the soul to activity towards thy fellow man. Let not the things of the earth disturb thee. Let not that which would make thee afraid come *nigh unto* thee! For *He is* thy guide, thy guard, and will defend thee against all that would make thee fearful.

Q-4. [*295*]: *Please give me a message on* Destiny *and tell me if I have made the correct decisions?* ([*295*] *withdrew from the group when she moved away. A-4, -5, -6 seemed to be a definite point of decision for her. She was present for 262-76 and 262-77 but her questions in the group readings ended with these answers.)*

A-4. Let *Him* be thy decisions. For thy destiny is in *Him.* Let *His* hand, His love, His strength, *guide* thee day by day. Thine own heart, thine own mind, will direct thee as to thy choice, as it is made in accord with— *and directed by*—Him.

Q-5. In accepting the teacher [Halaliel] or help promised, is there any reason to believe we shall not receive the highest and be guided by the spirit of truth as manifested through the Christ?

A-5. It has been given.

Q-6. Is this an opportunity for expanding spiritually, the acceptance of the help promised?

A-6. An opportunity for experiencing the presence of the Christ in thine own life is *ever* before thee. An opportunity rather that ye guide thyself first, then counsel others; but he that would *impel* shall indeed be impelled!

Q-7. [993]: Please give me a personal message.

A-7. Given. Ye that love the Lord know He is nigh unto thee, even in the pulsation of thine own heart that is the life flow of thine own body. Let each heartbeat, then, be as a greater love for thy fellow man. Let the glory of the Father be thine watchword, that He may use thee as He seeth fit; *not* as thou wouldst go but rather: "Let Thou me know, though the day may grow dark and the night stormy yet in Thee, O Lord, I put my trust. Thou *art* the haven of rest. Thou art the good shepherd. Thou hast the words of life. Thou art the living water. Let me drink deep, then, that *my* life, my body, my soul, may *shine* as a light for those along the pathway."

Q-8. [585]: Is there a message for me?

A-8. Keep the faith that there may be more and more awareness in thine daily life; not disregards to those things that are not understood. Take *time* to be patient with those that are in wonderment, yet harken to the voice that calls from within that ye make thine own paths straight that He may come and abide with thee. Know *only* true light may shine down the *straight* path.

Q-9. [341]: Is there a message for me?

A-9. Given. But: Know the truth and the truth shall make you free *in* the Lord; for he that is the law is no longer subject to the law; for being the law he hath put away fear, doubt, and those things that would hinder or make afraid. The Lord is in His holy temple; yea, in the temple where He has promised to meet thee—if ye will enter in and sup with Him.

Q-10. [*413*]: *Is there a message for me?*

A-10. Given; but know, he that endureth unto the end shall wear the crown of life; he that letteth little hindrances become stumbling blocks is not worthy of those things that are glories in His name—yet He heareth, ever. *Abide* ye in Him. Let the *glory* of thy love guide thee; for righteous is he that believeth and doeth as he believes.

Q-11. [*379*]: *Is there a message for me?*

A-11. As the Father hath loved Him, as His love hast guided thee, let *that* be the love ye show to thy fellow man. Let grace, mercy and peace be with those that ye bless; for many are blessed by thy very presence when ye call on the Lord.

Q-12. [*294*]:

A-12. Given; but know the promises that He has given in Him are ever nigh unto thee, and in and through thee; if ye will keep thy paths straight, many may be blessed.

Q-13. [*288*]:

A-13. Given. Glory in the *Son* and His promises, as He gave "Ask in my name, believing, and ye *shall* receive." Let the love of *God*, not of self, constrain thee ever.

Q-14. [*538*]: *May I have a message that will help me?*

A-14. As thou hast chosen in thine heart so be it unto thee. For the power, the glory of the Son that He sheds upon the sons and daughters of men is as He gave: "I, not of myself but the Father that worketh *in* me, so I in you and you in me and I in the Father, may bring that peace, harmony, joy, that maketh for those activities in *every* experience that become the light to others."

To all: Let thy love for one another, thy love for truth for truth's sake, in Him, *guide* you—ever. His peace, His mercy, His glory, overshadow you day by day!

Study that ye may give as He gives unto you; not of yourselves but as thy Master, thy Brother, giveth thee, through the measure that ye mete unto thy fellow man.

We are through for the present.

ℵ 262-76 ℶ *This psychic reading was given by Edgar Cayce at his home on Arctic Crescent, Virginia Beach, Va., on January 18, 1935, at 11:30 A.M. This reading was voluntarily given by Mr. Cayce after the suggestion for awakening was given upon conclusion of reading 795-1. Those present were: Edgar Cayce; Gertrude Cayce, conductor; Gladys Davis, steno; L. B. Cayce and Mildred Davis.*

[Background—See 262-71 through 262-75.]

Mr. Cayce: It would be very interesting for those who are going about to make a collection of such things to notice the vibrations and variations in vibrations of various cities, or those conditions that make for the abilities of the proper association or connections through the mental activities of individuals in relationship to information of such natures.

As has been seen from here, what has been given as to the influences or forces that should be combined through periods of activity—or a certain element for a combination of the mental influences and forces—is not irrelevant to the better influences for this particular individual or body at this time. But the attitudes, desires not only of those surrounding or seeking information but of the one who is receptive—or to act in the capacity of being receptive for such things—these are well in the present.

[Gladys Davis's note: The second paragraph seems to be referring to Edgar Cayce's physical and mental condition, also to those closely surrounding him during the readings—particularly to Gertrude Cayce in this instance.

Could this also be referring to 262-71 which indicated that Halaliel was being sent to the group through their own desires? All the rest of the readings seemed to be counseling the group *against* accepting any other sign or guide along the way except Jesus, the Christ.

Now 262-76 is seeming to say that the obstruction in the mind of Edgar Cayce and those around him has been removed, and that all is well. In my mind the above seems to be somewhat of an apology for the allowing of such interferences to enter from time to time.]

This psychic reading was given by Edgar Cayce at the Edmonds' home, 611 Pennsylvania Avenue, Norfolk, Va., on January 20, 1935, at 4:20 P.M., in accordance with a request made by those present: Edgar Cayce; Gertrude Cayce, conductor; Gladys Davis, steno; Hugh Lynn Cayce, Mildred Davis, Edith Edmonds, Florence Edmonds, Ruth LeNoir, Frances Y. Morrow, Helen Storey, and Esther Wynne.

⊰ 262-77 ⊱

[Background—See 262-71 through 262-76.]

Mrs. Cayce: You will have before you Norfolk Study Group #1, members of which are present here, seeking further guidance in preparing the lesson, Destiny, *and answers to their questions on same.*

Mr. Cayce: Yes, we have the group as gathered here and their seeking respecting the lesson. In considering further, then, that which has been given from that promise set, that the destiny of those that have named the name of the Christ is set in Him:

That individuals may of their own volition choose the exaltation of self, or the aggrandizement of self's own ego, is apparent. This makes for what many have termed and do term their karmic conditions, that may then be seen.

Those who are in that way or attitude of "Let the words of my mouth and the meditation of the heart be acceptable in Thy sight" are in the way of truth.

Those that kick against the pricks—even as thine own teacher, thine own writer, Paul, saw the error and turned therein. Was it destiny that he was to be called? Or that the gift of the Son set a way, a vine, a water, living water, and that he chose to meditate and thus give that destined to work upon? For, as given, this material life is of those energies that make for the adherence to the laws that pertain to this material plane. And the spiritual laws are interpenetrable with those activities that make for the will of the Father that no soul should perish but that there may be the burning of the dross that it may be sifted as wheat, that it may be purified even as He through suffering in the material things that *are* for the soul's edification.

Then, in this may each be enabled to look only to Him, knowing that He *is* the light, He *is* the way; those things which come to bear in the experience are that there may be known those things necessary for those who seek, for only those who seek may find.

For, as has been given, there be nothing in earth, in hell, in heaven, that may separate the soul from God save the individual soul.

Then, what is destiny? That the soul who seeks shall the sooner find; that the soul who puts into practice day by day that which is known may the sooner enjoin itself to that which *is* hope and peace and happiness and love and joy in the earth.

That there should be those who should know heaven on earth or in the earth, or in flesh, is the destiny of those that are willing, who have had their minds, their bodies, their souls cleansed in the blood of the Lamb. How? By being as He, a living example of that He, the Christ, professed to be.

Then, that which hinders most—this group, any group, the world—is speaking one thing and living in the inner self another. This destines to bring confusion and turmoil and strife and want, and a reckoning with that which makes for tears, sorrow, and that is of the earth earthy. And ye are, as He gave, servants of—workers with—*that* force whom ye serve.

In presenting self, then, as has been given, come to the altar of truth within thine own self. There He through His promise, *in* His promise, will meet thee, and it shall be shown thee that which is the way, the manner.

Individuals in their understanding falter here and there, for they have been told and have listened from their own observation, rather than experience, that this way, that way, the prayer at this period or at that period, the stars at this period have meant or do indicate or do mean that this number from the name, this day means this or that; and in the application comes confusion. These—as has been given—are signs, are omens; but how gavest He? "The heavens and the earth will pass away, but my word shall not pass away."

The signs, the omens then, are to be used as stepping-stones for an *understanding;* not to be confused with nor given— through that gift in thee of constructive forces from the Father-God Himself—other power than they contain within themselves. For each soul that meets and encounters and accredits receives the same in return. How gave He on this? "He that receiveth a prophet [Halaliel?] in the name of a prophet hath a prophet's reward." This does not indicate that the prophet received is of God, an angel of heaven or of hell; but in the name, in the manner, in the way as received so cometh the reward. *That* is destined! Why? In the seed of thought, whether of body, mind or soul, *is* the seed thereof; and it bears fruit which is of its own kind and nature. Said He, "Ye do not gather grapes from thistles; neither may ye expect to do evil looking for good." For the destiny is in that which has set the world, yea, the earth and all that is therein, in motion. And ye in thy blindness, thy foolishness, thy *desire* for self, look for some *easy* way; when all the ease, all the hope, all the life there is *is* in Him! [Possible warning against accepting Halaliel's offer given in 262-71.] Then, *His* way is the easy way. What is His way? "He that would force thee to go one mile, go with him twain; he that would sue thee and take away thy coat, give him thy cloak also." Did He say whether justly or unjustly? Who did He say is the judge? "Judge not that ye be not judged." For, "As ye do it unto the least in the earth, ye do it unto me."

Then, when ye seek to do His biddings and do otherwise than thou would have Him do unto thee, thou alone maketh the way harder for thyself. For the will of the Father is *life!* It is life eternal to as many as will accept, as many as will view that which they hear from the still small voice as they meet Him within. For ye are made up of mind, body, soul. The soul is the God-part in thee, the *living* God. The manifestations that ye make in thy mind make for that growth which is manifested in the body in the earth and in thy soul in the everlasting.

So, know ye the way; point it out. For, as He has given, though ye come to the altar or to thine church or to thine group or to thine neighbor pleading not for self but for others, and it is that ye may be exalted, that ye may be honored, that ye may be spoken well of, for others; He cannot hear thy petition. Why? Because there has another entered with thee into thy chamber, thy closet, and He thy God—that answers prayer, that forgives through His Son—is shut out. In His name, then, only; for, as He gave, "They that climb up some other way are thieves and robbers."

Then, today, will ye not rededicate thyself, thy body, thy soul, to the service of thy God? And He that came has promised, "When ye ask in my name, *that* will be given thee in the earth." Then, do not become impatient that ye are counted in this day as a servant, as an humble worker, as one that is troubled as to food, shelter, or those things that would make thy temporal surroundings the better. For ye grow weary in waiting, but the Lord will not tarry; eternity is *long,* and in that ye may spend it in those things that are joy and peace and harmony, make thy self sure in Him. How? "As ye do it unto these, my brethren, ye do it unto me." Just being kind! Thy destiny is in *Him.* Are ye taking Him with thee in love into thy associations with thy fellow man, or art thou seeking thy *own* glorification, exaltation, or thine own fame, or that ye may even be well-spoken of? When ye do, ye shut Him away.

Enter thou into thy chamber not made with hands, but eternal; for there He has promised to meet thee. There alone may ye meet Him and be guided to those things that will make this life, now, happiness, joy and understanding.

As ye have received, love ye one another even as He has loved you, who gave up heaven and all its power, all its glory, that thine mind can conceive, and came into the earth in flesh that ye through Him might have the access to the Father, God. In Him there is no variableness or shadow made by turning. Then, neither must thy thoughts or thy acts cause a frown or a shadow upon thy brother—even as He. For He gave, "Be ye perfect, even as thy heavenly Father is perfect." Ye say, "This cannot be done in this house of clay!" Did He? Ye say, "This is too hard for me!" Did He grumble, did He falter? To be sure, He cried, "Father, if it be possible, let this cup pass." Yea, oft will ye cry aloud, even as He. Ye cannot bear the burden alone, but He has promised and He is faithful, "If ye put thy yoke upon me, *I* will guide you."

Then, when we come in our sorrows alone and there comes the peace, the quiet, and then those periods of joy and gladness when we forget—we carry the thought of others, of those that would make merry, and wonder why the joy has passed. It is because we have left Him outside.

Take Him, then, in thy joys, in thy sorrows, in *all* of thyself; for He alone hath the words of life.

Ready for questions.

Many there be among you for whom changes will shortly come to pass. Be ye strong. Be ye steadfast.

Q-1. Please explain, "may become as a light to many who have stumbled upon those signs in their activities, in their efforts here and there." [See 262-75, p. 1, par. 6.] *What signs are referred to here?*

A-1. It has just been explained. Those who may not read this are blind indeed!

Q-2. Please give a message on destiny for [404].

A-2. Study to show thyself approved in all things, if ye would know peace and harmony and joy now. For He *is* thy destiny; He hath not willed that any should perish. Why will ye make thy will, then, in opposition to His? Keep the *little* things, and there will grow and grow the greater joys in thy service to thy fellow man.

Q-3. [462]:

A-3. Let thy going in, thy coming out, be acceptable in the best that is in thee. For as thou hast seen and heard, as thou hast meted to others so may it be meted to thee. How readest thou? Are ye to be judged by the manner, the purpose, the aim, the desire toward thy fellow man? Then, be sure these in word, in act, in thy meditation, are as He gave.

Q-4. [341]: *Please explain the relation of heredity and the destiny of the physical body within man's control.*

A-4. This would rather come in body as related to *destiny.* Let's don't get ahead; we've got to have *mind* yet! Mind builds for the body; both physical and the soul, and the body is of the hereditary influences through the relativity of activity of soul and mind. Comprehend?

Q-5. [993]: *Please explain the following passage from a recent reading: "That no one mention who, though the name and the activities of any desire may be given thee, but when thou speakest outside thine own group, thou hast cut thyself aloof."* [See 262-71, p. 1, par. 7.]

A-5. Ye have not chosen! Then, remember Lot's wife! Ye chose not for a dweller among thee, save in the spirit of the Christ! It is as He gave when He brought that which separated the physical body from the possession of that which brought ill, or dissension. What was His command? "See that thou tellest *no man!*" Tell God, from within. Live it from without!

We are through for the present.

[Gladys Davis's note: In discussing group work with [993] she often made the statement through the years that she thought we might have progressed faster if we had decided, as a group, in favor of allowing Halaliel to give us information for the lessons. Apparently she was never convinced, as most were, that it was wrong to accept less than the Christ.]

≫ 262-78 ≪

This psychic reading was given by Edgar Cayce at the Edmonds' home, 611 Pennsylvania Avenue, Norfolk, Va., on March 3, 1935, at 4:25 P.M., in accordance with a request made by those present: Edgar Cayce; Gertrude Cayce, conductor; Gladys Davis, steno; Edith Edmonds, Florence Edmonds, Ruth LeNoir, Frances Y. Morrow, Helen Storey, and Esther Wynne.

Mrs. Cayce: You will have before you the Norfolk Study Group #1, members of which are present, and their work on the lesson Destiny. *You will give at this time further discourse on this subject which will aid in the preparation of this lesson. You will answer the questions which will be asked.*

Mr. Cayce: Yes, we have the group as gathered here, as a group, as individuals, and the lessons that are in preparation — *Destiny.*

In gaining that which may be helpful in preparation of those tenets that may be applied in the study and the experiences of selves and of others, as respecting the lesson *Destiny,* study first well that which has been given in reference to same in the varied approaches that have come from time to time.

As to that portion of same respecting mind and destiny, this — to be sure — will be as a portion or a lesson in itself, including mind in relation to the varied attributes of the physical, the mental and the spiritual bodies.

Mind in itself, then, is both material *and* spiritual.

That which finds itself expressed or manifested in material things is of the physical, for matter is an expression of spirit in motion to such a degree as to give the expressions in materiality.

That which is expressed or manifested in spirit, without taking body or form, is of the spirit; yet may be manifested in the experience of an individual.

As may be seen by the reference to those here, to those that are students, to *What Is My Ideal?* Here we find it expressly given that it, the ideal, must have its inception in, from and with that which is an unseen force, or in that we may worship as a God.

Mind, then, may function without a form or body. Hence we

-310-

will give, at this particular portion of this, that as an outline
of those conditions, experiences or manifestations that may be
had by the mind irrespective of the body:

In the beginning God created the heavens and the earth.
How? The *mind* of God *moved,* and matter, form, came into
being.

Mind, then, in God, the Father, is the builder. How much
more, then, would or should mind be the builder in the experience of those that have put on Christ or God, in Him, in His
coming into the earth? For as He has given, "Let that mind be
in you which was in the Christ, who thought it not robbery to
make Himself equal with God," but living in materiality in the
earth, in matter, as a body; but with the mind, with the thought,
with the manifestations of a Creative Force all together.

Then, destiny as related to that mind: Mind as related to
destiny must conform, must confine, must be amenable to, must
be as one of the immutable laws that has been set by that *mind*
calling into being worlds, the universe, the earth, man, giving
man a portion of Himself, and furnishing man — as it were —
a channel, an access, to that throne of grace, mercy, truth, that
mind of God itself; the soul, the ultimate, the only portion that
may be in accord with or in the presence of Him. For, as has
been given, flesh and blood does not inherit eternal life. Flesh
and blood is merely an expression, and in all its attributes
carries with same those portions, those movements, those
urges; just as each atom is made up of urges according to the
movement of and with what? That which in its final analysis
is the mind of that Creative Energy which has called into being
the mind that is a portion of self. And what is its destiny? Is
it that as the man thinketh in his heart so is he? or as ye sow,
so shall ye reap?

That ye think, that ye put your mind to work upon, to live
upon, to feed upon, to live with, to abide with, to associate with
in the mind, *that* your soul-body becomes! That is the law. That
is the destiny. That *is* as from the beginning, that each thought
of the Creator bore within itself its *own* fruit as from the beginning.

How does matter, how does the seed of the oak or of the grass
or of the flower or of the tree or of the animal or of the man,

find within itself that which impels, propagates the specie? the activative force that moves on in its realm of activity in whatsoever sphere it may find itself, giving expressions of that first thought of the Creative Forces? That is its destiny, which the easterners say was set in the first. But, as ye see, this is only half a truth. For if the mind dwells upon the spiritual things, then it follows that it becomes what it has dwelt upon, what it has lived upon, what it has made itself a portion of. But if the mind dwells upon self-indulgence, self-aggrandizement, self-exaltation, selfishness in any of its forms, in any of its variations, then it has set itself at variance to that First Cause; and we have that entered in as from the beginning, that of making the will—through the mind—at variance to Creative Forces before it has come into matter, into the movements in matter that we know as physical, material, as those things that are of the earth-earthy.

Yet we find the law, the same law, applying throughout the universe. For what was that which enabled man, or a mind, to first comprehend? "Know, O ye people, the Lord thy God is *One!*" *One* from the beginning to the ending, to those that use, to those that become constructive in their thinking, that are ever constructive in their minds, in their indwellings, in their resting upon, in their thoughts, in their meditations, and *act in the same manner,* to build towards that which does make, that creates in the experience of each and every soul that knowledge. How easily, then, must it have been said, that it hath not yet entered the mind of man as to the unspeakable glories of him who has washed his raiment in the blood of the Lamb, who has made himself one in thought, in deed, in body, one with that thought, that purpose, that mind, of God.

So as ye contemplate, as ye meditate, as ye look upon the mind, know the mind hath many windows. And as ye look out of thine inner self, know whereunto thou art looking, thou art seeking. What is thy ideal? What would you have your mind-body to become? For that upon which it feeds it becomes, that either by thought, by assimilation, by activity, by radial force, by atomic influence, by the very influence of its activity in *whatever sphere* that activity may be within. And in the material mind it is the same.

Hence, as turning then to the physical mind: This becomes necessary, as is set by some, for the application of the mind, for the preparations for its activity in the material world. Yet these become so intermingled, so much a portion—in the body and out of the body, that oft one becomes confused as to what is of spiritual import and what is of the material or the necessities of same. Yet ye are seeking in this to know what is the destiny of the mind. What has been set? Where is thy destiny? It is in what one does about that one knows that one becomes in oneself. For it is oneself from one's portion or activity of that first movement of mind from the spiritual aspect or from the material aspect.

Many questions, to be sure, will arise in the minds of many as respecting spiritual healing, materialization, and all phases of such activities. But if ye are well-grounded in those tenets, in that truth which has been presented here for thine own consideration, for thine own application in thine individual experience, then ye may set many a mind aright; and let, and have, and see their lives becoming more and more constructive in their daily experience, with their fellow man and in relationships with those they meet day by day.

For what is applicable to one is in the same relationship to self. For when those activities become such that the mind of the individual, of the soul, finds itself expressing itself in the physical, in the mental, the body will take on what? Immortality! In the earth? Yes; reflecting same that it may bring what is as the tree of life in the garden, that its leaves are for the healings of the nations; that are the leaves that may fall from thy lips, from thy activities to thy fellow man, in whatever sphere or realm of activity. Why? Because of thine own self, because thou art grounded in the water of life itself, as ye grow upon those inflowings and outflowings of the spirit of Him that gave, "Let that mind be in you which is in me, that as I abide in the Father and ye abide in me, we may be one with Him," which is the destiny of those that love His coming.

We are through for the present.

This psychic reading was given by Edgar Cayce at the Edmonds' home, 611 Pennsylvania Avenue, Norfolk, Va., on March 10, 1935, at 4:15 P.M., in accordance with a request made by those present: Edgar Cayce; Gertrude Cayce, conductor; Gladys Davis, steno; Hugh Lynn Cayce, Edith Edmonds, Florence Edmonds, Helen Ellington, Ruth LeNoir, Frances Y. Morrow, Helen Storey, and Esther Wynne.

⊰ 262-79 ⊱

Mrs. Cayce: You will have before you the Norfolk Study Group #1, members of which are present here, and their work on the lesson Destiny. *You will give such further material as may be obtained at this time. You will answer the questions that may be asked.*

Mr. Cayce: Yes, we have the group as gathered here, as a group, as individuals; and their work on the lesson *Destiny*.

In considering that portion of same that has been given concerning destiny as related to the mind, there may be added—as has been given—that if there is the concept gained here, ye may through these lessons set many aright as respecting same. [See 262-80, A-1.]

Consider these phases or portions of same in the present:

"As a man thinketh in his heart so is he," and "Thou canst not by taking thought turn one hair white or black, nor add one cubit to thy stature."

These in their various manners present the correct interpretation, then, of the destiny of the mind. Mind is, as has been given, both physical and spiritual; is amenable to laws that govern same in its phase of manifestation. Mind is the motivative influence in expression as to the growth in which the inward self would make for its expressions in materiality or in matter. What meaneth, then, those that spoke as given, "As a man thinketh so is he"? So does the growth become. For in the material things, as we shall find as respecting the destiny of the body, as a man eateth so is he also—the physical man. As a man thinketh so is he also; destined that that which is the growth of those influences in the experience of the individual for its accomplishing, its fulfilling that purpose for which it came into being.

Then the question, naturally, is asked: Is the destiny of a

mind set at the time of its birth into materiality? as to what it will think, as to what its environs will be, as to the length of its period of expression in the earth? Is it destined to lose a tooth on a certain day, a hair on a certain day, an arm, or this or that experience? These are in those signs that have been indicated, that as ye *are*, as ye were, so will ye be by or through that which has been accomplished in the experience of the body, of the mind, of the soul; that it, the soul (the only living portion of same), might be one. It is destined that it will pass through that experience necessary to give it, the soul, the greater opportunity for its becoming one with that purpose for which it came into being. For God hath not willed that any soul should perish but with each temptation hath prepared a way, a means of escape. This, then, would indicate that as the soul, or as the man, or as the mind works at in its thinking it becomes.

Then does this belie that the Master gave, "Ye cannot by taking thought add one whit or one cubit to thy stature, nor turn one white hair black"? This then rather indicates, rather assures those that accept what He has given, that it—the thought—is a growth by that which is (and will be seen the more in that which may be expressed or given as concerning) the destiny of the body.

But for that which may illustrate to each of you in your own experience as to the destiny, or what thought or what mind may do as determining the *soul's* destiny:

There is the mind of the soul. There is the mind of the physical being. There is ever that battle between the flesh and the spirit, which has been from those periods when man projected himself into flesh through the power given him and partook of flesh in such a manner as that flesh, as all matter, dieth in the matter or physical plane. Yet the spirit or the soul-man dieth not, for it is the gift of God.

Then as the mind dwells upon that in materiality or in the flesh or of the earth-earthy, to satisfy, to make for growth within the flesh, this—as the Master has given—does not find itself in that of growth but rather as He gave, "Seek first the kingdom of God within you; *then* all of these things may be added *unto* you." Not as thou seest fit, not for thine own indulgences, but that ye may indeed and in truth be one in Him with the Father, and thus fulfill in each experience that which is the fulfillment of that destined for thee. Hast thou then aught to do with thy days in the earth? How readest thou? "Honor thy father and thy mother, that thy days may be long in the earth which the Lord, thy God, giveth thee." Honor, then, to whom honor is due destines that greater opportunities for an individual soul in an individual experience will be the result of such activity. How doth honor come? First by the *thinking*, the meditating upon; so that in the acts, in the words, these bring honor, bring that which is honor to such in a material manifestation. How, then, dost thou read as respecting that the fulfilling of the law as concerning that thou wouldest do in thine experience day by day will bring into the mental, the material, the spiritual, the soul experience of each that which may, which will, which *does* fulfill that for which *that* entity, that individuality, is destined? By whom? Is it within self? Is it within the gift of the Father? Both! For if ye labor one with another, ye cannot serve two masters; for ye will love one and hate the other. If ye live for thyself thou fulfillest the destiny for self-love, self-glorification. If thou thinkest and livest the life of love in Him that *is* life, *is* love, thou fulfillest that destiny for which He has given thee. Thou must be purged so as by fire, for eventually ye must pass under the rod.

Ready for questions.

We are through for the present.

≥ 262-80 ≤

This psychic reading was given by Edgar Cayce at the Edmonds' home, 611 Pennsylvania Avenue, Norfolk, Va., on April 28, 1935, at 4:00 P.M., in accordance with a request made by those present: Edgar Cayce; Gertrude Cayce, conductor; Gladys Davis, steno; Hugh Lynn Cayce, Edith Edmonds, Florence Edmonds, Helen Ellington, Ruth LeNoir, Frances Y. Morrow, Helen Storey, and Esther Wynne.

Mrs. Cayce: You will have before you Norfolk Study Group #1, members of which are present here, and their work on the lesson Destiny. *You will continue the discourse on this lesson, and answer the questions that may be asked.*

Mr. Cayce: Yes, we have the group as gathered here; as a group, as individuals—and their work upon the lesson *Destiny*.

As has been presented for the consideration and the study of the group, in presenting this subject and its divisions, and those tenets or understandings that have been given, this group should present that which shows the variations in that presented as of old and that yet older than they—yet by Him that is to this group the *only* way.

In the portion of this study as pertains to destiny as related to the mind, then, does there come the *real* import—or where there are the divisions of same by some as respecting that presented by Him, the Master, the Christ.

Mind is, as has been given, both spiritual and physical. In the material world, where we find expressions of the physical and of the spiritual, we find mind. Yet what is known as the group mind—or that of the plant kingdom, the mineral kingdom and the animal kingdom or group—returns (as its destiny) to the Creative Force which is its Author, its Maker. *Man*—the free will agent; man made to become a companion to the Creator through the purification, by manifestation of the love of God as may be manifested in the earth—makes his destiny as to whether his mind (that accompanies his soul) is one with or in opposition to the Creative Forces. For he, for weal or woe, gives expression of same in his activity. And his destiny—his mind's destiny—is in Him if he, man, will but make the mind one with that which is creative in its essence, in its activity, in its flow. For mind is the dividing line between that which is human, that

which is man, and that which is animal—or of that division
of a group soul or consciousness. Hence the variation in that
He taught as He gave to Nicodemus, "Know ye not ye must be
born again?" Born of water and of blood; that is, of the spirit
—yet the spirit making manifest in the flesh the last command,
the whole command as He gave, "A new commandment I give,
that ye love one another"—that ye be of one mind, of one
purpose, of one aim, of one desire. That each must approach
from his or her own vision, his or her own status of development, does not alter that as has been spoken, "As the man
thinketh in his heart, so is he." So does the mind bring health,
wealth, happiness; in that it is made *one with* Constructive
Force, one with the Creator; and thus fulfill its destiny—to
become one in Him, one with the Father. Not by other than that
"abiding in me, as I in the Father, ye in me." And what ye ask,
what ye seek, what ye live, what ye *are,* will be one with that
force. Thus is the destiny of mind. Thus is the variation that
lies between East and West; that of the old tenet yet ever new,
presented in *mind is the builder.* Yea, mind is that which makes
for the destiny in the experience of all; not by denial alone but
rather by an active, positive assurance of the mind's activity
being One in Him. As He abides in the Father, ye may abide
in the Father also. For as He is the way, He is the light, He is
the bread of life, He is the water of life, He is the vine, we abide
in that mind, that flow of life as of Him, and we then are one
with Him.

Ready for questions.

*Q-1. Please explain that given in reading of March 10, 1935,
"If there is the concept gained here, ye may through these lessons
set many aright as respecting same."* [*See 262-79, p. 1, par. 2.*]

A-1. As has just been given; that those thoughts, those expressions of creation, those expressions of manifestivity in materiality—in flesh, in matter, in activity—are the variations. Not
that which entereth into the man defileth, but that which
cometh out of the man— *in* thought, in act, in word. As He gave,
then, set others aright.

We are through for the present.

This psychic reading was given by Edgar Cayce at the Edmonds' home, 611 Pennsylvania Avenue, Norfolk, Va., on May 12, 1935, at 4:00 P.M., in accordance with a request made by those present: Edgar Cayce; Gertrude Cayce, conductor; Gladys Davis, steno; Hugh Lynn Cayce, Edith Edmonds, Florence Edmonds, Ruth Le-Noir, Frances Y. Morrow, Helen Storey, and Esther Wynne.

⊀ 262-81 ⊁

Mrs. Cayce: You will have before you the Norfolk Study Group #1, members of which are present here, and their work on the lesson Destiny. *(I hold in my hand a compilation of the material on the* Destiny *of the Mind.) You will comment on this material, suggesting proper arrangement and presentation and give such further discourse on this subject as will be helpful at this time. Answer questions.*

Mr. Cayce: Yes, we have the group as gathered here, as a group, as individuals—and their work upon the lesson *Destiny*.

As to the data gathered here, as we find, these are very good. It has been indicated from the first portion of that which has been given that there would be set forth rather the preamble, as to how this lesson is to be considered in its various phases; mind, body, soul; the mental, the physical, the spiritual man. Also what pertains to that portion or relation of the mind as to the body, and how it bears relationships to that dealing with the physical forces, the physical aspects and the physical relationships in the individual's activity; and a creative force making the correlations of the various portions of the data respecting same.

Then there is the mind as the spiritual aspect or consciousness, in the material, in the soul or mental body; and the mind that is the portion of the awareness within, that is made for its constructive forces in the individual aspects of the soul. Here again we come to those mooted questions as to the portion that becomes the personality and individuality of the mind in its relationships to what becomes a constructive influence in the activity of the individual or the entity in its entirety.

So we have or meet those various aspects in the experience of each individual; for where there has been the constructive or destructive aspects in the experience of each individual, they

-319-

must be met in that same sphere or plane of activity in which they have been in action in the experience of the entity—and met according to that which is to be meted. For what saith the law? As ye mete, so shall it be meted to thee in thine *own* experience, in thine own activity. So, as individuals in their material or mental experience in the material world find that they are in the activity of being mistreated, as from their angle, from their own angle have they mistreated. If harshness has come to thine own experience, so has there been in thine own activity that which makes for same; and so is the experience in each phase.

Some may ask, some may say, how or when does one become aware of that mercy, grace? As the individual in the Christ is under the law of grace and mercy and not of sacrifice. Then indeed does each soul, each individual, in same become aware of the saving grace—or the purpose for which the Holy One gave within self that sacrifice such that all through Him may become aware, in the *spiritual* plane, through the grace of the Christ, of the manner in which the individual has met in the material. For He hath forgiven thee already. Only in thine brother—as ye are to be judged before Him by the deeds done in the body-*physical*. For once for all has He entered in that ye are forgiven by Him already.

Then, in the preparation, prepare same in the present manner as has been indicated and outlined for the various phases. And then as there is the undertaking in the destiny of the mind, the destiny of the soul—as these are given and their tenets and truths correlated, they need only those changes that make them as *one*. For the Lord thy God is one. One Lord, one Christ, one faith, one hope, one baptism—in the Christ; putting on Christ.

Ready for questions.

Q-1. How should we define the following in this lesson: First, what is gospel?

A-1. News, tidings, understandings; that which bespeaks the sounding of warning, knowledge, awakening—if there will be the considering in the mind of the hearer. Gospel. Glad tidings.

Q-2. Second, what is truth?

A-2. That which makes aware of the divine within each and

every activity; that is of the mental, the material, the spiritual self—and is a growth in each and every soul.

Q-3. What is judgment?

A-3. With what judgment shall ye be judged? Law is love; love is law. Judgment is weighing love, law, according to the intent, the purpose of the activity in its relationships to thyself and to the force that impelled same. A weighing of evidence in an activity; as law is that through which, by which, in which all are judged.

Q-4. [993]: May I have a message from my Elder Brother, the Christ?

A-4. Abide thou in the way that has been chosen by thee. Meet oft in thine inner self, in judgment upon thyself in Him. For ye keep the way open for many.

Q-5. Is there a message for the group as a whole?

A-5. Let that thou doest in thine application of that being presented thee, for the edification of thy brethren, be done in humbleness of heart, in singleness of purpose, in service *through* thy Lord's meeting oft with thee. And as ye do it in this manner will He abide closer, closer—Lord, to thee. Let thy prayer and thy meditation be,

"IN THEE, O LORD, DO I TRUST. IN THEE WILL I PUT MY FAITH, MY HOPE, MY ALL."

Continuing, then, upon thy lesson as related to the destiny of the body—it has been indicated in thine outline as to how there are the manifestations of those things in the earth that become the expressions of the movement of the spirit bringing into being that which is matter in its various expressions. Also it has been indicated how that matter in its group form, or in its various forms, appears, disappears, dissipates into that from which it came. Yet in man, as we find, the soul, the individuality of the soul, becomes more and more apparent through the manner of life—or manner of its expressions in its activity, in its awareness within whatever sphere of activity in which it may find itself. Hence, as we find, of man—upon whom much has been bestowed—much is required. In all the universe, the celestial, the terrestrial forces, in summer, in fall, in winter, in spring, in *every* manifestation we find the beauty of the Lord, of the Christ—the *glory* of those. Only in man may we see—

through his relationships to his brother—selfishness, un-comeliness, the desire for self-aggrandizement or for self's own gratification without thought or concept of what may be the result of its activity. Hence man in his destiny makes for, in the body, that which he as an individual, as a personality, must meet in personality or in the flesh—or in the manifestations of same, with the awareness of that as may be builded in and through those various activities through which the body in its varied environments, its varied activities, may find itself. And what makes for the change? *Will!*

What, then, is *will?* That which makes for the dividing line between the finite and the infinite, the divine and the wholly human, the carnal and the spiritual. For the *will* may be made one *with* HIM, or for self alone. With the will, then, does man destine in the activities of a material experience how he shall make for the relationships with truth. What is truth? That which makes aware to the inmost self or the soul the Divine and its purposes with that soul.

So does the body—whether it is sown in this or that environ, this or that plane of activity—become one with His purposes, through the making of the will one with the spiritual import or activity; or it makes for the separations—that are to be met only in the material experience.

Hence the necessity; hence the judgment; hence the mercy, the justice shown by the all-wise Creative Force—that is so beautifully illustrated in the spring, the summer, the fall, the winter—the returning again and again of the body of man for its purification.

Has not man demonstrated how that the elements in the earth are purged of the dross by the fires of the furnace for their purification? Have not the weaklings in the flock or the un-healthy plants been made sturdy in their relationships of beauty in nature, by purging, pruning, and making for those advancements again and again? And yet some deny that the all-wise, the all-merciful Father would be so gracious to the sons of men who have erred in this a little thing! What hath the Maker of the heavens and the earth said? They that are guilty of the least are guilty of them all!

So, in the destiny of thy body, make the *will* (How? Through the mind of the body!) at-one with Him; knowing in thine self that what has been set, what is *is*—as God. Yet in Christ may ye meet *every* trial, every temptation. For how hath He spoken? That though offenses must come (and woe be to those by whom they come!), He hath not allowed those to be tempted beyond that (in the body), above that which they are *able* to bear. How *great*, then, is the trust that He hath put in thee, that *thou* should bear the glad tidings of a *risen* Lord, an *alive* God in thine own experience! *Ye* that have chosen Him, as He hath chosen you, to be lights unto the sons of men. Quit ye yourselves, then, as He hath trusted in thee; trust *ye* in Him!

We are through for the present.

This psychic reading was given by Edgar Cayce at the Edmonds' home, 611 Pennsylvania Avenue, Norfolk, Va., on May 26, 1935, at 4:10 P.M., in accordance with a request made by those present: Edgar Cayce; Gertrude Cayce, conductor; Gladys Davis, steno; Hugh Lynn Cayce, Edith Edmonds, Florence Edmonds, Helen Ellington, Ruth LeNoir, Frances Y. Morrow, and Helen Storey.

≫ 262-82 ≪

Mrs. Cayce: You will have before you the Norfolk Study Group #1, members of which are present here, and their work on the lesson Destiny. *You will continue at this time the discourse on the section pertaining to the destiny of the body, and answer questions.*

Mr. Cayce: We have the group as gathered here; as individuals—as a group—and their work upon the lesson *Destiny*.

In continuing with what has been given, it would be *well* that they each put into practice or application in their own experience that which has been outlined. For, as given, thus will their expression find that which will answer in the experience of others in *their* various phases of development.

For, as outlined in that portion of the lesson relative to the destiny of the body, their individual activity is destined much from the varied experiences in the earth.

Have ye not read as He gave, that he who is guilty of one jot or tittle is guilty of it all? Have ye not read that ye shall pay to the uttermost farthing? Yet it is not the same as considered by some, that ye have builded thine own karma—and that the blood, the debt, the law of grace is of none effect. But as He has given, if thine activity is made that ye may be seen of men, or if thine purpose, thine aim, thine desire is for self-glorification, then ye are none of His. Then, the meeting of the deeds done in the body is by relying upon, the faith in, Him; the activity that makes for an exemplification in the flesh of that faith, of that mercy. If ye would have mercy, be ye merciful. If ye would be faithful, show thyself by thy acts that ye trust in Him. How readest thou? "Consider the lilies of the field, how they grow; they toil not, neither do they spin; and yet I say unto you that even Solomon in all his glory was not arrayed like one of these." Hast thou put on the Christ, then, in thine activity with thy neighbor, with thy brother, with those of thine own house? Know ye within thyself. Hast thou met with Him in thine inner chamber of thine own temple? Ye *believe* that your body is the temple of the living God. Do ye act like that? Then begin to put same into practice, making practical application of that thou hast gained, *leaving* the results with thy God.

Thou believest He is able to keep that thou committest unto Him. Dost thou live like that? Dost thou cherish the thought, *"I am in Thy hands. In Thee, O God, do we live and move and have our being in the flesh: and we as Thy children will act just that"?* Speakest thou evil of thy friend, thy foe; or as thou wouldst speak if thou wert in the presence of thy God? Ye are continually in that presence, within thine self. He with the Father, He in thee. Will ye keep the faith that is accounted to thee for righteousness, that thy body in its purging—through the varied experiences in the earth—may *ever* be a channel that points to the *living* God?

What will ye do about same?

Ready for questions.

Q-1. [*993*]: *Explain, "He hath not allowed those to be tempted beyond that (in the body) they are able to bear."* [*See 262-81, p. 3, par. 6.*]

A-1. As an illustration: When the earth came to be the dwelling place of sin, there came the Son—that the earth and all therein might see, might know, might experience, that the Son, the love of the Father, the glory of the Son might be manifested in flesh. This is an illustration of how that ye are not tempted beyond that ye are able to bear. It hath been said again, *"God hath at no time tempted man."* But again as the Master hath said, "Had I not come ye would not have *known* sin." Hence man in his awareness of sin, of the Christ Spirit, of that which makes him in all the phases of his experience awakened to that, may become aware of God's destiny for the soul. Shall it return empty-handed or bearing *thy* name? As it has already been given, the destiny of the soul is to return to the Giver, the Maker. To man, in the body, does there remain the destiny of whether it, that soul, shall return (as of the creation) empty, or bearing the name. For hath He not said, "I have called ye by name"? If *God* hath called thee, and *thou* hast harkened, then thou *knowest* Him. He that hath not heard, he that hath preferred what man terms being tempted, has given in to same and preferred the filth of the carnal experience to that *glorious* association and oneness with the way, the life, the light, the water of life. Hence, as given, He hath prepared the way. The *will* of man is either to become one with that way or cast from it.

But ye would come, bearing *what* name? In the name of Him that hath given Himself in the world as a ransom for the world, that we in that name may stand justified before the throne of mercy or peace and light.

Then how precious should be that cross, that name, to *every* soul; that it should stand instead of thy shortcomings, that it shall stand instead of thine own selfish ways! But ye *must* make the attempt. The attempt is righteousness. He will bear thee up; for as He has given, He hath given His angels charge concerning thee. And He, thy Brother, standeth before the face of God to make intercession. How great is the mercy! How great is that, "He hath not allowed me to be tempted beyond that I am *able* to bear!" in that name.

Q-2. [379]: *Please explain what is meant by Jesus being tempted in all points like we, yet without sin. Does this refer to more than one incarnation?*

A-2. That as the Son entered into the earth throughout the ages, as man counts time, there was the growth; the growth that made for that purposefulness that the world, the earth and the fullness thereof might be a *living* example of the *glory* of the Son. And as man counteth shortcomings *many* there were, yet tempted in all—even in that experience when "yet without sin" He presented His body before the throne of grace and mercy (as is the promise of every man) and offered it up— without question; offered up the blood of that body, in same becoming pure. So does every soul that offers its body, its mind for a cleansing, become pure in that thing. He, through all, grew to where, "This is my beloved Son; hear ye him," for He hath the words of life.

Q-3. [341]: *Please explain heredity in relation to the destiny of the body. Do we draw to our bodies the same atomic structures used in other bodies?*

A-3. This is rather confusing in its questioning.

There is a compliance with those things, ever, set as immutable laws. *Like begets like!* Heredity, then, is the association of that within the minds, the bodies, the atomical structural forces of a union which hath drawn for its *own* development as well as for that which comes *as* an activity of a unison of purpose. Hence we have a choice, yet the *choice* of that as we have built; for as the tree falleth so shall it lie. If the blind lead the blind *both* shall fall into the ditch. But He, the Lord, the Master, the Maker, maketh the paths straight to those, for those, that seek to have *Him* lead the way.

Q-4. [303]: Is there a message for me?

A-4. Let His strength sustain thee. Thou hath grown in grace and in knowledge and in understanding. Be not overcome by those things that rise that would make thee afraid; for He will bear thee up as He hath promised. Put thy trust *wholly* in Him. *Know* that He will do thee good.

To all: Let thy daily associations, the words of thy mouth, the activities of thy hands and of thy bodies, be in accord with that thou wouldst give thy brother to live by.

We are through for the present.

This psychic reading was given by Edgar Cayce at the Edmonds' home, 611 Pennsylvania Avenue, Norfolk, Va., on June 9, 1935, at 4:15 P.M., in accordance with a request made by those present: Edgar Cayce; Gertrude Cayce, conductor; Gladys Davis, steno; Hugh Lynn Cayce, Edith Edmonds, Florence Edmonds, Helen Ellington, Ruth LeNoir, Frances Y. Morrow, and Helen Storey.

⊅ 262-83 ⊄

Mrs. Cayce: You will have before you the Norfolk Study Group #1, members of which are present here, and their work on the lesson Destiny. *You will continue at this time the discourse on the section pertaining to the destiny of the body, and answer questions.*

Mr. Cayce: Yes, we have the group as gathered here, as a group; as individuals, and their work of the lesson *Destiny*.

In considering further what has been given relative to the destiny of the body, much of this for the individual needs clarification. But unless effort is made with the mental application of same by the individuals, little clarification may come.

As has been indicated, that each may make the lessons living truths, make personal application of same. For the body being of the earth earthy, true indeed is the destiny as is set; that as in Adam ye all die, so in Christ are all made alive.

In *this* statement does it appear as to whether this has reference to the natural body or to the superficial body. With what manner of body hath man appeared, and doth man appear? *Body* is form. *Form* is pattern. By what hast thou patterned thy body? What dost thou use as thy measurements? But if ye count time, ye know not the manner of that ye build. For in Him hath He said that ye shall become aware of all that hath been from the foundations of the earth. As in Him ye all live, as in the first Adam ye all die, so in the last Adam are all made alive.

Keep that pattern which is set before thee in what are and are to be the effects, the results, the essentials, the elements, the mode and manner of thy divinations. What are the attributes of that body which ye as individuals, as souls, would present to thy Maker? Who put on flesh, put on a body, that ye might have the greater knowledge, the greater understanding? What is knowledge, what *is* understanding, if ye apply it not in thy daily life?

Ready for questions.

Q-1. [993]: Please explain what was meant as given in an early reading, that anyone taking up this work would have to give up the world for a season. Does this mean a preparation? Explain.

A-1. Take that illustrated by Him; that if ye are *of* the world and in the world then ye are the world's, but that if ye are in the world and of the Lord ye *are* the Lord's. Then as may be said, in making the personal, practical application of the tenets, the truths, the life, the light, the understanding that may be presented to thee through these sources, these channels, if ye would abide in them ye are *not* OF the world—only *in* the world. Hence that given, ye that would take up this as a *practical* thing, or ye that would become channels of blessings to thy fellow man, give up the world. Not that there is not to be the use *of* things material. Even thy Master paid His tribute to Caesar.

Q-2. Gladys Davis: Please explain how physical conditions may come to pass as dreamed of at times regarding individuals. Are such conditions set at the time dreamed of? Why would one dream of any given condition? [See detailed dream at end of reading.]

A-2. The law of cause and effect is immutable, by choice in individual experience. Or choice is the factor that alters or changes the effect produced by that which is the builder for every experience of associations of man, in even material experience. Hence as thought and purpose and aim and desire are set in motion by minds, their *effect* is as a condition that IS. For its end, then, has been set in that He, the Giver of the heavens and the earth and those things therein, has set the *end* thereof. *Dream* is but *attuning* an individual mind to those individual storehouses of experience that has been set in motion. Hence at times there may be the perfect connection, at others there may be the static of interference by inability of coordinating the own thought to the experience or actuality or fact set in motion. Hence those experiences that are visioned are not only as has been given to some, to be interpreters of the unseen, but to others dreams or as dreamer of dreams, to others as prophecy, to others healing, to others exhortation, to this and that and the other; yet all are of the same spirit. Hence this is the manner as may be seen. This has little reference to *body-destiny,* but much with the *mind.*

Q-3. [585]: *Would the conflict between spirit and flesh cause one to be affected physically, to become tired or even ill?*

A-3. *Relatively* so. As He gave, "For whether is easier, to say, 'Thy sins be forgiven thee'; or to say, 'Arise and walk'?" Or again when confronted by that which had become as a disease, as a temperament of the body, as the wantonness of the flesh, He said to the woman, "Where are those thine accusers?" — "No man, Lord" — "Neither do I accuse thee; but *sin no more.* " What took place then in the experience of those individuals spoken to by *Life,* Light and Immortality? These were concentrated and centralized upon the activity of what? What has ever been the builder, body, mind and spirit? As given, the expressions are in the physical, the motivative force is the spirit, the mind is the builder. What was builded? Those bodies had dwelt as individuals do (as may be illustrated in habit) with the inter-consciousness of the necessity of the expression of something within self which brought dis-ease, the natural result of what? An at-variance to the divine law! Hence it may truly be said that to be at variance may bring sickness, dis-ease, disruption, distress in a physical body. It is true then that the mind may heal entirely by the spoken word, by the laying on of hands, dependent upon the *consciousness* of the motivative forces in the individual body. Yet those requiring material expression to create a balance may necessitate drug, knife, water, heat, electricity, or *any* of those forces that are yet what? What is the spirit? The *manifestation of God!* The *Creative* Force working in, with and upon what? The awareness, the interconsciousness of the *body,* the mind, the spirit, as separated in individuals! O that all would gain *just* that! and not feel, "Yes, I understand — but my desires and my body and my weaknesses — and this or that — and I didn't do it." Who else did?

This may be a hard statement for many, but you will eventually come to know it is true: No fault, no hurt comes to self save that thou hast created in thine consciousness, in thine inner self, the cause. For only those that ye love may hurt you.

Q-4. [*307*]: *Any message for her at this time?*

A-4. Keep inviolate that thou knowest. Love the Lord and His ways. Put thy trust wholly in Him. He is able to bear thee up and to present in thine inner self that awareness which will make thee anew. Those that look only to the god within may become idol worshipers; for the expression that is of thy concept is what one does *about* that concept!

Q-5. *Any message for the group as a whole?*

A-5. Be ye joyous in thy service to thy fellow man, in the *name* of Him who is able to keep thy ways. Count thy hardships, thy troubles, even thy disappointments, rather as stepping-stones to know His way better. Be ye joyous; be ye happy in *His love.* For He hath loved us, even when afar. How much more when we try, though we may stumble and fail! For the trial, the test, the *determination* creates that which will rise as faithful, true, and as righteousness before the throne of grace. For thou art under a dispensation of mercy. Be ye merciful. Be ye unhurt by hard words. For *thy* hurts are His! Bear them, then, with Him in thy dealings with thy fellow man. If ye would have love, show thyself lovely; not only to those that speak kindly to thee —for what profit have ye? Are ye seeking the easy way? Did He? Come! Be joyous in thy love for thy friend, thy foe, thy loved ones, thy enemies. For *all* are His; and as ye do it unto the least ye do it unto Him.

We are through.

[Gladys Davis's detailed dream referred to in A-2:

In late January of 1934 Edgar Cayce, Hugh Lynn Cayce, and I were visitors for the weekend at the Ladd home on Long Island. Late Sunday night Mrs. Ladd was telling me about her husband's financial difficulties; his job was insecure, and they were about to lose their home. As I got in bed I remember wishing I could do something to help the Ladd family. It turned awfully cold that night and I was very uncomfortable. Although the little modern cottage was steam heated, I was from the South and it seemed mighty cold to me. Early the next morning, January 29, 1934, I was awakened by this dream:

"A knock on the door. I said, 'Come in.' Mr. Ladd stood there with a coal scuttle in his hand, and wearing a lumber jacket. (I had never seen him in anything but a business suit.) He came in and made a fire in a little coal stove which stood in the room, saying, 'Now the room will soon be warm so you can get up.' "

On the train back to New York later that morning I told Mr. Cayce and Hugh Lynn about the dream, when relating what an uncomfortable night I had experienced. We all laughed and attributed the dream to my discomfort. Still, I remember remarking how strange it was that the room should be different from the one I was occupying—which had cute little radiators on two sides of it (too cute and too little).

In early April of 1935 while on a business trip to New York the three of us were spending the weekend as guests of Harold J. Reilly at his Sun Air Farm, Oak Ridge, N.J. On Sunday morning, April 7, 1935, when I said "Come in" to a knock on my door, there stood Mr. Ladd in his lumber jacket, a coal bucket in his hand, and he said, "I thought you'd like to have a little fire in your stove to take the chill off while you get dressed." I immediately noticed that the little room was exactly the same as I had dreamed it over a year ago.

You see, Mr. Ladd had become manager of Sun Air Farm in January of 1935, a year after we visited him in Long Island. If he had not come to my room to make the fire, I would never have remembered the dream nor recognized the room. So many questions arose in my mind as a result of this dream coming true that I sought the answer in above reading 262-83, A-2.]

≈ 262-84 ≉ *This psychic reading was given by Edgar Cayce at the Edmonds' home, 611 Pennsylvania Avenue, Norfolk, Va., on June 23, 1935, at 4:35 P.M., in accordance with a request made by those present: Edgar Cayce; Gertrude Cayce, conductor; Gladys Davis, steno; Hugh Lynn Cayce, Edith Edmonds, Florence Edmonds, Helen Ellington, Edna B. Harrell, Ruth LeNoir, Frances Y. Morrow, and Esther Wynne.*

Mrs. Cayce: You will have before you the Norfolk Study Group #1, members of which are present here, and their work on the lesson Destiny. *I hold a compilation of the first section on* Destiny *of the Mind in my hand. Please comment on this and continue with the discourse on* Destiny of the Body. *You will answer the questions that may be asked.*

Mr. Cayce: Yes, we have the group as gathered here, as a group and as individuals; and their work on the lesson *Destiny.*

In commenting upon that as compiled here, well that in the prelude or a prelude—there be presented rather more of that as was the *beginning* of the lesson, or more of that as was presented in the first discourse on same.

Then compile rather in the order as was then indicated; as to how that the mind in its different or the various phases— which at times make for confusion to many—is ever the builder, and that the key should be making, compelling, inducing, having the mind one with that which is the ideal.

So few there be who have a singleness of purpose, having a mind with an eye single to service that the destiny of the mind, of the body, of the soul, may be in keeping with that which was purposed from the beginning.

What saith He? "Heaven and earth shall pass away, but my words shall not pass away."

Again what hath He said respecting the individuals who would come to abuse, to make a show of that they would do with their lot? "Many will say to me in that day, Lord, Lord, have we not prophesied in Thy name? and in Thy name have cast out devils? and in Thy name done many wonderful works? And then will I profess unto them, I never knew you; depart from me, ye that work iniquity."

What meaneth then these as respecting or in application respecting the destiny in the mind?

Lest those err that would make for a show, lest those come into disrepute, *know* what thou hast believed and be ye consistent in that ye say, that ye do. For that ye think, that the mind dwells upon, that ye do become.

In gathering the data which have been given, know that much is here.

To those that have failed to contribute their portion, what think ye—that ye would amiss be in thy service to thy fellow man? For as has been given here and there, the need has been and is that you each present your own experiences. For the experiences of all are worthwhile. Compile these, then.

In giving further that as respecting the destiny of the body, begin—in thy compilations—with questionings respecting same. For *all* have not understood that as He gave; as to how ye should consider what manner of man ye are; for many are likened unto whitened sepulchres, *beautiful* to behold from their walks before men, but within the mind harboreth those things that are vile, unkindly, and will make for that as must be met in themselves. For He hath not willed that any soul should perish, but hath prepared a way of escape.

Who, then, will separate you from the knowledge, the application, the understanding of thy relationship to thy God? None save thyself.

For, as has been given oft, nothing in heaven or in hell may separate man from the knowledge of the Father save himself.

What, then, may separate thy body? What then is the destiny of thy body?

Ye read, ye have heard it said, "I believe in the Father, the Son and the Holy Ghost. I believe in the resurrection of the body; the communion of saints." What meanest thou?

Hast thou set aught in thine own experience against these words that He hath given? "Who *is* my mother, or my brethren? Whosoever shall do the will of the Father, the same is my mother, my brother, my sister."

These bespeak the activities of the body before thy fellow man. Hast thou in thine meditation, in thine prayers and thy supplication kept the faith that thou art His? that in Him ye live and move and have your being? *This* ye say; *this* ye may do. How, ye ask?

Love one another.

Ready for questions.

Q-1. Any special message for the group at this time?

A-1. Ye have work of love, of joy, of peace before thee. Keep the faith, by *living* same. They that set themselves as knowing become stumbling blocks; for he that would be the greatest among you, let him be the servant of all. Serve ye one another, in love—as becomes the children of faith. Let thy words and thy meditation be, as ye present thy bodies, thy lives, thy activities before others:

"LORD, USE ME IN WHATEVER WAY OR MANNER THAT MY BODY MAY BE AS A LIVING EXAMPLE OF THY LOVE TO THE BRETHREN OF OUR LORD."

We are through.

This psychic reading was given by Edgar Cayce at the Edmonds' home, 611 Pennsylvania Avenue, Norfolk, Va., on July 21, 1935, at 4:05 P.M., in accordance with a request made by those present: Edgar Cayce; Gertrude Cayce, conductor; Gladys Davis, steno; Hugh Lynn Cayce, Edith Edmonds, Florence Edmonds, Helen Ellington, Ruth LeNoir, Hannah Miller, Frances Y. Morrow, Helen Storey, and Esther Wynne.

⪼ 262-85 ⪻

Mrs. Cayce: You will have before you the Norfolk Study Group #1, members of which are present here and their work on the lesson Destiny. *As I present each section of the part on mind, comment on same. You will answer the questions.*

Mr. Cayce: Yes, we have the group as gathered here, as a group and as individuals, and their work on the lesson *Destiny*.

In the presentation of that portion of same as given here, as a whole we find it is very good. In the various sections, as in one and two, there is an overlapping of subject matter; yet this in this individual way or manner we find very good.

There is *not* sufficient in the preamble of that which should be taken from the first lesson as given in the presentation of *why destiny* should become a portion of the lessons at this time.

These are the only changes as we find, though of necessity there must be some putting together in a little more concise form, in sections, after their associations as one to another.

Q-1. Is it necessary to comment on each section separately?

A-1. Only in the preamble should be the comment. The next comment would be upon the second portion of the lesson as a whole, or *Destiny of the Body.*

Q-2. Is the outline correct?

A-2. This is very good.

Q-3. Please explain, given in reading [922-1, p. 1, par. 5] of May 10, 1935, "Try the spirits."

A-3. As indicated, or in making the interpretation, reason from thine conscious mind from the first premise which is the basis of all the lessons: All force, all power, is of the *one* source, even as was given by the Master when questioned by Pilate, "No power is given over me save from the Father."

So in the experiences, as indicated oft, there are those activities from the outside of the physical body, through the mental,

-336-

through the spirit of those as disincarnate influences or forces. *These* try! as to whether there is the force or power of that constructive nature as given. They that deny that the Christ has come in the body are not of Him.

Q-4. Please explain, "Try the aspects." [*See 922-1, p. 1, par. 5.*]

A-4. The same may be applied in *their* phases of the same expressions. These may lead to the questionings in the own mind; hence *try* the aspects, from whence do they arise? What are the promptings and what is the seat thereof?

For, as has been given by Him, there is the way that seemeth right unto a man but the end thereof is death.

This is the aspect of an individual, or collective experience. Yet oft may there be sufficient of truth to keep alive, yet feedeth only on the egotism of the individual.

For each spirit that may make manifest must be as the complement of the Creative Forces or God, or of that which would lead to destruction. And how spake He? In the mouth, in the experience of two or three witnesses is the fact established.

Q-5. Please give examples and explain, "a mental-physical experience and a spiritual-mental force."

A-5. Very well in just those conditions that have been used as the phase of experience, and of the spirit as may be tried in the experiences of individuals.

But that these may be more specific, we may use that which is the common error in and among men:

There may be the biological urge of a body for the gratifying of that which is of the ego or of self. And the one or body so urged may use same as the justification that it, or the force, is of the Creative Energy. Sure, but the end thereof—unless of a unison of purpose with the spiritual attributes of the body or bodies—must bring eventual destructive forces.

Yet that urge that may arise from the oneness of purpose with the spirit of truth, of life, in being a help to an individual or body in loss of hope, in the disturbing factors even of the biological influences, is of the Creative Forces. The other may be only material.

Q-6. Explain the "superficial body."

A-6. That which is of the earth-earthy; that channel, that house, that piece of clay that is motivated in material forces as the dwelling place of the spirit or the soul. That is the superficial body.

The soul body is the motivative power within, that has either grown in the constructive forces in its associations or activities, or to the gratifying, satisfying of the superficial emotions or urges.

Q-7. Is it possible for our bodies to be rejuvenated in this incarnation?

A-7. Possible. For, as the body is an atomic structure, the units of energy around which there are the movements of the atomic forces that—as given—are ever the sentiment or pattern of a universe, as these atoms, as these structural forces are made to conform or to rely upon or to be one with the spiritual import, the spiritual activity, they revivify, they make for constructive forces.

How is the way shown by the Master? What is the promise in Him? The last to be overcome is death. Death of what?

The *soul* cannot die; for it is of God. The body may be revivified, rejuvenated. And it is to that end it may, the body, *transcend* the earth and its influence.

But not those standing here may reach it yet!

Q-8. Is it true that "destiny is the result of will's activity on karma"?

A-8. It is and it isn't. Depends upon the approach or the phase of same. What has been thy lesson? The *body*-destiny depends upon the will, by the use of the mind, that is of the spirit.

If the mind is to gratify the body without the consideration of the spirit, that destiny is made, see?

For to say the body of an individual, or an entity, is soul and then to say God hath not *willed* that any *soul* should perish, is not conformity. For will the *will* of man override God, or will man be *ground* to that *necessary* for his own awakening?

Ye that worry and are troubled, ye that are doubtful and fearful, who hath brought this upon you? God? *God* hath not at any time tempted man, but if ye will but accept it He hath prepared with every temptation, with every fault in man, a way of escape.

And the will of man is *just* combative. But the end of the soul *must* be back to its Maker.

But what manner of body ye will carry depends upon thy will, yes.

Q-9. Explain, "If thine eye be single, thy whole body shall be full of light." [Matt. 6:22, 23] [Given as "moral perception" in Bible notes.]

A-9. It explains itself. The I AM, the I Self, the I Consciousness, the eye as in those things James has given; the eye that hath looked on, the eye that hath observed, the eye that hath desired in the heart. *That* eye.

If thine eye be single thine whole body is then full of light. Just as indicated in that given, as the Master gave to him that became the teacher to many peoples, how hard it is to kick against the pricks. Or in other words, how hard it is to make thine eye single, or thyself to say, "Lord, have *Thy* way with me."

Q-10. [585]: Please explain the experience I had on the morning of July 17th, in which I saw a pyramid of smoke over my head and then a burning bush within. What do these symbols mean?

A-10. The awakening to that as must be a portion of the experience necessary for the full cleansing, the full awakening to the possibilities that lie within.

How hath He given that ye shall be purged? Even as by fire. This, to be sure, then, is emblematical; that thy service may rise as sweet incense from the altar of service in thyself.

So long as ye look upon a service done, a good deed, as a lesson, as a duty, as a service, so long are ye subject to same.

When to do good is the joy, when to deny self is a pleasure, *then* thou wilt know the I AM is awakened within.

Q-11. Please give a discourse on destiny as related to the body.

A-11. Much has been given. Apply *that* first; then seek ye as has been given. For ye have sufficient material that unless ye apply same ye must indeed live it.

Q-12. [404]: Please give me a message at this time.

A-12. Let the light of His countenance, as it comes before thee in thy service with thy fellow man, keep that hope burning in thine heart for the joy of the privilege of serving in *His* vineyard.

In this then be joyous that thou art counted as worthy to be a channel of blessing to many, to bring before the face of those that opportunity of the knowledge that may purge their minds, their bodies, for a greater channel of service, of blessings to others—those ye contact day by day.

Q-13. Any message for the group as a whole?

A-13. Hold ye one to another in thy prayer, thy meditation, thy service; for in union is strength, even in Him.

We are through for the present.

≫ 262-86 ≪
This psychic reading was given by Edgar Cayce at the Edmonds' home, 611 Pennsylvania Avenue, Norfolk, Va., on August 11, 1935, at 4:15 P.M., in accordance with a request made by those present: Edgar Cayce; Gertrude Cayce, conductor; Gladys Davis, steno; Hugh Lynn Cayce, Edith Edmonds, Florence Edmonds, Edna B. Harrell, Ruth LeNoir, Hannah Miller, Frances Y. Morrow, Helen Storey, and Esther Wynne.

Mrs. Cayce: You will have before you the Norfolk Study Group #1, members of which are present here, and their work on the lesson Destiny—*section on body. You will continue the discourse on the destiny of the body and answer the questions which will be asked.*

Mr. Cayce: Yes, we have the group as gathered here, as a group, as individuals; and their work on the lesson *Destiny.*

In the approach upon the subject, let's make a little different approach; that much of that which has been intimated that should be asked as questions by individuals of this group may have, perhaps, (with thought) the wherewithal to approach same.

First there is the destiny, as we have indicated, of the mind; that is both material and spiritual.

Then there is the destiny of the body, as we have indicated. And it is held by some that, the body being of the earth-earthy it is born into the earth, dies and returns to earth. This has been set by the sages of old, and would indicate that the body—being of that phase of experience or existence—remains in its sphere; that while changes come about, it remaineth.

Yet the pattern has been shown by Him who entered into the earth that we through Him might know life, and in having life have life more abundant.

As the question has been asked, when ye say "I believe in the Father, the Son, the Holy Spirit; I believe in the holy church, in the resurrection of the body," what meanest thou? The spiritual body or the material body? What meanest thou also (as will be approached, for it must be all a portion of the one) as to the communion of the saints? Bodily? With what body? Spirit? With whose spirit; their own or God!

-341-

In the body, then, we have the body, the mind, the soul; each representing a phase of man's experience or consciousness.

The destiny that is spoken of in these, then, is of the body-physical; that which is manifested in the earth in materiality, in matter; that has taken form, represented by an individual that has been given a name to designate its body from other bodies of similar nature.

What of it?

As the body (this body spoken of) is the temple of the living soul, the temple of God—What of it? Is it to become dust again and again; yet being associated with the soul, the spirit of the individual that had been lent such, or had used such in creation as the abode of their existences, their experiences? Is it to see corruption? Is it to be lost entirely? Is it to be glorified, spiritualized? How was *His* body?

As the body is a portion of the structure in which the manifestations of the individual, as a portion of the whole, are carried on, it, that body—is then in the keeping of its *keeper*. So what wilt thou do with same?

God hath not *ordained* that any *soul* should perish! What of thy body? Hast thou ordained, hast thou so lived, hast thou so made thy temple that being untenable thou dost not care for its glorifying?

Ye attempt, rightly, to adorn thy body for thy fellow man. Dost thou care less for thy God than thy fellow man? Dost thou purge the body, as He hath given, that it may be made whole for thine soul?

What is to come depends upon what thou hast done, what thou wilt do with the opportunity which is, has been and will be *thine* for the glorifying of same.

If ye would be like Him, then so live, so conduct thyself, that *thy body* may again and *again* be brought into such relationships that it may be raised; a glorified body to be known as thine very own!

That thou mayest have been called, this, that and the other name may make for confusion to many. But when ye say Creative Force, God, Jehovah, Yahweh, Abba, what meanest thou? One and the same thing, carrying through in the various phases of thine own consciousness; or of those who in their activities

seek, as thou (if thou seekest aright), to be one with Him yet
to *know* self to *be* self, *I AM,* in and with the *GREAT* I AM.

The destiny of the body, then, lieth with the individual.

Ready for questions.

*Q-1. Should we study to present with this lesson an under-
standing of the Book of Revelation? If so, how?*

A-1. Not necessarily; for one is as the spiritual body, that is
given in symbolic activity for the learned, while we are beginning with babes!

*Q-2. At the change called death is the entity free of a physical
or material body?*

A-2. Free of the material body but not free of matter; only
changed in the form as to matter; and is just as acute to the
realms of consciousness as in the physical or material or carnal
body, or more so.

*Q-3. What is meant by the resurrection of the body? What
body?*

A-3. That body thou hast taken in thine individuality to draw
upon, from matter itself, to give it shadow or form, see?

As may be seen by a study of the information which has been
given through these sources as to the various appearances of
an individual soul-entity in the earth, sometimes the body is
six foot two, again four foot five; sometimes fair of hair, sometimes of very dark complexion. What has the Book written on
same? *Man* looketh on the outward appearance; *God* looketh
on the heart.

This is the same, but why the change?

In entering into materiality, that thou hast used of spirituality or Creative Force makes for the development that has been
in the experience of thy entity or soul-body, see?

Then as it appeareth in the earth, what has been the builder
ever? *Mind!* Mind of what? Of the *entity!* as associated with
Creative Forces drawn by those environs into which it has come
in its various experiences. The matter is drawn, as it were, of
the soul and of the soul-entity. Hence with what body shall ye
be raised?

The same body ye had from the beginning! or the same body
that has been thine throughout the ages! else how could it be
individual?

The *physical*, the dust, dissolves; yes. But when it is condensed again, what is it? The *same* body! It doesn't beget a different body!

Q-4. Is the body aware of the destiny of the physical body at birth?

A-4. God Himself knows not what man will destine to do with himself, else would He have repented that He had made man? [Gen. 6:6] He has given man free will. *Man* destines the body!

Q-5. Moses taught the laws of health to the children of Israel. If we should strictly follow these or similar laws, would it make for a perfect body, a better mind and more soul development?

A-5. It may make for a better body, a better mind. As to the soul development, this depends upon the use of same in thy experience. Did the high office of priesthood make Nadab or Abihu better, or have more soul development? They used that they had for their own destruction! Did the office of being chosen by God Himself to be the king over his brethren make Saul a better man? Was he better as the prophet, as the king, or as the dead king?

Q-6. Is the destiny of woman's body to return to the rib of man, out of which it was created? If so, how; and what is meant by "the rib"?

A-6. With this ye touch upon delicate subjects, upon which *much* might be said respecting the necessity of that *union* of influences or forces that are divided in the earth in sex, in which all must become what? As He gave in answer to the question, "Whose wife will she be?" In the heavenly kingdom ye are neither married nor given in marriage; neither is there any such thing as sex; ye become as *one*—in the union of that from which, *of* which, ye have been the portion from the beginning!

Q-7. [585]: Do the dreams I had last night and night before bear on the destiny of the body?

A-7. Bear on the destiny of thy *own* body!

Q-8. As I call each name, you will give each a personal message on the destiny of the body.

A-8. Of their *own* body!

Q-9. [288]:

A-9. Keep thy mind, thy body, more in accord with thy own ideal, if thou wilt know that thou *art* one with Him.

Q-10. [*585*]:

A-10. As thou hast been shown the necessity of the purges within thine mind, thine body, that thou may know the glory of Him who took His own body that ye might have a pattern, so keep ye the way.

Q-11. [*307*]:

A-11. Let the Lord and His ways *ever* be thy guide. Let *not* the word of man, in any form, turn thee aside from that thou hast been shown in thy heart.

Q-12. [*560*]:

A-12. Let the ways which lie before thee be kept ever open that ye may know more and more the glory of the risen Lord, that *thy* body may be one with Him.

Q-13. [*379*]:

A-13. Unto him that hath shall be given. Keep the ways of the Lord before thee. Bind them upon thy forehead, that ye may see and hear and know only that which is good.

Q-14. [*303*]:

A-14. Let the law of the Lord be as a lamp unto thy feet, that ye err not in thy walks before thy fellow man. Thus shall ye keep the way and walk therein.

Q-15. [*993*]:

A-15. The light of the Lord is precious in thy sight. Let *nothing* deter thee nor make thee afraid. For ye shall see Him as He *is*.

Q-16. [*341*]:

A-16. *Thou* hast seen the way; thou hast known that which maketh men afraid; thou hast known that which easily besets the ways of those that would harken to the vicissitudes of life. *Keep* the faith thou *hast* had!

Q-17. [*404*]:

A-17. The law of the Lord is perfect, converting the ways that seemeth awry, making straight the paths of those that love His coming. Keep in those paths as thou art shown from day to day.

Q-18. [*462*]:

A-18. In the Lord's house are many mansions, and they that

keep His ways shall dwell therein; in those bodies that they *build* with their fellow man day by day! Know the Lord, that He is good.

Q-19. [*413*]:

A-19. In the way of the Lord the earth seems afar off. In the way of the earth the Lord seemeth afar off. Keep, thou, close to the ways of the Lord.

Q-20. [*295*]:

A-20. The Lord's ways are not past finding out, if ye will seek them. They that seek for the satisfying, for the gratifying of the *material* forces, know *not* the Lord. Let *Him* have His way with thee.

Q-21. [*294*]:

A-21. The Lord keep thee; the Lord bless thee, and cause His face to shine upon thee and bring thee peace!

Q-22. [*538*]:

A-22. Unto those that trust in the Lord, He *maketh* the paths straight. Unto those that trust in the might of their own counsel, or their own strength, it cometh to naught. Trust ye in the Lord!

Q-23. [*264*]:

A-23. Present in this room: The Lord's ways thou *knowest.* Keep them, if ye would know *Him* the better. Let not the cares of thy body, of thy mind, of thy life in the earth, deter thee. For the Lord loveth those that are *just kind* to His children.

Q-24. *Any message for the group as a whole?*

A-24. As has been given, study that thou hast had presented to thee; lest thou experience much that would show thy short-comings.

We are through for the present.

This psychic reading was given by Edgar Cayce at the Edmonds' home, 611 Pennsylvania Avenue, Norfolk, Va., on August 25, 1935, at 4:10 P.M., in accordance with a request made by those present: Edgar Cayce; Gertrude Cayce, conductor; Gladys Davis, steno; Hugh Lynn Cayce, Edith Edmonds, Florence Edmonds, Helen Ellington, Ruth LeNoir, Hannah Miller, Noah Miller, Frances Y. Morrow, Dorothy L. Wright, and Esther Wynne.

⊰ 262-87 ⊱

Mrs. Cayce: You will have before you the Norfolk Study Group #1, members of which are present here, and their work of the lesson Destiny. *You will continue the discourse on the section, destiny of the body. You will answer the questions that may be submitted.*

Mr. Cayce: Yes, we have the group as gathered here, as a group, as individuals; and their work on the lesson *Destiny.*

Following those suggestions that have been made, you each should present yourselves as channels of blessings to others; in that others may receive a better concept of the necessity of presenting their bodies as a living sacrifice, as a living example. Each should understand that sacrifice does not necessarily mean a giving up; rather a glorifying of the body for a definite purpose, for an intermediary, for an ideal, for a love. Along this line should the idea be, rather than that there should be a refraining from this or that. The choice must be made as to the purposefulness for which the activity is to be; and in keeping with what has been presented, that the bodies *are* the temples of the living God. So, the activity should be such that the self, the ego, the I AM would present same to the God, the Father, the Universal Influence, the Creative Energy, the I AM THAT I AM, in such measures and manners as to be a glorifying of that the body, the entity, the soul would present as its portion of the whole. Thus may you each of this group, in presenting your experiences through the application of that which has been given, make for those ways, means and manners in which others, seeing, knowing, hearing, may take the initiative necessary for the awakening of *their* own purposefulness in any given experience; that may make for the turning of hate to love, the turning from strife to a purposefulness towards peaceful-

ness that may bring to all mankind—at *this* time—that necessary in the influence of all. For thoughts as they run have their
activity in the experiences of all, and thus create the environ,
the atmosphere of thought upon which those who are active in
their various spheres of experience and of expression must
draw for that which will be a portion of the motivative influence
in their experience.

Thus may you each here contribute of yourselves through
your expressions in those thoughts presented in this lesson, the
destiny of the body; and that which has been presented should
be sufficient at this time for not only the completing but for the
presenting of that which has been the experience. For as given,
seek and ye shall find; knock and it shall be opened unto you.
For the spirit is willing, flesh *is* weak. But if ye glorify that flesh,
that body, in the service of the spirit of truth, that truth may
indeed quicken same; and may it not be glorified before thy
brethren?

Ready for questions.

Q-1. Was the Apostles' Creed man-made or inspired?

A-1. What is inspiration? From the standpoint of the seeker
(for all haven't sought this), it was man-made. From the standpoint of many another present, it was the interpretation
prompted by the inspiration to make a united effort in the
purposefulness of one line of thought.

To be sure, this answers to some and to others does not.

The Apostles' Creed as presented, to be sure, as would be
judged by those who are orthodox, is inspirational; and comes
from those sources that to many a man are considered au-
thoritative.

As to the experiences of the apostles themselves, this—to be
sure—was created or put together some ninety-seven, yes a
hundred and sixteen years later than the last of their activities;
yet it was the expression that came from the activities. The
belief of all the twelve apostles? No, not as written; but the
experience in the minds and hearts and souls of many who
sought as best they understood to present a solid front, with
each naming that for which he stood in his own life.

Most of these expressions presented in the Creed may be the
experience of each and every soul. And to no soul does any

expression become a portion of self until experienced; *experienced* by the soul! Many may find here and there a word, a phrase, a sentence, a line that answers to something because it has been the experience or is the answer to a longing that has not yet been satisfied wholly. For until there is an answer that to the soul is the *justification* of that which is *thought,* it is not even a good axiom to the soul!

Q-2. With whose spirit, mentioned in the Apostles' Creed, would we commune; with ourselves or God's?

A-2. Within ourselves to God. For, as intimated elsewhere, "My Spirit beareth witness with thy spirit." Whose spirit? There is only *one* spirit—of truth. There may be divisions, as there may be many drops of water in the ocean yet they are all of the ocean. Separated, they are named for those activities in various spheres of experiences that are sought to be expressed here. The communion of the spirit of the divine within self may be with the source of divinity. This is what is meant by the communion of saints, of those that are of one thought, for all thought for activity emanates from the same source, and there is the natural communion of those who are in that thought. This may be expressed by that indicated oft, that unless a helpful experience may be presented in an individual's activity as a parallel, as a complement, as a positive and negative force that may be united in one effort, it does not run true. For *opposites* create disturbance, dissensions, disruptions, devilment. A union of force makes for strength and power. Thus, the communion of saints means that all who have one purpose, whose thoughts and motivative forces are one, may communicate; whether those in the material plane, in the borderland, or those that may be upon the shores of the other side of life.

What meaneth the interpreters of the experiences in that, "Ye as standing here shall see glory; and after six days he taketh with him Peter, James and John and goeth apart into the mountain and there was transfigured before them"? What saw they? A glorified body? The glory of the body brought what? Communion of saints! For who appeared *with* Him? Moses; that to those present meant a definite undertaking which set them apart from other peoples, which had made for the first association or communication direct with a creative force or God through the activative forces in their experience. And Elijah (or John the Baptist); representing that they, too, would become as messengers to a waiting world, ready, ripe unto the harvest as he had told them. Then this *indeed* was the communion of saints.

It is the natural state that the intent and purpose of activity in whatever environ or sphere ye may find self, is attuned with that sought by the soul. When may such a communication be given? Seek and ye shall find; knock and it shall be opened unto you—that attunement to which thou hast brought thine self! Hence more and more is the admonition given that if ye would know God ye must be godlike to some poor soul. If ye would have friends, be a friend to a friendless one. If ye would know peace and harmony, *bring* peace and harmony to the experience of another soul. Yes, be even as He; who showed His glory to His disciples in the mount; facing death, facing even the denial by one to whom He was showing Himself that he had any part in that which He would give to others.

Let it be so in thine ministry, in thine activity; in the preparations of thy body, thy mind, thy knowledge concerning that which may bring to thine self those awarenesses of the spirit of truth, those things that make for the experiences of each and every soul. Seek not the experience until—and unless—ye know from whence and how and to whom it is given!

Q-3. What is the Holy Church?

A-3. That which makes for the awareness in the heart of the individual. It is as He that was set as the head of the church is the Church. The Church is never a body, never an assembly. An *individual* soul becomes aware that it has taken that Head, that Son, that Man even, to be the intermediator. *That* is the Church; that is what is spoken of as the Holy Church.

What readest thou? "Upon this I will build my church."

What church? The Holy Church? Who is the head? That One upon whom the conditions had been set by that question asked. For here ye may find the answer again to many of those questions sought concerning the Spirit, the Church, the Holy Force that manifests by the attuning of the individual; though it may be for a moment. He asked, "Whom say men that I am?" Then Peter answered, "Thou art the Christ, the Son of the living God!" Then, "Upon this I will build my church, and the gates of hell shall not prevail against it." He said to Peter, "Flesh and blood—*flesh* and blood—hath not revealed this unto thee, but my Father which is in heaven." Heaven? Where? Within the hearts, the minds; the place where truth is made manifest! Wherever truth is made manifest it gives place to that which is heaven *for those that seek* and love truth! but a mighty hell for those that seek gratification of their own selves! And these are those things which become stumbling blocks to many an individual that becomes more and more material-minded. For these must be seen; yet they heed not what *has* been seen and heard and given of old. Who communicated, ye want to know, to Peter when he gave this confession? Whom did He say is thy father, thy mother, thy sister, thy brother? He that doeth the will of the Father in heaven, the same is thy *earthly* father, thy *earthly* mother, thy earthly brother and thy sister. They that love *truth* rather than the satisfying, the gratifying of *fleshly* desires. This does not indicate that no beauty, no joy, no happiness is to be in the experience of those who claim to seek to be the channel of blessings, or the source of inspiration to others! Who is the father of joy? Who is the father of happiness? Who is the father of peace? The same that thou would serve in showing forth the Lord's death till He come again. For he that is long-faced, he that is sorry for the world is sorry most for himself; and of such has He said, "Though in my name ye cast out demons, though ye heal the sick, I will say Depart from me, I never knew you." Why? For ye have your own glory when such is done that it may be seen and known and heard among men alone.

But love thy neighbor. Love thine enemy. Love those that despitefully use you. For what profit hath thou if ye love only those that love you?

Q-4. Should the outlines of this portion of the lesson on destiny, the physical body, be in the form of questions?

A-4. In the form of questions and answers, as indicated.

Q-5. Please explain how the physical body may be cleansed.

A-5. Read rather that presented in *Meditation*. Here it is given. What may be cleansing for one will only partly be found so by another. *What* is thy standard?

Q-6. Why did Jesus say, "Touch me not," when He first appeared to Mary after the resurrection?

A-6. For the vibrations to which the glorified body was raised would have been the same as a physical body touching a high power current. Why do you say not touch the wire? If ye are in accord, or not in touch with the earth, it doesn't harm; otherwise, it's too bad!

Q-7. Please explain Romans 8:23, "And not only they but ourselves also which have the just fruits of the spirit, even we ourselves groan within ourselves, waiting for the adoption; to wit, the redemption of our body."

A-7. Just as given, as to the manner in which the glorified body, though still of clay, was shown before those witnesses that were to bear the evidences within themselves and their activities. Read this within the light of that given, and ye will understand.

Q-8. Please explain I Cor. 15:51. Is the reference here to body? "Behold, I show you a mystery. We shall not all sleep, but we shall all be changed."

A-8. Referring to the body; though the individual here speaking (Paul) *looked* for this to happen in his own day, see? For what is the stumbling block to us today? If we do a good deed we want God to repay us tomorrow! So did Paul! Did he not groan continually that the mark, that scar in him, was not removed? Did he not bring those things as said by Peter concerning same? That, "He speaketh many things hard to be understood, that many wrest with to their own destruction." To what did he refer? That their idea (of many who spoke) of time and space was limited; for they had even less conception of same than the weakest among you here!

Q-9. Any message to the group as a whole?

A-9. Let this be in thy minds, thy hearts and thy lives, as ye go about preparing that as will be thy contribution to this lesson which will go to many. For, as given, the time will come when these things written here ye many may study again; and will be as Bibles are to many in the present. But let thy light so shine among thine own associates day by day that ye are indeed *not ashamed* to speak that thou hast heard in the manner of thy living, in the same breath with that ye do and say to thy fellow man.

We are through for the present.

≫ 262-88 ⪦

This psychic reading was given by Edgar Cayce at the Millers' home, 3217 Verdun Avenue, Norfolk, Va., on September 8, 1935, at 3:40 P.M., in accordance with a request made by those present: Edgar Cayce; Gertrude Cayce, conductor; Gladys Davis, steno; Hugh Lynn Cayce, Edith Edmonds, Florence Edmonds, Helen Ellington, Ruth LeNoir, Hannah Miller, Noah Miller, Frances Y. Morrow, Helen Storey, and Esther Wynne.

Mrs. Cayce: You will have before you the Norfolk Study Group #1, members of which are present here and their work on the lesson Destiny. *You will give any suggestions that will be helpful in completing the section on destiny of the body, and continue with a discourse on the destiny of the soul. You will answer the questions that may be asked.*

Mr. Cayce: Yes, we have the group as gathered here and the work on the lesson *Destiny,* as a group and as individuals.

That which has been gathered from the information, from the experiences, as compiled, is very good—as we find. There needs be only, then, a correlating or tying together—as it were —of that which has been compiled or gathered together; as of the mind and of the body, for these are as one. For mind ever is the builder; hence man in the mental sphere, man in the material sphere, must make for that experience where the body and the mind are as one and not warring one with another; so that the consciousness of the spirit of truth is ever the motivative influence in the experience of the individual in its activities. How was He in the hour of trial, of temptation? He gave the lesson as to how that even though the body would be destroyed, in three days it would be raised again. He gave the lesson as to how there should be the thought of the fellow man, when those upon whom He had depended to be the ministers in His stead failed to catch the vision of what it was all about. He healed even His enemies, thus making the mind and the body as one; even in those hours when the change and the dissolution, the enlightening, the resurrection, were taking place within the activities of the *mental* body, expressing themselves through the activities of the material body.

So ye in making for that which may be helpful to thy fellow man in the application of the lesson, let all be of one mind—

-354-

even as in Christ, who thought it not robbery to be equal with God, yet desiring ever that *His* followers, *His* brethren, *His* friends, be one with Him, equal to and one with the Father.

So may ye, in the manners as indicated that the activities of the body bear within themselves the fruits of the spirit, attune the material forces in such ways and manners that the *mind* changeth ever to become in accord with, in attune with, whatever, wherever, in whatever manner it is presented with those influences that reach *in,* that are from without, that must be coordinated; that the body, the mind, may be carried to the Creative Forces—in what?

The destiny, then, of the soul. Each individual as a child of the Creative Force came into being that it, that child, might be a companion with the Creative Force, God, in its activity; given by the very breath, by the desire, by the will of the Father that with which it might be one with the Father. Not the body as manifested in the flesh; not the mind alone that may partake of all those environs through which it passes; but the soul, which is as lasting as eternity, as the Creative Force, as the Creative Energy, as God Himself; that we through Him might know ourselves to be one with Him. He hath not willed that any soul should perish.

Then, the destiny of the soul—as of all creation—is to be one with Him; continually growing, growing, for that association. What seeth man in nature? What seeth man in those influences that he becomes aware of? Change, ever; change, ever. Man hath termed this evolution, growth, life itself; but it continues to enter. That force, that power which manifests itself in separating—or as separate forces and influences in the earth, continues to enter; and then change; continuing to pour in and out. From whence came it? Whither does it go when it returns? [See also 262-92, A-3; 262-99, A-6.]

So the soul's activity in the earth, as it is seen in this or that phase of experience, is that it may be one with the Creative Forces, the Creative Energies.

Many questions, then, are brought to thine own consciousness that must be answered *within* thine inner self; having to do with thine own experiences.

Then, seek ye within thine own consciousness. There may

then be given that as may be helpful in thine interpretation of thine experiences; that may bring a consciousness to thy fellow man of the awareness of His presence and of the soul's returning to that oneness with Him.

Ready for questions.

Q-1. Will you please give more information on the resurrection of the body?

A-1. This is seen in that ye have as thine instructions as to how He, thy pattern, resurrected the body, *quickened* the body. So within thine own self must come that which through Him may overcome death, overcome that transition, overcome that which is the change—save the conscious change of being in *all* matters, *all* phases, *all* experiences, one with Him.

Q-2. Please suggest the outlines for the destiny of the soul.

A-2. First the soul's creation; the soul's association with those influences of mind, of body; and its activities in the material influences that are seen in the activities of a body through a given experience. And then the questions and experiences of each.

Q-3. Please explain what difference was made in the body of the Christ by ascension to the Father as necessary before Mary could touch Him?

A-3. As the presence of the Father, as the presence of the Christ Consciousness is everywhere present, the change that was in place was the consciousness rather in Mary than in the body Himself. But the expression ye have, that she was not to touch Him, was rather the same as would be in *any* expression given to interpret spiritual things into material understanding, or infinity brought down to the finite understanding, see? That is, "I have not yet ascended to my Father" would to some indicate that the heaven and the Father are somewhere else—a place of abode, the center about which all universal forces, all energies must turn or give off from. Hence "up" may be rather from within, or to the within—of which each soul is to become aware. For heaven is that place, that awareness where the soul —with all its attributes, its mind, its body—becomes aware of being in the presence of the Creative Forces, or one with same. That is heaven.

In thine studies of the destiny of the soul, then, let this be the constant affirmation:

"Lord, let me—my mind, my body, my soul—be at one with Thee: That I—through Thy promises in Him, Thy Son—may know Thee more and more."

We are through for the present.

≫ 262-89 ≪

This psychic reading was given by Edgar Cayce at the Edmonds' home, 611 Pennsylvania Avenue, Norfolk, Va., on September 29, 1935, at 4:00 P.M., in accordance with a request made by those present: Edgar Cayce; Gertrude Cayce, conductor; Gladys Davis, steno; Hugh Lynn Cayce, Edith Edmonds, Florence Edmonds, Helen Ellington, Ruth LeNoir, Hannah Miller, Noah Miller, Frances Y. Morrow, Helen Storey, and Esther Wynne.

Mrs. Cayce: You will have before you the Norfolk Study Group #1, members of which are present here, and their work on the final section of the lesson Destiny, *a copy of which I hold in my hand. You will comment on this and continue the discourse on destiny of the soul. Answer questions.*

Mr. Cayce: Yes, we have the group as gathered here, as a group, as individuals, and their work on the study of the lesson *Destiny.*

In commenting on that prepared here, it is very good; only needing, as we find, those correlations as we have indicated under the varied heads—and then the addition of the experiences that may be had from those comments by each individual.

As to commenting upon the subject destiny of the soul: As man finds himself in the consciousness of a material world, materiality has often, in the material-minded, blotted out the consciousness of a soul.

Man in his former state, or natural state, or permanent consciousness, *is* soul. Hence in the beginning all were souls of that creation, with the body as of the Creator—of the spirit forces that make manifest in using same in the various phases or experiences of consciousness for the activity.

It has been understood by most of those who have attained to a consciousness of the various presentations of good and evil in manifested forms, as we have indicated, that the prince of this world, Satan, Lucifer, the devil—as a soul—made those necessities, as it were, of the consciousness in materiality; that man might—or that the soul might—become aware of its separation from the God-force.

Hence the continued warring that is ever present in materiality or in the flesh, or the warring—as is termed—between the flesh and the devil, or the warring between those influences of good and evil.

As the soul is then a portion of the Divine, it must eventually return to that source from which, of which, it is a part. Will *thy* name be written there?

Ready for questions.

Q-1. [294]: How does partaking of the emblems instituted at the Lord's Supper supply food to my soul?

A-1. In that they are the emblems, or emblematical of the body and the blood, the spirit *moving* upon same brings the life flow. As has ever been given, in Him we live and move and have our being. Then the partaking of those emblems—or of that body and that blood—supplies or becomes food for the soul.

Q-2. [993]: Please interpret the experience that I have been passing through the last few weeks. Does it have any connection with the experience I had on Aug. 12, 1935, and my appearance when associated with Jesus Christ when He was the son of Mary? Or is it the destiny of the soul? Please give me a message of comfort at this time.

A-2. When these experiences are viewed in the light that they each become, as it were, an opening of the way for the understanding as to the relationships of the soul with the Christ, then there should become rather the understanding that in Him is thy destiny—if thy trust is put wholly in Him.

The ways indicated in the experience, then, though from the purely material angle, or to the conscious mind or physical-conscious mind alone they appear unreasonable, in Him are made one with the purposes set in that He has given thee, "Ye abiding in me and I abiding in the Father, ask that in my name and it will be done unto thee."

Q-3. [379]: Please explain: "For thy star has not set but arises in Him, for the way is clear before thee!"

A-3. As has been given by Him, He hath given His angels charge concerning thee. This is simply a transformation of the same understanding. That there has not been withdrawn, then, as it were, that strength in those blessed assurances that His angels have charge concerning thee and shall bear thee up. And ye shall ask and ye shall seek and know, and ye shall be comforted.

Q-4. Do we have to have a knowledge of all branches of education to reach the final goal?

A-4. Education is only the manner or the way. Do not confuse the manner or the way with that of doing what ye *do* know! Not when there is a more convenient season, or "When I have attained unto a greater understanding I will do this or that." Knowledge, understanding, is using, then, that thou hast in hand. Not to thine own knowledge but that all hope, power, trust, faith, knowledge and understanding are in Him. Do that thou knowest to do *today,* as He would have thee do it, *in thine understanding!* Then tomorrow will be shown thee for that day! For as He has given, *today* ye may know the Lord! *Now,* if ye will but open thine heart, thine mind, the understanding and knowledge will come!

Q-5. Was it necessary for me for my development to study the different lines of thought, such as Unity, Theosophy, etc.?

A-5. If these have that which has helped thee to understand. This must be judged from thine own self. For what is the law? Seek and ye shall find! *Knock* and it shall be opened unto you! In seeking through all understandings, all interpretations, there may be gained something; if ye will not become confused by those who say, "Here! This way!"

Because thou hast seen the vision of the mount, because thou hast seen the heavens opened in an understanding way, cry not this or that. Harken not to here or there, but turn to thine temple where He has promised to meet thee ever. It is not who will ascend to bring Him down, nor who will come from over the way—even though the Beyond. For how said He? If they hear not Moses and the prophets, they would not heed though one rose from the dead!

Think ye how gracious has been the gift to man, that only those who have crossed the border through being glorified (and *Glory* shall be thy next lesson) have vision. For they that are on the borderland are only in that state of transition. If they were to speak to all, how terrible would be the confusion!

Q-6. Is our lack of material necessities due to the fact that we have not first sought the kingdom, or lack of faith in not speaking the word?

A-6. Both. For what saith the law? Seek ye first the kingdom of God and all things shall be added unto thee thou hast *need of!* Most of us think we need a great deal more than we do!

When there was given the bounty to man through the activities of the law of the Lord, did He prepare other than that needed for the sustenance of all? In the preparation at the feast of Galilee in Cana what supplied He? The meats and the viands of the table? No, only that lacking. When He supplied the needs to the thousands that were weak and ahungered and troubled, did He use other than that at hand? That *at hand* was multiplied in the blessings!

Be patient, all. For all will pass through, in material experience, the greatest bounty of all. When ye fail here or there, ye must learn thy lessons. Humility, patience, faith. These make for the proper relationships of the *mind;* that is the builder for the body, for the soul.

Q-7. Please give a discourse on the Creation.

A-7. As has been given, souls were made to be companions with the Creator. And through error, through rebellion, through contempt, through hatred, through strife, it became necessary then that all pass under the rod; tempted in the fires of flesh; purified, that they may be fit companions for the *glory* that may be thine.

Glory, then, is thy next lesson; and *this* thy affirmation:

"OPEN THOU MINE EYES, O GOD, THAT I MAY KNOW THE GLORY THOU HAST PREPARED FOR ME."

We are through.

This psychic reading was given by Edgar Cayce at the Edmonds' home, 611 Pennsylvania Avenue, Norfolk, Va., on November 3, 1935, at 5:10 P.M., in accordance with a request made by those present: Edgar Cayce; Gertrude Cayce, conductor; Gladys Davis, steno; Hugh Lynn Cayce, Edith Edmonds, Florence Edmonds, Helen Ellington, Ruth LeNoir, Hannah Miller, Noah Miller, Frances Y. Morrow, and Helen Storey.

⋈ 262-90 ⋉

Mrs. Cayce: You will have before you Norfolk Study Group #1, members of which are present here, and their work on the lesson Destiny, *especially as related to the soul. You will give anything which is needed at this time in completing this lesson and an opening discourse on our next lesson,* Glory. *Answer questions.*

Mr. Cayce: Yes, we have the group as gathered here; as a group, as individuals, and their work on the lessons, *Destiny, Glory,* and others.

In that which has been given should be found that necessary for the completion of the lesson, or that portion of same, destiny of the soul. The whole theme or the whole purpose in that portion is the awareness of the soul's association in such a manner with infinity in its activity in the finite world, yet in such measures for the soul to know its association and its fulfilling of the purposes.

In giving that as may be the opening presentation of the lesson, a lesson, on *Glory:*

These that present this should within themselves experience, then, that which to each *is* glory.

What manner or form, then, shall it take in each *experiencing* —during this lesson, this preparation of same—that which will be, that is, *glory* in each one's experience?

These lessons to many have become at times as yokes; yet some have learned and are learning what He meant when He gave, "Take my yoke upon you and learn of me; for my yoke is easy, my burden is light."

Then, as ye approach this glorified Savior, this glorified Christ, *glory* in thine *own* experience that ye as individuals are *being* a channel of blessing to others; that ye are serving in such a manner that the service is no longer as a servitude but rather

-362-

as that which brings *joy* in the activity, a longing for the association, the opportunity, the manner in which self may be in some measure or some manner a channel of blessing.

Does the glory then as in Him shine out unto others? Does it become in thine own experience only a cross in the flesh? Is it not rather that same experience which He had in entering into His glory? that is, the completion of those activities in the material world when His glory was shown? And He asked that they—that all those who would make of their lives, of their experience, a channel of blessing to the fellow man—might know His glory; that they might know their *own* glory; that there might come that glory in the experiences of those who had consecrated, dedicated their lives and so *lived* them as to become living examples known among men for their good work in being a channel. Think it not strange, then, that ye should look for that glory. For has it not been given that ye have been chosen, even as ye have chosen Him? Thinkest thou that His prayer will not be answered *in* thee, and in thine experience? [See also 262-93, A-3.]

Then, rather than the opening of that as would be presented to others, rather would we give here that *ye* rededicate, reconsecrate yourselves; that ye may know, that ye may experience, this glory.

How—ye ask—and in what way?

How has He asked ever? "What seekest thou?"

Then, shall this glory be known and experienced in the realm of spiritual awakening, of mental attunement, or of material benefit?

All are of the Lord. Choose thou.

We are through for the present.

≈ 262-91 ≈

This psychic reading was given by Edgar Cayce at the Edmonds' home, 611 Pennsylvania Avenue, Norfolk, Va., on December 22, 1935, at 3:15 P.M., in accordance with a request made by those present: Edgar Cayce; Gertrude Cayce, conductor; Gladys Davis, steno; Minnie Barrett, Hugh Lynn Cayce, Edith Edmonds, Florence Edmonds, Ruth LeNoir, Hannah Miller, Noah Miller, Frances Y. Morrow, Helen Storey, and Esther Wynne.

Mrs. Cayce: You will have before you the Norfolk Study Group #1, members of which are present here, and their work on the lesson Glory. *You will give a further discourse on this lesson, giving especially a Christmas message to the group as a whole, and answer questions.*

Mr. Cayce: Yes, we have the group as gathered here; as a group, as individuals, and their work on the lesson *Glory.*

In considering the lesson at this time, glory is that which is sought in the experience of each and every individual. It, glory, is the natural expression also of every thing, condition, circumstance that gives to man and his mind a concept of Creative Forces as they manifest in materiality.

Hence this, then, is the natural seeking of man. Yet, as with *every* phase of man's experience with conditions that deal with the fellow man, this may be turned into that which may become a stumbling block to self or to others.

Glory, then, in all its phases in man's experience, and as related to the Creative Forces in the manifestations in the earth, is to be studied.

That this particular season brings to man the time when there is the expression of the glory of the Father through the Son in the earth, is manifested in the experience of all present.

Then, we may find glory in those activities, those expressions that may bring joy, peace, happiness, understanding, knowledge, wisdom, in the experience of all. These be the expressions of man in glorifying not self but that purpose, that ideal, for which the season, the period stands in the experience of each that seeks to know the glory of the Father.

For, as was given of old, the glory of God shall be manifested among men; for He, God, hath spoken it, hath promised it to the sons of men.

Yet this glory must become aware in the experience of each in the same order, the same manner, as every law of the Lord. They that would know God or His glory must believe that He *is*, and a rewarder of those that diligently seek Him.

If ye would know God, if ye would know His glory, *do good* unto thy fellow man! Give expression of that love as the Son gave in His ministry among men; who went about doing good, giving praise and glory. Not to self, not to a period, not to an ideal, but to God. For, as He gave, "Of myself I can do nothing, but that the glory of God may be manifested among men—for this cause, for this purpose came I into the world."

Then, if ye would make this glad season of effect in thine own experience, show forth *that* LOVE in thy dealings, in thy relationships, in thine words, in thine acts.

For as He gave, "As ye do it unto the least of these, my brethren, ye do it unto me."

Not, then, that self may be well-spoken of. Not that there may be this or that of thine own convenience, of thine own satisfaction. But that the glory of God may be manifested among the sons of men! In this manner, then, ye may know the glory of the Father, of the Son, at this glad Christmas time.

For, "As ye abide in me and I in the Father, so may the glory of the Father through thee be made manifest in the experience of thy brethren."

Ready for questions.

Q-1. As I call each name, you will give an individual message for them relative to this lesson and their part in this group work. [*413*]:

A-1. Let the glory of service to thy brother, in the Christ, show forth thy life, thy mind, thy heart; that the light of the whole body may be strengthened in Him.

Q-2. [*585*]:

A-2. Let the glory of the Father, through thy efforts in thine dealings with thy fellow man, bring thee joy, bring thee peace. For like begets like. As ye sow, so shall ye reap. Keep the faith that is set in Him, and press *on* to the mark of the higher calling set *by* Him.

Q-3. [*404*]:

A-3. The glory of the Father, of the Son, keep thee in the ways that thou shouldst go day by day. Realize in thine daily experience that indeed in Him ye have life, in Him ye move and have thy being.

Q-4. [462]:

A-4. The glory of the Father, of the Son, keep thy days, thy ways, that there may be no shadows, no faults, in thine inner self. For He is the light and He is the way. Follow where He leadeth thee.

Q-5. [303]:

A-5. Let the glory of the Father, of the Son, be as the light to thy feet, to thy ways. When the turmoils of life, the turmoils of associations trouble thee, look rather to Him who hath given, "Put thy burden on me—*Learn* of me and thy burden will be light, and thy way will be straight."

Q-6. [307]:

A-6. Let that glory thou hast seen in thy service to thy fellow man strengthen thee in the way that He leadeth thee. For He faileth not those who put their trust in Him.

Q-7. [379]:

A-7. Let that glory of service, of understanding, be as *wisdom* in thy dealings with thy fellow man. Not as knowledge alone but as wisdom, that giveth the manner, the way, the how, the when, to speak His name—in and before thy fellow man.

Q-8. [560]:

A-8. The glory of the Father, of the Son, shadow thee in all thy going in, thy coming out. Let the voice as thou hast heard, as thou mayest hear calling, be as those experiences that make more and more aware of His abiding presence with thee. For whom the Lord loveth He directeth.

Q-9. [993]:

A-9. The way of the Lord is not past finding out. And the glory that thou hast had, thou mayest have in His presence, abides nigh unto thee. Glory, then, in the Father, in the Son; that His name, His promises, may be sure to the sons of men.

Q-10. [295]:

A-10. Let the glory of the Lord abide with thee. Know that he that calleth but harkeneth not is as they who build their house on the sand. When He calls, answer—and give forth that which may be in glory for the purposes, for the service of the Son.

Q-11. [288]:

A-11. Let the glory of the Father, of the Son, suffice thee. Not what man thinketh, or what man sayeth. For man looketh on the outward appearance, but God looketh on the heart. Know that as thou hast purposed in thy heart is that which comes before the glory of God, that may be manifested *in thee*—for as He abides in thee and in thy fellow man, then not to the glory of self but to that spirit of love, of truth, that abides with Him.

Q-12. [341]:

A-12. Let love be without dissimulation. Abhor evil. Cleave to good; that the glory of the Son in the Father may—through thine efforts among the sons of men—be more and more glorious in the eyes of those that seek to know the way.

Q-13. [294]:

A-13. Let the heart be not troubled. Let it be not afraid.

Q-14. [538]:

A-14. Let the glory of the Father *ever* be before thee. For whom the Lord hath called, they will be borne upon those glories that may become as shining lights before men. Keep the faith that *His* ways may become more and more as the ways of those ye meet day by day. For with the measure ye mete, it will be measured to thee again—either unto the glory of the Father or to thine own confusion. Let the Lord guide and direct thee.

Q-15. [69]:

A-15. Let that thou hast held in thine heart keep thee ever. For the glory of the Lord is nigh to those that seek Him. For He hath given, "If ye will be my children, I will be thy God." Let that seeking, then, be the glory of thy purpose, of thy desire.

Q-16. Is there a message for the group as a whole?

A-16. Keep the purposes thou hast been called to do. For as ye have purposed, then to that end will He bear thee up—if ye will but remain *true* to the purposes in thy love for Him. Ye may indeed glory, for ye have been called of Him.

We are through.

This psychic reading was given by Edgar Cayce at the home of Mrs. Helen Storey, 2709 Lafayette Boulevard, Norfolk, Va., on January 12, 1936, at 3:50 P.M., in accordance with a request made by those present: Edgar Cayce; Gertrude Cayce, conductor; Gladys Davis, steno; Hugh Lynn Cayce, Edith Edmonds, Florence Edmonds, Ruth LeNoir, Hannah Miller, Frances Y. Morrow, Helen Storey, and Esther Wynne.

➢ 262-92 ≮

Mrs. Cayce: You will have before you Group #1, members of which are present here, and their work on the lesson Glory. *You will give further discourse on this lesson and answer questions.*

Mr. Cayce: Yes, we have the group as gathered here; as a group, as individuals, and their work on the lesson *Glory.*

In giving that as may be helpful in the study of the lesson, and in presenting that which may be helpful to others:

Oft in the interpretation of glory we find those conditions that become disturbing, or the incorrect understanding of glory.

There may be given, then, that premise from which those interpretations may be presented to others. So we would give, here, the manner in which this group would present this lesson, *Glory:*

Glory is the ability of the individual, the object, the personality, the God-force, to *serve.*

Then, when this is considered from this phase or angle, we find that oft there is *vain*glory. When that spoken so oft by the sages, the prophets of old, is considered, as to how the glory of the Lord would fill the earth, it is seen as to how vain becomes the experiences of individuals who have lost sight of that purpose for which those individuals, groups or masses spoke—or were spoken to—as to the glory that might be theirs.

As it has so oft been given from the first, *know* that the Lord, thy God, is *one! Know* that thy ability, thy service, begins first with *cooperation* in BEING that channel through which the glory of the Lord may be manifested in the earth!

For, "The earth *is* the Lord's, and the fullness thereof—Day unto day uttereth speech, and night unto night sheweth knowledge."

If ye would, then, fill that whereunto thou hast been called,

-368-

let thy glory—let thy knowledge—let thy *wisdom*—be in the
Lord!

Ready for questions.

Q-1. Please give an outline for the lesson Glory.

A-1. There have been many outlines for the varied lessons.
Would you change these? Is not this outline the same as the
others; that pertaining to the various phases of glory?

As has been given in the first, there is the glory of the mind,
the body, the soul. In all of these phases there are presented
the various activities through which there may be the interpretation of glory in those that would be glorious, or the interpretation of glory in those that would show forth the glory of the
Lord.

Q-2. Please give a discourse on the creation of the soul.

A-2. This will come in its own time, in *Wisdom*—that is the
second lesson from this. *Knowledge, Wisdom.*

Wisdom, then, begins with the recognition and acknowledging of, the knowing of, the application of, the soul in its development.

*Q-3. Please explain the following excerpt from group reading
[262-88, p. 2, par. 1] given Sunday, Sept. 8, 1935: "That force,
that power, which manifests itself in separating—or as separate
forces and influences in the earth, continue to enter; and then
change; continuing to pour in and out. From whence came it?
Whither does it go, when it returns?"*

A-3. Here we find those influences are spoken of that come
as a portion of the whole, that are separate—as companion-
ships to the whole; and are given their individuality through
their activities in and through material manifestations. In
other words, the soul—that is the motivative influence in the
activities in a manifested form in the earth, in its expression
of that thou art studying in the present.

These influences, or interpretations, will become confusing
unless kept in their *own* sphere.

*Q-4. [585]: What is meant by paradise as referred to by Jesus
in speaking to the thief on the cross?*

A-4. The inter-between; the awareness of being in that state
of transition between the material and the spiritual phases of
consciousness of the soul. The awareness that there is the com-

panionship of entities or souls, or separate forces in those stages of the development.

Q-5. What is meant by Jesus in John 21:23, "If I will that he tarry till I come, what is that to thee?"

A-5. The answer to the disturbed soul of Peter, who recognized the condition existent in the transition of the thought or the mind, or the experience of that which had been asked, "Lovest thou me?" And the *man* felt that the love shown to the beloved disciple was such that there *might* be that change. Hence the setting of that aright, to that which had been before given, "to sit on my right hand, and on my left, is not mine to give," but is earned, is given, is prepared, for those that "shew the Lord's death till he come."

Q-6. Any message for the group as a whole?

A-6. Much of that ye seek, ye ask, may become confusing — unless it, the information, the interpretation, the *application* of same in thine experience is kept in its *own* realm.

For, as has been given, the interpretation of spiritual laws is in spirituality; the interpretation of material laws is in materiality.

Confuse not thyselves, but study to show selves approved; not by wisdom, not by might, but in that which is the perfect law of the Lord, "Thou shalt love the *Lord* (thy God) with all thy heart, and with all thy soul, and with all thy mind, and with all thy body, and — thy neighbor (thy brother) as thyself."

For, as He gave, this is the whole law — and there *is* no other!

We are through for the present.

This psychic reading was given by Edgar Cayce at the Edmonds' home, 611 Pennsylvania Avenue, Norfolk, Va., on March 8, 1936, at 4:10 P.M., in accordance with a request made by those present: Edgar Cayce; Gertrude Cayce, conductor; Gladys Davis, steno; Hugh Lynn Cayce, Edith Edmonds, Florence Edmonds, Helen Ellington, Ruth LeNoir, Hannah Miller, Frances Y. Morrow, and Helen Storey.

⊰ 262-93 ⊱

Mrs. Cayce: You will have before you Group #1, members of which are present here, and their work and study of the lesson on Glory. *You will give a further discourse on this subject, and answer questions.*

Mr. Cayce: Yes, we have the group as gathered here, as individuals and as a group; also their work and their study on the lesson *Glory.*

In summing up that which has been given respecting the manner in which individuals should apply themselves in relationships to activities for the glory of the Father through the Son in their activities with and to their fellow man, we find:

The activities should come to be less and less for self, but more and more that self may be the channel through which the glory of the Father may be manifested in the earth.

Then, the activities of self become less and less towards the glory of self, less that good may come to thee. For being one with the Father, even as He has given, "As ye abide in me and I in the Father," then there may be that glory, that consciousness of the oneness that thou didst occupy before thy advent or before the world was. Even as He prayed, "Now, glorify Thy Son, that he may have the glory that was his before the worlds were."

Hence, be—individuals in this group—as individuals preparing others that they, too, may know that glory in their activities, in their lives. Not unto the glory of self that thou may be only well-spoken of; for they that do such have indeed their own reward within their *earthly* experience. But they that do service *in* His name, for the glory of the Father, may indeed know the glory the Lord hath prepared for them that serve Him.

Quit ye yourselves like the children of the Father, knowing

that His love, His glory, abideth with those who love His ways, that keep His commandments, that *glory* in the cross and in a service to their fellow man.

Ready for questions.

Q-1. Explain what is meant by "glorified" in John 14:13, "And whatsoever ye shall ask in my name, that will I do, that the Father may be glorified in the Son."

A-1. If we as individuals will but look about us, as to the ways of man and his knowledge of those things that go to make up the elemental influences in the earth, we can see and experience that as the Master gave; that the children of this world are wise in their own conceit; again, that the children of this world are wise even unto those that are the children of light.

Hence as He gave to those lacking in worldly wisdom and in the wiles of those that would make for deceitfulness in any of its phases or experiences of man's activity, the glory of the Father may manifest through the prayer, the activity, the seeking of those though they may be to the worldly wise as but babes in understanding.

Thus as He has given, those that run may read that the glory of the Father is made manifest in those that seek to know His ways.

Q-2. Explain John 17:12—"and none of them is lost, but the son of perdition." What is meant by lost in this sense, and just what would be meant by saved?

A-2. He had chosen rather to seek his *own* ways and to deceive others into seeking to follow their own manner rather than that there should be credence or credit or loyalty or love shown to that source from which life, consciousness or manifestations emanated.

Hence that spoken of him that rebelled against the throne of heaven, and manifested in the flesh in the one who betrayed Him.

Then, all are sons of perdition—or allow that force to manifest through them—who deny Him, or who betray Him, or who present themselves to be one thing and—under earthly environment or for personal gain, or for reasons of gratification—do otherwise; for they do but persecute, deny, betray Him.

Q-3. [993]: In the reading of Nov. 3rd, [262-90, p. 2, par. 1] where it said, "Thinkest thou that His prayer will not be answered in thee, and in thine experience?" what connection has this with the prayer of Jesus Christ recorded in John 17? What bearing does this have with my experience which I had while on the lesson Glory? *Please explain.*

A-3. As we find, one is a parallel or an explanation—as it were—of the other. In the prayer that He gave, "I pray not only for these but for those that may hear through the words of these." Or it is an inclusive prayer for every soul that names the name of Christ *as* the example, *as* the way, as the water of life, as the Savior, as the Son. Yet all of these are ever conditional, even as He gave. "If ye ask in my name, that will be given unto thee— *if* thou believest, *if* thou art faithful." Yet He said again, "Hadst thou the faith, the belief, even to the grain of the mustard seed, thou would say to this mountain 'Be thou removed and cast into the sea.' " And yet these we turn in our minds to mean spiritual or mental implications and not truths, literal in our own experience!

So in the implication as given in thy own experience, as thou saw, as thou understood, as the promises were given in thee, so may they be—so will they be—fulfilled according to thy faith. For how spoke He to they? "What seekest thou? Be thou healed according to thy faith."

What *is* thy faith? How readest thou, in thine self, that the glory of the Father may come to another but not to thee? Why? Art thou not His child? Art thou not His alone, even as He has called? Be not dismayed, but know that in thee, in thy service, in thy activities, many will be drawn close to an understanding.

And let him know that hath saved a soul he hath covered a multitude of sins.

Q-4. Any message for the group as a whole?

A-4. Draw nigh unto Him who hath called thee. For thou hast seen, thou hast experienced, thou will know within thine own self the nearness of His presence among thee. For His words faileth not. For as He gave, "Though the heavens and the earth pass away, my words shall *not* pass away."

So, as He hath called thee into service, be thou willing, be thou *glad* to be led by His presence, *His* presence alone. For the Lord is mighty and maketh known His ways unto those that seek to be gentle and kind, to be patient and long-suffering, to be one that showeth forth brotherly love.

For, "Inasmuch as ye do it unto the least of thy brethren, ye do it unto me—if ye do it in my name, saith the Lord of hosts!"

We are through.

This psychic reading was given by Edgar Cayce at the Edmonds' home, 611 Pennsylvania Avenue, Norfolk, Va., on March 22, 1936, at 4:00 P.M., in accordance with a request made by those present: Edgar Cayce; Gertrude Cayce, conductor; Gladys Davis, steno; Edith Edmonds, Florence Edmonds, Helen Ellington, Ruth LeNoir, Hannah Miller, Frances Y. Morrow, Helen Storey, and Esther Wynne.

⊰ 262-94 ⊱

Mrs. Cayce: You will have before you Group #1, members of which are present here, and their work on the lesson Glory. *You will give further discourse on this lesson and answer questions.*

Mr. Cayce: Yes, we have the group as gathered here, as a group and as individuals; and their work on the lesson *Glory*—in giving that as might be helpful to each of you in applying yourselves as individuals, and in giving and supplying that as may be helpful to others in their study and their seeking for the ways and manners in which they, too, as individuals, may know and manifest the glory of the Son in the Father.

In adding to that which has been given, or in summing it all up, KNOW that to *know* the glory indeed is to—self—be a part of that glory; that which would come through thy efforts. Not as an honor, but as thy honoring the Christ—for His name's sake. Not that ye may be well-spoken of or looked upon by the world as something set aside. Rather as He gave, *"in the world but not *of* the world"* yet manifesting that which becomes the glory of the Father among the children of men.

Not that self, thine own ego may be satisfied, but rather that the spirit of truth—as exemplified in the manner, the way the Master, thy Savior did manifest—may be *through thee* manifested before and toward thy fellow man. For it was spoken of Him that He went about doing good. *No* one could speak evil of Him, yet *we* say, *ye* say, evil was done Him. Yet He said, "for that purpose came I into the world, that I might overcome the world," and thus that the glory of the Father, of the Creator—yea, of thy Elder Brother—might be manifest.

As has been declaimed by a teacher, there is one glory of the sun, another of the moon, another of the stars; each differing in their glory according to the purpose for which they each have been established. For what? That man might in himself see the

-375-

glory of the Father being made manifest by they each performing their purpose in *their* cooperation, in *their* activity, before Him.

So, in thine own life, in thine own relation, in thine own associations one with another, how speakest *thou*—how readest thou? that ye do this or that in order that ye may be well thought of? or are ye fearful of what another will say because thou art called to do this or that?

Does the sun fear the glory of the moon, or the moon the sun?

Do the stars fail to shine because the sun is in *his* glory?

Yea, these should be to each of us that example, even as He gave, "Abide in me, I in thee, and ye shall have and *know* the glory of the Father."

Ready for questions.

Q-1. What did Jesus mean when He spoke of "the glory I had with the Father before the world was"?

A-1. The opportunities; as glory is only the means of opportunities for expressing that purpose, that duty, that love, that law which is before each soul.

Q-2. Please explain the veil within the holy of holies.

A-2. This is far afield, yet may be seen as that given by the Master, "These I have spoken in parable lest they see and are converted." What meaneth this? That those individuals' times, purposes, intents, had not been completed or sufficient unto where they would be stable in their use or application of the glory or the opportunity or the factor itself.

So with the veil in the holy of holies, which might not be entered save by him who had been dedicated to the office of representing or presenting the purpose, the mind of the people as a whole—and *then* only after consecrating himself for that period or act of service.

So within man's own experience, as has been indicated, step by step through that which has been given thee, as ye approach the Father KNOW the way by putting into *practical* application that thou hast *gained* day by day!

What brought death to him that put forth his hand to steady the Ark that, in *order,* sat behind the veil? That which had brought to that individual material prosperity, laudation among his brethren; yet the soul had accepted all without dedicating his body, his mind, his purpose to that service — breaking through the veil to accept and yet not showing forth that which was in keeping with those commands, those promises. For it had been said and given, "He that putteth forth his hand *beyond* that veil shall *surely* die! "

Q-3. Please explain Hebrew 9:28, "So Christ was once offered to bear the sins of many, and unto them that look for him shall he appear the second time without sin unto salvation."

A-3. As it reads, so *is* it; in spirit and in truth. For, combine each promise in same to that the *Master* Himself spoke. And we will find that the promises are, "He that abideth *in* me hath indeed then put *on* Christ, hath indeed become one with Christ and is no longer subject to the temptations of the earth, of the world," and hence becomes one with Him and is *in* that attitude, that plane of oneness. To such there is no returning to the flesh.

Q-4. As I call their names, you will please give a personal message to each of the group that will be of help at this time. [413]:

A-4. Keep thy paths before thee as brightened with the promises of thy Christ, and the ways will open for thee in thy service to others, through Him.

Q-5. [585]:

A-5. Let the words of *His* mouth be as lamps to thy feet, that the glory of the Lord may shine roundabout thee.

Q-6. [404]:

A-6. Keep the mind, the heart, *open;* that the light of the Lord may enter in and abide *with* thee. For He *will* do thee good.

Q-7. [379]:

A-7. Let the words of thy mouth and the meditation of thy heart coordinate with thy purposes in Him. For in such does the light and the glory of the Lord shine.

Q-8. [560]:

A-8. In the Lord is thy hope, thy trust; in Him there is builded about thee the light of the glory of the Christ. *Keep* Him in thy heart.

Q-9. [993]:

A-9. Let the ways of the Lord come nigh unto thee day by day; for in thy meditations ye walk along "this way," and He, thy Christ, thy Brother, is the light thereof.

Q-10. [*303*]:

A-10. Keep thy mind, thy heart, as one in Him; knowing even as He, the faults in others ye *cannot* correct of thyself. Only open the way; let the *Lord* have *His* way with thee.

Q-11. [*307*]:

A-11. The glory of the Lord shineth roundabout thee when ye put thy trust wholly in Him. The ways of the Lord are not past finding out; neither do they become as a mystery to those that make their purposes, their desires, *clean* in the sight of the Lord.

We are through.

This psychic reading was given by Edgar Cayce at the home of Mrs. Helen Storey, 2709 Lafayette Boulevard, Norfolk, Va., on May 10, 1936, at 3:55 P.M., in accordance with a request made by those present: Edgar Cayce; Gertrude Cayce, conductor; Gladys Davis, steno; Hugh Lynn Cayce, Edith Edmonds, Florence Edmonds, Ruth LeNoir, Hannah Miller, Frances Y. Morrow, Helen Storey, and Esther Wynne.

⊁ 262-95 ⊀

Mrs. Cayce: You will have before you the Norfolk Study Group #1, members of which are present here, and their work on the lesson Glory. As I call the heading for each section, comment on same. You will then answer the questions which will be asked. 1st. Introduction.

Mr. Cayce: Yes, we have the group as gathered here, as a group, as individuals, and their work on the lesson Glory.

The introduction is very good.

Q-1. 2nd. Glory of the Mind.

A-1. This is very good. There needs be some minor changes in the first portion of the first paragraphs. The rest is very good.

Q-2. Glory of the Body.

A-2. Very good, save lose not sight of that which is the whole purpose; the body is the manifestation, the movement of the mind, of the soul, through the mind that expresses itself in materiality. Not from materiality back, but up from soul through the mental processes of application in those things material.

Q-3. Glory of the Soul.

A-3. Very good.

Q-4. Experiences and Questions.

A-4. In the experiences some need to be transposed, but on the whole very good.

Q-5. Please give the affirmation for the next lesson, Knowledge.

A-5. LET THE KNOWLEDGE OF THE LORD
SO PERMEATE MY BEING THAT
THERE IS LESS AND LESS OF SELF,
MORE AND MORE OF GOD,
IN MY DEALINGS WITH MY FELLOW MAN;

-379-

THAT THE CHRIST MAY BE IN ALL,
THROUGH ALL, IN HIS NAME.

Q-6. What should be our approach for the preparation of this lesson?

A-6. That each may be conscious of that stated and implied in the affirmation.

Knowledge is power, yet power may become as an influence that brings the evil ways. For the expression of self is that which hinders man in the knowledge of the more perfect way.

Hence becoming more and more aware of that desire, that purpose within self, that as was given of old, "I am determined to know nothing save Christ and Him crucified."

As He in His death in the earth exemplified that *His body* was broken, we—too—must put away *self* that we may indeed *know* God. For knowledge is being—*being*—the channel through which God, that influence, that force, manifests in—and motivates—the earth.

For as the heaven is His throne, the earth is His footstool, so may we at His feet learn, know, become aware of, the knowledge of His ways. For He is not past finding out. For is God, the Father, so far away that He answers our pleas, our prayers, as from afar? Rather is His presence felt when we become aware of His force, His power, His love; the knowledge of His presence in our lives, our experiences, our undertakings in His name.

Q-7. What should be the basic principles in our thought on this lesson?

A-7. Knowledge as of God; knowledge as a workable experience in the affairs of individuals, of groups, of nations; that may *arise* from the motivative forces of the knowledge and power of God. Knowledge as a material experience, and how that knowledge as pertaining to the laws of a universal nature adds to the conditions in the experiences of man, even as to the conveniences of man; and how that the misapplication, the misinterpretation of such knowledge brings into the experiences of individuals, of groups, of nations, that which exalteth man's power and he forgets God.

The correct evaluation then of knowledge in all its phases of man's experience and the application of that knowledge in his relationships and dealings with his fellow man.

Study these. Make thyself more practical in the application
of that thou hast attained. Know that each step, each lesson
as a step, has opened and does open the way for each student,
each individual, to apply the next lesson, to make the next step.

These, with all those experiences that will be in the life of
each as you study are worthy of acceptation; and most of all
keep them in thine own heart and ponder them well.

We are through for the present.

[Mrs. [903], visiting the group and meditating with us on the
lesson *Glory,* had this personal experience during meditation
on the lesson:

"I realized that the soul (made aware to us by or through its
longings, its needs, its urges) is not contained in the body; it is
not contained in the mind. The I am that I am is in accordance
with the state of consciousness I have attained, but I know that
my soul is that centralized part of the Great I AM, which finds
expression through the instrument which is my mind and body.
I realized that if I could live *in* the realization that there is only
that one source of light, I would be living in a state of cosmic
consciousness—or glory."

Personal experiences such as the above were submitted by
Group #1 members throughout the period of preparing the
lessons. Only a few are included here and there in detail,
though many were printed into the lessons, word for word, or
briefed. Some may be found in studying personal files of Group
#1 members, under their case numbers, where they will be
indexed to tie in with the lessons.]

This psychic reading was given by Edgar Cayce at the Edmonds' home, 611 Pennsylvania Avenue, Norfolk, Va., on May 24, 1936, at 4:05 P.M., in accordance with a request made by those present: Edgar Cayce; Gertrude Cayce, conductor; Gladys Davis, steno; Hugh Lynn Cayce, Edith Edmonds, Florence Edmonds, Helen Ellington, Ruth LeNoir, Hannah Miller, Noah Miller, Frances Y. Morrow, Helen Storey, and Esther Wynne.

⊰ 262-96 ⊱

Mrs. Cayce: You will have before you the Norfolk Study Group #1, members of which are present here, and their work on the lesson Knowledge. *You will continue the discourse on knowledge and then answer the questions which will be asked.*

Mr. Cayce: Yes, we have the group as gathered here; as a group, as individuals, and their work in the preparation of lessons—now *Knowledge.*

As has been intimated in the outline, there will come the experiences to each (who seeks, in truth), during the study as in the preparation of the lesson, unusual experiences; to each according to your own attunement. To each has been given, ponder these well within thine own heart before giving expression even of same to others. Meet with thy Master as respecting same. He has promised to guide, to guard, to direct thee in thine uprisings, in thine downsittings. For to each many experiences will come.

In the study of data as respecting knowledge, this question in the present presents a threefold manner; secular knowledge; worldly knowledge; individual application—the interpretation of self of the knowledge of the body, the knowledge of the mind, the knowledge of the spiritual forces.

May to each it come, then, as was given by him who would reason, would help, would direct you through these experiences; not instead of thy Master, the Christ, but as the beloved of Him in the earth; that ye may be one in mind, in purpose, that the day of the Lord may draw nigh unto each, and that ye may have the greater love, the greater patience one with the other.

For His mercy, *His* patience, endureth forever, and ye would be like Him if ye would know Him, if ye would be His.

As I gave, then, that we have received, that we give, God is a God of knowledge. For He judgeth man by his activities. He *is* light, and in Him is no darkness at all.

Dwell ye then in the light as ye study to show thyselves, each, approved unto God; a workman not ashamed of those things that bespeak thy sincerity, thy earnestness, in the study of the knowledge of thy God. Remembering this:

The first *don't* was, "Thou shalt not eat of the tree of the knowledge concerning good and evil, for in the day thou eatest thereof thou shalt *surely* die."

In this beginning, then, must we undertake to give that concept that man has so long, it seems, appeared to make become as ridiculous in the eyes of the Maker; flaunting his knowledge of things that be, that always have been. Yet man in his greed, in his own selfishness, has set himself so oft at naught by the very foolishness of his own wisdom.

For the soul had understanding before he partook of the flesh in which the choice was to be made. [See also 262-99, A-2, -3.] The choice, or the road, or the path, once taken, then the end thereof was (and is) tribulation, toil, misunderstanding. And this expression came into such measures that there arose the periods when man came as *one* and said, "We will *build,* we will go to now and make those conditions that will prevent any such confusion again among men." [Gen. 11:4]

And then came the diversity of tongues and confusion arose. For the very selfishness of man had brought this confusion, this defiance to a God of love, of mercy, of patience, in such a measure that He gave that expression, "There is nothing beyond the scope of man's ability unless he misinterpret his brother's words."

Then come ye now, beloved of Him, and know that—as before ye entered into materiality—ye were at one with Him; but ye have made thy choice, ye *are* aware of those experiences brought about in the confusions of thy dealings with thy fellow man. Know that true knowledge is God, and as ye judge thy fellow man, as ye judge thy brother, ye are *assuming* the offices of the Lord Himself.

Did thy Master (and mine) judge any man? Rather did He give, "Peace be with thee, peace I give unto thee."

Even when His brethren sought that He might condemn the

activities of those that gathered not with His group, what said He?

As given by the prophets even of old, "Who hath taught the Lord judgment?"

With whom did He counsel? Yea, as is written there, as I gave to you, "Without Him there was nothing made that was made. The WORD *was* knowledge, and the Word was made flesh, and the Word dwelt among men," that they, too, might know that in the *humbleness,* in the *humbling,* in the *subduing* of self they (ye) might know their (thy) God.

For God *is* knowledge, and as He gave, "Judge them not," for they that be for us are above those with their own *worldly* wisdom. They *shall* excell for the moment, but dost thou grudge their excellence even for naming the name? Dost thou make to thyself such a condemning that ye become rather worse than they?

These, then, be the *spirit,* be the manner, be the purposes within thy heart, thy mind, beloved.

Empty thy minds, *empty* thy hearts of all that thou hast held that is of a secular nature, if ye would know the *true* knowledge of thy God.

For as ye hold to those things, to those conditions, to those experiences, yea to those ideas that have formed concepts that ye should not do this, ye *should* do that, ye should make this, ye should lend that, these are but barriers if ye would know the true knowledge of *why,* of *how* thy Brother, thy Lord, thy Master, came into the earth; and what He would have thee do with that which may be poured out to thee in thy seeking.

For as has been said of old, if the Lord be with *one* He shall put ten *thousand* to flight.

What, then, will *ye* twelve do? Ye *are* as lights unto many. What is *thy* choice?

The tree that is of knowledge is before thee. Thy choice in the heart of each is to be made.

Remembering His mercy, remembering His prayer as He gave, "Yea, Father, that they may be one, even as I and Thou art one, that the world may know that Thou didst *send* me."

Wilt thou choose then, wilt thou not come as He has chosen each of you, to be a light to those that sit in darkness? Thus

He may through thy feeble efforts (as they appear to thee, though in the power of His might they may) move mountains of doubt and fear in the hearts of those that are crying—crying that they may know the Lord, that they may understand the knowledge of God.

For the way is open, even to thee, my beloved. Faint not for doubts that arise. For He, thy Savior, is thy strength, is thy power, yea *thy knowledge,* if ye will but *empty* thyselves of those secular forces that have made and do make for differences between ye even in thine own meetings.

Let the love that He has shown, that He would pour out to thee, be sufficient unto thee. Not in the trust of self, not in the awareness that thou art naked before thy God, but rather in the promises that He hath given:

Love the Lord; *eschew* evil; be kind to thy fellow man. Not some great deed! For art thou able to stand the disappointments even of thy secular life without doubting thy brother, thy loved one, thy neighbor?

Let the strength of His might make thee strong in purpose, in desire; that the knowledge of the Father in the Christ, thy Brother, may be known to thee, to thy neighbor, to thy brethren *everywhere!*

Keep the faith that sustains thee in the love of God.

We are through.

This psychic reading was given by Edgar Cayce at his home on Arctic Crescent, Virginia Beach, Va., on June 7, 1936, at 4:15 P.M., in accordance with a request made by those present: Edgar Cayce; Gertrude Cayce, conductor; Gladys Davis, steno; Hugh Lynn Cayce, Edith Edmonds, Florence Edmonds, Helen Ellington, Ruth LeNoir, Hannah Miller, Noah Miller, Lillian B. Whitmore, and Esther Wynne.

≫ 262-97 ≪

Mrs. Cayce: You will have before you the Norfolk Study Group #1, members of which are present here, and its work in the preparation of the lesson Knowledge. *You will continue the discourse on this subject and answer the questions which will be presented.*

Mr. Cayce: Yes, we have the group as gathered here, as a group, as individuals, and their work on the lesson *Knowledge.*

In continuing with what has been given, first let each examine themselves as to whether they as individuals have pondered that which has been presented, and answer within themselves —has the choice been made within self that ye have as an individual emptied self of those petty malices, those set ideas as to this or that, and are ready to open thy mind, thy heart, to the true knowledge?

For knowledge is power; and all force, all power, emanates from the one source.

Has thy mind been able, then, to be empty and ready for that which may be given each? Thus ye as individuals may be awakened to the influence of the love of the Master that *cleanses,* that makes pure, that brings within thine own experience the knowledge of the Father as thy God, thy stay, in whom ye may indeed trust.

For His promises are sure, and the knowledge of these promises being thine—not someone else's—may indeed be experienced. Not that thou art the judge of thy brother, of thy neighbor, of any purpose; but that ye as true sons and daughters of the Father are willing, are ready to receive Him as thy guide, thy understanding.

For thou art His. Hath He not said, "Are not two sparrows sold for a farthing?" Doth He not give to those that ask? And yet ye in thine little understanding, in the weakness of thy knowledge of man, of thy brother, of the worldly conditions about thee, trust rather in circumstance, in favors, in this or that in thine experience rather than in the knowledge that "I am Thine, and Thy Son's promise has been that what I ask in His name, that will be done in my experience; that experience necessary that I be one with Him."

This then is *true* knowledge. Not that the understanding of what the world terms knowledge is that cause and effect exist, that there is this or that law in effect, this or that experience that comes into the affairs of individuals that brings this or that effect into the experiences of others. Are not the interpretations of these laws in essence a comprehending of the true knowledge of the *love* the Father hath for His children?

Those that accredit same to other forces, or of nature, or of this or that influence in the experiences of man and say that these are natural because they follow as the day follows the night, and that these have existed from time immemorial and consequently remain, are becoming much as he whom the Master gave as an example, that he was the simple one, the fool, for "This night thy soul will be required of thee."

What then cometh of thy barns, of thy store of riches, of thy power, of thy money, of thy position, of thy exalted place; yea, even of thy good name, lest it be that having been in the true knowledge thou has been indeed a channel that hath opened the eyes of those that had been dimmed by the vicissitudes of life that brought fear and distrust; lest thou hast brought to others a knowledge, an understanding in thy daily life, in thy daily dealings with thy fellow man, that "First seek the Lord while He may be found, and all these things will be added unto thee in their order, in *their* place, in *their* time."

Because of the worldly knowledge, then, many have become faint, many have fallen away.

What saith He to you who have emptied yourselves of traditions, who have emptied yourselves of malice, who have emptied yourselves of hate? Encourage those that are weak, strengthen the fainthearted; in *these* be the true knowledge; in these be the perfect understanding that *His* ways, thy God's ways are not past finding out—if ye will but seek Him while He may be found.

In the knowledge of the mental life, that this or that experience through thy association or activity has come to thee, does this bring thee peace—or confusion? Doth this bring harmony, or does it bring strife? By its fruit ye shall know whether it be the true knowledge of God or not. For ye gather not figs from thistles; neither doth there spring living waters from those that are dried or dead within themselves to the true knowledge of the living water.

These be the influences that true knowledge is that those correct interpretations of experiences, other than thine own, are what hath it wrought in the experience of those that apply same in their dealings with their fellow man day by day? Not whether it has brought riches or fame, or those things that are even well-spoken of by those of the world, but has it made in the experience of the individual a better neighbor, a kindlier friend, a more long-suffering one with those that would hinder? Doth it bring patience? Doth it bring love in any manifested form? *This* shows as to whether the true knowledge is manifested in the experience of any individual.

So in applying this in self, if that ye have heard, that ye have seen, that ye have experienced, that ye have pondered in thine heart makes of thee a better father, a better mother, a better friend, a better neighbor, more gentle with those that are cross, more loving to those that are dishonest, more patient with those that storm here or there, then ye are experiencing the true knowledge of the Father.

If it has brought not this, if it brings not in thine own experience the fruits of the spirit, then it is not of God; neither is it countenanced by thy Brother, thy Savior, who prayed that He might, that ye might, that all men everywhere might be of the one mind *in God!*

What was the confusion? That there was the misinterpreting, the selfish motive, the lack of understanding. These brought confusion, but the true knowledge is "not of myself but the Father that worketh in me and through me." It is the knowledge that maketh alive, that maketh not afraid, that meeteth each day with the love of the greater opportunities, that maketh for the meeting of each ache, each pain within thine own body with that fortitude that makes for the removal of same through the knowledge that *He* is God of the weak, of the great, of the lowly, of those that are in power, of those that are oppressed. And He heareth the voice of those that cry unto Him.

What art thou doing about removing the oppressions, about giving an understanding to those that are in power as to the source from whence they obtained same? and as to what is in store for those that forsake His ways day by day?

This is knowledge, that ye show *thyself* approved unto that which is set in Him that hath shown thee the pattern, that hath made the way straight; that those who seek Him may not be confused therein, that they who love His coming will just act as those that are in close communion with Him from day to day.

This is knowledge, that ye love one another, that ye show forth in thy dealings with thy fellow man day by day that thou carest, thou understandest, thou art willing to take a portion of the burden of those that are so heavily burdened with the cares of life, the cares of the world, the deceitfulness of riches; that thou art willing to aid those in distress, thou art willing to feed those that are hungry—not just materially. For the world is crying for that knowledge.

It is opened to thee that have made the choice that ye will empty thyselves of those little differences that breed hate, contempt, and those things that *hurt* and *hurt* in thy dealings with thy fellow man.

Forgive, if ye would be forgiven. *That* is knowledge. Be friendly, if ye would have friends. *That* is knowledge. Be lovely, if ye would have the love even of thy Father; for He is love. This indeed be knowledge.

We are through for the present.

This psychic reading was given by Edgar Cayce at the Edmonds' home, 611 Pennsylvania Avenue, Norfolk, Va., on July 19, 1936, at 4:00 P.M., in accordance with a request made by those present: Edgar Cayce; Gertrude Cayce, conductor; Gladys Davis, steno; Minnie Barrett, Hugh Lynn Cayce, Edith Edmonds, Florence Edmonds, Helen Ellington, Ruth LeNoir, Hannah Miller, Frances Y. Morrow, and Esther Wynne.

⩔ 262-98 ⩔

Mrs. Cayce: You will have before you Norfolk Study Group #1, members of which are present here, and their work on the lesson Knowledge. *As I call each name of members you will give a personal message on the lesson* Knowledge *which will help them to understand and contribute to this lesson.*

Mr. Cayce: Yes, we have the group as gathered here, as a group, as individuals, and their work on the lesson *Knowledge.* Ready for questions.

Q-1. [*307*]:

A-1. Let the emptying of self make thee indeed ready for the receiving of the knowledge of the law of the Lord. For His ways are not past finding out to those that seek to know His face through the Christ. Let love be without preference. Let thy yeas be yea, thy nays be nay. *Know* the Lord in *all* things. For He will keep thee, if ye will be guided in *every thought,* in every act, by the knowledge of the Lord.

Q-2. [*303*]:

A-2. The ways of the Lord are only hard to those who have set themselves in ideas. Let the *ideal* of the Christ guide thee. For He hath given His promise, "Take my yoke upon you, and *learn* of me." In *this* knowledge of Him, thy Savior, as thy companion, the way becomes easy, the burden becomes light. For as He hath given, take not thought or fret thyself not concerning tomorrow, looking not back but ever upward, onward, into the face, into the love of the Christ. And ye will find His presence giving thee strength for the daily conditions, the daily disturbances. And He will keep thee as in the hollow of His hand. For as He hath given, He hath given His angels charge concerning thee, but the Christ has given, *"I*—even I— will be *with* thee." Then trust in Him, for this is indeed knowledge.

Q-3. [*379*]:

A-3. The Lord is thy strength and thy redeemer. Then let not the cares of the world or the turmoils of those about thee upset thee, nor cause thee to be afraid. For the earth *is* the Lord's, and those that love the knowledge of the Lord keep His ways. And they that keep His ways need not fear. For harm of a *destructive* nature *cannot* come nigh to those that love Him. Though the ways of the earth may appear dark, though anxiety may make thee fretful, the patience and the knowledge that patience maketh for the awareness of thy unity with Him will keep thee ever.

Q-4. [*404*]:

A-4. Let mercy, grace and peace abide in thee, through the knowledge thou hast of His promises. For as He hath given, though the heavens and the earth pass away, His promises remain. Then *believe,* then be guided, then hold fast to that thou hast seen, thou hast known. Doubt not the love of the Father. Fear not those that may make for disturbing influences in the material life. But know the knowledge of the Father through the Christ sustaineth those that trust *only* in Him.

Q-5. [*560*]:

A-5. The beauty of service is the understanding of the knowledge of God. And as God is knowledge, let that service, let that love that hath been shown thee be given *in* love, in mercy, in justice, even to those that are doubters, that are fearful, that even say unkind things. For to love those only that love thee, what profit hath thou in the knowledge of the law of love in the Christ? For He loved those that hated Him. He died for those that would take His life—in the earth. Then, in thy knowledge and in thy love for Him, let nothing make thee afraid. For the love of the Christ sustaineth those that put their trust in Him. And as He hath given, ye shall know, ye shall have knowledge of the truth and it shall make thee free indeed in Him. Then keep the faith, for knowledge maketh faith easy.

Q-6. [*993*]:

A-6. The knowledge in Christ of the love to the world, as a universal love, maketh the hearts of men glad—if they do not become hedged about by schisms or those forces that cut short the fruits of the spirit. Then let the love in the Christ be thy mantle, thy cloak; yea, let it shod thy feet—that maketh for the pathway before men; glorious in the knowledge that ye walk with the Christ! For He keepeth those that love their brethren. He abideth with those that have the knowledge that the love of God constraineth all at all times. Then, *in* the knowledge that He is thine, thou art in Him—and in Him in the Father, be thou sustained and strengthened day by day. For the night is spent and the day of the Lord is nigh to those that *know* His ways and keep them before their brethren. [See also 262-99, A-4.]

Q-7. [*413*]:

A-7. The cares of the world, the bickerings of those that are fearful, cause thee to wonder. But let these not shake thy *faith*. Let them not make or cause in thy answers other than *love* that casteth out fear; that heapeth upon the heads of those that are fearful that ointment as of the Lord that bringeth healing to those to whom it may be given. And they that in their weakness are strong in the Lord are ministers of mercy in the Father through the Son. For He hath shown the way, and He will keep thee and sustain thee—if ye will hold fast to that knowledge of Him that ye have heard, that ye have seen, that ye have experienced in thine own daily life. For to love the Lord is indeed knowledge. And in the ministering of those things, those influences that He hath given thee is indeed knowledge—and will bring to thee, to thy house, to thy hands, to thy mind, to thy heart, peace and harmony that passeth understanding.

Q-8. [*585*]:

A-8. Mercy and justice and faith and patience are in the hearts and minds of those that deal with their fellow man in the *knowledge* of the Father through the Christ. They that seek for self, for self-satisfaction, for self-gratification, are unwise; but they that judge their brother, they that find fault with the things of life *lack* the knowledge and *understanding* of the mercies of God. Then if ye would find mercy before the Father, be merciful to those that even smite thee, that even use thee, that even abuse thee. For in being merciful thou doth indeed obtain mercy before the throne of grace. If ye would know the love of God, if ye would know the abiding presence of the Savior, show in thy dealings to thy fellow man the love even as He. Oft thou findeth in thy experience that there appears to be lack of appreciation of thy efforts. Forget not how that those whom He healed even forgot to say even "Thank you." Give thanks then for the pattern, for the knowledge of Him that thou hast in thine experience. And *hold fast* to that knowledge. For in giving it out ye obtain the greater understanding; yea, the greater knowledge.

Q-9. [*288*]:

A-9. The cares of the world, the thoughts of others in their indifference to that thou holdest as thy ideal should not *worry thee;* for thou may not add one whit or one tittle to the *power* of God or of knowledge. Do *thy* duty, do thy love, day by day. *Leave* the fruits, the increase, the change, in the hands of the Father. For *He* knoweth thy worries. Then *love* the Lord, *love* the opportunities for expression; but give *only* the love of *Christ,* give *only* the ideals as He set. They are *not* of the earth, though they may manifest in same. For ye see them in the face of nature, in the beauty of a rose, in the smile of a baby. Then fret not thyself that it will not find expression. Do that thou *knowest* to do and find not fault with thy neighbor. For he that doeth such is not wise, neither is it of wisdom. For He sendeth His blessings on the just and the unjust, hoping—hoping that thou in thy knowledge of Him will aid thy fellow man and leave the *blessings* to God.

Q-10. [*294*]:

A-10. Let mercy and peace abide with thee in thy knowledge of the Lord. Boast not of thyself. Rather know that only in Him, through Him, may help come to thy brethren, to His children. For he that would be the greatest is the servant of the meekest, the lowliest of His children. Then the knowledge of God constrain thee in that the *doing,* the being of a channel, is thy opportunity for the *showing* of thy appreciation, of thy love, for His blessings to thee.

Q-11. [*341*]:

A-11. Let thy understanding make thee strong in being more humble, more patient, more long-suffering with those that fear neither earth nor the powers in same, that regard not God nor His love for man's estate. In the knowledge of Him *guide* those that are weak, comfort those that are fearful, direct those that are doubtful. And keep thine own conscience, thine own mind, thine own body, as one with Him. Thou hast seen His might in the earth. Thou hast seen the mighty fallen. Thou hast seen the wicked arise to places of position, yet these in the knowledge of the Father have been brought as naught or as one. For only in doing the fruits of the spirit may ye *attain* to the use of the knowledge and the fruit thereof. To have love, give it; to have patience, show it; to have long-suffering, be it; to have the love of God, live close to His ways.

Q-12. [*538*]:

A-12. Empty thou thine heart and thine mind of those things, those experiences, those ideas, that would separate thee from the true knowledge of Christ, of God, in Him. For though He were in the world and subject to and saw *all* the little petty malices, strifes, and wept over them all, He gave—and *gave*—and GAVE until the blood flowed even from His body. These be opportunities, then, in thine experience; that ye may indeed be clean in thy living, thy words, thy life before thy Brother, thy Christ. For He *will* give thee knowledge. He will give thee understanding, if ye will embrace Him now—while the light of thy life is in the making, while the blessings of His love are roundabout. For the knowledge of the Lord is doing even as He. Though the world may mock, though the world may sneer, thou *knowest* in *whom* thou hast believed, and know He is able to keep thee against *any* experience if ye will hold fast to His hand.

Q-13. [*462*]:

A-13. Unto him that hath the knowledge of the Lord is given greater knowledge in the ways to meet those influences of the earth that would make men afraid. To him that beareth with his neighbor, to him that overcometh those things that are fearful, is given the greater knowledge of the Father in those ways and those manners that bring harmony in the life, that bring peace and bring *activity* of the kind, of the nature that He did. For the life of the Master in the earth in *any experience* was a life of ACTIVITY, a life of service. So in thine experience be ye up and *doing* with a heart that is set in Him as the light to thy feet, the lamp to thy ways; as a city that the buildings and makers of same are of God. For thou hath much work to do.

Q-14. [*295*]:

A-14. Fear and the uses of same in thine experience maketh thee afraid. Let the knowledge of the Lord constrain thee day by day. Fear not those things of the flesh, of the body, that would hinder in thine understanding, thine knowledge of thy God. Though ye be in the midst of tempestuous forces of the earth, if the knowledge, if the love of the Christ be thy guide, ye will be strong, ye will be steadfast, ye will be patient.

Q-15. [*69*]:

A-15. The knowledge of the Lord is only the *beginning* of wisdom. The application of knowledge in thy experience is to do *good* to—those of the household of faith? Yea, to those that berate thee, to those that speak unkind of Him, to those that fear not man nor regardeth not God. Let love and patience and mercy be *with* thee. For in doing these ye have that knowledge that surpasseth all the wisdom of the earth. For who is wise? He that loveth the Lord and doeth His ways.

Q-16. Any message for the group as a whole?

A-16. As ye have received, as ye are moved, as ye apply that ye receive, give to those that seek. Be patient, be kind. Speak not unkindly of anyone. Let not gossip nor unkind things, either in thought or deed, be in thine experience. And ye will find the true knowledge of the Christ in the Father being close to thee.

We are through.

This psychic reading was given by Edgar Cayce at the Edmonds' home, 611 Pennsylvania Avenue, Norfolk, Va., on August 16, 1936, at 4:00 P.M., in accordance with a request made by those present: Edgar Cayce; Gertrude Cayce, conductor; Gladys Davis, steno; Malcolm H. Allen, Hugh Lynn Cayce, Edith Edmonds, Florence Edmonds, Ruth LeNoir, Hannah Miller, Frances Y. Morrow, and Esther Wynne.

ぇ 262-99 ⫞

Mrs. Cayce: You will have before you Norfolk Study Group #1, members of which are present here, and their work on the lesson Knowledge *— a copy of which I hold in my hand. You will give any further suggestions to be incorporated in this lesson and such information as will be of help to this group at this time. Answer questions.*

Mr. Cayce: Yes, we have the group as gathered here, as a group, as individuals and their work on the lesson *Knowledge.*

That which has been given and as gathered here is very good, needing those correlations of ideals, experiences, purpose, intent, and then the application of same in the experience of those that would make knowledge as a part of themselves, in their search, in their way, in their application of that as may be manifested in their experience *in* the application of that as has been given.

For this, as you each will find, do find, should be in your experience a real turning point in your *individual,* personal experience; as you each have emptied yourselves, as you each have laid the groundwork as it were of that indeed as was given to man, "*Subdue* the earth." For all therein has been given for man's purpose, for man's convenience, for man's understanding, for man's interpreting of God's relationship to man. And when man makes same only a gratifying, a satisfying of self, whether in appetite, in desire, in selfish motives for self-aggrandizement, self-exaltation, these become—as from old—stumbling blocks. But he that hath put off the old and put on the new is regenerated in the new Adam, in the last Adam, in the Christ. And as many as have done so may find in themselves that knowledge of His presence abiding with them; so that things, conditions, circumstances, environs, no longer become stumbling blocks—rather have they become stepping-stones

-396-

for the greater view wherein they each may gain at least in part first, gradually growing in grace, in the understanding to know those glories, those beauties God hath prepared for them that know the way of the cross *with* the Christ as the good shepherd. For He will call each by name, for He knoweth His sheep and He is the good shepherd to those that put their trust, their lives, their troubles, their joys, their sorrows, their understandings, in Him. For He hath taken the burden of the world. Will ye then join with Him in this acceptable year of the Lord and know that to do good is knowledge?

Ready for questions.

Q-1. Are the outlines for the lesson correctly made out?

A-1. Just as has been given. Follow those; correlating the various groupings as has been indicated, coordinating the activities and those that are as tenets, those that are as visions, those that are experiences, and then make for that manner in which there may be a practical application. For unless each lesson, each comprehending of that as intended to be presented through same is a *workable* thing, something that may be experienced, something that may be applied by *any*, in *any* environ, in *any* walk of life, it is as nothing!

For as given, the way the Master has shown is so simple that he who runs may read. It is so mighty that the powers that be in the earth become subservient to same. It maketh the weak strong; it maketh the strong humble.

Q-2. Please explain the following from reading [262-96] May 24, 1936: "For the soul had understanding before he partook of the flesh in which the choice was to be made." Why (if the soul had understanding) the necessity to take flesh in order to make the choice?

A-2. Considereth thou that spirit hath its manifestations, or does it *use* manifestations for its activity? The Spirit of God is aware through activity, and we see it in those things celestial, terrestrial, of the air, of all forms. And *all* of these are merely manifestations! The knowledge, the understanding, the comprehending, then necessitated the entering in because it partook of that which *was* in manifestation; and thus the *perfect* body, the celestial body, became an earthly body and thus put on flesh. (The explanation to some becomes worse than the first!

This, then:) (This has nothing to do with knowledge, or it is too much knowledge for some of you, for you'll stumble over it; but you asked for it and here it is!)

When the earth became a dwelling place for matter, when gases formed into those things that man sees in nature and in activity about him, then matter began its ascent in the various forms of physical evolution—in the *mind* of God! The spirit chose to enter (celestial, not an earth spirit—he hadn't come into the earth yet!), chose to put on, to become a part of that which was a command not to be done!

Then those so entering *must* continue through the earth until the body-mind is made perfect for the soul, or the body-celestial again.

Q-3. *Please explain, from same reading* [262-96], *what is meant by "any such confusions" referred to when it was said, "We will build, we will go to now and make those conditions that will prevent any such confusions again among men." Why did they think a tower would help?*

A-3. The tower was after the flood. This is very simple—to reach above. Why do you build houses? Why do you build boats, those things that become "above the flood"? It was just the same! Same concept—that it might reach even to that which would *not* be destroyed by flood again.

Q-4. *Please interpret from the reading* [262-98, A-6] *July 19, 1936, "For the night is spent and the day of the Lord is nigh to those that know His ways and keep them before their brethren."*

A-4. It is a fact, as God is, as good is, as virtue hath its own reward, as the seed sown *is*—has within same the fruit thereof —it is the law, see? For when those that seek have begun, the seed is sown, do they keep same as the Master gave in the parable in good ground, in stony ground? Do they allow the things of the world, as the fowls of the air, to gather same and carry same away? The day is spent. The evening is nigh for those that *seek*, for those that *do* as has just been given. Unless each of you in this group are regenerated by the very lesson learned and applied, ye are slipping—ye are slipping!

Q-5. *Please comment on, "The fear of the Lord is the beginning of knowledge." Proverbs 1:7.*

A-5. Of wisdom, not knowledge. *Wisdom* is our next lesson!

Q-6. Please explain this excerpt from group reading [262-88] Sept. 8, 1935: "That force, that power, which manifests itself in separating—or as separate forces and influences in the earth, continue to enter; and then change; continuing to pour in and out. From whence came it? Whither does it go, when it returns?"

A-6. Just as has been explained in how spirit sought projecting; chose to enter that as had been the creation of the Father as manifestations, that still is as manifestations; and thus enters, leaves, enters, leaves, or incarnates through the lessons gained in each experience.

For each experience in the earth is as a schooling, is as an experience for the soul. For how gave He? He is the vine and ye are the branches, or He *is* the source and ye are the trees. As the tree falls so does it lie. *There* it begins when it has assimilated, when it has applied in *spiritual* reaction that it has gained.

Q-7. Any message for the group?

A-7. Stand ye steadfast in Him, knowing—knowing—believing, acting what ye profess!

We are through.

This psychic reading was given by Edgar Cayce at the Edmonds' home, 611 Pennsylvania Avenue, Norfolk, Va., on September 13, 1936, at 4:00 P.M., in accordance with a request made by those present: Edgar Cayce; Gertrude Cayce, conductor; Gladys Davis, steno; Hugh Lynn Cayce, Edith Edmonds, Florence Edmonds, Ruth LeNoir, Hannah Miller, Frances Y. Morrow, Helen Storey, and Esther Wynne.

⊁ 262-100 ⊱

Mrs. Cayce: You will have before you the Study Group work of the Association for Research and Enlightenment, Inc. You will consider the outlines and plans for group work as prepared and presented by Esther Wynne and Hugh Lynn Cayce, present in this room, and as each idea or plan is read you will comment and give advice regarding it.

Mr. Cayce: Yes, we have the work of the Association for Research and Enlightenment, Incorporated, and that phase of same as may be presented through the Study Group work, with those as individuals and as a group as gathered here.

In considering first the selection of teachers, leaders, helpers, aiders, in the Study Group work, make haste slowly. For it is not by might nor by power but by "My Spirit" saith the Lord of hosts.

As has been given oft in considering the work of the Association, and this applies to each phase of its activity, first to the individual. As each individual in the group that has added to those preparations for a study group course *has* applied and does apply those truths in his or her *own* life, so may that individual or any individual—whether it be two or ten that would select or choose or pray for or pray with others that were seeking some manner, some way of expression— *hope* to attain to that which will be as the lessons have purported and do purport to be—living truths in the minds, the hearts, the lives, the *daily* life of individuals seeking—through the study of themselves and their relationship to their Creator and their fellow man—to make for those conditions, those manners in which same may be presented.

Hence the burden of the preparation, then, lies with those that *have* prepared, do prepare, the Study Group lessons.

As for that manner of seeking a selective group or individual members of the Association in various spheres, various walks of activity, do not choose; let *them* choose! Invite each individual who is, who has been a member of the Association to become a part of such a group as would prepare themselves to be channels of blessings for others in their finding *their* relationship to their Creator, their fellow man, in their respective spheres.

This as we would find would be well then:

Outline, from the manual, lessons, that which is to be presented. And this is the burden of the whole outline: Those that would seek to know better their relationships to the Creative Forces that manifest in and through them from spiritual (not spirit, but *spiritual*) sources, and their relationships to their fellow man. That would be well for a beginning.

Q-1. Each prospective teacher would be asked to study the following:

1. *Teacher's Manual.*
2. *Selected Bible readings as suggested through this channel from time to time.*
3. *Lessons (1st series).*
4. *Oneness of all force, meditation—(simple and complete forms)—Atlantis.*
5. *Selected books recommended in manual—Hudson, James, and others.*
6. *Correspondence with Esther Wynne.*

Comment on this program and make suggestions if needed. [*See 262-100 Supplement.*]

A-1. This as has been outlined, as has just been given, is well; but do not *select* your group! Let *them* select *themselves* and let it be a letter to each and every member that has been and is, of *any* nature and character!

Q-2. Any other suggestions for preparing teachers and leaders for group work?

A-2. You'll have your hands full if you'll do this; not as individuals but as a group *and* as individuals!

Then let there be selected, given a period, a definite period —15th of October—when all must be *in* that would choose to become a part of a group for preparations, see, for the study. *Then* have the week, two weeks, month or six months of prayer.

Q-3. Give suggestions for additions, changes or corrections in Teacher's Manual, a copy of which I hold in my hand. [See 262-100 Supplement.]

A-3. This is too big a job to correct all of this! This should be edited first, *then* corrections made.

Q-4. Any suggestions for additional subjects?

A-4. Enlarging upon those that have been set here would be preferable to making additional ones in the present. For let this be ever: Know that the activities of the Association are—as to the work or service of each individual—a growth; as truth, as knowledge, as wisdom, as love *is* in the experience of those that seek to know the way.

So should be those activities. But *do not* allow these to become other than supplementary aids to individuals in their preparation for service in their *own* selected manner; that is, do not become a schism, an ism, laying down laws as to the morals or as to any set rules. For those as have been set have *one*—the Christ! Let those, those manners be, then, so that—whether these be the Parthenians, the Jews, the Catholics, the Protestants, the atheists or the agnostics—all will be seekers for truth, and seeking to know the *individual* relationship to Father-God and the relationship to the fellow man. These should be the burdens and these then find only those activities that correlate denominations, correlate the schisms, correlate the thoughts for a greater service for the fellow man; for in same, as has been the theme throughout the lessons, "As ye do it unto the least of thy brethren, ye do it unto thy Maker."

Q-5. Parallel material for study group work.

A-5. The Bible is the best parallel, especially the admonition by Moses after he had finished all of his own egotism and had come to realize that there was not to be the experience in self for the enjoying of that as had been builded, owing to that weakness of selfishness. Also the great leader. That's the last chapters of Deuteronomy, of 30th on. Also the study of Joshua, not only as the soldier but rather as the leader, as the commander that would give as few, "Let others do as they may, but for me and my house we will serve a living God." Then the Psalms, especially the 1st, the 2nd, the 24th, the 91st, the 23rd, the 67th, the 150th. All of these become as portions of *this* part of parallel work. Then all of those that are *now* being prepared for presentation each Sunday upon the radio. Also James, Hudson, the research upon Palladino, also the findings of various individuals as have studied into individual interpretations; these should be part of parallel work. Do not leave out those, to be sure, of the 14th, 15th, 16th, 17th chapters of John, of 3rd John, of Jude, of Revelations.

Q-6. Preparation of a simplified paper on meditation which will be studied for six months by a new student. Comment on this.

A-6. This is very well, but this is a natural procedure. If you will pray with—which you will have some 16 or 18 in the group —for 6 months the meditation will be there, in the experience of those 16!

Q-7. Comment and give suggestions on studies of meditation now being made by Norfolk Group.

A-7. These are very good but add to same six months *every day* a given period for one hour, and it will be there! Many will seek and know. Do not seek to know the experience other than thy relationship to thy Maker, thy relationship to thy brother.

Q-8. What is the best time for that hour?

A-8. Either 11 to 12 in the day or 11 to 12 in the evening, or the *best* time is 2 to 3 in the morning! [Group joined to pray at 2 A.M. for 6 months.]

Q-9. Expansion of present paper on meditation; especially by additions of examples and experiences. Comment.

A-9. This as has been given. Let's leave this until the experience of these has *prepared* individuals. As has been given, make haste slowly!

Q-10. A study of the phenomena as manifest through Edgar Cayce.

A-10. These are very well, as it should be in others. Study that rather as manifested through the Christ. Study what happened when the water turned to wine, what happened when He took her by the hand and lifted her up, what happened when He walked to His disciples upon the sea, what happened when He called Lazarus, what happened in the garden when His disciples—even His closest friends—slept while He fought with self; what happened on the cross when He commended His mother to John, what happened when He spoke to Mary Magdalene; what happened when He spoke to Thomas, to the other disciples; what happened when He arose, "Go ye into all the world and preach the gospel." What was that gospel? Not much that is being given so oft over and over. For He combined it all into one, "Thou shalt love the Lord thy God with all thy heart, thy mind, thy soul; thy neighbor as thyself." For this is the *whole* law—the *whole* law. Hence ye would study to show thyself approved unto thy concept of thy God. What *is* thy God? Let each answer that within self. What *is* thy God? Where is He, what is He? Then ye may find yourselves lacking in much. How personal is He? Not as Moses painted a God of wrath; not as David painted a God that would fight thine enemies; but as the Christ—the Father of love, of mercy, of justice. And man meets it in himself! How *can* it be then that ye do not understand God loves you, why do you suffer? It is mercy, it is justice to thy soul! For those things that are cares of the flesh and of the earth cannot inherit eternal life. Hence life alters, life changes in the experiences of individuals through their sojourns in the earth, and thus ye learn thy lessons, even as He; for though He were the Son, though ye are His sons and daughters, yet must *ye* learn obedience through the things that *ye* suffer. For ye having partaken of *sin,* not *in* Adam but *as* Adam must as the new Adam learn that God *is* merciful, is love, is justice, is patience, is long-suffering, is brotherly love; for these are the law, not *of* the law but *the* law. And the law is love and the law is God. The law is not individual; *ye* make individual application of same in that ye are His sons, His daughters, ye are seeking the way. Then that ye give to others, that ye have; that ye have spent ye never have; that ye would save you have already lost.

We are through.

This psychic reading was given by Edgar Cayce at the home of Mrs. Helen Storey, 2709 Lafayette Boulevard, Norfolk, Va., on October 4, 1936, at 4:25 P.M., in accordance with a request made by those present: Edgar Cayce; Gertrude Cayce, conductor; Gladys Davis, steno; Hugh Lynn Cayce, Helen Ellington, Ruth LeNoir, Hannah Miller, Frances Y. Morrow, Helen Storey, and Esther Wynne.

ℵ 262-101 ℵ

Mrs. Cayce: You will have before you the Study Group work of the Association for Research and Enlightenment, Inc. You will consider the outlines and plans for group work as prepared and presented by Esther Wynne and Hugh Lynn Cayce, present in this room, and you will continue the discussion of group activity begun in reading of Sept. 13, answering the questions which will be asked.

Mr. Cayce: Yes, we have the purposes, the aims, the desires of the presentation of the Study Group work by those that have prepared the outline. Hence this is another approach.

In considering the outline, as we find, the ideals and the purpose of the Association for Research and Enlightenment, Inc., as are set forth should be more closely followed.

There should be first, as has been indicated, the preparation of an invitation for each and every member that has been and that is of every nature and character, but in the preparation of such invitation consider their own development, their own desires in relationship to the ideals and purposes of the Association.

Hence it should be rather as in *this* line, through the Study Group Committee, Esther Wynne and Hugh Lynn Cayce, *of* the Association:

Presenting then that which has been found helpful in those Study Groups that have used or prepared the lessons for same. That the ideals and the purposes are that this group may in some manner aid those seeking to know *their* relationship to their Creator, and the manner of expressing or manifesting same in their dealings with their fellow man. And that the course as may be presented in this outline, that has been used by others may be used as a manner or way or means for this preparation, for this understanding. And not as that they as individuals become teachers, leaders, ministers or whatnot for the Association but for themselves and for *their* God! If the study with this leads them *to* that, *well*—but dictate not. For ye have Jew, Parthenian, Greek, and those of every cult, and they each have their ideal. But how few have found or know *their* relationships to Creative Forces as may manifest through them as individuals! as has been presented to those who have used these outlines to know *their* Maker, their Savior, their selves, their brother, the better! Ready for questions.

Q-1. What explanation should be given regarding meditation for those who desire to join in the hour meditation from 2 to 3? Give an affirmation if needed.

A-1. As the paper or data upon meditation, as has been given, is to be a part of that to be sent each individual, then in the beginning this would be rather as a prayer, as a oneness of purpose, desire on the part of each that may take part. While they each may present their own petition in this way or that way, let it be rather as He gave, "When ye pray, pray in *this* manner." Let that be for the beginnings. And then let there be rather the growth of this as may be presented through these channels if so sought as the developments progress. For if they each that join are sincere in seeking to know their relationship to the Creative Forces, that they may know themselves the better, they *will* become seekers. And as has been given from the beginning, they that seek may find.

Q-2. For how long should this hour meditation period be observed?

A-2. Each in their own way, but at least thirty minutes or the hour.

Q-3. For how long at a period?

A-3. How long has it been given? Six months or a year? How long does it become necessary? Some will want to continue, some will be through in a few days; for it will be as the sower going forth to sow.

Q-4. Consider the preparation of parallel pamphlets covering such subjects as follow for 30-minute parallel study of same for each group period: Dreams, Auras, Mental Telepathy and Power of Thought, Numerology—

A-4. [Interrupting] Leave off.

Q-5. [Continuing] Astrology—

A-5. Leave off.

Q-6. [Continuing] Palmistry—

A-6. Leave off.

Q-7. [Continuing] Spiritualism, Spiritual Healing. Comment on this plan and suggest other subjects or indicate any that should be omitted during period of first twelve lessons.

A-7. Those as indicated leave off. Those additions that may be made may arise from questions naturally arising upon the various subjects that are being treated. For this will not be a one-man job, nor the two that have set themselves in order! There will be many others necessary to handle it, if handled properly!

Q-8. Would it be wise to undertake in groups comparative studies of isms and philosophies as Yogi, Rosicrucianism, etc. Comment and suggest. The idea would be to point out good points, not to find differences.

A-8. This is preparation rather of individuals. Hence comparative studies, isms, schisms, Yogi philosophies and all would become a part of the preparation. For this will lead the individuals who join as a group to become missionaries, emissaries for something! For the world, for the people are seeking—seeking oft they know not what. Ye that have begun, then become greater channels, and ye will find that as has been given as to what portions of this or that land ye will become the more efficient in meeting the problems of those in those particular portions of the land.

Q-9. Any other suggestions regarding parallel work in groups?

A-9. This is getting the cart before the horse, and may become confusing. Remember that you have begun for the *preparation* of groups, and you haven't gotten to the groups yet!

Q-10. Comment on the proposal to prepare a small pamphlet for general distribution on the purposes of group work. Give suggestions for this if advisable.

A-10. This *should* be short enough to be in the letter that is to be sent to each and every old member, new member, present member of every nature—as has been suggested.

Q-11. Please interpret the dreams had by [540] of 2638 Harrell Ave., Norfolk, Va., on Aug. 27 and 28th regarding the blessing that could come to Study Groups—directed to Esther Wynne.

A-11. This is as a vision of that which might or could come, or is what may be called the etheric activity of the proposed work that may be made a mental and material expression in material relationships.

Q-12. Give advice and counsel for direction of the following groups: Group #2 [397]:

A-12. As has been indicated, the type of data and of study that would be the more comprehensible, the more sought for, and that they should follow. This then, rather than becoming—for this particular group—as a routine or as rote will offer for its membership a study of those phases of experience that become more acceptable in their own relationships. For unless every phase of human experience is answered in the life of the Christ, He is not their guide nor their light, nor their way. But that phase of the activities of individuals should be kept in that as has been given. We do not find the natures of any have changed.

Q-13. Group #3 [473]:

A-13. This should be rather the studies that make for the answering of those problems that have become the stumbling blocks in the ways of denominationalism, schisms, cults and the like. For these seek to find an answer for each of these. Do not study their differences but rather their correlating of those activities in each as pertain to the tenets or lessons or truths (dependent upon the manner of presentation as to the term) as given through the lessons as compared with that of Jesus. And then the lessons from each faultfinder.

Q-14. Group #7 [792]:

A-14. Practical application of the tenets that are set forth by the lessons in the *experiences of* each member of the group. For in this group practicality and *not* mere theory must be the answer for each individual.

Q-15. Group #6:

A-15. This is a new combination, a new seeking, and quite a divided one at present. Hence the ideals of presenting the purposes of the group work and the lessons as presented should be rather in that line of knowledge as taught in *Knowledge;* wisdom as may be presented in that as given, "First seek ye to know God and then the rest will be added in its proper order";

and as to how those suggestions, those experiences of those that have prepared such lessons may apply in the individual experience of each of those studying or applying same. This, to be sure, will make for the lives of many of Group #1 to be held up as patterns. And how some will find the light shining through without any shadow, and others very shadowy. But these are needed for those as represent or present Group #6 in the present, for these seek—as the number indicates—to know *why* people think as they do!

Q-16. Any suggestions for handling the introductory material for the Virginia Beach Group?

A-16. The preparations as we find that are being made in the mind, in the actions of those that may present themselves— first the approach from the varied angles and then as to what has been done. For in those periods of the activities there will be many questions as to what the Association and the Study Groups have done and are doing *about* making known that they have found helpful in their experience. Then the preparation would be not only of those authors, writers, lecturers or speakers that may be presented, but as to how many of the questions that are treated by the individual author are answered in the experiences of individuals who have sought or who do seek daily the information through those channels that the individual presents.

Q-17. Any advice and counsel to Esther Wynne at this time regarding group work?

A-17. Again we would give that as has been given. Ye have been called, ye have chosen, ye are worthy. Just be faithful.

Q-18. Any other suggestions regarding group activity?

A-18. As has been given regarding the activities of Group #1, there falls—with the opening of the proposal to assist and aid others—a greater service that may be rendered.

Let all count themselves not in themselves worthy but through the grace and the mercy and the glory and the promise of thy Brother, the Christ, ye *can* accomplish all.

We are through.

This psychic reading was given by Edgar Cayce at his home on Arctic Crescent, Virginia Beach, Va., on November 1, 1936, at 3:50 P.M., in accordance with a request made by those present: Edgar Cayce; Gertrude Cayce, conductor; Gladys Davis, steno; Hugh Lynn Cayce, Edith Edmonds, Florence Edmonds, Helen Ellington, Ruth LeNoir, Hannah Miller, Frances Y. Morrow, Helen Storey, Helen Kerr Vincent, and Esther Wynne.

≫ 262-102 ≪

Mrs. Cayce: You will have before you the Norfolk Study Group #1, members of which are present here, and their work on the lesson Knowledge, *a copy of which I hold in my hand. As I call each section you will comment on same and give suggestions for changes or additions that will make this lesson a more effective treatment of this subject. Questions.*

Mr. Cayce: Yes, we have the group as gathered here, as a group, as individuals; and their work on the lesson *Knowledge.* Ready for questions.

Q-1. Section I—Introduction.

A-1. Very good.

Q-2. Section II—Knowledge is of God.

A-2. Very good.

Q-3. Section III—Knowledge is Power.

A-3. Very good.

Q-4. Section IV—Knowledge as a Workable Experience in the Affairs of (a) Individuals (b) Groups (c) Nations.

A-4. Very good.

Q-5. Section V—Knowledge as a Material Experience.

A-5. Should be rather a change in the caption. Knowledge as May Be Applied in the Individual Experience, would be better.

Q-6. Section VI—Correct Evaluation of Knowledge (a) Man's Experience (b) Man's Application.

A-6. This is the better portion of same. Very good.

Q-7. Section VII— We May Have the Knowledge of His Presence.

A-7. Very good.

Q-8. Section VIII—Experiences in the Study of Knowledge.

A-8. Very good.

Q-9. Please comment on the lesson as a whole.

A-9. This as we find, as has been indicated, is very good; and as may be seen by the close study of the lessons that have preceded same, they are as a wheel or the spokes in same that lead step by step in the practical application of the mental, the spiritual, for the physical development of individuals' opening their understanding to the application in their experience of the truths as presented by Him.

Q-10. You will give the affirmation for preparation of our study of Wisdom.

A-10. OUR FATHER, OUR GOD, MAY THE LIGHT OF THY WISDOM, OF THY STRENGTH, OF THY POWER, GUIDE—AS WE WOULD APPLY OURSELVES IN THY SERVICE FOR OTHERS. IN HIS NAME WE SEEK.

In the preparation for or of the group activity upon this lesson, let there be a very careful analysis of each individual as you approach the throne—in self—of God, for the more perfect understanding. For this should be as a crowning experience in the life of each and every one. For the wisdom of the Father is that to be sought which should make each individual *free* from worry, care, and *know* within thyself thy relationship to the Father—through the Son—in this experience.

We are through for the present.

This psychic reading was given by Edgar Cayce at the Edmonds' home, 611 Pennsylvania Avenue, Norfolk, Va., on December 20, 1936, at 3:20 P.M., in accordance with a request made by those present: Edgar Cayce; Gertrude Cayce, conductor; Gladys Davis, steno; Hugh Lynn Cayce, Edith Edmonds, Florence Edmonds, Helen Ellington, Hannah Miller, Frances Y. Morrow, and Helen Storey.

ᚼ 262-103 ᚴ

Mrs. Cayce: You will have before you the members of the Norfolk Study Group #1 who have gathered here seeking a reading which will give them a better understanding and deeper appreciation of the birth of Jesus, the Christ, which will be celebrated this week as Christmas 1936.

Mr. Cayce: Yes, we have the group as gathered here and their desires and their seeking as a group, as individuals.

In giving to these, then, that seek to know more of that circumstance, those conditions as surrounded that ye call the first Christmas: Do not confuse thyselves. While to you it may be a first Christmas, if it were the first then there would be a last; and ye would not worship, ye would not hold to that which passeth.

For time never was when there was not a Christ and not a Christ mass.

But in giving that interpretation of what this season means —that birth of Jesus as became the Christ—to this world: In giving the circumstance, much has been recorded as respecting this by the writers of the Gospel, especially by Luke; but little perfect concept may be gathered except ye as individuals seek to experience what such an advent meant or means to thy life as an individual.

For knowledge of a thing or a condition and the wisdom that is presented in that happening are two different things. What ye hear ye may believe, but ye will rarely act as if ye believed it unless ye have experienced and do experience that "God so loved the world as to give His Son" to enter into flesh, that flesh, that man, might know there *is* an advocate with the Father; and that—as ye in thy material experience see—life coming from out of nowhere to enter into materiality, to become a *living* expression of those promptings of the heart.

-412-

That has been the experience of that *soul* in its varied spheres of consciousness, to give such an expression. That is the purpose for which it has entered—to give the more perfect concept of the relationships of man to the Creator.

Such we find as that happening in Bethlehem of Judea ages and years ago, when that channel had so dedicated itself to the service of her Maker as to become *mother,* wherein the whole world is shown that this must come to pass in the experience of those who would make themselves channels through which the Holy Spirit of God may manifest; that the world may know that He, God the Father, keepeth His promises with the children of men!

And the hour approaches when nature is to be fulfilled in the natural courses in the experience of the mother, and His star has appeared—and the angels' choir, and the voices of those that give the *great message!*

Who heard these, my children? Those that were seeking for the satisfying of their own desires or for the laudation of their • own personality? Rather those close to *nature,* to the hours of meditation and prayer, and those that had given expression, "No room in the inn!" For no inn, no room, could contain that as was being given in a manifested form!

For He came unto His own. For there was nothing made that was made to which He had not given life, to whom He had not given, "Be ye fruitful, multiply—" in *thyself; in thyself* may there be the propagation of thine own specie, of thine own self!

Only then to those that sought could such a message come, or could there be heard the songs of the angels, or that music of the spheres that sang, *"Peace on earth—good will to men!"*

For this, then, is in *every* birth—the possibilities, the glories, the actuating of that influence of that entrance again of God-man into the earth that man might know the way.

Thus this comes at this time to bring to the hearts and minds of those of that glad period the fact that not only 1900 years ago but *today,* He may be born into thine own consciousness, thine own understanding; He comes unto His own!

Art thou His? Have ye claimed Him? Have ye put on the Christ, even as was and is exemplified in that life, that birth, that death of Jesus, the Christ?

For He is thy Elder Brother, He *is* the babe in thy heart, in thy life; to be then even now—as then—nourished in the heart, in body, in mind. And indeed do His words become more and more then of meaning, "As ye do it unto the least of these, thy brethren, ye do it unto me!"

For as ye behold the face of thy friend, of thy neighbor, of thy foe, yea thine enemy, ye behold the image of thy Savior.

For ye are all His, bought not only with the birth of the God-child into flesh but with the death—that ye might know that He, thy Brother, thy Savior, thy Christ, has been and is the way to the Father in this material plane.

For as He chose to enter, so *ye* have entered. As He chose to live, so may ye live. As He chose to give of Himself that there might be a greater understanding, a greater knowledge; yea, the showing forth of the wisdom of God that God *is* love, poured forth upon the children of men in this experience.

And as these changes come and as ye make known that as has been the raising of that consciousness of His presence in *thine* experience, by thy dealings with, by thy conversation with, by thy life with thy fellow man, so may ye hasten the day when *He, Christ,* may come into thine own heart, unto His *own* peoples, to reign; yes, in the hearts and lives!

Then indeed should each of you at this glad season make the hearts of others merry by thine own happiness in the birth, the life, the death of thy Jesus, thy Christ!

Know this had no beginning in the 1900 years ago, but again and again and *again!* And it may be today, He may be born into thy consciousness; not as a physical birth—but each moment that a physical birth is experienced in the earth is an *opportunity* for the Christ-entrance again!

Then what are ye doing about it in thy daily life, thy daily conversation? For not by might nor in power, but in the still small voice that speaks within, ye may know as He hath given so oft—"Peace—it is I! Be not afraid, it is *I,*" thy Savior, thy Christ; yea, thy*self* meeting that *babe* in thine own inner self that may grow even as He to be a channel of blessings to others!

For as ye do it unto others ye do it unto Him.

May the peace, the joy of His consciousness, His presence,

His joy be thine this day; yea, all thy days in the earth! For He is nigh unto thee, He is in thy midst!

Praise ye the Lord that gave, then, His Son; that ye might know Him!

We are through.

This psychic reading was given by Edgar Cayce at the Edmonds' home, 611 Pennsylvania Avenue, Norfolk, Va., on January 10, 1937, at 3:55 P.M., in accordance with a request made by those present: Edgar Cayce; Gertrude Cayce, conductor; Gladys Davis, steno; Hugh Lynn Cayce, Edith Edmonds, Florence Edmonds, Hannah Miller, Frances Y. Morrow, and Helen Storey.

⋈ 262-104 ⋉

Mrs. Cayce: You will have before you Norfolk Study Group #1, members of which are present here; and their work on the lesson Wisdom. *You will continue with such information as will be of help in preparing and presenting the lesson on this subject. You will answer questions.*

Mr. Cayce: Yes, we have the group as gathered here; as a group, as individuals, and their work upon the lesson *Wisdom.*

In the preparation of this, much as has been preconceived ideas in the minds of many as of knowledge, so of wisdom. Knowledge, as has been in the interpretation of that presented, is not always power unless wisdom is used in the application of same. Or, as has been given, the fear or the knowledge of the Lord is the beginning of knowledge *and* wisdom. Wisdom then is the application of that as is the understanding, as is the concept in the *light* of that which is the ideal of the individual who applies knowledge and wisdom.

Hence as we find, the greater, the deeper concept, and the manner in which wisdom should be interpreted, should be presented, is first in the experience of each individual in the group. For wisdom then becomes first a matter of choice, second a matter of will; in the light ever of that which is the ideal as respecting the application of that to which the individuals may apply themselves, as toward an object, an experience, a goal sought. For ever these become as a triune in the experience of each individual.

The understanding, the concept, the will, the application. If in any of the approaches to wisdom it is then an exaltation of self, as an aggrandizement of self's own motives, this is a lack rather than an application of wisdom of the Lord.

But rather that in the application self is not abased but used

-416-

in selflessness, in the ideals of the glorifying, the exalting of the Prince of Peace, the glory of the Father and not of self.

This is the approach, this is the beginning. For as has been indicated, in the knowledge or in the fear is knowledge and wisdom of God. Then the willingness to be abased that the name that is above *every* name may be exalted.

For how hath He given? The whole law is to love God with all thy mind, thy body, thy soul; thy neighbor as thyself; that He, the Father, through the Son—or the Father in the Son—may be exalted, may be made manifest in thy life, thy experience, thy application of that thou hast gained in thy search for God.

And as has been given from the beginning, as has been given to each individual—whether those that were raised to be leaders, sages, directors, ever has it been—"Use that thou hast in hand *today."* For it is little by little, line upon line, precept upon precept, that the individual becomes aware of the wisdom of God; that to man becomes—in his own self-knowledge—as to some—even stumbling stones. For oft *ye* have found, ye have felt, ye have even reasoned, how can God love us so and yet allow us to suffer in body, in mind, in the needs of the day, in the needs of the body, and bring into the experience of individuals those things that to *us* become not understood?

This indeed then is such knowledge as brought the experience to those who rebelled against the wisdom of God, and went about to establish that which was satisfying, gratifying for the moment, for the experience, for just the raising of those things that were pleasant in the immediate experience.

How again hath He given? Ye had not known sin unless the Son had come and shown thee the way [John 15:22]. This is then the wisdom that is shown in the life, in the experience of each soul. It is through the variations, through those activities that make for the thinking, the analyzing, the seeking for God and God's wisdom, that man is brought to the closer understanding; making for that consciousness within the experience of each soul that in patience, in long-suffering, in brotherly love, is wisdom. Yet as judged by man in the earth, and of the earth, becomes as that which is weakness. But the weakness of man is the wisdom of God. Just as the knowledge of God, the wisdom of God applied in the daily experience of individuals, becomes strength, power, beauty, love, harmony, grace, patience, and those things that—in the lives of those who are applying same —make for a life experience that is worthwhile, even in the turmoils of the earth and those activities of sin and sorrow and shame and want and degradation; as worthwhile experiences, that the glory of the Father in the Son may become known and read and seen and understood by others—that would take counsel of that ye *are* in thy daily activity in the earth.

For as He hath given, he that giveth a cup of water in the *name* of the Christ loseth not his reward. He in wisdom then that giveth same doeth it not that he as an individual may be well-spoken of, thought kindly of or considered magnificent or in any of those phrases of earthly experience, but he that giveth same that the glory of the Father may be made manifest—and that He may be the director, the ruler, the influence that prompts the activity, that prompts the desire, that prompts the act itself. This then is wisdom.

As ye study then, first study those things that have been given thee as respecting all the varied phases of the relationships of man to man, in the various forms of endeavor as a unit, as collective activity, as that necessary for thought, as that necessary for expression, as that necessary for the very activities.

Now ye come to that which is the individual nature of the application of the knowledge, which is the wisdom; the choice, the will, the faculties of the mind, the faculties of the spiritual forces that would be directed in the relationships. And ye have not that which may be touched with hands. Ye have sought, ye have said—each of you—"I seek a city without foundations, whose builder and maker is God." *That* is wisdom!

Then as ye go about to apply this thou hast gained, this understanding, this concept of thy relationships with thy fellow man, thy relationships with thy Maker, ye seek, ye pray, ye meditate upon that as would direct thee. For as ye meditate ye feel, ye see, yea ye hear the voice, the spirit, the moving influence in thy life. And yet when ye go to apply same in thy conversation with thy brother, thy friend, thy neighbor, ye forget what manner of voice ye heard, what vision ye have seen, what is the prompting! For the things of the moment crowd in to such an extent that indeed ye find the spirit willing and the flesh weak.

Then the wisdom is ever that as He hath given, "Not my will but Thine, O God, be done in and through me." Let thy conversation ever be, "If the *Lord* is willing — if the Spirit of the Christ directeth — " These as the purposes, these as the inclinations, these as the directing forces may become more and more in thine experience the wisdom of the ages, the wisdom of God, the promptings of who hath given and whom thou settest as thine example. Ye say ye believe, but do ye show wisdom in acting that way? "I, thy Brother, thy Christ, will stand in thy stead."

Wisdom then is the divine love made manifest in thy daily conversation, thy daily advocation, thy daily acts as one to another. *This* is wisdom. This as ye apply, this as ye make known in thy conversation, in thy acts, will become more and more part and parcel of thy *very* self.

And though the earth may make for the calls, for that which is the satisfying of the moment, the glorifying of self, the exalting of self — if thou hast the divine love ye will find that in the application of thy knowledge, thy wisdom, the glory of the Christ is brought forth in thy conversation, thy daily life, thy daily activity among thy fellow men.

Choose ye then this day *whom* ye will serve. The Lord holy and righteous, or the self who is weak and unworthy of the love? unless ye show forth His love as thou hast seen in thine experiences, to thy fellow man.

What is love divine? That the Father and the Son and the Holy Spirit may direct thee, does direct thee, *will* direct thee in every thought, in every act!

And judge not others, condemn not others. This is not love divine, neither is it wisdom. For it builds barriers, it destroys, it undermines the life of self first and then in the hearts and minds and experiences of others brings sorrow, disappointments, and those things that maketh the hearts of men afraid.

And the fear of the Lord is the beginning of the wisdom. Not that fear of disappointment, of contention, of strife, of fault.

Consider the thoughts of thyself even for the period ye have listened here. If ye were condemned by the Christ Consciousness, where would thy mind, thy thoughts, be? For even as He when they spat upon Him, when they condemned Him, He saith not a word; that ye might know in His example, in His experience, that thou—too—would know suffering, but have a balm in Him; thou, too, would know disappointment, but have in Him the fulfilling of all thy wishes, all thy desires; thou, too, would have pain but in Him have strength and power and might; thou, too, would know suffering in body, suffering in mind, but in Him would have strength!

The wisdom then of the Lord thy God is shown thee, is exemplified to thee, is *patterned* for thee in the life of Jesus of Nazareth, Jesus the Christ!

For He indeed in thy wisdom is *wisdom* indeed!

How gave He? "If thy brother smite thee, turn the other cheek. If thy brother seeketh or taketh away thy coat, give him the other also. If he forceth thee to go one mile, go with him twain."

Are these but sayings? Are these but things not understood? Dost thou say in thine heart and thy mind, "Yea but He was the Son of the Father and thus had the strength that is not in me"? But ye are foolish! For not only art thou sons and daughters of the Father but hath the strength in the promises of Him who is life and light and the way and the water and the understanding!

Then the practical application of the Christ-life in thy daily experience is wisdom indeed.

This then is not a thing afar off. Not that ye would say as of old, who will bring down from heaven a message that we may know wisdom, or who will come from over the sea that we may hear and understand; for Lo, it is in thine own heart; it is within thine own power, yea within thine own might! It is the application of that *thou knowest* to do in the light of the pattern as set in the Christ. *That* is applied wisdom!

As is shown in the experiences of the sages of old, those whose material lives ye look upon oft and say—in the light of thine understanding—these were *beastly* men! Looketh thou in thine own heart? When thou knowest that the Christ, Jesus the

Christ, hath died—yea *liveth*—that ye might *have* the greater understanding! And yet ye speak uncomplimentary, yea ye speak *vilely,* yea ye condemn, yea ye hate thy brother. Who is the greater beast? He that knoweth to do good and doeth it not, or he that cried day in and day after day, "Not my way, Lord —but cleanse Thou me from all unrighteousness; purge me that I may know the Christ-way!"

Ye are chosen, ye are sufficient—if ye will but apply that ye know.

For as ye apply day by day that ye know, then is the next step, the next act, the next experience shown thee. Because thou hast then failed here or there, do not say, "Oh, I cannot —I am weak." To be sure thou art weak in self, but O ye of little faith! For He is thy *strength!* THAT is wisdom!

Let no *one* then again ever say *"I cannot."* It's rather, if ye do, saying "I *will* not—I want *my* way." This is foolishness; and ye know the way. For He is strength, He is love, He is patience, He is knowledge, He is wisdom.

Claim ALL of these, then, *in HIM!* For He is in thee, and the Father hath not desired that any soul should perish but hath prepared a way of escape; a way of love, of peace, of harmony for every soul—if ye will but claim same, live same, in Him.

We are through for the present.

[Edgar Cayce's letter to Mr. 470 and Mrs. 1100 in re experience he had during above reading:

"All are fair here. Had the loveliest experience yesterday I almost ever had when giving the reading for the group here. Joined the Christ with three of His disciples and heard a beautiful talk from Him. Possibly much of what we received was from that talk, but the reaction to my body was wonderful. Never felt as well and as really rested in my whole life."]

[Edgar Cayce's letter to Mrs. 1100: "Am most anxious about the next reading (262-105) on the same subject, as had a dream about same recently, and certainly makes me wonder. Anyway, do know it has given me a physical strength that had thought was not for me any more, for have felt better even with all the extra work, and some continuous extreme, hard cases. Well, the praise is all to *Him.*"]

This psychic reading was given by Edgar Cayce at the Edmonds' home, 611 Pennsylvania Avenue, Norfolk, Va., on January 24, 1937, at 3:55 P.M., in accordance with a request made by those present: Edgar Cayce; Gertrude Cayce, conductor; Gladys Davis, steno; Hugh Lynn Cayce, Edith Edmonds, Florence Edmonds, Helen Ellington, Hannah Miller, Frances Y. Morrow, Helen Storey, and Esther Wynne.

⊰ 262-105 ⊱

Mrs. Cayce: You will have before you Norfolk Study Group #1, members of which are present here, and work on the present lesson, copy of which I hold in my hand. You will continue the discourse on the lesson Wisdom.

Mr. Cayce: Yes, we have the group as gathered here; as a group, as individuals, and their work upon the lesson *Wisdom.*

In continuing with the discussion upon the wisdom of the Father, let first each of you attune yourselves to that consciousness as may be had through attuning self in this meditation:

"OUR FATHER WHO ART IN THE HEAVEN OF OUR OWN CONSCIOUSNESS, SO ATTUNE MY MIND, MY BODY, WITH THE INFINITE LOVE THOU HAST SHOWN TO THE CHILDREN OF MEN, THAT I IN BODY, IN MIND, MAY KNOW THE WISDOM OF THE FATHER IN JESUS, THE CHRIST."

Then it behooves each to be more aware of that love as brings into the experience of each soul the understanding that we as individuals cannot bear the cross of life alone but that the Father in His wisdom has given to each an ensample, a promise to the children of men—"which is indeed mine now if I will but choose the love of Jesus in my daily life, in my walks among my fellow men."

In wisdom thou wilt not find fault. In wisdom thou wilt not condemn any. In wisdom thou wilt not cherish grudges. In wisdom thou wilt love those, even those that despitefully use thee; even those that speak unkindly.

"In the wisdom of Jesus do I claim the promises of God and know His presence. Though in those things that are not always understood, it is His wisdom that makes for the changing of the affairs of the material experiences, the environs, the opportunities for those who profess their faith to give of themselves in body, in mind, that they may indeed know the wisdom of God in their experiences."

Know that the wisdom of Jesus—that is the promise to all —is a part of the daily life, and not to be put on as a coat or a cloak but to be part and parcel of each and every entity.

This is the wisdom to know, "As I purpose in my heart to do, it is in accord with that I profess with my mouth." It is wisdom that the acts of the body, of the mind, be in accordance with that proclaimed to thy children, to thy neighbor, to thy friend, to thy foe.

For life is in its material activity the wisdom of the Father that men may everywhere manifest, that they—too—may be a part of the consciousness of the Cosmic Consciousness.

For as the ways of life become more complex individuals see rather the material than the mental and spiritual.

Yet to thee, to whom the Book of Life—yea, the record of thine experiences—has been opened, there is the awareness that ye are indeed the children of God. And as children in thy wisdom ye may approach boldly the throne of mercy. For the prayers of the righteous are heard, for they have attuned in wisdom to the God-Consciousness within, and have come to the realization that they are not alone but that He walketh and He talketh with those who have called upon His name, and who day by day show forth in their conversation their love. For Jesus is the Way, Jesus is the Christ, Jesus is the Mediator, Jesus is Wisdom to those who will harken to do His biddings.

And as He hath given, "If ye love me, keep my commandments; for they are not grievous to bear. For I will bear them with thee, I will wipe away thy tears; I will comfort the broken-hearted, I will bring all to those in the ways that are in the wisdom of God for thy expressions through each experience, in each activity of thine."

For thy soul in its wisdom seeketh expression with Him. Smother it not in the doubts and the fears of materiality but in the spirit of love and truth that encompasseth all, and that is open to ye who have set thy hearts, thy faces, toward the love that is in Jesus, thy Friend, thy Brother.

These, my brethren—yea, these my beloved children—know

that in Him is the truth, the light. Ye have seen a great light. Ye have touched upon the wisdom of the Father, as is shown in the Son.

Then make thy paths straight. Let thy conversation, thy wishes, thy desires be rather as one with Him who thought it not robbery to be equal with God.

Ye know the way. Do ye stumble in ignorance or in selfishness? Do ye doubt for the gratifying of thy body or for the fulfilling of the body-appetites?

Ye know the way. Let, then, that love of the Infinite fire thee to action, to *doing!* And indeed live as hath been shown.

Study to show thyself in body, in mind, approved unto that thou hast chosen in the words of Jesus thy Master, thy Brother —in dividing the words of life in such measures that all who know thee, yea that contact thee, take cognizance of the fact that thou walkest and thou talkest with Jesus day by day; keeping thyself in body, in mind, unspotted from the world.

This is the wisdom of God and is thine if ye will but claim it as thine own.

And may the grace and the mercy and the peace of a life lived in thine own consciousness be thine through Him that is able to present our lives before the throne of God spotless, white as snow, washed in the blood of the sacrifices made in our own daily experience—even as He has shown us the way.

We are through.

This psychic reading was given by Edgar Cayce at the Edmonds' home, 611 Pennsylvania Avenue, Norfolk, Va., on February 14, 1937, at 3:00 P.M., in accordance with a request made by those present: Edgar Cayce; Gertrude Cayce, conductor; Gladys Davis, steno; Hugh Lynn Cayce, Edith Edmonds, Florence Edmonds, Helen Ellington, Hannah Miller, Helen Storey, and Esther Wynne.

ༀ 262-106 ༁

Mrs. Cayce: You will have before you Norfolk Study Group #1, members of which are present here, and you will continue on the lesson Wisdom; *answering the questions that may be. asked.*

Mr. Cayce: Yes, we have the group as gathered here, as a group, as individuals, and their work upon the lesson *Wisdom.*

In continuing with the subject, first we would admonish each that you apply yourselves that you would give to others regarding the subject. Preach not that which you would not yourself practice. Do not insist upon others trying that in their experience ye have not tried. And each of you finds this means *you* —if ye will but look into thine own heart! Not that any would be condemned, for ye go part the way but not all; else ye would never hear a grumble from any.

Try in thine own experience, each; that ye speak not for *one whole day* unkindly of any; that ye say not a harsh word to any, about any; and see what a day would bring to you—the next lesson, *Happiness.*

This should be a crowning of that ye each have gained, if ye apply wisdom as has been shown you.

The next lesson after *Happiness* is *Spirit*—and if ye finish it this year you will do well!

Happiness:

OUR FATHER, OUR GOD, IN MY OWN CONSCIOUSNESS LET ME FIND HAPPINESS IN THE LOVE OF THEE, FOR THE LOVE I BEAR TOWARD MY FELLOW MAN. LET MY LIFE, MY WORDS, MY DEEDS, BRING THE JOY AND HAPPINESS OF THE LORD IN JESUS TO EACH I MEET DAY BY DAY.

We are through.

≈ 262-107 ⮜

This psychic reading was given by Edgar Cayce at the Edmonds' home, 611 Pennsylvania Avenue, Norfolk, Va., on March 7, 1937, at 4:05 P.M., in accordance with a request made by those present: Edgar Cayce; Hugh Lynn Cayce, conductor; Gladys Davis, steno; Gertrude Cayce, Edith Edmonds, Florence Edmonds, Helen Ellington, Hannah Miller, Noah Miller, Frances Y. Morrow, Helen Storey, and Esther Wynne.

Hugh Lynn Cayce: You will have before you Group #1, members of which are present here. At this time the group as a whole and as individuals seek guidance and understanding in making practical application of wisdom and putting it into expression for the lesson for others.

Edgar Cayce: We have the group as gathered here, as a group, as individuals; and their work on the lesson *Wisdom*—also their choice to give to others that which has been helpful in their experience.

Then, this should not be lost sight of; that what has been helpful in thine own experience will bring to others a light, a hope.

For remember, it is a part of His promises to thee, that God giveth the increase, God giveth the help.

It is thy purpose then, in the comprehending of thy experience, in the study of that which has been given thee as to how it is wisdom, to put away strife; it is wisdom to manifest love and patience and long-suffering.

For ye have been and are called to put into practice that ye have experienced in thy material life.

Then in the simplicity of thy faith in the promise, give expression to same; that those who read, those who meditate upon same may take hope.

Have ye forgotten as to when that ye are preparing may become even the textbooks to many, the way for many to know, to have a greater understanding?

Be not then overcome by those very experiences that have shown thee the wisdom of thy choice in God, in Christ, in Jesus as thy pattern.

Remember thy first lesson, *Cooperation*—how that you each contributing of yourselves will add to the strength of those who are in darkness, who are disturbed by the worldly wisdom of many.

For it is as has been given, oft the foolishness of man is the wisdom of God.

Then is it true that the Lord thy God is One?

Be in singleness of purpose, then, not that thy own self is to be glorified. What has been thy concept of glory? Glory signifies that ye are able to suffer. Only those who have suffered much may ever be glorified.

Do ye seek glory? Then ye must be willing to suffer; and if ye count thy suffering, thy disappointments, thy heartaches, thy misunderstandings, as judgments upon thee, ye are unwise. For whom the Lord loveth He chasteneth and purgeth every one, that ye may bring forth fruit in *due season!*

Would ye have thy glory without thy purification? Would ye have thy wisdom without thy preparation? Would ye have thy happiness, or seek thy happiness, without being able to comprehend, to understand? If this be so, ye have not gained thy lesson of wisdom.

Then how may each of you here make a practical application of wisdom? Ye all, *every one,* in your own experience have been called upon to manifest that ye have chosen, even as He hath chosen thee.

Then go the whole way with thy Master. Give expression, each of you, to that which has helped thee in those periods of not only disturbance but distress, in periods of disappointment, in periods of lack of that self-exaltation, even of that of self-expression, until ye have lost—some of you—even a hope in thine ability to do this or that.

When thy friends, when thy family, when thy brother would cast thee out, yea and condemn thee—*then* the Lord will bear thee up.

Was the Master, Jesus, come to the self-righteous of Israel or to the lost sheep?

Ye are His sheep, yea every one of you. For ye have named the name of the Christ, and He calleth each of *you* by name!

Will ye then, at this time, fail those who may in the days, the years to come be given hope and cheer by that ye have experienced in thy walks with Jesus, in the garden of wisdom?

In the periods of purifying, of testing, know ye *will* take thy part. For it *is* a practical application of wisdom in thine own experience.

Then *indeed* ye may be lifted up to that new vision in the happiness of the presence of thy Lord, thy Christ.

We are through.

This psychic reading was given by Edgar Cayce at his home on Arctic Crescent, Virginia Beach, Va., on April 25, 1937, at 4:00 P.M., in accordance with a request made by those present: Edgar Cayce; Gertrude Cayce, conductor; Gladys Davis, steno; Hugh Lynn Cayce, Helen Ellington, Carrie S. House, Hannah Miller, Frances Y. Morrow, Helen Storey, and Esther Wynne.

ॲ 262-108 ᕮ

Mrs. Cayce: You will have before you Norfolk Study Group #1, members of which are present here, and their work on the lesson Wisdom. *As I call the heading of each section you will comment, giving any suggestions that will assist in improving this lesson. Questions.*

Mr. Cayce: Yes, we have the group as gathered here, as a group, as individuals; and their work on the lesson *Wisdom.*

This as we find in the main is very good.

As has been indicated, to be complete, it is to be a part of the experience of each member of the group. For to be consistent in all things is wisdom, but to be growing also. For ye grow in grace, in knowledge, in understanding—in wisdom, of God, the Father, and the relationships as ye experience in the application of that thou hast known, thou hast seen, thou hast heard, thou hast experienced in the application of His love. For love is wisdom, as love is God.

Ready for questions.

Q-1. Section I—Introduction.

A-1. This we find very good.

Q-2. Section II—The Approach to Wisdom.

A-2. Yes, very good; only a few minor changes or a transposing here of the approaches as relate to the activities of the individual in the applying of that known in the experience.

Q-3. Section III—Let Each Examine Himself.

A-3. Very good. For this may be ever kept before every individual: God is one, and in the examining of self it is to be, in wisdom then, to realize self—in desire, in purpose, in aim—to be at one with that which is the representing of, the application of, God in the experience of each.

Then this necessarily becomes self-examination. Not self-condemnation, nor self-glorification, but—as the mind is the builder, as the will is the meter or measure, and as the law of love is that to be builded—it is wisdom to be at one in same.

Q-4. *Section IV—Application of Wisdom.*

A-4. This is very good.

Q-5. *Section V—Closing.*

A-5. This is very good; only the more of the individual experience—in the application and in the personal experience of that as becomes a part of the individual experience of each one who studies or reads same, as a consciousness, an awareness.

Then indeed does there come happiness into the experience. Happy are they that know the Lord in their daily lives. Not unto self-glory, but just being willing for self and self's abilities to be used even as He—"Not my will but Thine, O God, be done in and through me."

Think ye that Jesus went happily to the cross, or that He went happily from the garden where there had been apparently so little consideration by those of His followers as to what the moment meant? when they slept as He wrestled with self in the garden?

Think ye then on thine own disturbances that are of the moment, though ye may have them in thy consciousness constantly, and worry as to this or that, the shortcomings of those ye love. How was He with those He loved? Yet He gave them His blessings.

So in wisdom, so in happiness, bless them that despitefully use thee, that speak unkindly, yea though they deny thee of that thou knowest is thy part, even in the daily experiences. Bless them if ye would be wise, if ye would be happy or if ye would have happiness in thine own life.

For as He hath given, bless and curse not if ye would know God, if ye would know the Father. For as He sendeth His blessings upon those that are righteous and those that are unrighteous, do ye become envious that the unrighteous receive even those material blessings as ye consider thy daily needs, and thus find fault with thine own concept or thine own righteousness? Unwise are they that do such!

Though ye may mourn for their unrighteousness, happy is the man that blesses those whom the Lord does smile on even in their weaknesses.

For ye know in whom ye have believed, and His promises are sure. Doth ye find in thy heart that one son or daughter is not as kind or as gentle or as patient or as loving as another? Do ye not show the more gentleness to those who are weak, that thy very strength may touch them? From whence gained ye such wisdom? From the earth or from God?

So does He in His mercy, His patience, His loving-kindness —but ye are wise that love the law and the understanding of same.

Q-6. You will give the fundamental principles for our study of the next lesson on Happiness.

A-6. These have been given, as has just been outlined, that if ye would be happy:

No envy, no strife, no faultfinding, no heckling—but rather the *joy* of the Lord, and in seeing beauty and grace in *every* thing!

How hath it been given? Unless ye can see in those that dislike thee, that despitefully use thee, that ye would worship in that ye would call a manifestation of God, can ye know happiness?

Then, only those who make happiness in the lives and the experiences of others may indeed know what it is to be happy.

Have ye made anyone happy that was discouraged, that was disturbed, that was misunderstood? Not that ye condone anything, but the love of God that taketh away sadness and sorrow. What is the life in the presence of the Christ depicted as? That He shall wipe away every tear, and no sickness and no sorrow shall be in that happy land.

So the fundamentals are: Casting out fear first in thine own heart, and aiding others to aid themselves—in gaining an insight into *their* relationships with the Creative Forces or God.

Tell them of the happiness in the Christ Way, in the manner that Jesus showed Himself to be the Christ; and the joy and happiness in keeping *His* ways, His promises, His joys, His life before thee and before them always.

This is the mission of those who would bring happiness into the experience of others; and as ye share, ye become happy in the way.

What—in thy study, thy experience, thy understanding—

made the man Jesus the Christ? His willingness in the flesh to give Himself instead of the world for the knowledge and help of others! *This* brought into the individual experience the kingdom of God.

What, then, is the variation between the kingdom of God and the kingdom of heaven?

In the finding out of these, in their variation, is the happiness of ye that seek the way.

We are through for the present.

This psychic reading was given by Edgar Cayce at the Edmonds' home, 611 Pennsylvania Avenue, Norfolk, Va., on June 20, 1937, at 4:20 P.M., in accordance with a request made by those present: Edgar Cayce; Gertrude Cayce, conductor; Gladys Davis, steno; Edith Edmonds, Florence Edmonds, Helen Ellington, Ruth LeNoir, Maud Lewis, Hannah Miller, Noah Miller, Frances Y. Morrow, Helen Storey, and Esther Wynne.

ᕃ 262-109 ᖾ

Mrs. Cayce: You will have before you the Norfolk Study Group #1, members of which are present in this room. You will continue on the lesson Happiness, *answering the questions that will be asked.*

Mr. Cayce: Yes, we have the group as gathered here, as a group, as individuals, and their work and their study on the lesson *Happiness.*

Happiness is abiding in the infinite love.

Then to each individual here there comes the necessity of making infinite love compatible with the material surroundings day by day.

Hence we will find that it is as the Master gave, first keeping self out of the way, less of self, more exaltation of the Father-God, more patience, more kindness, more gentleness, more brotherly love.

These, as you all say, we have heard before. Have you put them in practical use day by day?

What said He? If thy brother sue thee and take away thy coat, give him thy cloak also. Have you tried that? or have you sworn and said there is no justice, "This one has done me wrong, and that one has done another wrong"?

These are the children of the earth that speak such, and know not happiness.

Happiness then is knowing, being in touch with, manifesting in the daily life, *divine* love.

Being glad when you are persecuted for His name's sake, being in that attitude of forgiving those who speak unkindly, being in that mind that was in Him when He gave, "Father, forgive them, they know not what they do," and not saying under your breath, "Poor saps! I'm the one persecuted but they

-433-

are the ones that must receive the damnation," for you have turned it then on self.

These then are, as given of old, in His precepts, His love, in mind, in spirit. Bind them upon thy brow. Let them be thy hands, thy feet; that you do His biddings, that you walk in His ways, that you keep His precepts.

For it is only those who know divine love that know happiness.

Happy are they, then, who love the Lord's ways.

Ready for questions.

Q-1. Are the outlines on the lesson Happiness *correct? If not, please advise what changes we should make.*

A-1. These as we find are very good. The natural form of filling in the outline will in manners adjust itself more as there are definite contributions of the individuals of the group putting into expression their own experiences in a soft word, a kindness when rough words or unkind words or hatreds have been expressed, when unkind things have been said for thy very purpose's sake.

When ye have put into practice the fruits of the spirit and have experienced. For has it not been given you that from henceforth more and more you will, each of you, experience the very things, the very phases, the very activities that you would encourage others to study?

Then do not berate self nor others for the experiences, but use them for *what they are* to bring happiness and joy into thy own experience of life.

And give the expressions of the experience as a portion of thy contribution to the lesson in hand.

For each experience is as a help, as a step to someone else. It is, if true in thy spiritual life, the leaven that leaveneth the whole lump. It *is* as He has given, you being the channel, "Heaven and earth shall pass away but my words, my promises, my laws shall not pass away."

And happiness is as much a law as is error or goodness or day and night; for without it man is a dreary being indeed.

And as has been set to song, if you will count your happiness, your blessings day by day, they are many more than that you have even any right to find fault in.

For if the earth is the Lord's, and if your brother is in the image of your Maker, have you any right—ever—to find fault? or to speak unkindly? much less unjustly?

And what is the first law? Like begets like! For in the act, as in the seed, is the full grown blossom of what you do, what you think, what you are! Hence if you sow happiness will you reap turmoil? or riot? Rather in the still small voice, do you find the song of happiness, the blessings of divine love directing, guiding, keeping your ways.

What matter if there is no new dress, hat, shoes, or even the house rent paid? They are of the moment. If you are happy that you are alive, you still have the opportunity to say, "Blessings be on thee," and these are what live forever. Shadows pass. Only the light and truth lives on. Disturbances and distresses pass. For you say "God is in His holy temple, let all the earth keep silent." What do you mean? Is it just a saying because you have heard it oft, or do you really believe it?

Then, as His children, *act that way!*

Q-2. As I call the names of members of the group, you will please give each a personal message that will be of help on the study and application of the lesson, Happiness. *First:* [*413*]:

A-2. Keep thy heart singing, for there is music and joy in the happiness of knowing that you may be—and are—at a oneness with Him. Though there may come disturbances, shadows, turmoils, these must pass in the light of patience, persistence, loving kindness.

Q-3. [*404*]:

A-3. Let others do as they may but for thee and thy house, love a living God. Keep His precepts. Thou knowest the way and that it is good. Then seek and ye shall find, knock and it shall be opened unto thee day by day. For others look to thee oft for counsel. When ye least suspect ye are an example for others.

Q-4. [*303*]:

A-4. Let the ways of the earth pass over thee and reckon not them by the spiritual truths ye have seen. Rather magnify in thy life, in thy labors, in thy dealings with others, the love, the patience, the joy, the *happiness* ye find in service to a living God —even when others speak unkindly, even when there is that which is the least in man's knowledge—the lack of appreciation of the service one does. Know ye look not to the earth for thy reward. For only *one* can give, does give, that peace that brings joy and happiness in thy experience. This is only accomplished in doing that thy hands find to do in His service day by day.

Q-5. [*379*]:

A-5. The ways of the world, the joys of living, are before thee oft as questionings, as disturbing factors in the experiences of those you would direct. Let others do as they think; only sow the seed. Some fall on stony ground, some fall by the wayside, some fall among the thorns and briars; but much on goodly ground. For as you keep the faith, God alone giveth the increase and He addeth—daily—such as may be, should be, will be saved in this experience.

Q-6. [*993*]:

A-6. Let not the little things of the material mind so unnerve, so disturb, that the greater things are overshadowed. Much joy, much happiness you bring to others. Does it not bear the same fruit in you? Keep that thou hast sown *nourished!* Let it not die by neglect, nor by forgetfulness. For as you do sow, so shall you reap—if you keep the way clean. In many ways, even as He gave, let the thorns and the wheat grow together, but in *thy* life, to know love, to know joy, to know happiness is to make it in the experience of others.

Q-7. [*560*]:

A-7. The light and love draws near to thee, and thy ways are close to His ways. Keep faithful in the little things. Be not unmindful that persistence is a whole sister of patience, and if ye would know the greater joy, the greater love of the Christ Consciousness, these ye must keep in thy daily life. Grow not weary, then, in well-doing, but let the love divine, the beauty sublime, the joy as of the Lord, keep thee. This does not mean there are no joys in the material surroundings or in the material associations, but they must be in the spirit of truth.

Q-8. [*462*]:

A-8. In thy Father's house are many mansions. All are not for the one nor the other; each according to the use of his abilities is meted that with which he is attuned. Keep thy purposes then, keep thy aims, thy desires, of a material, of a mental, of a spiritual nature, attuned to that *you* would occupy for aye, for aye, forever. For these temporal things must pass away, but that spiritual house, that temple—that cleanliness so akin to godliness—is that which lives on and on. It ever was, and you have drawn close to His ways. Then steer thy course to that thou knowest that brings peace, and the calm that brings happiness in thy daily life.

Q-9. [*585*]:

A-9. Let the joy of the Lord keep thee. For His ways are not past finding out. For as He has given, search and ye shall find; be *still* and ye shall hear the Lord. For He is nigh unto thee. Though there come discouragements, disappointments, disagreements in thy experience, know that thy purposes, know that thy desires are of and for the Lord—of as well as for the Lord; and ye shall know the happiness of the divine love as He sheds to those who keep His ways.

Q-10. [*307*]:

A-10. In keeping the law of the Lord, take it never as a hardship upon thee, for then it is law alone. And it is mercy and grace and love ye seek, and would show in thine experience one to another. In thine experience, have you found ever that to "get even" with anyone made thee happy? To forgive them is divine and brings happiness to all. *These* things *sow* in the lives, in the hearts, in the minds of others. "Grace and mercy, Lord, not sacrifice—nor judgment."

Q-11. [*288*]:

A-11. The heart that seeketh the Lord may find same only in day by day, step by step, living that you preach to others. For the law of the Lord is not as a precept but is as a living thing, known of those who deal with thee day by day. Is love, is mercy sown? or is judgment or questioning or discouragement? They that become discouraged are not worthy of the mercy and the merit of true knowledge or true happiness. For *happy* is the man that loves the Lord and His ways, not thy ways.

Q-12. [*294*]:

A-12. Let mercy and judgment and honor be as one in thy dealing with thy fellow man. For he that showeth mercy may obtain mercy, he that brings happiness into the lives of others will know happiness. And only by the sowing of the seed of that nature that ye desire the full activity of in thy life may ye accomplish or accede to such an experience. For what you *are* speaks so loud, few hear what you say.

Q-13. [*538*]:

A-13. Let mercy and justice be thy watchword rather than judgment upon others. For "Judge not that ye be not judged" is the same as saying show mercy to those that are wayward, to those that are awkward, to those that are unkind, to those that are rude—if you would have God show these to you. For in thy awkwardness, in thy stumbling, ye oft find fault in thine self. Do not judge thyself. Let God's mercy and love rule thee.

Q-14. [*341*]:

A-14. In knowing happiness ye find that it is the little things, the little "I thank you," the little patience, the little mercy, the little kindnesses that bring it to the lives of others. So does it grow in thee. Then let grace and mercy and patience be thine. For in patience ye become aware of thy soul, that ye are indeed a soul in a material world; though stumbling oft, following blindly at times. The way is narrow, yet it is the happy way. Only in happiness may one indeed *know* Jesus. *Only* in *happy way* may one know Jesus. For He is the way, as thy soul knoweth; and He was happy even to the cross. Not that moments of discouragement do not arise in thine experience, for as He gave—and these are His words, and His words, though the heaven and the earth may pass, do not pass away—"It must indeed be necessary that offenses come, but woe to him by whom they come!" Then never be in the way of being an offense to anyone. Let mercy and patience keep thee.

Q-15. [*1391*]:

A-15. In the house of the Lord ye find His offices, His steps of understanding, of comprehending. Sing thy joys of thy Lord. Know in whom ye believe as well as in what ye believe. Know the source of thy knowledge and ye may know the end thereof. Know the laws—or the love; for the law of God is *love* of God, and is not a hardship. For the law as man's law killeth, but the love of the law as of God maketh alive—every one. And thy Lord, thy God, is God of the living. Make thy life and thy love of thy fellow man a living thing in thine experience day by day. Smile oft. Speak gently. Be kind.

Q-16. Any message to the group as a whole?

A-16. Happiness is the love of God made manifest by those who love God's ways.

We are through.

This psychic reading was given by Edgar Cayce at the Edmonds' home, 611 Pennsylvania Avenue, Norfolk, Va., on July 11, 1937, at 4:00 P.M., in accordance with a request made by those present: Edgar Cayce; Gertrude Cayce, conductor; Gladys Davis, steno; Hugh Lynn Cayce, Edith Edmonds, Florence Edmonds, Ruth Le-Noir, Hannah Miller, Noah Miller, and Frances Y. Morrow.

⊱ 262-110 ⊰

Mrs. Cayce: You will have before you the Norfolk Study Group #1, members of which are present here and their work in preparing the lesson on Happiness. *You will continue the discourse on the material for this lesson.*

Mr. Cayce: Yes, we have the group as gathered here; as a group, as individuals; and their work on the lesson *Happiness.*

In continuing with the discussion, as has been given, you each shall analyze yourselves and that given you as a helpful measure towards your comprehending or embracing happiness in your individual experience.

You each will find, if it is but applied, that which will enable you to give to others a greater vision of what and how happiness may be in the experience of others; and—as doers of the word and not hearers only—become more and more in accord with that which has been designated as true happiness.

To be sure, many find the inclinations for quiet or rest, or laziness, to become oft your meter or standard; but these, too, are—as has been given—far from true happiness. For happiness is being busy about the Lord's work; not in other peoples' business, not in that of stirring up strife, but rather as He brought to the world that of peace and happiness in going about doing good.

That is the business, that is the activity, that is being doers of the word; that is showing forth faith by the works.

In this then, let you each arouse yourselves to that which will enable you as individuals to give in your daily dealings with others a greater expression of joy, and not of those things that build for offenses of one nature or another.

For offense is absent from joy or happiness. And when there are resentments, when there are petty jealousies, when there are those things that are contradictory to happiness and joy

-440-

that are a part of the activity, these build those things that hinder those who would know the peace and the joy and the happiness of just being kind, just doing that which brings to the experience of others that of joy, peace, happiness to all.

Ready for questions.

We are through for the present.

This psychic reading was given by Edgar Cayce at his home on Arctic Crescent, Virginia Beach, Va., on August 22, 1937, at 3:50 P.M., in accordance with a request made by those present: Edgar Cayce; Gertrude Cayce, conductor; Gladys Davis, steno; Edith Edmonds, Florence Edmonds, Helen Ellington, Hannah Miller, and Esther Wynne.

⊁ 262-111 ⊰

Mrs. Cayce: You will have before you Norfolk Study Group #1, members of which are present in this room, and their work in preparing the lesson Happiness. *You will continue with that needed on this lesson, answering the questions that will be submitted:*

Mr. Cayce: Yes, we have the group as gathered here, as a group and as individuals; and their work upon the lesson *Happiness.*

It is well that you each — in the study of that which was given as necessary for your better concept of happiness as applied in your personal experiences — think, too, on the difference between pleasure and happiness. It is like the spiritual and the material. We oft see things beautiful, and they come out of that which may be very murky, very bad-appearing yet that necessary for the beauty.

So with happiness. Only when one has lost sight of self, in the appreciation of the love, beauty and hope in the Creative Forces and their activity, may one indeed know happiness.

That which gratifies only the sensuous self, or as an aggrandizement of physical pleasure, *rarely* brings happiness. Out of the dregs of same may *grow* happiness, but in themselves they are only passing.

To illustrate: The road to Gethsemane, to the minds of those who look upon their own Gethsemane, was as a road of thorns; the perspiration, the sweat of blood and all appear anything but happiness — yet the kind words spoken, even on the way to Calvary, were indeed those that brought happiness.

And as there were the words from the cross, these — though filled with all of the horrors of spite, fear, by the very activities of others — were such as to bring happiness into the hearts and minds of those who seek to know His way.

It is again as infinite love and divine love. Infinite love is the love of God, while love divine is that manifested by those in their activities who are guided by love divine. These bring happiness and the experiences of joy; not mere pleasure, not gratification of any of the material things. But differentiate—or, as has been given—put the proper value upon the proper phases of one's experience.

Because we see one smile, or with the outward appearance of pleasures and the gratifying of the worldly seekings, does not always indicate happiness. The gratifying of the worldly seekings may bring pleasures, but very rarely indeed do such pleasures being happiness with them. For it is indeed as has been said, there are ways oft that appear to be good but the end thereof is death, separation, dissension, anger, all those things that make for strife.

Happiness, then, is of love divine; manifesting in the experiences as one gives a cup of water in His name, that may bring much greater happiness than to he that taketh a city, or to he that ruleth even a nation. You each are endowed, to be sure, with power only from one source, but to know happiness—then —is to do the biddings of the Father; or as He gave, "If ye love me, keep my commandments" [John 14:15]—"they are not grievous—" [I John 5:3].

Ready for questions.

Q-1. What was meant by Him when He said, "If thy brother sue thee and take away thy coat, give him thy cloak also"?

A-1. Go to the other extreme in being kind and gentle, or— Because ye have little ye say, "I must save—that I be not in want"—but there are those who need what little thou hast! For it is indeed as has been given here. If you say, "If I were so and so—if I had this or that—O how much I would give to charity, to the needy" and give not in your present estate, you would not give any at all if you had all at your command! Then His command was as this: If what you have is taken away, give the *all*—that you may be *filled!* For how has it been said? "That alone you give away, that do you possess."

Q-2. What is the variation between the kingdom of God and the kingdom of heaven?

A-2. As has been indicated, one is within while the other is the activity of the Infinite upon those influences that bring to bear the experiences of the kingdom within the lives of the individuals. For He has so oft likened it to the various experiences that may be in the emotions of the individuals; as: The kingdom of heaven is likened unto him who has the hundred sheep and one was lost, and he left the ninety and nine and went to seek that which was lost. Or the kingdom of heaven is likened unto she that lost a penny and tore up the whole house and called on the neighbors to rejoice because she had found that which was lost. These are examples of the kingdom of heaven; while the kingdom of God—they that enter in have known the happiness of the kingdom of heaven in their *own* experience.

Q-3. *Please explain that given in the affirmation, "Bring the joy and happiness of the Lord in Jesus."* [*See 262-106, p. 1, par. 7.*]

A-3. It has just been illustrated or given, as the example of how and out of what grows happiness. Then, as the suffering of the Master brought happiness to Him and to thee, so indeed out of thy disappointments, thy trials, thy tribulations, do ye know happiness.

Such then is that as given in the affirmation; and again is it illustrated in that as you see it in and as you do it to your fellow man, so may the measures of happiness and joy be yours. For, "As ye do it unto the least, ye do it unto me," ever has been, ever is the relationship-conditional. And in the loss of doing or being for self, but rather for the glory of God, does the knowledge and the wisdom and *happiness* come. They that know not what have been the measures given for the bringing of life into existence know not the happiness nor the joys therein. They that have known not the sorrows, the disappointments for righteousness' sake, know not the joy and the happiness in the Lord. Hence as has been the warning to many: Look not upon the things of the world and the pleasures of things therein as a measure or standard as to the joy and the happiness in the Lord.

Q-4. *Please explain from the 5th chapter of Matthew, "Happy are they that mourn."*

A-4. Happy are they that have known sorrow, for their joy

will be filled if they trust in the Lord. For He *is* the force, the power, the might that *comforts* those that mourn for those things even as He wept over Jerusalem and mourned for the cities about same; yet might He not by His own power have commanded that all who would seek not to know be blotted away? Yet man's will, man's desire is that which makes him at a oneness with the knowledge of God. And to seek and to know and to be *filled* is that as comes from those who mourn over those things which they may be able to help but are powerless through the very will of others.

Q-5. *Please explain "Happy are the poor in spirit, for they shall see God." Who are the poor in spirit?*

A-5. They that have not allowed and do not allow themselves to be directed by other influences than that of Godly-Force itself. They that are not acquainted with the familiar spirits but with the divine. They that are meek yet proud in their meekness and their humbleness. These are they that are poor in spirit.

Q-6. *Comment on "Where your treasure is, there shall your heart be also."*

A-6. This is emblematical; as indicated in that whatever influence or force draws the material mind may also draw the mental and the soul experience. What you desire and seek after mentally and spiritually, and what you desire and seek for in the material things are not *always* from the same promptings; but where the heart or the treasure is, there is the desire. Hence again is the injunction given that you know in *whom* you believe as well as in *what* you believe; so that you know whether or not thy treasure is laid in that where moth and rust doth not corrupt, and where thieves do not break through nor steal —that is in the spirit of truth, in the Christ, in Jesus.

Q-7. *If we completely surrender ourselves to God's will, and become a channel of blessings to others, do we not then possess true happiness?*

A-7. You then possess true happiness.

Q-8. *Please differentiate between being conscious of and being aware of.*

A-8. Being conscious of and being aware of may be synonymous to some; and these may differentiate to some, dependent upon the individual experience. It is much in the same way as being aware of and being satisfied with, or being convinced and being aware; but they each are dependent upon the *activity* to which the motivative influence works upon the individual self. For you may be aware and do nothing about it! You may be conscious, so conscious it is necessary to do something about it!

Q-9. When one we love is floundering and unhappy, apparently lacking in spiritual purpose, how can we influence such a one to become conscious or aware that He is the way?

A-9. We may only sow the seed. Remember *ever* it is *God* that gives the increase. It is not *anything* that an individual may *do*, except keeping in that it knows to be the right. For the knowledge or the vision or the comprehension is the *gift* of the *Father*. As was illustrated by the life and experience of John [John the Baptist?], one may be great, one may understand, and yet *not* comprehend. Only the spirit of truth may awaken. One can only pray and hope, one can only mourn and be glad; one can only live and experience that which is to him and to his activity the fulfilling of it all. You cannot force upon any soul your *own* estate. The Christ died that all might be saved, but those that may be saved must seek to know Him of *themselves.* Not *He* only making the way; for He is the light and the way and the truth, the vine, and all—the water and the bread. But unless we *partake,* we do not have the awareness, the sustenance, the life, the knowledge, the hope. We *must partake!* For how gave He when they fainted, when even many of His disciples turned away? "Unless ye eat of my body, drink of my blood, ye *cannot know* the way!" And they all said, "How can this be —lest we partake of Him we may not know?" Then for our loved ones, for our acquaintances, yea for our enemies, we only so live—as in persistence, in patience, in hope; for the prayer of the righteous shall save many. Even as one plead that there be spared a city, if there were only the ten! How *great* are the mercies of the Father! Then faint not though ye may see those of thy loved ones floundering. Is it not again illustrated in just that given? On the way to the cross the world seemed black, for darkness covered the whole earth. Yet out of it came joy and happiness, the renewing of man's relationship to God and the closer communion. For ye have an advocate in Him. Faint not at thy well-doing, nor find fault with those because they have not grasped hold even as thou. For "In my father's house there are many, many mansions"—many, many consciousnesses.

We are through for the present.

This psychic reading was given by Edgar Cayce at the Edmonds' home, 611 Pennsylvania Avenue, Norfolk, Va., on September 12, 1937, at 4:00 P.M., in accordance with a request made by those present: Edgar Cayce; Gertrude Cayce, conductor; Gladys Davis, steno; Hugh Lynn Cayce, Edith Edmonds, Florence Edmonds, Helen Ellington, Ruth LeNoir, Hannah Miller, Frances Y. Morrow, and Helen Storey.

⋊ 262-112 ⋉

Mrs. Cayce: You will have before you the Norfolk Study Group #1, members of which are present here, and its work on the lessons Wisdom *and* Happiness. *You will answer the questions which will be asked.*

Mr. Cayce: Yes, we have the group as gathered here; as a group and as individuals, and their work on the lessons *Wisdom* and *Happiness.*

Ready for questions.

Q-1. Please comment on the second division of the lesson on Wisdom, *The Approach to Wisdom. This has been changed as recommended. Copy I hold in my hand.*

A-1. The changes as we find are very good and more in keeping with the body of that presented in the rest of the lesson.

Q-2. Please comment and give suggestions and correction on divisions of lesson on Happiness, *as I call them:*

A-2. One: This we would not change materially. This we find very good. Two: This very good. The only revision as we would give would be in some of the wording, and this as we find will be corrected as it is copied or revised or put together. Three: Very good. Four: Very good. Five: Very good. It would be well if all would make this portion of the lesson a part of their activities. Six: Very good. Seven: Very good. Eight: Nothing except it's all low [?], and all there—it's very good. Nine: Very good. Ten: Very good. Eleven: Very good. Twelve: Very good. Thirteen: Very good. Ands and thes not always necessary in some of these. Fourteen: Very good. Fifteen: Very good. Sixteen: [Mumbling . . .] That is, it's different. Very good. Seventeen: Very good. Eighteen: Somebody's been left off here that should have been put in; otherwise very good.

Q-3. Any suggestions or comments on the lesson as a whole?

A-3. This as we find—more and more as those that do give

-448-

of themselves as channels to bring others the interpretations
through the study of the lessons, they are gaining within themselves a security, a surety of their purposes in this experience.
Those that are failing to carry through are losing that which
would bring the experience of happiness in their own selves.
Learn, in the application of the purposes, that the first lesson
is well to be applied in each meeting. Seek not thy differences
but rather the ways, the means of the cooperation with those
though they become overanxious, and with thy own manifold
duties and activities ye become somewhat peeved. But ye have
been called—*get up! and work!* For it's the workers and not the
shirkers that the blessings come to.

*Q-4. Please give the words of the Master (in English) of the
verse, "Blessed are the poor in spirit," Matthew 5th chapter, if
not translated correctly.*

A-4. This has been dwelt upon at length and is in literal
English as given, "Blessed are the poor in spirit."

Q-5. [585]: Please give me a message that will help me.

A-5. Let thy heart be opened to the beauties of the service
in the Lord. Let not anxieties or indifferences on the part of
others cause thee to lose thy hold upon thy vision. For whom
the Lord loveth He keepeth in the ways that bring joy of service
in Him. The way is being opened. Follow thou in the way of the
Lord.

Q-6. Any message to the group at this time?

A-6. In the study, in the work, in the service of the preparation of the lessons, grow not weary. For if you each will but
become introspective of the experiences that have been thine
through the varied conditions that have arisen through the
period of time ye have given in the service, ye will find that it
has opened thy way of understanding, it has opened thy mind,
thy heart to the greater attunement that ye may attain with
the Creative Forces that manifest in the experiences of those
who serve an ideal in as near an ideal manner as circumstances
permit in their lives. Then grow not weary in well-doing. For
ye all *have* attained unto happiness in that peace has come into
the hearts and experiences of ye all.

Then as ye begin that study wherein ye must look as it were
into the very depths of the heart of God, and again see the

vileness of the evil influences that may come to bear in the experiences of all, be not fearful. For remember what was said to Peter; he bid that the Lord call him. Ye have bid that ye be channels of blessings. Then trust in the Lord. For He will *hold* thee and sustain thee if ye will but put your trust in Him.

And as He gave, "If ye love me ye will keep my commandments." And what is His commandment? "That ye love one another, even as I have loved you, that the Father may be glorified in you."

These keep in remembrance.

We are through for the present.

This psychic reading was given by Edgar Cayce at his home on Arctic Crescent, Virginia Beach, Va., on September 26, 1937, at 4:00 P.M., in accordance with a request made by those present: Edgar Cayce; Gertrude Cayce, conductor; Gladys Davis, steno; Hugh Lynn Cayce, Edith Edmonds, Florence Edmonds, Helen Ellington, Ruth LeNoir, Frances Y. Morrow, Minnie J. Williams, and Esther Wynne.

≥ 262-113 ≰

Mrs. Cayce: You will have before you the Norfolk Study Group #1, members of which are present here, and its work in preparing the Study Group lessons, especially in relation to the beginning of their work on the lesson Spirit. *You will give a discourse on this subject and also give the affirmation for this lesson.*

Mr. Cayce: Yes, we have the group as gathered here, as a group, as individuals; and their work in the preparation of lessons.

In the beginning of the preparation then of the lesson *Spirit,* this is the beginning and the end of all matters that pertain to the individual development in the material experiences.

For as the individual entity, or soul, is spirit, so its end—or at the beginning and the end—is spirit.

Then as ye seek in each experience for that which may be given as a help in thine individual activity, ask. Not as for knowledge alone, but how and what may be given that will aid or strengthen or give a better understanding to each of you as ye seek.

For this should be, in the experience of each, a greater awakening to each of you in thine application of thy opportunities in this material experience.

For unless ye are happy in the knowledge of thy opportunity, ye have lost hold on love, on the understanding of self, and what cooperation means.

For as has been given, God is not mocked; and whatsoever each of you sows, *that* must ye also reap.

And as the door has been opened to you, as ye know the Lord thy God is one in thee, hence body, mind, soul must be in the spirit of truth at all times.

Hence the affirmation at this time would be:

-451-

FATHER, GOD, IN THY MERCY, IN THY LOVE, BE THOU WITH US NOW. FOR WE KNOW AND WE SPEAK OF THY LOVE.

AND HELP US THEN TO PUT AWAY, FOR THE HOUR, THE CARES OF THIS LIFE; THAT WE MAY KNOW IN TRUTH THAT THE SPIRIT AND THE LAMB SAY, "COME."

LET THEY THAT HEAR ALSO SAY, "COME."

LET ALL THAT WILL, COME AND DRINK OF THE WATER OF LIFE.

We are through for the present.

This psychic reading was given by Edgar Cayce at the Edmonds' home, 611 Pennsylvania Avenue, Norfolk, Va., on October 10, 1937, at 4:15 P.M., in accordance with a request made by those present: Edgar Cayce; Gertrude Cayce, conductor; Gladys Davis, steno; Hugh Lynn Cayce, Edith Edmonds, Florence Edmonds, Helen Ellington, Ruth LeNoir, Hannah Miller, Frances Y. Morrow, Helen Storey, and Esther Wynne.

ⅹ 262-114 ⅹ

Mrs. Cayce: You will have before you Group #1, members of which are present here, and its work on the lesson Spirit. *You will continue the discourse on this lesson and answer the questions.*

Mr. Cayce: Yes, we have the group as gathered here—and their work on the lesson *Spirit.*

As has been indicated, this is the beginning, the end of self-development—*if* it is applied in the experience of the individuals.

Then it behooves us that we give an interpretation, an explanation, of what is in reality meant when many of the accepted terms are indicated in the individual expression.

This to be sure is a question then within the realm of the metaphysical as well as in the material.

Then we should be able to answer ever for the cause, the purpose that we have within us, for every question that may arise respecting such.

The spirit of the times! What do we mean?

The spirit of the age! We here speak of the spirit of America, the spirit of '76, the spirit of the pioneer! What do we mean?

We hear again of the spirit of Fascism, the spirit of the Japanese. What do we mean?

The Spirit of God, the Spirit of Christ, the spirit of the Church, the spirit of truth—what do we mean?

It has been given, has it not, that there is *one* spirit?

Then what is the meaning of this confusion of words?

When we speak of the spirit of the departed, what do we mean? From whence arose such terms?

Again it has been given that we know nothing that we have not experienced in this material world. What is meant?

When the Master spoke to Peter and said—". . . flesh and

blood hath not revealed *it* unto thee, but my Father which is in heaven"—was that an indication that the spirit is divided? Is the same meant when He said a few minutes later "Get thee behind me, Satan—thou savourest not the things that be of God (the spirit), but those that be of men (the earth)"?

What is the spirit of the earth? What has He given?

These then must be questions; not only questions but answers. For as they have been asked of us here, they must in truth be answered in such a manner that we—each of us—may make them practical, applicable, practical in our experiences day by day.

Then we must begin, my beloved, at the beginning of how, where, when such things came to be a terminology; or expressed in such manners that there appeared to be, or *appears* to be, or *may* appear to be, a diffusion, a separation; that only those who *have* the desire for the seeking and knowing the truth *may* correctly interpret.

For remember, as has been given by Him, flesh and blood may *not* reveal it unto us—it is the gift of the Father; that we may be lights unto the children of men, to those that sit in darkness, to those that are confused, to those that have made their opportunities stumbling stones rather than stepping-stones.

But these must then answer, ever, in all good conscience, to all that seek to know.

Then the basic or first causes, as spirit came to materiality, must be sought out. And to be understandable to man, to be comprehended by all, they—the first causes, the answers—must conform to that which has been ever given, in *any* condition, in *any* experience of man in his seeking in this material world. They must answer for that which was, that which is, and that which will be.

Then we must know from whence we came; how, why; and whence we go—and why.

In God's own purpose, spirit is His presence then. For the Spirit of God moved and that which is in matter came into being, for the opportunities of His associates, His companions, His sons, His daughters. These are ever spoken of as one.

Then there came that as sought for self-indulgence, self-glorification; and there was the beginning of warring among themselves for activity—*still* in spirit.

Then those that had made selfish movements moved into that which was and is *opportunity,* and there came life into same.

Then what was the spirit that moved that made rebellion? The Spirit of God or the spirit of self?

This becomes self-evident even when we look about us in our own experience day by day. They that have the Spirit of God have the spirit of truth, have the Spirit of Christ, have the spirit of construction.

They that have the spirit of rebellion have the spirit of hate, the spirit of confusion; and seek self-glory rather than peace, harmony and understanding.

Thus as has been indicated, the spirit pushed into matter— and became what we see in our three-dimensional world as the kingdoms of the earth; the mineral, the vegetable, the animal —a three-dimensional world.

And that which beareth witness is the spirit of truth, the spirit of light. For He said, "Let there be light; and there was light."

Then indeed there is no power that emanates that is not from God.

Then what is this spirit of rebellion, what is this spirit of hate? What is this spirit of self-indulgence? What is this spirit that makes men afraid?

Selfishness! Allowed, yes, of the Father. For, as given, He has not willed that the souls should perish but that we each should know the truth—and the truth would make us free. Of what? Selfishness!

Then we should each know that the sin which lies at our door is ever the sin of selfishness, self-glory, self-honor.

Hence as the Master has said, unless we become even as He, we may not in *any* wise enter in.

Enter to what? To the consciousness that our Father would that we be even as that spirit of truth manifested by the Son of righteousness, that—even as those souls—took on flesh in this three-dimensional world; becoming a part, a parcel of what? Those kingdoms of which the earth is a part; or that by their very presence is in existence.

Hence we find He had come, is come, ever has come into the experience that He might through love—not force, not hate, not by command but by edification and justification—bring that soul that is dominated by the spirit to understanding.

Thus we find His intervention in man's attempt throughout the eons of time and space. For these (time and space) become portions of this three-dimensional plane. And what is the other? Time, space, patience!

For God has shown and does show us day by day, even as His Son gave, that in patience we become aware of our souls, of our identity, of our being each a corpuscle, as it were, in the great body, in the heart of, our God. And He has not willed otherwise.

Then what is the Spirit of God? *Patience, time and space* in the material understanding.

This then is our first premise; that God *is*—in the material experience of man—*time, space, patience!*

For have not even our own wise ones conceived that those elements between that which is and that which will be are of the same? What? God, the Spirit!

We in our seeking then have seen the movements in the earth, by the very activities of those influences, by what? "Where two or three are gathered together in my name, there am I in the midst of them." Either to do good or to do evil, according to our individual application of the spirit of truth or of Creative Force in our material experience.

Who then is the aggressor? He that seeks to glorify self, to make the selfish motives guide the progress.

And as has so oft been given in times past, God has winked at and God has allowed such things to pass; yet ever is calling —calling—to the sons of God; that we make straight the paths! For He will not *always* hold to those things that rend the heart of God.

For when we are raised in power we know, as we have seen, that our spirit beareth witness with *His Spirit* that we are His children.

What then is the spirit of patriotism, the Spirit of Christ— yes, the spirit of knowledge, but that—as they are individual- ized by the activity of those that seek to know and make the paths straight—they take on that power, that might, yes that glory, that is the magnifying of that spirit of truth that is God in any individual group, nation or experience of man?

These then become those basic beginnings.

Now we, in our individual selves, seek—for what? Self-glory, self-understanding; or that we may be in His place as an emissary, a missionary, a *channel* through which *others,* too, may know that the consciousness of Christ is but that we have effaced self and are again one with Him—to be a purpose in the scheme of redemption for those souls whose spirits are a portion of the God as ourselves?

Let us indeed know then that God is not mocked, and that what we sow we must meet in our own selves. For He calls always unto all men to come— *come*—and take of the water of life.

What is this water of life? What is this that the spirit and the bride, or the spirit and the Lamb, say to come and take of freely?

Patience, time, space! That we may know ourselves to be His; that our spirits, our souls, bear witness in the things that we do in which we bear witness of Him.

For that which has a beginning must have an ending. Hence rebellion and hate and selfishness must be wiped away, and *with it* will go sorrow and tears and sadness. For *only* good shall rule. For it is the Spirit of God that will move over the face of the earth, and Lo, His Son—even Jesus, the Christ—has borne in Himself all these things, and has committed unto us the keeping of His sheep, His lambs, till He come to make an accounting with each of us.

Where—where—where will we be?

This psychic reading was given by Edgar Cayce at the Edmonds' home, 611 Pennsylvania Avenue, Norfolk, Va., on October 24, 1937, at 4:00 P.M., in accordance with a request made by those present: Edgar Cayce; Gertrude Cayce, conductor; Gladys Davis, steno; Hugh Lynn Cayce, Edith Edmonds, Florence Edmonds, Helen Ellington, Ruth LeNoir, Hannah Miller, Noah Miller, Frances Y. Morrow, and Esther Wynne.

≽ 262-115 ≼

Mrs. Cayce: You will have before you Norfolk Study Group #1, members of which are present here, and their work on the lesson Spirit. *You will continue the discourse on this lesson, and answer the questions asked.*

Mr. Cayce: Yes, we have the group as gathered here; as a group, as individuals, and their work on the lesson *Spirit.*

In continuing with that which has been given, it would be well—as has been outlined—that we each ask within ourselves that which would enable each of us to correlate these interpretations with our experiences.

For as has been given oft, unless we are able to make the lessons practical in our own experience, how will we ask others to interpret or apply them?

In answering then the questions that pertain to spirit and its relationships to man in his *present* estate in the material plane:

All *spirit* is *one.* How?

Just as all force, all power emanates from that influence, that essence, that consciousness, that awareness which the consciousness of man—or man as the image of the Creator—worships.

How then is man a part of spirit? How does he live, move, have his being in that Creative Force?

How does man differ from other animate, inanimate beings or matter in the material plane?

As has been given, error or separation began before there appeared what we know as the earth, the heavens; or before space was manifested.

This becomes hard to conceive in the finite mind; as does the finite mind fail to grasp the lack of or *no* time. Yet out of time, space, patience, is it possible for the consciousness of the finite to *know* the infinite.

Hence, then, the interpretations of spirit as it manifests to the sons of men must follow closely what we have chosen as Holy Writ.

Before this began (this not as history but as the basis of the interpretation), we have had how one Amilius with that projection of self brought into being the awareness of desires as related to relationships with the beings—or matter—about.

Hence there began what is *now* known as the correlating, or the cohesive activity, or the relativity of matter as it relates to what becomes positive and negative.

Remember, negative is only error.

Then, these make for this activity through those influences in thine own earth, thine own sphere, of which you have begun to catch a glimpse here or there as to their activities. And our own earth, our own sphere, as we realize more and more, is only a speck, only a dot in the universe.

Then why, as has been said, is God mindful of an individual soul?

Spirit! For our spirit, that is a portion of His Spirit, ever bears witness with His Spirit as to whether we be the children of God or not.

Then through Mu, Oz, Atlantis—with the breaking up of these—why, *why* no records of these if there were the civilizations that are ordinarily accredited to them by the interpreting of the records made by entities or souls upon the skein of what? Time and space!

But he only that has recognized patience within self may indeed make the record as an experience in the consciousness of any.

Each individual spirit then is only a portion of His Spirit. Not that God is separated. But in His love, in what we call infinite love, boundless, the unbounding grace and mercy and patience and love and long-suffering, these have brought to the Father the thought of the lack of, the wonderment of, companionship.

But we, as we see in our *own* experiences about us, must earn —yes, must measure up—yes, must conceive of its existence before we may enjoy, before we may know and have the awareness, the consciousness of the existence of such experiences in our *own* understanding, our own comprehension.

Then, as the sons of God came together and saw in the earth the unspeakable conditions becoming more and more for self-indulgence, self-glorification, the ability to procreate through the very forces of their activity, we find that our Lord, our Brother, *chose* to measure up, to earn, to *attain* that companionship for man with the Father through the overcoming of *self* in the physical plane.

By choice we know His companionship, and by will we exercise our choice. And He is ever willing, ready to give us all the power, all the influence to bring love, light, into our own active consciousness.

And He does so as we apply ourselves; not unmindful though is He of our weaknesses throughout our experiences in the earth, in the sojourns. For He came as those activities when man was in the beginning of what we have recorded as that God brought light.

What is light, then, in that sense? In that city, in that place, there is no need of the sun, nor of the moon, nor the stars; for He is the *light;* He *is* light, and in Him is no darkness at all!

"Let there be light," then, was that consciousness that time began to be a factor in the experience of those creatures that had entangled themselves in matter; and became what we know as the influences in a material plane. And the moving force and the life in each, and the activities in each are from the spirit.

Hence as we see, the divisions were given then for the day, the night; and then man knew that consciousness that made him aware that the morning and the evening were the first day.

What is our experience? Have we visioned, have we understood, have we even attempted to comprehend what is the meaning of the evening and the morning being the first day of an infant entering the material plane? a soul taking on flesh, its attributes, its whole experiences in heaven, in earth, in all the influences about the earth?

Let us each study same. We will catch a new vision of what time and space begin to mean. Then we know that with patience you mothers have waited and known from this or that experience those awakenings, those awarenesses of the activity; and we see the creation of the world, as the awareness of these influences that have become enmeshed, entangled into matter; that are seeking they know not what.

For that desire to procreate in self, or to hold to selfish interests, has grown—grown—until it *is*—what did He give?—the prince of this world; the prince of this world!

Know that He who came as our Director, as our Brother, as our Savior, has said that the prince of this world has no part in Him nor with Him.

Then as we become more and more aware within ourselves of the answering of the experiences, we become aware of what He gave to those that were the first of *God's* projection—not man's but God's projection—into the earth; Adam and Eve.

And then in their early day they were tempted by the prince of this world, and partook of same.

When we see that in ourselves, yes in our own sons, in our own daughters, in our own brothers, in our own husbands, in our own wives, we begin to see how, why that patience becomes a part of that which is the awareness in man of God's presence in the earth.

And we see the ways and means through which such activities were presented to those children that were bestowed with the very power of God, yet not aware of right and wrong. For they were *in* a world ruled by the prince of selfishness, darkness, hate, malice, jealousy, backbiting, uncomely things; not of the beauties, but that self might be taking advantage in this or that way or manner.

What moves the spirit of these activities? *God,* but—will and choice misdirected.

And these then show the mercy and the patience that He gives forth to each soul in this speck, this dot in the universe. Yet He would have each soul, each one of us, to become even as He—even as He prayed: "Father, may they be with me where I am; that they may behold the glory I had with thee before the foundations of the world."

What do these words mean to us? That the spirit has quickened us, so that we seek to manifest what? His mercy, His grace, His patience among our fellow men.

And He has given His angels charge concerning us, that they bear us up, if we will but make ourselves as one with Him.

Then, as there were the disputations in themselves, their blaming in the sons or among the sons of God in this material world, there became the peopling of the earth with what? That they had themselves made, even as Amilius, even as in those lands and countries where even with their worldly knowledge as children of God their activities had gone to seed in that which is selfishness, self-destruction.

We may see this, we know this in our own experience from the very fields, yes in our very homes: When that which has grown to seed and blossomed in our experience, if selfishness began it then the seed must be hate, avarice, those things that are the fruits of same. For these are the lessons that we see in those things which came to those children of men. Yet He but the second comes and He is known as He that walks with God. He preached, yes practiced, what? Love, patience, obedience; and the world knew Him not. Why? For as He has given, when He again and again has come into the earth, to the sons of men, the world knows us not.

Then seek not worldly fame, worldly recognition, you that are sowing the seeds of truth in your lessons, in your meditations. Because this day or this generation seeks not that as you may understand. *Know* that you cannot do but sow. God giveth the increase. But *cultivate* that you sow in your daily experiences.

We are through for the present.

This psychic reading was given by Edgar Cayce at his home on Arctic Crescent, Virginia Beach, Va., on December 19, 1937, at 3:45 P.M., in accordance with a request made by those present: Edgar Cayce; Gertrude Cayce, conductor; Gladys Davis, steno; Hugh Lynn Cayce, C. A. Barrett, Minnie Barrett, M. L. Black, Mildred Davis, Edith Edmonds, Florence Edmonds, Helen Ellington, Ruth LeNoir, Hannah Miller, F. Y. Morrow, Helen Storey, Esther Wynne.

⊱ 262-116 ⊰

Mrs. Cayce: You will have before you the various members of the Norfolk Study Groups assembled here. You will consider the study of spiritual laws as being made by these groups and give, as I call each name, at this time a personal Christmas message that may be of help.

Mr. Cayce: Yes, we have the group as gathered here; as a group, as individuals and their study of spiritual law.

First, we would give as a message for all:

As ye approach the season that to every student of Christian thought means so much, know that the birth of the Christ-child in Jesus has meant and does mean more and more in the thought and the activity of the world as a whole. And you each here may judge within yourselves as to whether the world is growing better or not according to that conviction, that feeling within thine own self that what the Christ-mass or Christmas spirit means is being manifested in thy daily life and thy associations with thy fellow men.

For unless this fact is a personal experience, then to you — as an individual — it is not being accomplished.

But you each here, with only few exceptions (and these ye know within thine own hearts), feel that the peace within — as comes from the meditating upon the desire to be what the Father-God would have thee be through the promises in the Christ-Jesus — *is* making thy life, thy associations with thy fellow man, more and more in keeping with the Christmas spirit; that commandment as He gave, "A new commandment give I unto you, that ye love one another, even as I have loved you."

Ready for questions.

Q-1. First, [1223]:

A-1. Let that light, that love, which was manifested in the

-463-

mother, the Child, be in thee; that thy lights may shine unto the earth, that needs the love that is shown in *thy* life.

Q-2. [*1223's husband*]:

A-2. Keep thy paths straight. Know in whom ye have believed, as well as in what ye believe. For the love as passeth understanding *can,* does and will make thy pathway brighter. Keep in that way.

Q-3. [*1003*]:

A-3. Let the beauty of thy joy, in manifesting the light and love as shown in the Christ Spirit, that makes for the new song in thy heart, *keep* thee in thy *daily* walks of life.

Q-4. [*585*]:

A-4. Let others do as they may, but as for thee and thy house, ye will love the *living* God. *Know* His love is sufficient to keep thee. No matter what may be the trial, His love abideth, and He is *not* unmindful of thy prayers.

Q-5. [*560*]:

A-5. The beauty of thy life riseth as a sweet incense before the altar of mercy. Yet it is not sacrifice but peace, grace and mercy that we would manifest among the children of men. For God is love.

Q-6. [*478*]:

A-6. Love mercy and justice, eschew evil; and keep thy heart *singing* all the while. For the joy of the service in the love of the Lord maketh the heart glad. Look not upon those things that make for disturbing influences, as of an evil force. For God so *loved* the world as to give His Son, that we through Him might know *eternal* life!

Q-7. [*462*]:

A-7. "In my Father's house are many mansions," saith the Lord of lords. And as we keep His ways we come to know *how* that out of sorrow cometh *joy*—if the peace of the Lord is *in* same. But if there is kept a hate, a grudge, it bringeth rust and corruption. Let the Lord's ways be thy ways, and the Christmas joy fill thy heart.

Q-8. [*5001*]:

A-8. As ye are trusted among thy fellow man, so hath the Lord put thee in the way to do good; even to those that may at times despitefully use thee. Then, let the love of the Father, as was manifested in Jesus the Christ, so rule thy life that love, mercy and peace replaces questionings and hate and grudges in thine own life. See not the mote in the lives of others, rather magnify the grace and good that is in *each* life, and speak evil of *no* man!

Q-9. [*2468*]:

A-9. Let patience, love and mercy be thy watchwords. *Practice* them in thy daily life. For in so doing ye bring into thy experience all the joy, all the expectancy, all the anticipation of a closer walk with Him—which is indeed the Christ-mass spirit.

Q-10. [*618*]:

A-10. Keep the faith thou hast set, for His love, His mercy, is able to sustain thee ever, and His grace—yea, His patience —endureth forever. Then be thou a little more patient, a little more gracious, and ye will find the love unchangeable, and His presence abiding closer.

Q-11. [*1467*]:

A-11. In the desire of the heart is there the activity of the mental self. Keep thy mind, then, attuned to "Not my will, O God, but Thine be done in and through me." And as ye hear the still small voice within, *answer "Here* am I, O Lord, *use me —send me!"*

Q-12. [*578*]:

A-12. Love and mercy and grace casteth out fear. Then, as ye magnify these in thy daily associations—yea, thy daily conversation—ye will find grace and mercy shown thee; and *His* presence—yea, His voice—coming close, closer—yet still, to thee.

Q-13. [*1970*]:

A-13. "Peace I leave with you, my peace I give unto you" saith He that *is* the Lord, the Master, the keeper of those that would know Him. Then let His laws, yea His precepts, be thine. Love the Lord thy God, with all thy heart, thy mind, thy body; and thy neighbor as thyself. For this is the whole law, and in it ye will find strength and grace and mercy sufficient to *keep* thee at all times.

Q-14. [*1834*]:

A-14. In the way of truth, in the way of light, is security and strength. And as ye walk therein, ye will find His hand guiding thee—if ye do so for the very love of Him that gave, "Come—learn of me, for my yoke is easy, my burden is light," to *those* that love the Lord!

Q-15. [*303*]:

A-15. Let thy light so shine that others taking note may take heart also. For the Lord loveth thee and keepeth thee in the shadow of His wing. Then let mercy and grace and peace abide with thee. Be not faultfinding ever, for when ye find fault, ye may be sure others find fault with thee. Let peace, then, and mercy, guide thy *words,* and thy activities, day by day.

Q-16. [*1374*]:

A-16. Study to show thyself approved unto God, a workman *not* ashamed but rightly dividing the words of truth, and keeping *self* unspotted from that ye question in thy neighbor. The Lord keep thee, the Lord bless thee—if ye will walk in the way that ye know!

Q-17. [*5773*]:

A-17. Let thy light so shine that it will lighten the way for those that are stumbling here and there about thee. For as ye hold His hand, that *is* the light, as He *was* lifted up, so will ye —with Him—draw many to the way of truth and light; and thus indeed do ye show the spirit of the Christ in thy life.

Q-18. [*993*]:

A-18. Let thy heart be glad in the service of thy Father, thy Brother, yea in the light of Jesus' way. For He walks with thee and talks with thee when ye open thy mind, thy heart, in a service for thy fellow man. Then even as He, *lose* self in service. For "He that would be the greatest among you, let him be the servant of all."

Q-19. [*307*]:

A-19. In trials, tribulations, temptations even, there may be seen the hand of the Lord—if ye do not blame others for same. Then let that thou knowest in the heart of God—mercy, justice, peace and love—be thine in thy *every* walk; yea, in thy every activity. For the Lord hath called thee to service, and will direct thee—if ye will keep His ways. For the Christ Consciousness awakens, arouses thy consciousness to a greater and greater service to others.

Q-20. [*379*]:

A-20. The strength of the Lord preserve thee, the blessings of His countenance shine upon thee! For though the days at times grow hard, and the way seems to be out of the direction sought, yet know He is mindful of thee, and will not allow thee to be tempted nor persecuted, nor disappointed, beyond thy capacity to serve. Then, let that love as is manifested at this season in the Christ-mass spirit be the light to thy feet and the guiding way to thy desires—in the Lord.

Q-21. [413]:

A-21. In love and mercy and justice ye see and know the love of the Father hath shown upon the children of men, yet the children of men wander so far afield! Yet into thy hands and to thy brethren's hands is given the ways, the means, the manners of making known this love unto others. For as ye live it, day by day, ye constrain others to seek to know His ways. The Lord bless thee, the Lord preserve thee, the Lord make thee glad in thy heart! For His ways are thy ways. *Keep* that faith!

Q-22. [1237]:

A-22. Let light and mercy keep thee. Let the spirit of love abide, as was shown by Him—who would have thee know the world is the Lord's and the ways are not past finding out if ye will seek to know them. For they alone bring joy, peace and love.

Q-23. [1129]:

A-23. In keeping the lights of love ye walk in the paths that thy Savior—yea, that Jesus—trod; to do good even when lightly and slightly spoken of; to show mercy and judgment even when considered to be a little "off"; to be kind and patient. This is keeping the Lord's ways, and though they may bring at times discouragement and wonderment, know He *is* mindful and will protect thee. For His promises are sure, and what ye ask in His name believing ye will have in thy experience.

Q-24. [361]:

A-24. His ways ye know. Then let the love of the Father direct thee in thy dealings with thy fellow man. And as the Christ-mass spirit brings the desire to forgive, the desire to make the paths bright, the desire to make for joy in the life, in the heart of someone, let that spirit keep thee day by day. For *His* ways are the *only* ways of eternal life!

Q-25. [263]:

A-25. In the love of the Father is all desire, all hope. And if ye will make His ways thy ways, then thy life, thy hopes, thy desires grow! For in giving happiness to others it grows in the giving. In finding peace within self ye are able to bring peace into the lives and the experiences of others. For God is not mocked, and as ye sow, so must ye reap. The Lord love thee, the Lord keep thee—in His ways!

Then to *all:*

Let that love, that beauty as was the message to the shepherds, be thine today: "Unto *thee* is born," yea unto thee—each one here—is given a knowledge, an understanding of the *life* of the Christ that will *renew* thy life, thy purposes—if ye will but *sing* that new song, "Love one another."

We are through for the present.

This psychic reading was given by Edgar Cayce at the home of Mrs. Helen Storey, 2709 Lafayette Boulevard, Norfolk, Va., on February 27, 1938, at 4:00 P.M., in accordance with a request made by those present: Edgar Cayce; Gertrude Cayce, conductor; Gladys Davis, steno; Hugh Lynn Cayce, Helen Ellington, Hannah Miller, Frances Y. Morrow, Helen Storey, and Esther Wynne.

⊰ 262-117 ⊱

Mrs. Cayce: You will have before you Group #1, members of which are present here, and their study of the lesson Spirit. *You will answer the questions that have been prepared on this.*

Mr. Cayce: Yes, we have the group as gathered here; and their work on the lesson *Spirit.*

There has not been the completion of that which has been outlined for the group study, nor for their work on same.

This then should be very much more complete, for you have only gotten the effects and are questioning these rather than the cause or the conception of that which moves the individuals in the activity of the study and presentation of that as may be helpful in the preparation to others.

Rather would we question those here, than be questioned:

What is *spirit?* God of heaven, of the universe, of the state, of the nation, of the home, of thyself?

Are these one in thy conception? Then *why* do ye not act like that?

What is thy relation to thy home, thy community, thy county, thy state; thy church, thy nation; thy God? Are these one? Then *why* is there not better cooperation in thy home, in thy relations to thy home, thy church, thy country, thy state?

What is that spirit that moves thee to find fault with thy brother, thy neighbor? Is that in keeping with what ye believe? Is that how ye will spend eternity? Is that what ye would have thy Savior, thy God, be? Then *why* is not thy life more in accord with that ye profess that ye believe? *God is!* Thy spirit is in the Maker. Then what are ye doing about that in thy daily conversation, in thy daily proclaiming of this or that as comes into thy experience?

Ye believe that good and right and justice live *on,* and are continuous in thy experience. Yet ye find fault with what this

-469-

or that person may have said, may have done, may have looked; or may have failed to say or do.

What manner of spirit, then, hast thou directing thy life? Look within. See thyself, that which has motivated thee in thy dealings with thy fellow man; or as to what ye have proclaimed is thy concept, thy thought of thy Creator.

Have ye opened thy heart, thy desires to Him? Are they in keeping with that thou would have meted to thee, to thy fellow man, to thy Maker, to thy Savior?

Does the Spirit of the Master and the Father abide with thee? This is His promise. "If ye love me, I will come and abide with thee." Have ye driven Him from thy home, thy church, thy state? yea, from thine own consciousness?

Have ye not rather entertained the anti-Christ?

Have ye considered as to *who* is the author of thy activities day by day? yea, in thy dealings with those in thy home, in thy neighborhood, in thy city, in thy state? Have ye not preferred one above another?

Is that the spirit of truth? Is that the consciousness with which He that is the author of thy faith ministered to those He met day by day?

Has He changed? Have the circumstances, the environs, the times changed? Are not time, space and patience in thy consciousness a manifestation rather of His love, His patience, His long-suffering, His activities with the children of men?

Art thou wiser in thy own conceit than He?

Do ye day by day, in *every* way, say *"Thy will, not mine, be done"*? Rather do ye not say, "Bless me and my house, my son, my children, my kinfolks; for we are a little better and we do a little better"? Do ye not excuse thyself?

Be these in keeping with spirit as ye now conceive, as ye now understand?

Then gather together, even as He gave; "Let not your hearts be troubled; ye believe in God, believe also in me. And I go to the Father, and if ye love me ye will keep my commandments. For my commandments are not grievous, but are *living* and *doing* day by day those things that ye *know* to do!"

Patience, love, gentleness! Not gainsaying, not finding fault!

These be the little things, yet bespeak that fact that ye have known, ye do know, and ye entertain the Spirit of the Christ!

If ye do these, then, there is no question as to whether "I shall do this or that," for the Spirit of the Christ will and does direct thee! if ye live the Christ-life!

We are through for the present.

This psychic reading was given by Edgar Cayce at the home of Mrs. Helen Storey, 2709 Lafayette Boulevard, Norfolk, Va., on April 10, 1938, at 4:10 P.M., in accordance with a request made by those present: Edgar Cayce; Gertrude Cayce, conductor; Gladys Davis, steno; Helen Ellington, Ruth LeNoir, Hannah Miller, Frances Y. Morrow, Helen Storey, and Esther Wynne.

 ⊰ 262-118 ⊱

Mrs. Cayce: You will have before you Group #1, members of which are gathered here, and their study of the lesson Spirit. *You will give to each at this time, as I call the names, that needed to enable them to understand and make practical application of this lesson:*

Mr. Cayce: Yes, we have the group as gathered here, and their work on the lesson *Spirit.*

As to that which may be helpful for each, we find they each have their individual problems which to them as individuals often supersede their activities as related to spirit manifestation in their lives—as related to others.

This may be that which has been referred to by some as the latent sin in all through Adam. Yet you as students, as seekers should have gathered—as has been indicated—that the more there is the effacement of self the more there may be magnified in your activity the spirit of truth.

What has He given? "If ye will love me, if ye will keep my commandments, I and the Father will come and abide with thee."

This does not signify, then, that your individual problems are to be neglected, forgotten nor thrown aside; but rather that you —as the spirit moves you in the *doing* of the commandments of the Son in the Father—*will* show forth, in your dealings with others, that your problems are *His* problems—and that you live as such.

What then are His commandments? He has given that "Thou shalt love the Lord with all thy heart, thy mind, thy body; thy neighbor as thyself." As He has given, this is the whole law.

Because ordinances of secular organizations have adopted this or that manner of expressing the adherence or the consecrating of self for service in His vineyard, these—as ye accept them as individuals—become a portion of thy individual experience. But the whole law is bound in that as He gave, "And a new commandment I give unto you, that ye love one another, even as I have loved you."

These are to many but sayings, so trite that ye have stumbled or do stumble over the spirit of same.

Ready for names.

Q-1. [*379*]:

A-1. Let thy meditation, thy prayer ever be: "Father, God! In that Thou hast given to me the Christ Consciousness, may I—in my daily walks before my fellow man—manifest the spirit of the Christ; in humbleness, in love, in patience, in long-suffering; that I indeed may manifest the spirit of the Christ Consciousness."

Q-2. [*404*]:

A-2. Let *thy* prayer be: "Lord, Thy will not mine be done in and through me! May I hear, may I see in those about me the love of the Father for the children of men! May I so act, so mete in my daily conversation, in my daily activity, giving the spirit of truth—even as the Son gave; and condemned no man! May I then condemn none, that I be not condemned."

Q-3. [*303*]:

A-3. Hold thou to this in thy prayer, set in the order with thy own problems: "Lord, let me fill that place, that purpose in the lives of those I contact day by day, that the spirit of truth as manifest in Jesus the Christ may be magnified in my speech, my activity; that others may see, may know that I walk, that I talk with thee often! Let that which has been be as passed. Let me look up, into the face of the Christ, with the pure purpose that each word, each act may be in the true spirit of the Christ-life."

Q-4. [*413*]:

A-4. Let thy conversation, thy prayer be: "Lord, here am I—use me in the way that I may be a living message known of those whom I meet, with whom I am associated day by day, as one who lives that professed in the heart and in the speech day by day." Not looking to sorrow or joy, but rather being glad

within for being counted worthy as one that may be an ensample before others of the truth and the spirit of the truth—as
shown in the Christ-life.

"Let my yeas be yea, my nays be nay, but with that graciousness, that beauty as He manifested in His speech with and in
His walks among men day by day. For I, O Father, would be
like unto Him!"

Q-5. [585]:

A-5. In thy problems, in thy cares, take them all to Him in
the spirit of truth and love that He expressed and manifested
to those with whom He walked and talked as in the flesh; "As
ye abide in me and I in you, so may the Father be glorified in
me." For in so living, speaking, acting before others is the spirit
of the Father—which is thy birthright—manifested. And what
does this bring into thy consciousness? That awareness, that
joy, that peace which He has promised, and that is a part of thy
inheritance in Him—the peace that passeth understanding;
the assurance that thou art His and that He is thine! Make thy
wants known to Him. For He is mindful of thy cries. Keep the
face, then, towards the light of the Christ, and the sorrow and
care will fade.

Q-6. [307]:

A-6. Ask and ye shall receive, saith the Lord who is thy
keeper. Then in thy prayer, thy meditation, call ye on Him. For
He is not afar off. And with the spirit of love that is His commandment to thee, "that ye love one another" ask in His name.

Sow the seeds of truth, but *do not* continue to scratch them
up—but leave the results, the increase to Him.

Sow that as ye would have thy Father do, and say, to thee.
For the Lord hath called thee to an excellent service, to thy
fellow man. Then let His ways be thy ways, His people be thy
people, His prayers thy prayers, His messages thy messages;
and ye *will* in the spirit of the Christ *bring* an awakening in
the minds and the hearts of those who seek to know Him.

Q-7. [560]:

A-7. In thy study of spirit and the application of same in thy
daily life, let thy prayer, thy supplication be: "Father, Thou
knowest my heart, my mind, my body. Make it all one with

Thee; that I may in Thy pleasure, in Thy purposes, be more and more a manifestation of Thy love to the children of men.

"Help me, O Father, to put away—more and more—the cares of this world and look to Thee as the author and the finisher of faith; as the manifestation of that which is good, which is holy, which is right in the earth. And let me, O God, in my dealings, in my conversation with and my invocation before men, be a living example of the truth of the *Christ* in the earth."

Q-8. [*993*]:

A-8. In thy seeking for wisdom, know that it is not of the earth-earthy. Then let thy prayer, thy meditation be—as ye study the lesson of *Spirit* and the activity in same be as this; for ye know it is not what is said but the spirit with which it is given that makes it a living thing or a burden to someone's soul. "Father, let that love Thou hast promised in the Christ be in me and my life—yea, in my conversation to my fellow man. Let me so forget myself—yea, the needs of the earthly body—that I may the more magnify the love that is shown in the spirit of the Christ-life.

"Let my activities be of such a nature that there is never a doubt shown, a fear manifested. For love indeed casts out doubt and fear. And may I live such an experience that the glory of the Christ Spirit directs—yea, builds—as the builder indeed— in the lives and the hearts of those I meet day by day.

"Let this be, O God, a living thing in my experience! For the spirit of truth *must* prevail! Let *me,* O God, be a channel through which the spirit is directed!"

Q-9 [*462*]:

A-9. In thy meditation, in thy seeking, know that the answer must come within. For His Spirit beareth witness with thy spirit, and ye know within thy own self as to whether ye are conscious of His abiding presence or not. Then let thy prayer be: "O Father, leave me not alone, but come, strengthen Thou me in my weakness! Make me strong in the might and in the purposes that Thou would use me, O God, in such a way and manner that others whom I meet day by day may be constrained to glorify Thee.

"The cares of life and of the earth at times grow heavy, yet Thou, O God, knowest the way! Be Thou the guide in my daily conversation, in my daily dealings with my fellow man. For the Christ promised that when we ask in His name Thou wilt not be slow to answer.

"Keep Thou my ways, O God!"

Q-10. [*288*]:

A-10. In thy study of spirit, know there is the influence of body, of mind, of soul. These are manifested in the material plane as an individual entity. Just as the Father, the Son, the Holy Spirit is an individual entity. Just as time and space and patience are the individual manifestation of that spirit-body in the experiences of man.

Then, as ye pray, and as ye think on these things, let thy cry —yea, let the purpose of thy heart be: "Lord, use Thou me in the ways and manners Thou seest that I may be the greater blessings—in my weak way—before the children of men! Lord, Thou knowest my heart! Make it one with Thee, even as the Christ in the material plane made His life one with Thee!

"In my weakness I often go amiss, I often am stirred to rebellion in the experiences I see in the children of men. Let me, O Father, be patient, be kind to such; even as the Christ was with those whom He not only blessed but upon whose bodies He poured out His love in such measures that others might be physically and mentally healed even by their presence.

"Thou art the same, O God, yesterday, today and forever! Then give to me that strength, that measure of love that Thou seest I may use in the *perfect* way in the Spirit of the Christ!"

Q-11. [*341*]:

A-11. In thy study, in thy meditation upon the activities of the spirit, thou seest in the lives of others the motivative influences that are of good and of bad. And yet the same spirit motivates these. For to each soul is given the choice as to whether it will be one with the Father or, even as the son of perdition, attempt to establish self in glory of self. Then as ye meditate and pray: "Father, keep Thou my mind, my heart open to thy calls! May I choose ever the Spirit of the Christ to be the author of my activities day by day. May I be patient and long-suffering. May I be gentle—yea, may I be humble. For

without these, the very activity may become a stumbling block.
Then, keep my heart pure. Renew the righteous spirit within
me, O God! day by day! May I hear again, as in the days of yore,
the voice of the Christ as He calls to men to *renew* their faith
and *manifest* their love of God in their dealings with their
fellow man.

"May I fill that purpose whereunto Thou hast called me into
service in the vineyard of the Christ, and may I fill it with that
spirit that He manifested when He gave, 'Father, I condemn
them not—they know not what they do.' "

Q-12. [*294*]:

A-12. We are through for the present.

This psychic reading was given by Edgar Cayce at his home on Arctic Crescent, Virginia Beach, Va., on May 22, 1938, at 4:20 P.M., in accordance with a request made by those present: Edgar Cayce; Gertrude Cayce, conductor; Gladys Davis, steno; Florence Edmonds, Helen Ellington, Hannah Miller, Noah Miller, and Frances Y. Morrow.

≫ 262-119 ≪

Mrs. Cayce: You will have before you Norfolk Study Group #1, members of which are present here, and their work on the lesson Spirit, *a copy of which I hold in my hand. You will continue the discourse on this lesson, and answer the questions that may be asked.*

Mr. Cayce: Yes, we have the group as gathered here; as a group, as individuals, and their work on the lesson *Spirit.*

In continuing with the discussion of that which may make the lesson and spirit understandable in the mind and the experience, much of that which has been given *should* be studied and dwelt upon—in the mind of each.

Remember, as ye do this, that which has been given; the spirit maketh alive, the mind is the builder, the application is the experience in the individual life.

Just so have we seen and comprehended how that there is the Father, the Son, the Holy Spirit. The spirit is the movement; as when God—the First Cause—called into being *light* as a manifestation of the influences that would, through their movement (light movement) upon forces yet unseen, bring into being what we know as the universe—or matter; in all its forms, phases, manifestations.

As it has been indicated and given of old, no man hath seen God at any time. Yet they who have seen and who now may experience the consciousness of the Christ-presence, as manifested in flesh in Jesus, have known *of* God, have seen the figure of Him in what the Christ purposed to do, in the desire with which He acted with and upon those influences and forces of the earth.

And as He gave or taught, we become aware of same through dwelling upon mentally and through applying physically those

-478-

things we know that partake of that which brings the awareness.

Yet we know, or find, that the kingdom of heaven is within;
and that the awareness, the awakening comes from within.

Then through faith, through the gift of the Son and the faith
in Him, we become more and more aware of the abiding presence of the spirit—the movement—as prompted by the Father;
and not of self.

Ready for questions.

*Q-1. Please comment on the treatment of the outline, page 3,
"From Whence We Came, How and Why."*

A-1. This has been commented upon heretofore. As has been
indicated, the purpose of the spirit entering into what we know
as matter is a different condition or phase of condition from the
purpose of entering into spirit as He is spirit.

As those influences or forces entered that took man away
from Him, then it was from that consciousness or spirit that
the individuality had its source, its essence, its influence that
might be made a personality in its activity.

Hence the entrance into matter became as the description
has been given by Stephen, by Philip, by Jesus.

"Know ye not that the Son must go up to Jerusalem, there
be tried, condemned, and die—even the death on the cross?"
Why?

That there might be indeed an advocate, a *way* to the Father
—from the lowest depths of man's desire, man's loathsome-
ness, even in matter.

For if God has not willed that any should perish but has with
every temptation prepared a way to meet it, *who* then—*what,*
then—is the way? The experiences through which man passes,
as God gave in other periods, to become aware of his purpose
for entrance into what we know as materiality. Then, the
awareness of the *way* comes through the *thought* of man, the
faith of man, the *desire* of man such as ever held by that One
who became *righteousness itself;* passing through all the phases
of man's desire in materiality.

Then, what meaneth faith—what meaneth hope—what
meaneth these things in man's experience. There must be the

arousing of that desire for same. Hence how has He put it again? "Indeed it must be that offenses come, but woe unto him by whom they come."

Not that man is awakened all at once, but here a little, there a little, line upon line, precept upon precept. Then as these are applied, as these become a part of the experience of the soul, there becomes the desire of the soul to find its rest, its peace, its hope in Him who is the Author of faith, of hope, of mercy, of love. Thus does the awareness come as to the purposes of man's advent into what we know as materiality.

Thus do we see and comprehend why it was necessary that He, the Son, the Maker, the Creator, come unto His own; who in their blindness, selfishness, hates, spites, have brought and do bring about those influences that keep the heart of man from seeking the way.

But He being the way, offers — whosoever will, let him come and take of the water of life freely.

What is meant then by "the spirit and the Lamb say come"? or "the spirit and the bride saith come"?

It means that whosoever will may take hold upon those things that take man's mind and heart and purpose and *being* away from those things that have made men afraid, that have brought all of these petty conditions, spites, heartaches and disappointments.

Hark ye, when ye are disappointed, when ye are confused, and think for a moment what it must have been for the Son, for Him who had made the earth and who had been given all power therein, to have His own to receive or understand Him not; yea, those of His own household — yea, those who had come through the channel even as He. Is it any wonder that He said (and do ye comprehend?), "Who is my mother, who is my brother, my sister? He that doeth the will of the father, the same is my mother, my brother, my sister"?

These words ye know, but have ye comprehended, have ye understood? For when there has come the slight here, the harsh word there, or the disappointment, have ye smiled and with a song upon thy heart said, "Thy will, O God, not mine, be done"?

Until ye do, ye cannot comprehend the purpose for which the

souls of men came into materiality; for periods of lessons, of examinations.

Know that to be absent from the body is to be present with thy conscience, thy god. What is thy god? Is it self or Christ? Is it self or the Lord? Is it thy own desires and wishes? Or is it that as He manifested when He gave Himself as the ransom, as the way, that He—too—when ye call—might say, "Come —I will give you rest—my yoke is easy, my burden is light"?

Then when ye have the least of earthly burdens do ye doubt that He understands; He who has passed through *so much* in materiality, in the *flesh* and blood even as thee? *He* knows! *He* understands! *He* hears thy call and bids thee *come, drink* of the water of life!

Q-2. For what was the earth created?

A-2. This has been answered so oft! If ye have not gotten this, ye are dumb indeed!

Q-3. Comment on "The devil and Satan, which deceiveth the whole world, he was sent out into the earth."

A-3. Did He not—the Christ, the Maker—say this over and over again? that so long as spite, selfishness, evil desires, evil communications were manifested, they would give the channels through which *that* spirit called Satan, devil, Lucifer, evil one, might work?

Also He has said over and over again that even the devil believes, but trembles—and that is as far as he has gone except to try to deceive others.

Then he that denies in his life, in his dealings with his fellow man, that the spirit of truth maketh free, denies his Lord!

Q-4. Explain the "sons of God—daughters of men—sons of man."

A-4. This, too, has been given again and again. As has been indicated through other associations, the influences of those souls that sought material expression pushed themselves into thought forms in the earth. And owing to the earth's relative position with the activities in this particular sphere of activity in the universe, it was chosen as the place for expression. *Think* —universe, eternity, time, space! What do these mean to the finite mind? More often than otherwise they are just names.

More often we think of spirit as just a name, rather than experiencing it. Yet we use it, we manifest it, we are a part of it. Taking *thought* doesn't change anything! It is the application of the thought taken that makes the change within ourselves!

Then, as those expressed they were called the sons of the earth—or sons of man.

When the Creative Forces, God, made then the first man—or God-man—he was the beginning of the sons of God.

Then those souls who entered through a channel made by God—not by thought, not by desire, not by lust, not by things that separated continually—were the sons of God, the daughters of God.

The daughters of men, then, were those who became the channels through which lust knew its activity; and it was in this manner then that the conditions were expressed as given of old, that the sons of God looked upon the daughters of men and saw that they were fair, and *lusted!*

What did the Christ say? "Ye say in the law that ye shall not commit adultery. I say unto you, he that looketh on a woman to *lust* after her hath committed adultery already!"

Understandest thou? Then, what did it mean? Only that such channels offered ways and means for the expression of those influences claimed by Satan, the devil, the evil one, as his.

But *He,* the only begotten of the Father, the Christ, has become the way, the light, the truth, the water, the bread, the vine! and all of those are *of* Him who become channels for manifesting, or through which there may be those expressions that are of love and faith and hope!

Hence the two influences that are ever before thee; good and evil, life and death; choose thou!

Q-5. *Were the ones projected by Amilius—*

A-5. [Interrupting] We are through!

This psychic reading was given by Edgar Cayce at his home on Arctic Crescent, Virginia Beach, Va., on August 28, 1938, at 4:00 P.M., in accordance with a request made by those present: Edgar Cayce; Gertrude Cayce, conductor; Gladys Davis, steno; Helen Ellington, Hannah Miller, Frances Y. Morrow, Helen Storey, Jane Williams, and Esther Wynne.

≥ 262-120 ≤

Mrs. Cayce: You will have before you the Norfolk Study Group #1, members of which are present here, and their work on the lesson Spirit —a copy of which I hold in my hand. As I call each division of the lesson presented today, please comment and give suggestions and correction. Then you will answer the questions that may be asked.

Mr. Cayce: Yes, we have the group as gathered here—as a group, as individuals, and their work on the lesson *Spirit.*

We would make comment rather as a whole, than as sections.

As has been indicated, here there is presented—or to be presented—all that has gone before, in the preparation of the lessons; and the analyzing of each phase of human experience and endeavor from the angle of spirit.

Then, take that ye have in hand to the present—compile it. Then let each member of the group read it, analyze it, comment one to another; and *then* present it *as* the comments will have changed same.

We will give the further instructions then.

Ready for questions.

Q-1. Please give an affirmation to be used by those who have agreed to hold a meditation during the time that Edgar Cayce is giving readings at the 10:30 A.M. and 3:30 P.M. periods daily.

A-1. GOD! IN THY MERCY, IN THY LOVE, BE THOU NIGH UNTO THOSE SOULS THAT SEEK A MANIFESTATION OF THY LOVE THROUGH ONE OF THY SERVANTS.

LET EACH OF THY CHILDREN KNOW THAT THOU ART NIGH— THROUGH THE HELP, THROUGH THE HOPE THAT IS AROUSED IN THE HEARTS OF THOSE WHO SEEK THY FACE!

Q-2. In the light of the readings on spirit in regard to the sons and daughters of men, why did Jesus so often refer to Himself as the Son of man?

-483-

A-2. Study this—each of you—in the light of that which is compiled here from the information which has been given thus far. Let each answer within the *own* conscience, and then ask again. It will mean more to you!

Q-3. After Jesus returned to the Father at the ascension, and sent the Holy Spirit into the world, do those who receive the mark of the Lamb through the Holy Spirit become the sons of God?

A-3. All that manifest the Christ-life, the Christ Consciousness, are the sons of God. "Who is my mother—who is my brother, my sister? He that doeth the will of the Father, the same is my mother, my brother, my sister."

Q-4. What did Jesus mean when He said that the least in kingdom of heaven *was greater than John the Baptist?*

A-4. John was still the doubter.

Q-5. Any other comments?

A-5. There might be a book full of comments!

This to each: Let thy heart be lifted up; for as thou hast chosen Him, He hath chosen you to be a light unto many peoples.

Then, to be a doorkeeper in the house of the Lord is greater than he that taketh a city or ruleth a nation secondarily.

Keep, then, the faith that has held thee to thy purpose, knowing that He standeth near to each of you. *Rely* on Him!

We are through for the present.

≯ 262-121 ≮ *This psychic reading was given by Edgar Cayce at the Warner Hotel, Virginia Beach, Va., site of the Association for Research and Enlightenment's Eighth Annual Congress, on June 18, 1939, at 3:55 P.M. Present: Edgar Cayce; Gertrude Cayce, conductor; Gladys Davis, steno; and members of the Congress.*

Mrs. Cayce: You will give at this time to each guest of the Eighth Annual Congress, as I call the name, a message concerning today and tomorrow in his or her spiritual and mental life.

Mr. Cayce: Yes, we have those who seek, those who would interpret in their own experience that which might be helpful. Ready for names.

Q-1. [470]:

A-1. In the interpreting of the desires and purposes in thy heart and thy life, keep ever first and foremost, "Lord, use me; not in my way but Thine, that there may in my day, my generation, come a greater awakening to the needs of Thy ways in the lives and hearts and minds of those I meet day by day.

"And may I live my life in such a manner as to constrain others to look to Thee, and not trust in those arms that are short by their very selfish purposes.

"Keep the ways that I choose in those directions that may bring this to pass in my experience."

Q-2. [1100]:

A-2. Today, hope; today, desire. Today those things that would make thee afraid are far, far away. Shadows and doubts and fears will arise in thy experience, but keep before thee the light of all good consciousness, of all good and perfect service to Him; and ye will find that the shadows of doubt and fear will fall far behind.

Let those things that cause the doubts and fears be far removed from thee, through just the little kindness, the little service ye may do here and there.

For as ye keep thy mind, thy body, in service that His kingdom may come in the earth, so will joy, peace, harmony come into thy experience.

Q-3. [1770]:

A-3. Joy, happiness in a life well spent in seeking, is in thy experience today. Keep thou the ways that thou hast known, checking as it were upon thy own self day by day. *Know* in what and in whom ye have believed. And be sure that He in whom ye have believed is able to keep every promise He has made thee.

Put thy trust, then, in Him rather than in those things that falter and fade away. Let love rule *thy* life!

Q-4. [*1387*]:

A-4. In thy experience comes material, spiritual, *mental* experiences. Be a thorough discerner of truth. Hold to that which *is* eternal and changeth not in its purpose or in its intent with the children of men. To be sure, individuals grow in grace, in knowledge, in understanding; and as they apply that they know, the next step, the next purpose is shown to them.

For the promise is, "I will be *with* thee always, even unto the end of the world." He *was* with thee in the beginning. Ye wandered away, as with those activities that brought the needs for the material experiences that grace might indeed the more abound; for it is not by works alone but by every word that proceedeth from the mouth of the Father—not others, but from the Father-God!

Keep thy purposes, thy desires, thy ways circumspect in thy own conscience.

Q-5. [*623*]:

A-5. "In the Lord's house are many mansions—if it were not so I would have told you." What meaneth this in thy experience today? How have ye furnished, how will ye furnish that place, that room, that mansion? Will it be with those things that fade away, or with that which is eternal? Only that which grows by its usage is eternal. Only that which is of the fruit of the spirit of truth is eternal.

Discern ye, then, the *spirit*. That which denieth He hath come in the flesh, have naught to do with same!

As ye seek, so will ye find. For this is among those promises that have been to the children of men since they sought to have their *own* way, their *own* desire, their *own* purpose.

Let thy might, thy strength then, be expended—yea, lost in Him. For He *is* the light, He *is* the way. And He standeth at the door of thine own heart and consciousness. Will ye not sup with Him?

Q-6. [*951*]:

A-6. As today is expended so will the morrow bring joy, hope, gladness or sorrow and doubt and fear. For God is not mocked among the children of men, nor in all the earth is there any other than the one God.

As ye then seek, as ye then give, let that blood that cleanseth from all doubt and fear be not given as naught for thee.

Great are thy abilities. Great are thy hopes. So, too, great are thy *responsibilities!* For of those to whom much is given is much required.

Then, let thy yeas by yea, and thy nays be nay. Be ye stable in thy purposes, in thy desires; and let thy prayer be, "Here am I, God; send me, *use* me!"

Q-7. [*1849*]:

A-7. That doubts, that fears in the material things come into thy experience is today a portion of thy lot. As ye have trusted wholly in Him, these fears, these doubts have faded away.

For His promises are, "Rely ye on the Lord, and see if He will not open even the windows of heaven to pour out a blessing upon thee!"

Then, let thy desires be in the ways that are in keeping with those activities that ye know indicate to self as well as demonstrate to others where thy heart and thy purpose lies.

For, though ye gain the whole world in *every* way of fortune, fame or whatnot, and lose hold of that love that cometh from just being kind and patient, ye have lost that harmony, that peace which comes from being at one with Him.

The way grows brighter, if ye will come with Him into the light of thy own understanding!

Q-8. [*1921*]:

A-8. As thy purposes have been from the mental as well as the spiritual purposes in thy life, ye have found, ye do find joy in the expression of life in thy experience. When those things have prompted thee to desire or to feel a slight when none was felt or given or intended, these have brought fears, these have brought disappointments.

So, look to Him who *is* the light, who *is* the joy of life itself. Being the water of life, the bread of life, feed then upon love of God *in* expression of just being kind to thy fellow man.

Q-9. [*1561*]:

A-9. Again would there be given, "Seek ye the Lord while He may be *found!*" For, they that put their trust in those things that fade away, those things where moth and rust doth corrupt, find that sorrow, disappointments, fears begin to take the place of joy in service.

And know, He that is the greatest among you is the servant of the more. He that would come to know the Lord and His ways must practice in the daily life those things that partake of the *spiritual* life.

Let joy fill thy heart, for the day grows in every way before thee.

Q-10. [1561's wife]:

A-10. Let that peace that has come today, in thine heart, find a resting place there. Not by thy relying upon just the sentiment of those hopes, but by creating by thy daily activity that hope in the heart and life, in the mind and purpose of those about thee. For the Lord will keep thee in that way which will bring greater blessings to thee, as ye give unto others that joy, that hope ye have found today.

Then, let thy life be so filled with that love, that tomorrow brings the greater joy, the greater glory, the greater beauty of a life of service.

Q-11. [1602]:

A-11. As today brings thee wonderment in thy own self, in thy own experience—and as ye analyze, as ye determine in thy own consciousness the purposes that prompt thee to activity— know the sources of same must arise only from wells of pure, living water of mercy and grace and peace and beauty. For, *with* those things that bring contempt or fear in thine own heart or mind, these are magnified by the very water ye would drink to understanding.

As ye grow, then, in the grace and mercy of thine own understanding, let this be magnified in the manner and way ye give to others that *expectancy,* that *hope.*

Expect much of thyself, and then go about to see that ye are *not* disappointed.

Q-12. [1564]:

A-12. Hold fast to that thou hast purposed in thy heart. As ye vision the lights of the lives ye have led, let them be as

directing lights to thee. For His promises have been to bring
to the remembrance of those who love Him the knowledge that
needs be for the souls to manifest in the material plane that
needed for not only their *own* development but for the very joy
and hope and life for the others that such will aid in their
activities through this material experience.

Think not more highly of thyself than ye ought to think. For
He humbled Himself and became as one with the lowest of men
—that love might be made manifest. So may ye, in the humbleness of heart, come to know the greater glory by and through
the greater service ye may render to thy fellow man.

Harmonize thy life as ye do the tones of nature itself; and
more joy and beauty will be in thy daily experience.

Q-13. [*1000*]:

A-13. As ye grow in appreciation of the love of thy fellow man,
and the needs of such in thy daily experience, give the praise
to the Father-God; that ye may be *used* more and more in a
service for others.

And this will bring less and less of fear, and more and more
of hope.

For remember, these *are* at war one with another—hope and
fear. Let not thy mind, let not thy body, let not thy purpose,
thy desire, entertain fear. For as ye entertain these that make
for the building within thy consciousness, so may ye grow in
that understanding and in thy purposes with those conditions
of every nature that ye meet day by day.

Q-14. [*1663*]:

A-14. As today ye come to those experiences of seeing, of
feeling greater hope and love, greater peace and beauty, so rest
ye in the Lord.

Oft hath He given, fret not thyself but stand still and see the
glory of the Lord. These apply in thy experiences day by day.
Keep in the way of the seeking—opening thy heart, thy mind
for a greater service to others.

Teach thyself in teaching others to be patient, to be content;
not satisfied but *content* in the ways of the Lord!

Q-15. [*1472*]:

A-15. Keep that thou hast purposed. As ye have taught, as
ye have aided others in searching out themselves, so search

thine own heart; putting away from same all those things that would hinder, and run the perfect race. Or, as has been indicated to thee, *turn* to the right—walk straight ahead!

Find not fault with others who have stumbled in the way. Lend a helping hand, and climb—climb to those heights of content upon those things ye have seen as failures in the lives of others.

Encourage those who are disturbed. Give strength and aid to those who falter. It isn't those who have attained that need thy counsel, but those who falter and fear.

Remember, He that is thy light came not to save those who are satisfied with the way they have chosen. Know the difference between contentment and being satisfied; not only in thine own life but in the lives and purposes of those ye meet day by day.

Call ye oft on the Lord, that He may draw nearer to thee. As ye walk then and talk with Him (for as ye walked then and talked with Him, as ye have counseled), so may ye counsel with thy fellow man—and look for and expect His strength to sustain thee throughout *every* activity—here and now!

Q-16. [*264*]:

A-16. Look not on that which has passed as that to be thought of or turned to. Remember Lot's wife. But lift up, look up; knowing that He hath said, "When ye call I will *hear*—and answer speedily."

So as ye keep in the way of *applied* understanding, so may ye grow in grace, in knowledge, in comprehension of what He would have thee do.

Say not in thy heart, nor in words, what *ye* would do, but rather "Lord, lead Thou the way."

Q-17. L. F.:

A-17. As ye seek, as ye knock, so may the way be opened unto you. For His ways are not past finding out; and as He hath given, "Seek me, try me," that ye may indeed find—the Lord thy God is mindful of thee!

For He calleth His own by name. As ye seek, then, so will ye find. Let *His* words be with thee, ever—"Come! Open thy heart, that the Father and I may abide with thee." Be satisfied with nothing less than those *promises* fulfilled in thy life and thy experience.

Hate not. Be not disturbed by those who seek through any other channel, but know that the Lord is thy strength and thy might. For indeed in Him ye live and move and have thy being. Trust Him, as ye would He would trust thee.

Q-18. R. M. B.:

A-18. Disturbances are thine today, because of the thoughts of and the desires for the application of others. Let rather that fill thy mind and heart which has been given of old—that it is not who will ascend into heaven to bring us a message—not who shall come from over the sea that we may hear and heed —for Lo, the answer to *all* thy problems is in thine own heart!

Set thy face and thy purposes toward the light of truth that is in the promises of God! Make them thine—not by just acclaiming same, but by so living in thine own heart, and in thine own activities with thy fellow man, that what ye have builded and do build becomes the fulfilling of those promises in the lives of others!

In this way alone may ye know the peace He hath promised.

Q-19. [257]:

A-19. Let that purpose, that desire which has prompted thee oft to approach the throne of mercy, continue in thy heart and mind today, tomorrow, forever. For the Lord is the same yesterday, today and forever. They that put their trust wholly in Him shall not want—neither shall their seed beg bread.

But do ye the will of the Father in thy relationships to others, in the office, in the home, in the street—wherever ye meet thy fellow man. Thus may they know, not by thy boasting but by thy gentleness, that ye walk oft with the Lord thy God.

Q-20. [2091]:

A-20. Thou hast purposed oft—thou hast sought oft. Ye are drawing closer and closer to that day of the greater awakening.

Then, let not discouragement, let not disappointments cause thee to falter in the ways thou hast chosen to serve thy fellow man; but give *God* the praise, and never threaten another by thy own might, nor by thy position.

For, know, each soul merits that condition, that position it *today* occupies! But be not *thou* the judge. Rather *open* the way that new hope, new light, new joy, new aspirations may be in the hearts and minds of those ye would serve.

Q-21. L. M. S.:

A-21. Fear and doubt have been a part of thy experience, because of the suffering, because of the fears thou hast seen in the experiences of those nigh unto thee. Put ye rather, then, thy trust in the Lord. For *He* is life, and health, and strength to those who put their trust in Him. Not everyone that saith "Lord, Lord," shall enter in, but he that doeth the will of the Father by just being patient, just being kind to others.

Q-22. K. L. T.:

A-22. Boast not thyself because of those experiences that have brought thee to be in that position of power over others. For with thy purposes ye may become the blind leading the blind, and both may fall in the ditch.

Let rather the love, that has been shown in the Father through the gentleness and patience with the children of men, be manifested in thy *own* life. Then may peace rest with thee indeed.

Q-23. C. A. Z.:

A-23. Much has been thy purpose, little at times has been thy activity in the Lord. Know that He is thy strength. Thy purpose, then, should be rather in those things that take hold upon the ways of the Lord. For if ye will but come into the more perfect knowledge of *Him,* the more perfectly ye may serve thy fellow man.

Q-24. I. B. Z.:

A-24. Ye have sought, ye have heard, ye have listened to the many who have cried, "Lo, here is the way—Lo, this is the direction—this is the manner of approach."

Rather turn ye to these: In the 30th of Deuteronomy *find* what is told thee—*thee*—to do! Turn again to that as found in the 150th Psalm, and give praise that He, thy Lord, thy God, has entrusted to thee that way, that belief innate in thy purposes.

Then turn to the 14th, 15th, 16th and 17th of St. John, and know that He speaks again with thee—and that in thine own heart, in thine own mind will come that peace of the way chosen —that leadeth to life everlasting, to *joy* that knows no confines, to peace that passeth understanding!

We are through.

This psychic reading was given by Edgar Cayce at his home on Arctic Crescent, Virginia Beach, Va., on September 24, 1939, at 4:00 P.M., in accordance with a request made by those present: Edgar Cayce; Gertrude Cayce, conductor; Gladys Davis, steno; Hugh Lynn Cayce, Florence Edmonds, Marsden Godfrey, Hannah Miller, Noah Miller, Frances Y. Morrow, Helen Storey, Thomas Sugrue, and Esther Wynne.

⋊ 262-122 ⋉

Mrs. Cayce: You will have before you Group #1, members of which are assembled here. They present the lesson on Spirit, *a copy of which I hold in my hand. As the subject of each topic is called, you will comment on that section, suggesting changes, thoughts that should be added, or corrections. You will answer questions.*

Mr. Cayce: Yes, we have the group gathered here; as a group, as individuals, and the work on the lesson *Spirit.*

There have been suggestions given as to how to better complete the study of the subject, and as to how the members of the group might make same more applicable in their own experience, as well as digestible to the mind and the purposes of those who might attempt to use same in their experience.

Still, then, we would give—rather than accepting or rejecting that which is compiled here; for you each have experienced much in your material, mental and spiritual lives in the study of this subject:

As has been given, this should be the beginning, the end, for those who would apply that in their experience day by day. Not the end as to material application, not the end as to materialization—but no question should ever be in the mind of any of this group as to *what* they believe, or as to what they practice in their daily lives and associations with their fellow man.

Then, take that thou hast in hand—as written; and in thy meetings week by week let two by two furnish the discussion; and the comments as are given by each individual, let these become a part of this lesson. Ye *must* practice, ye *must* make practical these concepts in thy *own* experience, that others may gain from same the better understanding of what spirit is in activity among men.

Ye see in thy daily life *something* motivating individuals, in

-493-

their conversation as respecting their home, their city, their nation, their neighbors. What prompts same? The spirit of what? These have not been fully—no, they have not been recorded here so as to be understood by him who reads.

Let this be done, then, in earnest, in sincerity, in truth.

Ready for questions.

Q-1. Please explain dream which [993] *had—*

A-1. [Interrupting] Let's keep these rather to the subject. Not that the dreams, the visions, the experiences of any are not a part of the understanding. Let's keep these in their relationships to *individual* comprehension. Not that they are not a part of the experiences that may be for all, but *all* will not understand.

Q-2. Any other advice to the group regarding action or study from this point on?

A-2. Begin *now!* And each week take a portion of that. Divide it into such measures that it will be a portion to each member of the group, two by two. As to who would be linked together, as ye would say—those that are in the positions of the least time that they call their own, with those who have the most; but each contributing their thought, their selves. For *in* this ye may find eternal truth, eternal life; that spark, that connection that may revitalize thy whole experience.

We are through—for the present.

This psychic reading was given by Edgar Cayce at his home on Arctic Crescent, Virginia Beach, Va., on March 10, 1940, at 3:50 P.M., in accordance with a request made by those present: Edgar Cayce; Gertrude Cayce, conductor; Gladys Davis, steno; Hugh Lynn Cayce, Florence Edmonds, Marsden Godfrey, Hannah Miller, Noah Miller, Frances Y. Morrow, and Esther Wynne.

⋊ 262-123 ⋉

Mrs. Cayce: You will have before you the Norfolk Study Group #1, members of which are present here, and its work on the lesson Spirit. *You will answer the questions which have been prepared on this lesson.*

Mr. Cayce: Yes, we have the group as gathered here, and the work on the lesson *Spirit.*

Ready for questions.

Q-1. Give a definition of spirit which may be given in the lesson.

A-1. Spirit is the First Cause, the primary beginning, the motivative influence—as God is spirit.

Q-2. How does spirit compare with mind?

A-2. Spirit is the First Cause. Mind is an effect, or an active force that partakes of spiritual as well as material import. Mind is an essence or a flow between spirit and that which is made manifest materially.

Q-3. Just how should we explain the division of spirit (into what we know as good and evil) in the spiritual realm before the earth was created?

A-3. God, the First Cause, in spirit, created in spirit the separate influences or forces that are a portion of, and manifested in the spirit of, God. In that essence, to become materially manifested through the evolution of the spirit of God, sin first began.

Q-4. Are we correct in assuming that the first spiritual beings created were made up of mind, spirit and will?

A-4. The first concept as may be had of that in materiality is that it is an essence, without form, save as it begins to manifest—as would be gas, odor, wind, smoke—yet that it has with it the will, the mind, the power to make manifest by that with which, in which, it manifests—as does also odor, gas, wind and the like.

-495-

Thus—as the activities came—we may assume that the First Cause was spirit, mind, will.

Q-5. How much of an explanation should we give of Adam and Eve as God's projection and how should we handle this?

A-5. As has been indicated, this should be the interpretation of each member of the group, as they as individuals have reacted or do react to same.

As to the presentation of same here, do not make same obnoxious but state it in such a manner that there is little or no ground for refutation of same.

Q-6. Are time and space concepts that exist outside of physical consciousness?

A-6. No. For the physical consciousness is an activity that uses such, as the divisions of space and time. And in patience only may ye become aware of the concept of either.

Q-7. Would it be wise to read the entire lesson and receive comments through a reading?

A-7. This should be according to the consensus of opinion of the group. If it is sufficiently satisfactory to each member as it is written, it may be presented as a whole. If there are questions in the mind of sufficient numbers, or the majority, so that they desire that there be the comment, then prepare same in that way and manner.

Q-8. What work should the group undertake after finishing this lesson?

A-8. Is this the end, because it is an explanation of the activity? Why not continue with such as *Righteousness versus Sin,* or any of those that may be presented from time to time?

What *is* sin? What *is* righteousness? Are they mere concepts, or is there an opinion or a line over which, from which there are deviations, so that it puts one upon one side and one upon another?

Who is the judge of sin, of righteousness? Is an act in the affairs of one individual sin, and in another righteousness?

Q-9. Any other suggestions for the group at this time?

A-9. Stand fast in that ye have purposed to do. For, he that remains faithful to the end shall wear a crown.

We are through.

This psychic reading was given by Edgar Cayce at his home on Arctic Crescent, Virginia Beach, Va., on March 31, 1940, at 4:40 P.M., in accordance with a request made by those present: Edgar Cayce; Gertrude Cayce, conductor; Gladys Davis, steno; Hugh Lynn Cayce, Florence Edmonds, Marsden Godfrey, Hannah Miller, Noah Miller, and Esther Wynne.

⋊ 262-124 ⋉

Mrs. Cayce: You will have before you Group #1, and their work on the lesson Spirit. *As I call each section of the lesson, comment on same and tell us if this is expressed and presented in keeping with the material given through the readings on this subject.*

Mr. Cayce: Yes, we have the group as gathered here, as a group, as individuals, and their work on the lesson *Spirit.*

In commenting upon the lesson here, as a whole, this is very good. As we find, the brevity of same is rather better than too many words without too much meaning.

There are some points not so well stated as might be, yet this is something that should be in keeping with the intent and purpose of the group—which is to arouse in the minds of others the greater desire to seek a knowledge of, and their relationships with, Creative Forces—or the spirit.

For, indeed the letter killeth—the spirit maketh alive.

And as seekers apply that indicated here, we find that their lives will grow better, their knowledge of their relationship to Creative Forces will be broadened, and their abilities to aid and be a channel of blessings to others will be increased.

Ready for questions.

Q-1. Please comment on the first section, the Introduction.

A-1. This as we find is very good, save that—as has been indicated—crystallization in consciousness, or crystallization of consciousness is not of spirit but by spirit or through spirit, per spirit. This is made more explicit in the examples used, as to what is the meaning of the spirit of America, the spirit of '76, the spirit of Germany or the spirit of Fascism or the like. It is the consciousness crystallized *by* the spirit, which is made manifest in those comprehending, living, accepting, being, do-

-497-

ing that which has so crystallized itself into a movement, organization, feeling or the like.

Q-2. Section 2, In the Beginning.

A-2. Change the Never to Now.

Q-3. Section 3, Man's Projection.

A-3. This as we find is very good. There may be some questions, or some confusions in the mind of some; yet *if* such seek
to justify their beliefs, whether they are accepting or rejecting,
they will learn more. For, as indicated, it is the spirit that
maketh alive.

Q-4. God's Projection.

A-4. This is very good.

Q-5. Time, Space and Patience.

A-5. This is very good, and possibly the best portion of same.

Q-6. Self the Barrier.

A-6. Very good.

Q-7. Experiences.

A-7. These to some will appear as being out of place, and yet
to others very necessary. These are very good.

Q-8. Closing.

A-8. This is very well.

As we find, with those minor changes, or notes or footnotes
or side notes as may be made to meet the experiences of some
(in this group here), this will be very good; and will find its place
among those being prepared.

Q-9. Any affirmation at this time for the next lesson? [A
Search for God, *Book III*]

A-9. CREATE IN ME, O GOD, A NEW PURPOSE, A RIGHTEOUS
SPIRIT: THAT I MAY, AS THY CHILD, BE A LIVING EXAMPLE OF THAT
I HAVE PROFESSED AND DO PROFESS TO BELIEVE, BY MANIFESTING
SAME AMONG MY FELLOW MEN.

In the studies of this subject—*Righteousness versus Sin*—we
will find that in the minds of many there will be quite a contro-
versy as to what constitutes righteousness, in or under this or
that circumstance, and as to what constitutes sin.

To be sure, the commonly accepted terms are light and darkness; that which walks in the light as righteousness, and that
which is in opposition to God's will as error or sin.

Hence the real study is to be:

"What is God's purpose, God's will, with *me?*" using that which has been presented to others through the proposed word, and not only history (sacred and profane) but also the observation and experience of individuals in their present-day life, their present-day experiences.

For it is the purpose, the desire of this group to aid others to walk more circumspectly, and not to confuse or disturb any in that with which they are satisfied, or in that which for *them* constitutes righteousness *or* sin.

We are through for the present.

[Gladys Davis's note: While five of the next six readings in the 262 series deal with subject matter of the first three lessons of a planned Book III of *A Search for God,* the material compiled by the Group #1 was not approved in a final reading for each lesson. Consequently when Book II was published in 1950 it was decided best not to include the material in that book. Although Group #1 met frequently after Edgar Cayce's death and worked on the readings in the new series for Book III, it was never agreed that the compiled manuscripts on those three lessons were ready for publication.]

This psychic reading was given by Edgar Cayce at his home on Arctic Crescent, Virginia Beach, Va., on October 13, 1940, at 3:40 P.M., in accordance with a request made by those present: Edgar Cayce; Gertrude Cayce, conductor; Gladys Davis, steno; Hugh Lynn Cayce, Florence Edmonds, Ruth LeNoir, Hannah Miller, Noah Miller, Frances Y. Morrow, and Esther Wynne.

⩗ 262-125 ⩗

Mrs. Cayce: You will have before you the Norfolk Group #1, assembled here to study the basic ideas and principles to be expressed in the lesson Sin versus Righteousness. *You will continue the discourse on this subject, answering the questions that may be asked.*

Mr. Cayce: Yes, we have the group as gathered here, and their work, their study, on *Sin versus Righteousness.*

It was given, "Except your righteousness exceed the righteousness of the Pharisees, ye shall all likewise perish." Here we find the presentation of righteousness in varying degrees; else it could not have been referred to as even a type or condition of righteousness.

What was the righteousness of the Pharisees, and what was their sin? How were the disciples to discern between the righteousness of the Pharisees and the righteousness as presented by the Teacher? Or, was that the type of righteousness referred to as being the righteousness of the Master's hearers at that time?

The righteousness of the Pharisee was that as indicated by the prayer offered in the temple; that he thanked God he was not like other people. Here we find, then, self-righteousness; not condemned, and yet "except your righteousness exceed that of the self-righteous, ye shall all likewise perish."

Perish here indicates sin. Thus we have the direct manner in which each individual, each hearer, might judge; not as judging another but as an analysis, a judgment, a looking within as to whether there were the promptings of the life, the spoken word, the activities, by self's desires, self's indulgence, self's aggrandizement, self's laudation, self's praise, self's activities, without respect to the fellow man.

Then there may be a lesson here gained by each—that sin

versus righteousness is that sin which is separation from God; and righteousness is adhering to, making at-onement with, God's purposes—even as indicated in the prayer of the publican, "God be merciful to me, a sinner." Or, as He gave in the prayer, "As I ask forgiveness, so I forgive others," or, "With what measure I ask for mercy, for care, for love, for thought, that love and care and consideration I seek to give to others."

Thus may we draw a lesson in our daily experience from this attitude, this condition, this experience through which each soul finds itself passing in a material world. The flesh is weak, the spirit is willing.

Will you each as individuals be led by the spirit of truth? or will self, the own ego, the own material desire, so outweigh that purpose, that hope, that mission for which each soul is given the opportunity in material expression, that it may be said of you, "except your righteousness exceed the life of the self-righteous, ye shall indeed perish"?

In that outline first indicated here, who is to judge as to what is sin and what is righteousness for the individual? As we remember, as has oft been given, "Study to show *thyself* approved unto God, a workman not ashamed."

Here we find much that may need analyzing, looking into, in our own individual experiences. Do we, as children of God, as seekers after God, have firsthand knowledge? or do we accept only that others have told us? Do we condemn any? Do we know, or is it only self-righteousness that speaks?

Are we living that life that exceeds the righteousness of the Pharisee; who gave his tithes, who attended to the offices of his position, who met regularly in those capacities for activity of guidance, teaching and directing of others? Yet, what lacked he? Did he teach the letter of the law and forget the spirit of same?

Let each ask self, "Do I manifest—in speech, in activity—that I sincerely believe? Do I give credit to the spirit where credit is due? Do I adhere to the spirit of brotherly love? Do I sow the seeds of kindness with a kindly feeling, or with merely a sense of duty? Do I have long-suffering because I just can't help myself, or because I am willing that God—through His Son, through the Master of masters, show me the way? Is my life, my speech, my activity among others, in keeping with such righteousness as *He*—the righteous Master—taught?"

He said, "Be ye *perfect*, even as my Father in heaven is perfect." Would we modify that? Would we say that such is only to be sought, to be tried for, to be desired in the experience, and is not attainable here or now, under the present environs, the present hates, the present fears?

Was *He* unreasonable? Was He kind to those who despitefully used Him? Did His righteousness come as boastings of what His abilities were, of what He knew within Himself; or rather under those conditions wherein He came unto His own and His own received Him not, yet He condemned none?

Ready for questions.

Q-1. Please comment on the outline, a copy of which I have in my hand.

A-1. This as we find is very well begun. Much filling in is to be done, as the interpreting progresses in the lives and the mental experiences of compilers.

Q-2. Define sin and original sin, or what was original sin? Please explain.

A-2. It may be defined in one word—disobedience!

In the beginning, the perfect man was given all the attributes of the Father-God, in ideal environments prepared by God for man's material manifestation. Let's draw the comparisons of man made perfect through experience, and man *willfully* being disobedient:

In the first we find man listening to those influences which were at variance to God's way. Then in the temple, even at twelve, we find the perfect man seeking, asking, and answering questions as to man's relationship to God.

Sin, then, is willful disobedience. Draw the comparison within thyself as to those experiences indicated in the 1st, 2nd and 3rd of Genesis and those in the 2nd of Luke—where we find our pattern, our lesson, and those illustrations that indicate sin versus righteousness—one willfully seeking to know the relationship to the Creator, or the answer, "Know ye not that I must be about my Father's business?" How different from that other, "The *woman* thou gavest me, *she* persuaded me, and I did eat"!

We are through for the present.

⊰ 262-126 ⊱

This psychic reading was given by Edgar Cayce at his home on Arctic Crescent, Virginia Beach, Va., on January 19, 1941, at 4:20 P.M., in accordance with a request made by those present: Edgar Cayce; Hugh Lynn Cayce, conductor; Gladys Davis, steno; Florence Edmonds, Marsden Godfrey, Hannah Miller, Frances Y. Morrow, and Esther Wynne.

Hugh Lynn Cayce: You will have before you the Norfolk Study Group #1, members of which are present in this room, and their work and study of the lesson Righteousness versus Sin. *You will continue with the discourse on this subject.*

Edgar Cayce: Yes, we have the group as gathered here—as a group and as individuals, also their work and study on the lessons.

In continuing with the discussion of the subject *Righteousness versus Sin*—we have here the individual considerations.

As has been indicated through these channels, it becomes an individual matter—dependent upon or relative to, first, the ideals of the individual, and as to what constitutes a deviation from the ideal; and as to what ideals are in relation to moral, spiritual and mental standards.

For, righteousness and sin—as in the minds of most individuals—are the extremes of an awareness in the consciousness of an individual. Thus it becomes a personal condition to be reckoned with by the individual.

Not that there are not laws, nor that there are not metes and bounds about either of the terms intended to be expressed in the very words righteousness and sin. Yet, as we have given, what may be righteousness to one may be sin to another; or what is sin to one might not be considered at all by another as a deviation from a righteous path.

What then (ye may ask) is the awareness or the consciousness that makes for the producing of that as may be called righteous in the experience of the individual? To be in an at-onement—in purpose, in will, in desire—with the ideal is to the individual a righteous state. Then to be conscious of deviating from that ideal, whether consciously or unconsciously, is a sin to the entity.

Make note of the variation here as to the premise from which

the inference is drawn. For, each soul, each entity, each conscious awareness of an individual, is the combination or the
composite of all the entity has thought or done in consciousness
of every sphere or phase of activity. So are those things that
would tend to lead an individual towards the abuse or misuse
of privilege or opportunity in its experience. So are the confusions that arise oft in the experiences of those who are *active*
in their thought as to righteous or sinful activity.

To be sure, many are active as illustrated in that pronounce-
ment of Paul, "I did in all good consciousness persecute the
church." This to him was sin, yet—according to the consciousness—righteous sinning; for when he was aware of his error,
through the call to service, he became as active in the defense
of that *as* he had persecuted in all good consciousness.

Then, one's consciousness—by the activity in those influences arising in the experiences—may sear, alter, make for
those choices by the individual of that which to another would
be considered, or would be, sin.

To be sure, this is an approach only from the individual
standpoint, the individual's activity; but considered in the light
of those influences of statements which we have made here—
that one had best be active and in error than not doing anything at all.

For, as may be drawn from the experiences of those who have
been, who are, or who may be called into service—if there is
the sincerity towards the ideal, they as individuals will be
shown, will perceive, will be awakened, will be aware of God's
purposes with them.

Then, in illustrating this—for this should be in the mind of
each one here considered and meditated upon, and applied in
the daily life—let each be sincere, be direct, in that calling. For,
ye each are chosen—as ye choose to serve Him in a definite
manner—to be a messenger, a director—by word, by example
to others—to point the way to the glorifying of the Christ
Consciousness in a material world.

When there had been fulfilled that preparation, or a part
preparation of material knowledge of Moses, he set about to put
into activity that purpose for which he had come into the earth.
Yet materially he chose an error, a sin, in establishing the

righteousness of his fellow men. Thus a full period was required
—as of earthly righteousness or earthly knowledge—to undo
or to coordinate that as was to be a working principle of righteousness versus sin. *Then* he was *called;* as was Paul in his
persecution of the church, conscious of a purpose but *active,*
doing something *toward* an activity which by education to him
(physically) was correct, yet sin.

He, too, was called and directed.

So, too, may each individual be active in principle, in purpose,
being sincere, being direct. Thus may the individual gain the
greater working knowledge of that which is righteous, versus
that which is sin.

Then, let each be not slothful, not putting off, not unmindful
that ye must be up and doing; working, *busy* at that which is
to thee, *now, today,* that as thy conscience directs thee to do;
in sincere, direct manner. And ye may be sure He counts that
try as righteousness; and the sin that may appear to self or to
others is but upon the reverse—which is righteousness.

We are through for the present.

This psychic reading was given by Edgar Cayce at his home on Arctic Crescent, Virginia Beach, Va., on April 23, 1941, at 3:30 P.M., in accordance with a request made by those present: Edgar Cayce; Gertrude Cayce, conductor; Gladys Davis, steno; Hugh Lynn Cayce, Ruth Denney, Florence Edmonds, Helen Ellington, Ruth Le-Noir, Hannah Miller, Frances Y. Morrow, Mae Verhoeven, and Esther Wynne.

᠈ 262-127 ᠄

Mrs. Cayce: You will have before you the first twelve lessons which we have revised for the book, A Search for God, *which we hope to publish. Please comment on each lesson, as I call the title, pointing out any changes or thoughts that should be added. You will then answer the questions, as I ask them:*

Mr. Cayce: Yes, we have the information as given, and the revision as indicated here. In most of these, as we find, there is accord between that attempted to be indicated and that as appears prepared for publication. Little or no change would we now make in any of the subjects indicated. While there should be the first twelve lessons submitted, and also that upon *Meditation,* we find that *Meditation* should come first; not as a preface or introduction but as to prepare the individual—or individuals—who would use the lessons as a study.

And each affirmation for the lesson should preface that lesson, or be upon a page alone facing the lesson.

The rest we would keep in the manner indicated, though we would discard the questions—or most of them.

To be sure, the material will receive a great deal of commendation and also a great deal of disputation. A great deal of anxious moments will be spent by some.

Only ask that each individual *try* living that as presented here, and there will be a real revelation to all who will use—not abuse; or to all who will apply that suggested here.

There is little, that has been offered for the student, as well prepared as this material.

Do not print in a form that is to be just thrown aside. It deserves a good house. Give it such.

Ready for questions.

Q-1. First lesson—Cooperation. Any changes, or thoughts that should be added?

A-1. Though this should be listed as the first lesson, put *Medi-*

-506-

tation in the front. Let each know what it is about. And the form and manner of the meditations as presented here is among the first of the occidental ideas of an oriental theme according to that presented by the Master.

Q-2. Any other comment on the paper on Meditation?

A-2. Publish it first—in the book.

Q-3. Cooperation — any suggestions for changes or additions?

A-3. Good.

Q-4. Know Thyself.

A-4. Very well.

Let each lesson be prepared so that the affirmation as given is presented first, on a page alone facing the title of the lesson.

Q-5. What Is My Ideal?

A-5. Very well.

Q-6. Faith.

A-6. Good.

Q-7. Virtue and Understanding.

A-7. Very well.

Q-8. Fellowship.

A-8. Very well.

Q-9. Patience.

A-9. Good.

Q-10. The Open Door.

A-10. Very good.

Q-11. In His Presence.

A-11. Good.

Q-12. The Cross and the Crown.

A-12. Good.

Q-13. The Lord Thy God Is One.

A-13. Very good.

Q-14. Love.

A-14. Excellent.

Q-15. Which of the questions and answers should be cut out, and what principle should be followed in selecting those to be used?

A-15. If any, add a great many more. We would leave out the questions.

Q-16. Should all Biblical quotations be listed as from the King James version or as just from the Bible?

A-16. Just from the Bible.

Q-17. Any other advice as to the publishing or distribution of the book?

A-17. There will be a great many manners and ways of distribution. A great many of various groups, of various institutions or stores, have asked; and many more will ask when other books are published.

Give them to commentators, critics, lecturers—many of them. Ask individuals to sponsor ones to be sent to ministers, to Bible houses—even though they send them back to you, offer them!

We are through for the present.

This psychic reading was given by Edgar Cayce at the office of the Association for Research and Enlightenment, Arctic Crescent, Virginia Beach, Va., on August 17, 1941, at 4:00 P.M., in accordance with a request made by those present: Edgar Cayce; Gertrude Cayce, conductor; Gladys Davis, steno; Florence Edmonds, Marsden Godfrey, Hannah Miller, Noah Miller, Frances Y. Morrow, Helen Storey, and Esther Wynne.

≈ 262-128 ⋉

Mrs. Cayce: You will have before you the Norfolk Study Group #1, members of which are present in this room, and a copy of the lesson on Righteousness versus Sin *which I hold in my hand. You will give further discourse and commentation on this lesson, answering the questions that may be submitted:*

Mr. Cayce: Yes, we have the group as gathered here; as a group, as individuals, and their work on the lesson *Righteousness versus Sin.*

In further comment, this would be stressed:

As indicated by Him, there is none righteous—save the Father. Thus all righteousness is bound in the attempt of individuals to make application of that in the material as termed good. And yet good appears in varied forms to man's consciousness.

Good being from the All-Good, or as He gave there is none good save God—then that which would be good for an individual might not be to another godly; and thus it would be sin to that individual.

Thus *Righteousness versus Sin* becomes again a personal application of the individual's awareness of God's purpose.

For, as may be illustrated: To the workaday mind of today, Abraham's offering of Isaac would appear foolish, yet—as stated—it was counted to him as righteousness, not sin.

This, then, is a personal application of the awareness that is in the consciousness of the seeker after God.

As to the lesson presented—well.

Ready for questions.

Q-1. Please comment on: "And when he had said this, he breathed on them, and saith unto them, Receive ye the Holy Ghost: Whose soever sins ye remit, they are remitted unto them; and whose soever sins ye retain, they are retained."

A-1. Little comment here is needed if it is analyzed in one's own mind in the light of what has just been indicated as to righteousness versus sin.

Here the Master—it having been accepted that "I have chosen you—you have not all chosen me"—was committing unto them that righteousness to which He had attained.

Q-2. Ex. 20:5: "for I the Lord thy God am a jealous God—" Comment on the word jealous here.

A-2. This has been commented on so often! Read that which has been given!

Q-3. I Cor. 13:7: "— believeth all things—"

A-3. This "believeth all things" refers to the *promises* of God to man.

Q-4. You will give a personal message to each member of the group, as I call the names. [307]:

A-4. Let that light be in thee as was in Him, who thought it not robbery to make Himself equal with God. Thus, as He said of Himself, "Of myself I can do nothing." Let that be *thy* theme, that of thyself—nothing; of Him, *all.*

Q-5. [404]:

A-5. Keep that faith which has prompted thy meting to thy fellow man righteous judgment to all, of love to all, of faith in Him, that He *is* the way and the light.

Q-6. [462]:

A-6. Let not thy heart be troubled. Ye believe in God. Believe also in Him, who hath given, "Lo, I am with thee always, even unto the end of the world." Though there may come disturbances and turmoils, know that peace cometh only in Him—and in doing that thou knowest *to* do.

Q-7. [993]:

A-7. Let that heart and that mind be in you as directed Him in the choosing of those and of that one to whom He would give even the keys of the kingdom, and to whom He could give, "Those that ye bless are blessed, those that ye curse are accursed." So live, then, as it is required of thee, that in thy judgments and in thy measures of administration there is none else but He as thy guide.

Q-8. [379]:

A-8. The peace that comes from Him comes only by abiding

in His word. What, then, is His word? Put away those things that would cause fear or doubt. *Know* in thy inner self that He *is* the way, the truth, the light. There is no other joy to compare with the joy which comes from being counted worthy of His recognition, and the knowledge that in His way ye abide day by day.

Q-9. [*303*]:

A-9. Let not thy heart be troubled. For He careth for thee. Would that all would come to know, "Jesus careth for me." If that is held constantly in the trials of the day, in the troubles of associations or activities, there need be little fear or doubt. Then, do with thy might what thy hands find to do day by day. For the Lord, the Christ—who came, who will save the world —careth for thee.

Q-10. [*413*]:

A-10. The law of the Lord is perfect. It converteth the soul of those who will harken, who will make daily application of that His word and His promptings bid them to do. Be not weary, then, with well-doing. For He will guide, will uphold those that carry on in His name.

Q-11. [*585*]:

A-11. Let that which has kept the way be in thy mind and thy heart, as ye minister day by day to those who would seek the Lord, to those that consciously know not the Lord. For He hath committed such to thee that they might through thy efforts be made aware of His presence in the earth.

Q-12. [*294*]:

A-12. Let not that as would hinder thee from keeping in the way deter thee from the righteous judgment. The law of the Lord *is* the way, and His truth and His way is not past finding out.

Q-13. [*341*]:

A-13. Remain thou faithful unto the trust that has been committed unto thee. For the law, the love of God should prompt, should direct thy ways day by day.

Q-14. [*538*]:

A-14. Love the Lord and His ways. Pass not judgment upon others, lest He judge thee for thine own judgments. Who art thou, that thou may tell others what they may think or do? Doest thou as well as they? The Lord hath loved thee, for He hath given thee that love in those that are nigh unto thee.

Q-15. [*288*]:

A-15. They that seek shall find. They that knock, it shall be opened unto them. Then, forsake not the ways that would bring to thee the wisdom of applying daily that thou hast learned of Him. For He keepeth thee, if ye keep Him in thy purpose, in thy heart.

To all: Let not that deter thee because of evil days that may come about thee. For when sorrow and sadness and joy come, these are of the Lord. For whom the Lord loveth He purgeth; that they may bear more fruit in Him.

We are through for the present.

This psychic reading was given by Edgar Cayce at the office of the Association for Research and Enlightenment, Arctic Crescent, Virginia Beach, Va., on December 3, 1941, at 3:30 P.M., in accordance with a request made by those present: Edgar Cayce; Hugh Lynn Cayce, conductor; Gladys Davis, steno; Ruth Denney, Florence Edmonds, Helen Ellington, Hannah Miller, Frances Y. Morrow, and Esther Wynne.

⩢ 262-129 ⩠

Hugh Lynn Cayce: You will have before you Group #1, members of which are present here, and their work on the lesson Righteousness versus Sin. *As I call each paragraph, please comment on it, giving any suggestions necessary for improvement:*

Edgar Cayce: Yes, we have the group as gathered here, and their work on the lesson *Righteousness versus Sin.* Ready for questions.

Q-1. First, Introduction.

A-1. This is very good. May be expanded more in portions, if by the collaborators it is desirable.

Q-2. What Is Righteousness? What Is Sin?

A-2. Very good. Very well are the compilations here.

Q-3. There Is a Way.

A-3. Very good.

Q-4. God's Purpose for Us.

A-4. Very good.

Q-5. Our Purpose in Life.

A-5. Very good.

Q-6. Conclusion.

A-6. Very good.

Q-7. Would you suggest any general improvements for this lesson?

A-7. Only as there might be some expansion in the first presentations that have been indicated.

Q-8. Please give the affirmation for the next lesson.

A-8. The next lesson as we find that would be well here, following this, would be: *God—Love—Man.* The affirmation for such would be:

LET THAT LIGHT BE WITHIN ME IN SUCH MEASURES THAT I, AS A CHILD OF GOD, MAY REALIZE HIS LOVE FOR MAN. MAY I LIVE THAT, THEN, IN MY LIFE DAY BY DAY.

Q-9. Would you give any basic thoughts for this lesson?

A-9. In this period of man's experience in the earth there is the greater need that he, man, consider the purposes (and the needs) of God in his daily life. There is the need for such thought, such meditation on this universal consciousness, this field, to be manifested by man's love, man's activity towards his fellow man. For, the basic truth that must be presented throughout the study of this subject, is: "Inasmuch as ye do it unto the least of thy brethren, ye do it unto thy Maker." Man's ability, man's consciousness, man's thought—then—must be directed more and more—by those in authority, those in power, those as leaders, those as teachers, those as fathers and mothers, those as associates one with another—to those principles *God—Love—Man.*

We are through for the present.

This psychic reading was given by Edgar Cayce at the office of the Association for Research and Enlightenment, Arctic Crescent, Virginia Beach, Va., on July 30, 1942, at 11:25 A.M., in accordance with a request made by those present: Edgar Cayce; Gertrude Cayce, conductor; Gladys Davis, steno; Hugh Lynn Cayce, Florence Edmonds, Helen Ellington, Hannah Miller, Frances Y. Morrow, and Esther Wynne.

⊀ 262-130 ↙

Mrs. Cayce: You will have before you members of Group #1, present here, and their work on the lesson God—Love—Man. *You will give a further discourse on this lesson and suggestions in completing it.*

Mr. Cayce: Yes, we have the group as gathered here; as a group, as individuals, and their work on the lesson *God—Love —Man.*

In giving further discourse on the subject, much might be given. In the declaration that is made in the subject there should be the defining of what this group interprets as God, in their own experience.

It is true that God is love. Is it true that He is to each as a father? Is it true that He is to each as law? Is it true that we each know that influence, that law, that love, as a personal thing in our own experience; and thus a personal God—not a personality but as a God that is known of self, that may be demonstrated in the life of the individual?

As may be interpreted by the individual from that which is the *accepted* word of God, given through those that were raised or edified by their close walk with Him, as individuals qualified by Him to give their interpretation of Him in man's experience —love is qualified as an attribute of that force, power or influence known as God.

Thus, as man makes application of love in his daily experience, he finds God a personal God—whether indicated in relationship to that force He calls God, or worships as God, or whether in relationship with his fellow man.

These should be the questions, these should be the answers in the experience of the individuals as comprise this group, if they would give this as a complete study or lesson to others.

This has been begun well. Then complete same, in the outline as indicated.

And let the next lesson be: *Man's Relationship to Man.*

And the affirmation:

FATHER, GOD! LET ME, AS THY CHILD, SEE IN MY FELLOW MAN THE DIVINITY I WOULD WORSHIP IN THEE.

LET ME IN MY DAILY LIFE BE A WITNESS TO HIM, WHO EXEMPLI-FIED FOR MAN, TO MAN, MAN'S RELATIONSHIP TO GOD, AND THE MANNER OF RELATIONSHIP THAT SHOULD BE AS MAN TO MAN.

FOR WE ASK IT IN HIS NAME, JESUS THE CHRIST.

Ready for questions.

Q-1. Any message to the group?

A-1. As ye have given unto others, so do thyself. Study to show *thyself* approved unto God, workmen not ashamed; rightly emphasizing the virtue, the faith, the love, the patience, in thy daily life and in thy dealings one with another; keeping self unspotted from condemnation; keeping self from condemning self or others.

We are through for the present.

[Gladys Davis's note: With the publishing of the book *There Is a River,* Edgar Cayce's time was so filled with appointments that he was unable to give further readings for the group.]

INDEX

Index

A.R.E., relationship of study group
work, 243, 244
Affirmations—See: *Supplementary
Index—Affirmations*
Angels—See Also: Ariel, Halaliel,
Michael
man may judge, 131
Anger, 101
explanation of "Be angry, but sin
not," 103
righteous wrath, 99
Animal kingdom, 317
Apostles' Creed, 341
explanation of "Communion of
saints," 349, 350
origin of, 348, 349
Application
affecting desire, 257, 258
apply that understood rather than
seeking further understanding,
28
apply what ye seek, 6
brings light, 28
brings understanding, 79
determining clearer understanding, 28, 29
dynamics of, 203, 204, 205
importance of, regarding lesson,
324
individual affecting group, 28
of beliefs necessary, 213
of lessons as fulfillment, 246
prerequisite to understanding, 35
related to cooperation, 12
related to ideal, 55
related to living perfect life, 103
related to mind of Christ, 12
related to truth, 55
related to truth earned, 83
related to understanding, 22
Approval, needed from God only, 236
Ariel, 224
Astrology
as signs, not destiny, 298, 305
influences, 265
planetary sojourns, 219

Atlantis, 163, 164, 165
Atom, analogous to thought, 74, 204
Atonement, definition, 182
Attitude of mind, 15, 16
Automatic writing, 101, 106
Awakening
defined, 95
explanation of process, 36
regenerated by spirit, 15

Bartimaeus, history of Mt. Seir, 37
Bible—See Also: *Supplementary In-
dex—Bible References*
changes from original, 241
gospel, 320
history of Mt. Seir, 37
spirit of that written, 241
truest statement, 220
Bible characters
Abihu, 344
Abraham, 221, 509
Adam, 224
Barnabas, 63
David, 221, 404
Elijah, 350
Er, 287
Eve, 214
Isaac, 509
James, 349
Jeroboam, 38
Job, 215
John, 404
John the Baptist, 350
John the Beloved, 349
Lazarus, 403
Malcham, 287
Malchus, 287
Mary, 413
Mary Magdalene, 404
Melchizedek, 215
Moses, 221, 239, 240, 349, 404
Nadab, 344
Nicodemus, 239, 240
Paul, 352
Peter, 142, 149, 349, 351, 352, 450,
453, 454

Philip, 479
Sanballat, 37
Saul, 344
Stephen, 225, 479
Thomas, 404
Uzzah, 287, 289
Zaccheus, 142
Zerubbabel, 37
Bible interpretation
Corinthians, II, 5:1, earthly house vs. eternal house, 240, 241
Corinthians, II, 5:21, "He who knew no sin," 235, 236
devil (Satan, Lucifer), 205, 206, 220, 224
false prophets, 128
"Feed my sheep; feed my lambs," 200
Genesis, 224
gospel defined, 320
Haggai 2:7, "I will shake all nations . . . I will fill this house with glory," 260
"If thine eye be single," 339
John 3:16, "God so loved the world," 185, 186
John 15:22, "Had I not come ye would not have known sin," 325
Luke 1:35, "The Holy Ghost shall make that within thee alive," 235
Luke 17, 160, 161
Luke 21, "As ye have seen Him go, so shall He come," 128
Matthew 10:39, "He who finds his life shall lose it," 161
Matthew 21:22, whatever we desire shall be given to us, 252
Matthew 24:34, "This generation shall not pass," 238
Master's statement to Nicodemus, 239, 240
ninety and nine, 223
Peter, II, 3:8, "A thousand years is but a day," 224
Psalms 91, "secret place of the Most High," 127, 128
Romans 5:8, "yet learned He obedience," 222
"The day of the Lord is at hand," 195, 196

"There is set before thee, good and evil," 206
Timothy, II, 2:15, "Study to show thyself approved unto God," 236
"Try the spirits," 336, 337
Bible parallel
Abraham, promise, 226
Abraham, symbology of, 118
blind leading blind, 327
"consider the lilies," 324
creation and destiny of woman, 344
See Also: Creation
Genesis, 253, 254
Gethsemane, 261
"give unto Caesar," 329
"Honor thy father and mother," 316
"I never knew you," 333
Israel, symbology of, 118
Jesus' answer to Pilate, 336
Jesus' question to Peter, "And who do you say I am?" 351
Jesus weeping over Jerusalem, 239
"laborers are few," 56, 57
lamb slain, 225
Last Supper, 93
Lot's wife, 115, 308
Moses, 60
Moses and Red Sea, 240
Nicodemus, 318
parable of talents, 60
Pentecost, 80
Peter sinking, 64
rich young ruler, 39
sacrifice, 287
Saul on road to Damascus, 225
"seek first the kingdom of God," 315
Sermon on Mount, 262
Sodom and Gomorrah, 61
Stephen, 225
temple, 154, 155
temptations of Jesus, 326
ten healed by Master, 92
thief, he who climbs another way, 185, 186
transfiguration, 155, 349, 350
whited sepulchres, 334
Bible study
Daniel, 214, 215
Mark 14, 214, 215

Moses and laws of health, 344
prophets, 201
recommended, 242
Revelation, 201, 343
Blessings
as cooperation in action, 14
come as we become a channel to others, 13
through cooperative thought, intent, purpose, 13, 14
Blood, of Christ, definition, 182, 183
Body
coordination, where to begin, 15
organs, functioning and desires, 32
physical, as reflection of desires and nature, 32
physical, delineations of expressions, 33
physical unison with mental and spiritual, 33
resurrection of, 343
superficial, definition, 337, 338
Books: Song of Sano Tarot, 8
Brain, analogy, 241
Brotherhood, 22
affecting destiny, 299
as shadow of fellowship, 95
compared to fellowship, 92
pattern of fellowship, 95
related to forgiveness, 131
Buddha, faith in, 65

Carnal influences, development of, 254
Change, effected by will, 322
Channel, being a channel makes for coordination, 15
Children of light, definition, 185
Christ—See Also: Jesus
birth, timeliness, 128
blood of, definition, 182, 183
Consciousness, 227, 260, 263, 278
Consciousness attained through application, 51
Consciousness defined, 120, 121
Consciousness differentiated from Christ Spirit, 120, 121
Consciousness makes aware of Comforter, 121
Consciousness related to freedom, 54

Consciousness related to unselfishness, 258, 259
forerunner of, to appear, 165
how to know His presence, 141
life, daily expression, 107
mind of, how to attain, 12
misuse of, 128
realization of His presence, 131
relationship to Michael, 118
sameness, analogy, 307
Savior, personal, 206
Spirit, defined, 113, 120, 121
Spirit is not the man, 113
Spirit, manifestation of, related to sin, 235, 236
Spirit of, 227
Church
Apostles' Creed, origin of, 348, 349
Holy Church, definition, 350, 351
relation to group work, 246, 247
Cities, vibrations of, 303
Clairaudience, 167, 168
Comforter, 99, 100
Christ Consciousness makes aware of, 121
Communion of saints, explanation, 349, 350
Condemnation of others, 239
Confidence vs. faith, 63
Consciousness—See Also: Christ Consciousness
as awareness related to day and night, 220
opening of, 34
related to subconscious mind, 49, 50
Contentment vs. satisfaction, 60, 101
Cooperation, 6-23
action needed, 14
analogy, 88
as first lesson, 5
as foundation, 15
as group cooperates they are lifted up, 11
as preparation, 9
as soul of any group, 14, 15
defined, 14
defined as offering of self to be channel, 13
essential to group work, 17

gaining in the attempt, 20
giving of self, 13, 14
importance in all phases of life, 17, 18
individual techniques, 7, 8, 9, 10
initiated by consciousness of the Master, 11
need for practical application, 12
outline of chapter, 18, 19
promise from, 9
related to accomplishment, 30
related to attitude of mind, 15
related to being a channel, 14
related to giving, 13, 14
related to ideal, 14, 119
related to selflessness and open door, 119
relationship to blessings, 14
why needed, 4
Coordination, where to begin, 15
Creation, 185, 203, 204, 205, 211, 217, 220, 221, 222, 224, 253, 254, 311, 312
analogy, 219
sex, 344
Creative forces
as basis of faith, 61
how to attune to, 12
kept in direction of life, hope, peace, understanding, 11
Creed, Apostles', 341
origin of, 348, 349
Cross
salvation of, 326
why choose, 148, 149
Cross and Crown, 148-165
lesson as turning point, 146
Cycle, 7-year, 87

Darkness, as unawareness of light, 221
Day and Night, 213-226
Dead, communication with, 105
Death, 338
symbology of, 293
Decisions, 301
Dependence, 9
not on another person, 25
on the Father, not on group members, 18, 21

Desire, 253-294
for physical things, to be spiritualized, 259, 261, 262, 263
how to spiritualize, 255
mental, 253
mental, basis of, 254
nature of, how to determine, 275, 276
of flesh, 270
of heart vs. desire of will, 260
offenses of, 101
origin of, 251
physical, 253
physical, basis of, 254
related to choice, 263
related to oneness, 269
Destiny
as law, 298
compared to omens and signs, 299
compared to predestination, 344
determination of, 298
immortality, 313
overruling will, 279
related to brotherhood, 299
related to heredity, 308
related to karma, 338
Destiny of the Mind, Body, Soul, 295-363
Devil—See Also: Satan
existence of, 220
explanation, 205, 206
Dimension, third, manifestations as shadows of the source, 96
Disease as "at-variance with law," 330
Doubt
affecting faith, 69
effects of, 39, 79
springs from impatience, 186
Dreams, 22, 33, 34, 35, 36, 41, 42, 79, 135, 136, 145, 146, 196, 247, 300
Edgar Cayce's relation to group activities, 24, 25
guidance, 6
indicating individual's part in group work, 9, 10
marriage and apple, interpretation, 276
mountain climbing, 258
nature of, 329
nature of, discussion, 258

precognition explained, 329
prophecy and interpretation, 22
related to group activities, 70
related to group experience, 14
responsible for prayer group, 8
seeing Master, 216
self-awakening, 36, 41
strangers, 220
symbols of spiritual awakening, 38, 39
   See Also: Symbology
testing of group, 25

Egypt, temple
   activity, 35
   records, 97
Elementals, 11
Enlightenment
   ideal of, 243
   starts with harmony, 18
Entity, definition, 47, 48
Environment, vibrations, 265, 303
Epictetus, quotation explained, 100
Eternity, 279
Evil
   as rebellion, 206
   existence of, 220
   powers of, loosed for a purpose, 128
Evolution of soul, mind, matter, 219
Experiences
   how to interpret, 97
   sources of, types of, 337
Eye, spiritual or third eye, 86

Faith, 73-80
   affected by doubt, 69
   affecting will, 68, 69
   affecting growth of soul, 69
   as creative principle, 73
   as living truth when applied, 73
   as the Son, 69
   brings awakening to virtue, 80
   brings working forces, 78
   compared to confidence, 68
   creative forces as basis, 57
   definition, 63
   determined by ideal, 63
   how to extend, 73
   how to increase, 57, 75
   how to strengthen, 76
   Jesus, Buddha, Mohammed, 65

not of the senses, 64
related to direction of soul, 68
related to enlightenment of others, 66
related to healing, 74
related to ideal, 58
spiritual, definition, 79
strengthen by works, 67
strengthened by tests, 76
sufficient for each trial, 67
techniques to strengthen, 65
vs. confidence, 64
Father—See Also: God
   definition vs. God, 224
   kingdom of, compared to kingdom of heaven, 120
   manifestations of, 229, 230
   throne of, explained, 120
   when glorified in a person, 56
   will of, as life, 306
Fear
   how to eliminate, 122, 123
   relation to becoming the law, 302
Fellowship, 91-101
   compared to brotherhood, 92
   extreme test, 93
   how to attain, 94
   how to determine experiences as signs, 97
   importance, 89, 90
   reflected in brotherhood, 92, 95
   requires unison of purpose, 91
Fire, cleansing by, 201, 339
Forces
   creative, as basis of faith, 61
   faith brings working forces, 78
   good and evil, 205, 214, 218
   mental, insight by introspection, 49, 50
   occult vs. psychic, 86
   psychic and spiritual, 86, 87
   reflected, 204
   unseen, as aiding group, 14
   unseen more powerful than seen, 35
Forgiveness, 89, 90, 131
   related to patience, 98, 99
Form as guiding element vs. faith and hope, 75
Freedom related to Christ Consciousness, 54

Fruits of spirit, 227
    bring awareness of infinite, 204
    law of love, 198

Giving of self is cooperation, 13
Glands
    lyden, 86, 87
    man has lost vision through, 86
    pineal, 87
    pituitary, 86, 87
Glory, 364-381
    when Father is glorified in a person, 55
Glossolalia, gift or developed talent, 13
God—See Also: Father
    approval needed only from God, 236
    as first cause, 203, 204
    depend on God, not on individuals, 9
    distinguished from Jesus, 141
    explanation vs. Father, 224
    manifestations of, 228
God the Father and His Manifestations, 227-252
Godhead, defined, 57
Golden cup, 87
Golden Rule, extreme test of fellowship, 93
Good and evil, 218
    compared to day and night, 214
    forces are one, 205
Gospel, definition, 320
    See Also: Bible
Grace
    law of, 320
    related to mind and will, 254, 282
Group—See Also: Cooperation
    accomplishment related to cooperation, 30
    activities related to church, 246, 247
    activities related to Spirit, 15
    activities related to work of A.R.E., 243, 244
    activities, vision of, 162, 163
    application of lessons stressed, 245
    as they cooperate they are lifted, 11

    contribution of each member, importance of, 18, 41, 43, 59, 85, 207, 208, 237, 286
    cooperation by application, 87
    cooperative effort, importance of, 20
    cooperative in purpose, need action, 14
    dependency on the Father, not on other members, 18
    dependent on one another, 24
    directive, mind should be not of elementals but of spiritual forces, 11
    directive re relationship with others, 22
    directive re understanding, 22
    dream—See Also: Dreams
    dream depicting relationship, 14
    dream of Cayce re activities of group members, 70
    dynamics, importance of contribution of each member explained, 85
    each called for a service, 279
    each called into service, 272, 273
    each called must answer in person, 91, 92
    each has passed through trials, 9
    each member as a standard, 24
    eliminate dependence on each other, 25
    evaluation of lessons, 246
    expressions of transformation, 31
    hindrance of saying one thing, living another, 305
    how to complete lesson (Cooperation), 10
    how to conduct meetings, 7, 8
    how to cooperate with and serve the group, 13
    how to get in accord with unseen forces, 14
    how to handle discouragement, 272, 273, 278
    how to serve the group, affirmation, 12
    ideal, how to realize, 56
    individual as link or spoke, not the whole, 88
    individual gifts, 3

individual, importance of each, 17, 21

individual part in lesson, 5

individual participation necessary, 88

individual's part indicated in dream, 9, 10

individuals called in respective spheres, 27

individuals chosen for specific tasks, 17

judgment, measurements, criteria, 24

leadership selection, 10

lesson depends on individual contribution, 85

lessons as experiences not merely tenets, 292, 293

material as living truth, living lesson, 19

meditation related to lessons, 19

member not independent, not dependent on another but on God, 9

member's aid or hindrance determined by application, 28

message from one to another, 8

mind, 317

new members, attitude, 247

new members, decision, 294

new members, how to approach, 247

new members, organization of new groups, 247, 248

organization, purpose necessary, 6

participation by desire and choice, 26

preparation, 9

promises, 3, 162, 163

promises, doing the will of the Father, 25

promises given re light to world, 10

promises, messages from one to another, 8

promises, powers from on high, 4

promises, related to cooperation, 9

promises, reward of cooperative effort, 20

promises, safety in His peace, 21

promises, seeking His face, 21

promises, sign to be given, 54, 55, 62

promises, using His strength, 21

promises, way being opened, 19

purpose of, 202, 245

relationship with Spirit, 14

sign as tests, opportunities, visions, 62, 63

sign given if cooperation, 4

soul, 317, 318

soul of any group is cooperation, 15

source of lessons, discussion, 8, 286, 287, 293

steps for becoming of one mind, 4

strong as its weakest member, 30

talents plus cooperation with ideal, 66

transformation in three expressions, 31

warning re turning back, 43

work, how to expedite, 21

work, importance of cooperation, 17

work, importance of ideal, 51

work, related to dream, 70

work, related to love, 56

Growth
  process defined, 75
  relationship of mind, 314
  slowness explained, 101

Habit, subconscious mind classified as, 49

Halaliel, 222, 224, 286, 301

Happiness, 433-450

Harmony
  active attitude of mind, 15
  related to enlightenment, 18

Healing
  development, 96
  group, determining individual's involvement, 12, 13
  group, prayer leader, 6, 7
  modes, 53, 330
  position for laying on of hands, 78
  spiritual, gift or development, 13
  techniques and process, 74

Heart
  defined, 68
  desire of, 260
  pure, analogy, 68

Heaven
    kingdom of, compared to kingdom
        of the Father, 120
    rebellion in, 224
Hell, created with desires, 169
Heredity
    definition, 327
    influence of, 254
    related to destiny, 308
Holy Grail, quest of, 145, 146
Hypocrisy, hinders the most, 305

Ideal
    activating, 76
    affecting faith, 58, 63
    as measurement, 54
    Bible parallel, 60
    brings awakening, 79
    dynamics of, 54
    how to realize group ideal, 56
    inception of, 310
    must be set in Him, 54
    not man-made, 51
    promise regarding sign, 55
    related to application, 58
    related to cooperation, 14, 119
    related to "Cooperation" and
        "Know Thyself," 55
    related to destiny of mind, 310,
        312, 313
    related to escape from trials, 108
    related to opportunity, 198
    related to will, 37
    self controlled by, 126
    spiritual, 55
    techniques, 53, 54, 55, 56, 57, 60,
        61
Imaginative self, 131
Immortality, 313
In His Presence, 133-147
Infinite
    affecting finite, 205
    awareness of, brought by fruits of
        spirit, 204
Introspection
    methods, 49, 50
    necessity of, 39, 40
Intuition
    manifested more in female, 86
    process explained, 86

Israel
    of the Lord, seekers, 126
    symbology of, 118

Jesus—See Also: Christ
    as Son distinguished from God,
        141
    awareness of, 121
    consciousness—"Not as I will but
        Thine will be done in earth as in
        heaven," 13
    consciousness of the Master initi-
        ates cooperation, 11
    definition of patience, 100
    faith in vs. Buddha, Mohammed,
        65
    life of, as study to know self, 12
    perfection in materiality, 226
    promises, 4
    promises fulfilled as we are faithful
        in caring for others, 13
    promises, "seek and ye shall find,"
        13
    promises, "they that seek My face
        shall find it," 13
    purpose and desires of, 280
    salvation by the Name of, 169
    Savior, personal, 206
    second coming, 196, 229
    second coming, forerunner of, 165
    temptations of, 326
Josephus' history of Mt. Seir, 37
Judgment
    defined, 321
    of self not others, 82

Karma
    caused by self-exaltation, 304
    change in influences as expression
        of transformation, 31
    related to destiny, 338
Kindness never offensive, 40
Kingdom
    animal, plant and mineral, 318
    of Father, explanation, 116
    of heaven, compared to kingdom of
        Father, 120
    of heaven, within, how to attain,
        120
Know Thyself, 20-54

Knowing self
  importance of lesson, 44
  instructions on steps to, 12
  related to eliminating dependence
    on another, 25
Knowledge, 379-415
  compared to understanding, 83

Law, 197, 217
  as love, 183
  becoming the law, not subject to,
    301, 302
  defined, 152
  disease caused by varying from,
    330
  how to fulfill, 316
  mind relating to, 319, 320
  of cause and effect, 329
  of mercy, not sacrifice, 320
  of sacrifice, 283, 287, 288
  one is subject to the laws of envi-
    ron, 252
  related to destiny, 298
  related to fear, 302
  relating to judgment, 321
  spiritual, effect of, 304
Laws affecting mind, 314
Lessons
  as experiences, not merely theo-
    ries, 292, 293
  as experiences, not tenets, 244
  distribution, 64
  each receives in own language, 80
  how to evaluate, 246
  importance of contribution of each,
    explanation, 85
  material as living truth, 19
  purpose of, 246
  relationship to church, 246, 247
  source of, 286, 287
  techniques in preparing, 10
Life
  actions of bespeak the thoughts of
    the heart, 198
  as will of the Father, 306
  definition, 161
  motivative forces are composite ac-
    tivity of Spirit, 130
Light, 218
  bearer of, 40
  brought by application, 28

children of, definition, 185
explanation of activity, 214
to a waiting world, not individual,
  10
Lindbergh case, 59, 60, 64, 76
Loneliness, 200
Looking back, 186
  analogy, 115
Lot's wife, experience explained,
  115
Lord Thy God Is One, 166-177
Love, 178-196
  as law, 183
  as renewing strength, 26
  brotherly love as aid to know self,
    40
  defined, 178
  expressions of, 181, 182
  first in importance, 186
  laws of, use in temple activity, 35
  lose self in love, 8
  of God, not of man, 300
  related to creation, 185
  relationship to group work, 56
  universal, necessary for unity of
    purpose, 6
Lucifer, 224
Lyden, 86, 87

Man
  as companion of Creator, 254
  carnal influence, development, 254
  instincts and desires, 254
  spiritualize desires, 254, 255
Master, consciousness of the Master,
  initiates cooperation, 11
Materialization as shadow of the
  source, 96
Matter, defined, 310
Meditation
  as communion with the highest,
    184
  as rest, 215
  experiences, 143
  group vs. individual techniques, 7
  makes group of one mind, one pur-
    pose, 19
  positions for, 74, 75
  prayer of protection, 11
  related to lessons, 19

source of virtue and understanding, 82
sunrise, 7
time recommended, 219
visions experienced and interpreted, 12
"What wilt Thou have me do, O Lord?" 4
Mental
desire, basis of, 254
forces, insight by introspection, 50
Mercy, law of, 283, 284, 287, 288, 320
Michael
message from, 112, 113, 118, 124, 144
relationship to Christ, 118
Mind
active attitudes of, peace, harmony, understanding, 15
affecting growth, 314
affecting materiality, 315
as the builder, explanation, 311, 317, 318
attitude of, related to cooperation, 15
attributes of, 310
children of the mind, 15
destiny of, 311
developed by will, 254
developed by will, explanation, 282, 283
divider between man and group soul, 318
divisions and expressions of, 310, 313, 314, 315, 316, 319
grace acts upon, 282, 283
group mind as animal, plant and mineral kingdom, 317
how to attune to Creative Forces, 12
laws affecting, 314
not of elementals but spiritual forces, 11
of Christ, how to attain, 12
of Christ, related to application, 12
of Christ, related to service, 12
of soul, as builder, explanation, 255
physical, 313
physical body as expression of, 311
purpose affecting, 333

subconscious and conscious forces, 68
training subconscious, 49
Mineral kingdom, 317
Mohammed, faith in, 65
Moral aptitudes make for shadows, 54
Mount, defined, 152, 154, 155

Name
each individual given by Christ, 146
given each according to specific calling, 154
salvation by, 169
salvation of, 325, 326

Occult forces, compared to psychic, 86
Omens
as signs, compared to destiny, 298, 299
how to use, 305, 306
Oneness, 173, 174, 175
as law, 312
how to become conscious of, 171
of force, 203
of good and evil, 205
related to desire, 269, 270
Open Door, 114-132
Opportunities
as signs, 62
definition, 197
lost, 117
Opportunity, 197-212

Passivity, definition, 163
Patience, 102-113
active not passive, 99, 107
as necessary activity, 102
beginning of, 100
dead, 235
deterred by satisfaction, 99
faults of others, 100
how to practice, 105
how to overcome daily harassments, 99, 100
lack of, initiates fear, 99
losing, 104
Master's definition, 100
must be experienced, 98

need to eliminate criticism, 100
related to forgiveness, 99
related to wisdom, 100
requiring trust, 103
technique to handle problems, 105
with those who disagree, 52
Pattern
as form, 328
as shadow, 95
in the mount, 152, 153, 154, 155, 283
Peace as active attitude of mind, 15
Phares, 60
Physical
body as expression of mind, 311
body as form and pattern, 328
body as temple, 347
body, destiny of, 341, 342, 343
body, effect of desires, 48
body, heredity defined, 327
body, rejuvenation, 338
desire, basis of, 254
plane, soul experiments in, develops, magnifies, 48
Physiognomy as expression of experiences, 32, 33
Pineal, 87
Pituitary, 86, 87
Planetary sojourns, 219
Plant kingdom, 317
Polarity, 204
Power, as expression of transformation, 31
Prayer
for those seeking aid, 50
given, 288, 289, 294
Group started by dream, 8
See Also: Healing Group
"I am in Thy hands," 325
"I cannot bear this alone . . ." 261
individual concept determines technique, 75
leader of prayer in healing group, 6
"Lord, use me . . ." 335
of protection, 14, 83
source of virtue and understanding, 82
"trust in the Lord," 321
Predestination, 344

Prediction
discoveries, 164
forerunner to be born, 165
of disaster, time not fulfilled, 111
Promise, answer given to "What wilt Thou have me do, O Lord?" 4
See Also: Group Promises; Jesus' promises
Prophets, false prophets, defined, 128
Psychic—See Also: Forces
automatic writing, 101, 106
clairaudience, 167, 168
communication with the dead, 105
development, 86, 87
forces, 86, 87
forces, compared to occult, 86
intuition, 86
source of information, explanation, 244
telepathy, 8
vision interpreted, 167, 168, 169
Purging
analogy, 322
by fire, 201, 339
Purifying soul through material suffering, 304
Purpose
of group, 272, 273
singleness of, 333
unison of, 91
unity of, universal love necessary, 6

Ram, 60
Rebellion
analogy, 48, 49
as evil, 206
in heaven, 224
in the Mount, 152, 153
Regenerating, awakening, 15
Reincarnation, 225
Rejuvenation, 338
Resurrection of the body, explanation, 343
Revenge, 262
Righteous wrath, 99
anger, 101, 103
Righteousness as the attempt, 326

Sacrifice, 320, 347
law of, 287, 288

Saints, communion of, explanation, 347
Salvation by the Name, 169, 187
Satan, 224
  explanation, 205, 206
  See Also: Devil
Satisfaction
  compared to contentment, 60, 101
  defined as self-glorification, 101
  deters patience, 99
Savior, personal, 206
  See Also: Christ; Jesus
Search for God
  manuscript approval, 20, 44, 45, 46, 47, 62, 67, 68, 77, 81, 82, 89, 98, 112, 130, 145, 158, 170, 184, 210, 223, 251, 281
Secret place of the most high, defined, 127, 128
Seeking, self as integral factor, 32
Self
  as integral factor in seeking, 32
  awareness as selfishness, 122
  bewilderment, 14
  desire for continuity of self, 37
  glorification, effects of, 324
  how to know self, 12, 39, 40
  judge self, not others, 82
  knowledge of, key to understanding universal law, 44
  measure by what ye can give, 25
  must have part in losing self, 8
  not gifts related to service, 39
  only what it receives from within and without, 24
  reasoning of, 32
  stand aside and watch self, 39
Selfishness
  as self-awareness, 122
  how to distinguish from unselfishness, 258, 259
Senses, activity of, related to desire, 254
Service
  don't judge results, 92
  greatest, 58
  involves self, not gifts, 39
  prayer of, 335
  related to mind of Christ, 12
  related to understanding, 58

requires sacrifice of carnal forces, 144
  sanctify self, 74
  to others, cooperation, 11
Sex, creation, 344
Sexes, explained, 344
  intuition greater in female, 86
  woman, destiny of, 344
Shame, affecting standard, 26
Sickness as conflict, 330
Signs, 315
  and omens compared to destiny, 298, 299
  as opportunities, tests, visions, 62
  experiences as, how to interpret, 97
  how to use, 305
  mistaken for law, 298
  only given to those who cooperate, 2
Silver cord, 87
Sin
  begins as desire for self-exaltation, 269
  original, 214
Soul
  as companion, 269
  as gift from God, 52
  attributes of, 107
  group soul, 318
  grows slowly, 101
  meets what it has built in the spiritual plane, 48
  mind of soul as builder, explanation, 255
  purified through material suffering, 304
  registering experiences and impressions, 33
  will as attribute, 68
Source of information in readings, 8, 293
Spirit, 9, 10, 451-502
  activity of in material world, 80
  ask for answers, 97
  composite activity of, as motivative forces of life, 130
  consciousness of indwelling, 104
  gives utterance through speech, 30
  is the true life, 121
  matter as expression of, 310

of the Master, works through life,
  53, 54
of the Creative Forces, 29
of Truth, cooperation of, 59
of unrest, 15
reacts to manifestation of love in
  daily experiences, 185
related to group work, 15
Spiritual
  eye, 86
  faith, defined, 79
  forces, 86, 87
  how to become more spiritual, 6
  insight, 56
  law, effect of, 304
Spirituality rather than materiality
  as expression of transformation,
  31
Standard of measurement for self, 22
Subconscious—See Also: Mind
  defined, 49
  mind, training, 49
Superficial body, definition, 337, 338
Symbology
  Abraham, 118, 221
  altar, 276
  blood, 95
  Christ, 221
  climbing, 258
  cross, 146
  David, 221
  day and night, 219, 220
  death, 293
  dream—See: Dreams
  eye, 86
  fire, 339
  Frankenstein, 87
  fruit, 276
  gold, 82
  heart, 68
  holy grail, 145, 146
  Israel, 118, 126
  lamb slain, 225, 226
  lambs, 200
  letters (Greek), 270, 271
  light, orb of, 168, 169
  lights, 95, 96
  marriage, 276
  Moses, 221
  mountain, 258
  night, 56, 57

oil, 53
pattern in the Mount, 154, 155
sackcloth and ashes, 61
scepter, 118
serpent, 206
sheep, 200
water, large body of water, 12
Symbols of spiritual awakening, 39

Tama, 60
Telepathy, group messages from one
  to another, 8
Temple activity, use of laws of love,
  35
Temptation, overcoming, 325, 326
Temptations of Jesus, 326
Tests
  extreme test of fellowship, 93
  faith strengthened by, 76
  signs, visions, opportunities as, 62
Thought, atom, analogy, 74
Throne of the Father, explanation,
  120
Time, 96, 224, 225
  all time is one time, 7
  and space, 226, 265
  fulfilled, 195, 196
Transformation, expressions of, 31
Trial
  faith sufficient for each trial, 67
  no test or trial without means of
    escape, 108
Tribulation works patience, 110
Truth
  application of, analogy, 59
  becoming living, 133
  defined, 83, 320, 321, 322
  earned, not learned, 83
  ideal, founded in, 51, 52
  oil of, as healing, 53
  relationship to desire, 270
  requires application, 59
  spirit of, 64
  spirit of, awareness of activity
    leads to attaining kingdom of
    heaven, 120
  white light of, 41

Understanding
  application rather than seeking, 28
  as active attitude of mind, 15

as seed, 80
comes from patience, 99
compared to knowledge, 83
determined by application, 28, 35, 79
related to application, 22
related to purpose, 79
related to service, 58
related to virtue, 78, 79
source of, 82

Vibrations
effect of, 303
of cities, 303
relating to environment, 265
that created must be met, 48, 49
Virtue and Understanding, 77-90
Virtue
and understanding, analogy, 79
as fruit of faith, 80
defined, 78, 79
determined by faith, 80
measured by spiritual, not material, 83
Visions, 96, 171—See Also: Dreams; Symbology
alpha and omega, interpretation given, 215
as signs, 63
become manifestations, 34
Christ, interpretation given, 259, 260
Christ on cross, all-seeing eye, interpretation, 80
Christ, shadow of, 219
Christ, the shepherd, interpretation given, 116, 117
drops of blood, 95
floating sphere, interpretation given, 168, 169
Greek letters, 270, 271
hand of Master, 36
interpretation, 167, 168, 284

lights, 96
pyramid of smoke and burning bush, interpretation, 339
sky and figures, interpretation, 276, 277
walking with Master, 218, 219
water, large body of, 12

Water
spiritual elements of, 116
vision of, interpretation, 12
What Is My Ideal?, 51-72
Will
attribute of soul, 68
defined, 422
desire of, 260, 261
given for choices in materiality, 206
of the Father, life, 306
overruled through destiny, 279
related to destiny, 338
relation to atonement, 182
relationship to ideal, 37
use of, develops mind, explanation, 254, 282, 283
Wisdom, 416-432
related to patience, 100
Woman
destiny of, 344
intuition greater, 86
Words
importance of words in being a channel, 15, 16
responsibility for every idle word, 173
wait before speaking, 21
Work, 56, 57—See Also: Group, work interpreted, 30
World affairs, 161
period of seeking, 133

Zan (Zend), 241

Affirmations

Cooperation, 11

Not my will but Thine, O Lord, be done in and through me. Let me ever be a channel of blessings, today, now, to those that I contact, in every way. Let my going in, mine coming outs, be in accord with that Thou would have me do, and as the call comes, "Here am I, send me—use me!"

Know Thyself, 21

Father, as we seek to see and know Thy face, may we each—as individuals, and as a group—come to know ourselves, even as we are known, that we—as lights in Thee—may give the better concept of Thy spirit in this world.

What Is My Ideal?, 52

God be merciful to me! Help Thou my unbelief! Let me see in Him that Thou would have me see in my fellow man! Let me see in my brother that I see in Him whom I worship!

Faith, 59

Create in me a pure heart, O God! Open Thou mine heart to the faith Thou hast implanted in all that seek Thy face! Help Thou mine unbelief in my God, in my neighbor, in myself!

Virtue and Understanding, 76

Let virtue and understanding be in me, for my defense is in Thee, O Lord, my Redeemer; for Thou hearest the prayer of the upright in heart.

Fellowship, 89

How excellent is Thy name in the earth, O Lord! Would I have fellowship with Thee, I must show brotherly love to my fellow man. Though I come in humbleness and have aught against my brother, my prayer, my meditation, does not rise to Thee. Help Thou my efforts in my approach to Thee.

Patience, 98

How gracious is Thy presence in the earth, O Lord. Be Thou the guide, that we with patience, may run the race which is set before us, looking to Thee, the Author, the Giver of Light [Life?].

Open Door, 112

As the Father knoweth me, so may I know the Father, through the Christ Spirit, the door to the kingdom of the Father. Show Thou me the way.

In His Presence, 127

Our Father, who art in Heaven, may Thy kingdom come in earth through Thy presence in me, that the light of Thy word may shine unto those that I meet day by day. May Thy presence in my brother be such that I may glorify

Thee. May I so conduct mine own life that others may know Thy presence abides with me, and thus glorify Thee.

The Cross and the Crown, 146

Our Father, our God, as we approach that that may give us a better insight of what He bore in the cross, what His glory may be in the crown, may Thy blessings—as promised through Him—be with us as we study together in His name.

The Lord Thy God Is One, 158

As my body, mind and soul are one, Thou, O Lord, in the manifestations in the earth, in power, in might, in glory, art one. May I see in that I do, day by day, more of that realization, and manifest the more.

Love, 176

Our Father, through the love that Thou hast manifested in the world through Thy Son, the Christ, make us more aware of God is Love.

Opportunity, 195

In seeking to magnify Thy name, Thy glory, through that Thou dost make manifest in me, O Lord, be Thou the guide, and—day by day, as the opportunity is given—let my hands, my mind, my body, do that Thou wouldst have me do as Thine own in the earth; for, as I manifest, may Thy glory become known to those through the love, the promises Thou hast made in Thy Son.

Day and Night, 211

In Thy mercies, O heavenly Father, wilt Thou be the guide in the study of the manifestations of Thy love, even as in "Day unto day uttereth speech and night unto night sheweth knowledge." So may the activities of my life, as a representative of Thy love, be a manifestation in the earth.

God the Father and His Manifestations, 224

May the desire of my heart be such that I may become more and more aware of the spirit of the Father, through the Christ, manifesting in me.

Desire, 242

Father, let Thy desires be my desires. Let my desires, God, be Thy desires, in spirit and in truth.

Destiny of the Mind, 294

Lord, Thou art my dwelling place! In Thee, O Father, do I trust! Let me see in myself, in my brother, that Thou would bless in Thy Son, Thy gift to me that I might know Thy ways! Thou hast promised, O Father, to hear when Thy children call! Harken, that I may be kept in the way that I may know the glory of Thy Son as Thou hast promised in Him that we through Him might have access to Thee! Thou, O God, alone, can save! Thou alone can keep my ways!

Destiny of the Body, 335

Lord, use me in whatever way or manner that my body may be as a living example of Thy love to the brethren of our Lord.

Destiny of the Soul, 357

Lord, let me—my mind, my body, my soul—be at one with Thee: That I— through Thy promises in Him, Thy Son—may know Thee more and more.

Glory, 361

Open Thou mine eyes, O God, that I may know the glory Thou hast prepared for me.

Knowledge, 379

Let the knowledge of the Lord so permeate my being that there is less and less of self, more and more of God, in my dealings with my fellow man; that the Christ may be in all, through all, in His name.

Wisdom, 411

Our Father, our God, may the light of Thy wisdom, of Thy strength, of Thy power, guide—as we would apply ourselves in Thy service for others. In His name we seek.

Happiness, 425

Our Father, our God, in my own consciousness let me find happiness in the love of Thee, for the love I bear toward my fellow man. Let my life, my words, my deeds, bring the joy and happiness of the Lord in Jesus to each I meet day by day.

Spirit, 452

Father, God, in Thy mercy, in Thy love, be Thou with us now. For we know and we speak of Thy love. And help us then to put away, for the hour, the cares of this life; that we may know in truth that the Spirit and the Lamb say, "Come." Let they that hear also say, "Come." Let all that will, come and drink of the water of life.

Righteousness versus Sin, 498

Create in me, O God, a new purpose, a righteous spirit: That I may, as Thy child, be a living example of that I have professed and do profess to believe, by manifesting same among my fellow men.

God—Love—Man, 513

Let that light be within me in such measures that I, as a child of God, may realize His love for man. May I live that, then, in my life day by day.

Man's Relationship to Man, 516

Father, God! Let me, as Thy child, see in my fellow man the divinity I would worship in Thee. Let me in my daily life be a witness to Him, who exemplified for man, to man, man's relationship to God, and the manner of relationship that should be as man to man. For we ask it in His name, Jesus the Christ.

Bible References

OLD TESTAMENT

GENESIS
1   211
1-3   502
1:1   311
1:3   196, 455
1:3-5   460
1:22   413
1:28   396, 413
2:2-3   224
2:7   254
2:9   313
2:17   383
2:21-22 344
3:3   383
3:12   502
4:7   455
6:2   481, 482
6:6   344
8:17   413
9:7   413
11:1-9 383, 398
15:6   208
18:32   446
19:26   97, 103, 115, 308
22:2-14 509
32:24-30 118
35:11   413
38:6-7 287
49:10   113, 118

EXODUS
3:5   60, 67
3:14   47, 53, 94, 136, 347
20:5   510
20:12   316

LEVITICUS
26:12   94, 228, 367

NUMBERS
4:15   337
6:24-26 346

DEUTERONOMY
4:24   110
4:29   13

6:4   131, 136, 203, 312, 320, 368
8:3   486
17:6   337
19:15   337
30:11-14 360, 420, 491
30:14   228
30:15   206, 208, 482
32:30   384

JOSHUA
24:15   122, 419, 435, 464, 482

I SAMUEL
4:9   295
6:19   376, 377
16:7   273, 275, 276, 343, 367

II SAMUEL
6:6-7   287, 376, 377

I KINGS
19:12   414, 435, 465

I CHRONICLES
2:3   287
13:9   287
13:9-10 376, 377
22:16   174, 269, 394, 504

II CHRONICLES
7:14   13, 38, 233

JOB
1:6   460
8:3   384
14:14   211
19:25   289
21:22   384
38:7   211

PSALMS
1:2   4
8:5   131
11:4   22, 302, 435
19:1-2 221
19:2   216, 368
19:7   345, 511
19:14   232, 304, 377, 391
23:4   142
24:1   174, 368, 391
27:14   4, 21, 38, 105

37:34   4, 21, 38, 105
46:10   47, 229
51:6   270
51:10   68, 477
82:6   258
84:10   484
90:4   224
91:1   127, 128
91:7   384, 391
91:11   132, 326, 359, 390, 461
102:2   277, 490
103:13   192
106:31   212
118:6   103
139:8   142

PROVERBS
1:7   398, 399
4:5   9
4:7   9
7:15   13, 192
14:12   337, 443
16:25   337, 443
19:17   74
20:22   4, 21, 38, 105
23:7   192, 205, 298, 311, 314, 318, 334
24:12   381, 382, 386
25:22   40, 290
27:19   29, 136, 201

ECCLESIASTES
9:8   31
9:10   13, 61, 182, 198, 229, 436, 511
11:3   48, 327, 399
12:6   87

ISAIAH
1:18   117
6:8   5, 11, 264, 276, 465
13:6   192, 195, 294, 299, 382, 392, 398
14:12   358
25:8   431
28:10   7, 13, 26, 53, 56, 101, 108, 113, 126, 159, 191, 234, 417, 480
28:13   7, 13, 26, 53, 56, 101, 108, 113, 126, 159, 191, 234, 417, 480
34:4   117
46:10   215, 216
55:6   269, 387, 488
55:8-9   191, 293, 294
66:1   380

JEREMIAH
7:23   94, 228, 367
11:4   94, 228, 367
30:22   94, 228, 367

EZEKIEL
20:37   240, 316, 361
36:28   94, 228, 367
43:11   11

DANIEL
12:7   195, 196

HOSEA
6:6   283, 287, 288, 320, 437

JOEL
1:15   192, 195, 294, 299, 382, 392, 398

MICAH
4:4   60

HABAKKUK
2:2   284, 397
2:20   22, 123, 269, 302, 435

ZEPHANIAH
1:5   287
1:7   192, 195, 294, 299, 382, 392, 398

HAGGAI
2:7   260

MALACHI
3:10   487

NEW TESTAMENT

MATTHEW
3:9   118
3:12   138
3:17   121
4:4   486
4:6   132, 326, 359, 390, 461
4:10   179
4:19   27
5:3   445, 449
5:4   444, 445
5:5   103, 445
5:8   103
5:11-12   427
5:15   169
5:16   75, 192, 196, 239, 267, 268, 352, 353, 463, 464, 466

5:18	324
5:20	500, 501
5:26	324
5:28	482
5:29	122
5:37	10, 122, 138, 185, 268, 279, 296, 390, 474, 487
5:40	262
5:40-41	306, 420, 433, 443
5:43	233
5:44	351, 430, 464
5:45	393, 430
5:46	391
5:46-47	351
5:48	307, 502
6:6	30, 187, 306
6:8	13, 123, 257
6:9	406
6:10	13, 25, 122
6:19	241, 445, 464, 488
6:21	198, 445
6:22	86, 339
6:24	316
6:27	30, 314, 315, 393
6:27-31	142
6:28-29	324
6:30	421
6:32	13, 123, 257
6:33	60, 315, 361, 408
6:34	22, 60, 390
7:1-2	54, 82, 92, 104, 131, 306, 383, 384, 419, 438, 511
7:2	320, 367, 501
7:3-5	122, 465
7:6	4, 59
7:7	4, 7, 10, 13, 22, 38, 39, 75, 137, 151, 171, 191, 209, 257, 258, 299, 305, 348, 350, 360, 406, 435, 486, 490, 512
7:12	90, 93, 192, 298
7:14	44, 84
7:16	80, 194, 227, 248, 306, 388
7:20	80, 194, 227, 248, 388
7:21-22	25, 227, 492
7:21-23	333, 351
8:26	421
9:5	330
9:12	92
9:13	283, 287, 288, 320, 437
9:29	373
9:37	56, 59, 192
10:8	43, 443
10:19	4, 67, 208, 278
10:22	208
10:24	186, 244
10:27	335
10:28	262, 300
10:29-31	386
10:39	8, 161, 404
10:41	65, 306
10:42	40, 75, 88, 182, 231, 232, 418, 443
11:11	484
11:15	185
11:21-24	61
11:28-30	481
11:29	117, 307
11:29-30	294, 362, 366, 390, 466
11:30	126, 137, 288
12:7	283, 287, 288, 320, 437
12:18	121
12:34	199, 230
12:36	173
12:39	4
12:48-49	27
12:48-50	46, 229, 334, 351, 480, 484
13:9	185
13:12	137, 290, 345
13:13	376
13:43	185
14:27	100, 167, 170, 187, 414
14:28	450
14:30-31	64
14:31	421
15:11	48, 318
15:14	47, 327, 492
16:8	421
16:13-18	350-351
16:15-18	299
16:17	287, 453, 454
16:18	198, 350, 351
16:21	479
16:23	179, 454
16:25	8
16:26	487
16:28	349
17:1-9	349, 350
17:5	121, 326
17:19-21	61
17:20	63, 64, 373
18:7	263, 323, 438, 480

18:9   122
18:12-13   92, 223, 444
18:20   9, 456
18:21-22   99, 235
19:17   84, 509
19:19   233
19:21   39
19:30   162
20:16   59, 162, 363, 484, 504, 505
20:21-23   27
20:22   4, 427
20:23   18, 294, 370
22:14   59, 363, 484, 504, 505
22:21   329
22:30   344
22:37-39   191, 248, 370, 404, 417, 465, 472
22:39   233
23:11   6, 291, 335, 393, 488
23:12   232
23:27   48, 334
23:37   209, 239, 445
24:23   492
24:24   128
24:34   238
24:34-36   111
24:35   48, 75, 117, 123, 236, 298, 299, 305, 333, 373, 391, 434, 438
24:36   229
25:14-30   60
25:21   99, 104, 110, 123, 126, 128, 137, 151, 152, 174, 190
25:23   104, 110, 128, 190
25:29   137, 290, 345
25:40   90, 104, 105, 134, 143, 180, 182, 190, 200, 259, 263, 266, 268, 277, 289, 293, 298, 300, 306, 307, 331, 365, 374, 402, 414, 444, 466, 514
25:45   90, 92, 134, 143, 180, 182, 190, 200, 259, 263, 266, 268, 277, 289, 293, 298, 300, 306, 307, 331, 365, 374, 402, 414, 444, 466, 514
26:26   446
26:26-28   146
26:26-29   359
26:41   109, 117, 118, 143, 261, 269, 315, 348, 419, 501
28:18   110
28:20   67, 138, 141, 142, 232, 486, 510

MARK
1:11   121
1:17   27
2:9   330
2:17   92
3:33-34   27
3:33-35   46, 229, 334, 351, 480, 484
4:9   185
4:11-13   376
4:20   8, 10, 25
4:21   169
4:23   185
4:24   54, 131, 320, 367, 501
4:25   137, 290, 345
4:39   127
6:50   100, 167, 170, 187, 414
7:16   185
7:20   48, 318
7:37   229
8:33   179
8:35   8
8:36   487
9:1-10   349, 350
9:7   121, 326
9:28-29   61
9:41   40, 75, 88, 182, 231, 232, 418, 443
9:47   122
10:21   39
10:31   162
10:37-40   27
10:39   294
10:40   18
10:44   335
12:17   329
12:25   344
12:29   131, 136, 203, 312, 320, 368
12:30-31   191, 248, 370, 404, 417, 465, 472
12:31   233
12:33   404
13:11   67
13:22   128
13:31   48, 75, 117, 123, 236, 298, 299, 305, 333, 373, 391, 434, 438
13:32   229
13:33   109
14:22   446
14:22-24   146
14:22-25   359

14:38   109, 118, 143, 261, 269, 315, 348, 419, 501
16:15   404

LUKE
1:35   235
2   502
2:7   413
2:11   468
2:14   413
2:19   187, 381, 382, 386
2:49   30, 440, 502
3:8   118
3:17   138
3:18   137
3:22   121
4:8   179
4:10   132, 326, 359, 390, 461
5:31   92
6:28   430, 464
6:29   262, 306, 420, 433, 443
6:31   90, 93
6:32   391
6:37   54, 82, 90, 92, 104, 241, 299, 306, 383, 384, 389, 419, 438, 501, 511
6:37-38   131
6:38   320, 367, 501
6:39   47, 327, 492
6:41-42   122, 465
6:44   306
6:45   199, 230
7:28   484
8:8   185
8:18   290, 345
8:21   27, 46, 229, 334, 351, 480, 484
8:28   53, 54
9:24   8
9:25   487
9:27-36   349, 350
9:62   43, 97, 186
10:2   56, 59, 192
10:13-16   61
10:20   359
10:27   191, 233, 248, 370, 417, 472
10:35   229
11:2   13, 25, 122
11:9   4, 7, 10, 13, 22, 38, 39, 75, 137, 151, 168, 183, 191, 209, 257, 258, 299, 305, 348, 350, 360, 406, 435, 486, 490, 512

11:33   169
11:34   86, 339
12:3   30
12:12   4, 208, 278
12:20   387
12:21   315, 316
12:25   30, 314, 315, 393
12:27-28   324
12:28   421
12:30   13, 122, 123, 257
12:31   60, 361, 408
12:34   198, 445
12:48   155, 191, 290, 321, 487
13:24   44, 84
13:30   162
13:34   209, 239, 445
14:11   232
14:28-31   108
14:35   185
15:4   92, 223
15:4-10   444
15:7   92, 223
15:18   153
16:13   316
16:31   360
17   160
17:1   263, 323, 438, 480
17:6   373
17:17   92
17:32   97, 103, 115, 190, 308, 490
17:33   8, 161, 404, 443
18:10-14   500, 501
18:13   75
18:14   232
18:17   455
18:22   39, 41
19:5-6   142
19:26   137, 290, 345
19:27   404
19:40   183, 226
20:35   344
21:8   128
21:19   103, 108, 129, 142, 179, 180, 235, 277, 438, 456
21:33   48, 75, 117, 123, 236, 298, 299, 305, 333, 373, 391, 434, 438
22:19-20   359
22:42   13, 15, 59, 75, 127, 143, 259, 261, 269, 280, 307, 419, 430, 465, 470, 473, 480
22:61   142

23:27-33   442
23:34   13, 239, 433, 477
23:43   369, 370
24:49   4

JOHN
1:1   186, 384
1:3   236, 277, 384, 413
1:11   246, 480, 502
1:11-12   413
1:14   384
1:45   126
1:46   245
2:3-11   361
2:19-22   354
3:3   239, 240, 318
3:5   318
3:7   239, 240, 318
3:8   47
3:14   13, 16
3:16   158, 159, 178, 185, 233, 412, 464
3:18   255
4:4-26   37
4:21   260
4:35   56, 59, 192
4:39-42   258
6:20   100, 167, 170, 187, 414
6:68   149
6:70   384
8:28   13, 14, 16, 117, 231, 236, 302, 365, 388, 510
8:32   158, 159, 179, 276, 301, 391, 455, 481
8:58   225
9:4   54, 57, 279
10:1   186, 306
10:3   29, 56, 117, 186, 198, 233, 267, 325, 326, 366, 397, 427
10:10   185, 236, 341
10:16   56, 117, 366, 397, 427
10:27   29, 56, 117, 186, 233, 267, 366, 397, 427
10:34   258
12:25   8
12:32   13, 16, 132
13:34   233, 270, 277, 450, 463
14:1   190, 300, 367, 470, 510, 511
14:2   267, 345, 436, 447, 464, 486
14:2-3   229, 232
14:3   229, 259, 260

14:4   117
14:6   53, 82, 83, 84, 117, 293, 366, 511
14:7   39, 180
14:10   120, 121, 388
14:11   57
14:12-13   3, 4
14:13   55, 230, 255, 372
14:13-14   302, 386, 387
14:14   359, 360
14:15   443
14:18   67, 99, 100, 121, 132, 135, 174, 177, 184, 277, 288, 290
14:20   25, 52, 175, 313, 371, 376, 474
14:20-21   472
14:21   126, 137, 142, 143, 176, 177, 180, 187, 190, 200, 233, 270, 288, 423, 450, 470
14:23   117, 121, 318, 365, 371, 376, 470, 472
14:26   55, 74, 117, 135, 142, 328, 489
14:27   67, 284, 285, 300, 367, 383, 465
14:28   229, 470
14:30   461
15:1-2   399
15:1-5   293
15:1-8   427
15:2   277, 463, 512
15:12   40, 46, 56, 270, 274, 277, 298, 318, 335, 450, 468, 473, 474
15:13   123
15:16   4, 230, 255, 386, 387, 510
15:17   40, 46, 56, 270, 274, 298, 318, 335, 450, 463, 468, 473, 474
15:19   280
15:22   325, 417
15:24   325, 417
15:27   117
16:24   474
16:33   122, 375
17   373
17:5   121, 371, 376, 461
17:8-11   384
17:11   280
17:12   372
17:16   280, 289, 329, 375
19:11   336
20:17   352, 356

20:22-23   509, 510
21:15-17   200, 370, 457
21:22-23   370

ACTS
1:11   121, 128, 196
4:12   56, 143, 154, 169, 187, 289, 300
7:33   60, 67
7:49   380
9:5   289, 304, 339
10:34   18
10:38   115, 121, 227, 252, 365, 375, 440
17:27-28   135
17:28   12, 122, 186, 325, 334, 335, 359, 366, 458, 491
26:14   289, 304, 339

ROMANS
1:20   14
3:3   208
5:3   110
5:11   182, 183
7:21   15
8:16   29, 40, 47, 67, 84, 121, 122, 134, 200, 236, 259, 349, 455, 456, 457, 459, 475
8:23   352
8:28   152
8:29-30   56
8:38   230, 262, 305, 334
11:33   191, 209, 267, 288, 346, 366, 378, 380, 388, 390, 437, 467, 490, 511
12:1   56, 123, 347, 424
12:3   228, 489
12:9   299, 367
12:10   100, 226, 263
12:16   372
12:19   262
12:20   40, 290
12:21   230
13:9   233
13:14   377
14:7   39, 46, 75
14:8   122
14:13   13, 80, 126, 364, 499
14:16   190

I CORINTHIANS
2:2   146, 380
2:9   312

3:6-7   14, 53, 269, 270, 273, 393, 426, 436, 446, 462, 474
3:13   221
5:6   7, 56, 111, 271, 434
6:19   44, 123, 240, 269, 325, 342, 347, 360
9:22   53
10:13   4, 53, 108, 221, 315, 323, 325, 326, 334, 338, 421, 467, 479, 480
10:26   174, 368
10:28   174, 368
11:23-29   359
11:24   446
11:24-29   145, 146
12:12   44, 45, 48, 49
12:28-30   13
12:28-31   3
12:29-30   74, 329, 330
13   183
13:1   199
13:1-3   186
13:2   83, 385
13:7   53, 510
13:12   39
14:40   8, 10, 21
15:9   504
15:22   328
15:31   293
15:45   396, 404
15:50   110, 121, 311, 404
15:51   352
16:13   295, 296, 323, 371, 496

II CORINTHIANS
3:6   438, 497, 498, 501
5:1   240, 241, 307
5:8   481
5:14   300, 302
5:21   235, 236
6:2   103, 360, 397
12:9   67, 90, 100, 171, 284, 289, 293, 385, 465
13:1   337

GALATIANS
1:13   504
3:6   208
3:27   377
5:9   7, 56, 111, 271, 434
5:14   233

6:2   4, 5, 12, 123, 389
6:7   83, 89, 90, 108, 205, 250, 277, 311, 365, 436, 451, 457, 462, 468, 487
6:9   87, 125, 189, 201, 277, 436, 446, 447, 449, 511

EPHESIANS
2:18   295, 307
4:5-6   320
4:11   3, 74, 329, 330
4:26   100, 103, 235
5:15   22
5:19   19, 26, 157, 173, 174, 209, 230, 231, 435, 464
6:11   179, 276
6:13   122, 179, 276

PHILIPPIANS
2:5   4, 12, 13, 92, 108, 141, 252, 280
2:5-6   311, 313
2:6   120, 121, 236, 255, 276, 355, 424, 510
3:14   31, 58, 108, 128, 187, 191, 365
4:7   54, 176, 177, 180, 392, 474

COLOSSIANS
1:15-16   14
3:16   19, 26, 157, 173, 174, 209, 230, 231, 435, 464
4:2   109

I THESSALONIANS   53
2:19   191
5:21   31
5:22   171, 188, 190

II THESSALONIANS
3:13   87, 125, 189, 201, 277, 436, 449, 511

I TIMOTHY
1:12   299, 300
5:8   97, 186

II TIMOTHY
1:10   98, 99
1:12   75, 80, 109, 127, 137, 208, 258, 280, 289, 293, 325, 334, 431, 438, 445, 464
2:15   53, 64, 101, 134, 138, 171, 188, 189, 198, 201, 236, 299, 308, 370, 383, 404, 424, 466, 501, 516
2:19   56, 108, 201, 221, 232, 287, 288, 304, 427

HEBREWS
2:7-9   131
5:8   185, 186, 222, 326, 404, 417
9:11   307
9:22   95, 182
9:28   377
11:1   57, 63, 67
11:6   13, 93, 135, 174, 231, 266, 365
11:10   418
12:1   99, 110, 122, 490
12:2   299, 475
12:6   107, 110, 201, 427, 449
12:29   110
13:2   167
13:8   476, 491

JAMES
1:1   115
1:12   82, 109, 156, 157
1:17   15, 93, 259
1:22   122, 440
1:27   26, 64, 74, 424, 466, 516
2:8   233
2:17   67, 135
2:19   481
2:20   67, 135
2:26   67, 135
4:8   231
4:17   263
5:8   104
5:9   115
5:12   10, 122, 138, 185, 268, 279, 296, 390, 474, 487
5:20   233, 283, 373

I PETER
3:8   4, 7, 17, 19, 318, 354, 382, 388
3:11   233, 291, 300, 385, 464

II PETER
1:17   121
3:9   134, 179, 220, 221, 298, 304, 308, 315, 334, 338, 342, 355, 421, 455, 479
3:16   352
3:18   6, 108, 122, 137, 159, 327, 397, 429

I JOHN
1:5   84, 267, 383, 460
1:7   268, 279
2:1   65, 120, 236, 412, 446, 479
3:8   127, 150

4:1-3   336, 337
4:18   54, 105, 392, 431, 465, 475
5:3   174, 180, 190, 192, 423, 443, 470

II JOHN
7   128, 486

REVELATION   160, 161
1:8   57, 215, 216
2:10   39, 82, 109, 192, 302, 496
3:3   111
3:20   25, 47, 114, 117, 118, 119, 174, 302, 486

6:14   117
7:14   233, 305, 424
7:17   431
12:11   305, 424
12:14   195, 196
13:8   225
14:13   75
16:5   203
21:4   431
21:6   57, 215, 216
22:2   313
22:13   57, 215, 216
22:17   294, 457, 480, 481

Association for Research and Enlightenment, Inc.

Chartered by the Commonwealth of Virginia in 1931 to engage in psychical research, this non-profit organization is interested in exploring and making practical use of the information that came through the almost 15,000 telepathic-clairvoyant readings of the late Edgar Cayce. These readings, by one of the world's most widely witnessed and documented psychics, are being preserved and indexed by the Association, for the purpose of investigation, experiment and verification. The records include material of a mental, physical and spiritual nature. Research undertaken includes studies in the fields of psychology, parapsychology, philosophy and religion.

A year-round program of conferences, seminars, and lectures is held in Virginia Beach and across the nation. Study Groups throughout the world are organized to study the Edgar Cayce readings and implement the philosophy in daily life.

The Association maintains an open-membership policy. Three types of membership—Life, Sponsoring and Associate—are available. Information on the further privileges and services offered to members may be obtained by writing to the A.R.E., Box 595, Virginia Beach, Virginia 23451, Attention: Membership Secretary.